ROMAN IMPERIALISM

INTERPRETING ANCIENT HISTORY

The books in this series contain a mixture of the most important previously published articles in ancient history and primary source material upon which the secondary literature is based. The series encourages readers to reflect upon a variety of theories and methodologies, to question the arguments made by scholars, and to begin to master the primary evidence for themselves.

Roman Imperialism

READINGS AND SOURCES

Edited by
Craige B. Champion

Blackwell
Publishing

Editorial material and organization © 2004 by Blackwell Publishing Ltd

BLACKWELL PUBLISHING
350 Main Street, Malden, MA 02148-5020, USA
9600 Garsington Road, Oxford OX4 2DQ, UK
550 Swanston Street, Carlton, Victoria 3053, Australia

The right of Craige B. Champion to be identified as the Author of the Editorial Material in this Work has been asserted in accordance with the UK Copyright, Designs, and Patents Act 1988.

First published 2004 by Blackwell Publishing Ltd

5   2006

Library of Congress Cataloging-in-Publication Data

Roman imperialism: readings and sources/edited by Craige B. Champion.
    p. cm.–(Interpreting ancient history; 3)
    ISBN 0-631-23118-8 (alk. paper)–ISBN 0-631-23119-6 (pbk.: alk. paper)
    1. Rome–History. 2. Imperialism. I. Champion, Craige Brian. II. Series.

DG209.R596 2003
937–dc21

                                 2003045393

ISBN-13: 978-0-631-23118-9 (alk. paper)–ISBN-13: 978-0-631-23119-6 (pbk.: alk. paper)

A catalogue record for this title is available from the British Library.

Set in 10 on 12 pt Galliard
by Kolam Information Services Pvt. Ltd, Pondicherry, India
Printed and bound in India
by Gopsons Papers Ltd, Noida

For further information on
Blackwell Publishing, visit our website:
www.blackwellpublishing.com

Contents

Figures and Maps

Acknowledgements

I am grateful to T. Corey Brennan, Arthur M. Eckstein, Erich S. Gruen, and Brent D. Shaw, all of whom commented on the book in its planning stages. Many of their recommendations have been incorporated, and these have greatly improved the book. Other suggestions I obstinately ignored, and of course these scholars are in no way accountable for the flaws that may have resulted in the final product. My graduate assistant Anthony Marcavage proofread most of the manuscript and helped to improve clarity of expression. David Faith, Davida Ofori-Sarpong, Michelle Orihel, Shrimoy Roy Chaudhury, Subramanian Shankar, Dow Smith, Matthew Smith, and Patrick Wilcox used the book in a Roman history graduate seminar in the Maxwell School of Citizenship and Public Affairs at Syracuse University. Their comments have helped me to make the book more "student-friendly." I extend special thanks to Al Bertrand, commissioning editor at Blackwell, who invited me to undertake the project and who exhibited constant enthusiasm for the book in every phase of its production. Thanks must also go to Angela Cohen and Cameron Laux, for their help with the production process, and to Jean Van Altena, for her expert copy-editing. Finally I reserve the greatest debt of gratitude for Martina, Laura, and Maya Champion, who have unfailingly shown the special love and patience which are necessary when one's husband or father also happens to be a scholar.

The editor and publishers wish to thank the following for permission to use copyright material.

Chapter 1

W. V. Harris, "On War and Greed in the Second Century BC," *American Historical Review*, 76, no. 2 (December 1971), pp. 1371–85. Reprinted by permission of the author and publisher.

Erich S. Gruen, "Material Rewards and the Drive for Empire," from *Imperialism of Mid-Republican Rome*, ed. W. V. Harris, Papers and Monographs of the American

Academy in *Rome* 29 (1984), pp. 59–82. Reprinted by permission of the author and the American Academy in Rome.

John Rich, "Fear, Greed, and Glory: The Causes of Roman War Making in the Middle Republic," from *War and Society in the Roman World*, ed. John Rich and Graham Shipley (Routledge, 1995), pp. 38–68. Reprinted by permission of the publisher.

Chapter 2

Michael H. Crawford, *Rome and the Greek World: Economic Relationships* (Blackwell, 1977), pp. 42–52. Reprinted by permission of the author. Further reflections on this material can be found in Michael H. Crawford, *Coinage and Money under the Roman Republic* (Berkeley, 1985).

Keith Hopkins, *Conquerors and Slaves: Sociological Studies in Roman History* (Cambridge University Press, 1978), pp. 1–19, 48–54. Reprinted by permission of the publisher.

Chapter 3

P. A. Brunt, "Laus Imperii," from *Imperialism in the Ancient World*, ed. P. D. A. Garnsey and C. R. Whittaker (Cambridge University Press, 1978), pp. 162–78, 183–91, 320–30. Reprinted by permission of the publisher.

Susan Mattern, *Rome and the Enemy: Imperial Strategy in the Principate*, pp. 194–210. Copyright © 1999 The Regents of the University of California. Reprinted by permission of the publishers.

Chapter 4

R. MacMullen, *Romanization in the Time of Augustus* (Yale University Press, 2000), pp. 124–37, 174–7. Reprinted by permission of the publisher.

G. Woolf, *Becoming Roman: The Origins of Provincial Civilization in Gaul* (Cambridge University Press, 1998), pp. 238–49. Reprinted by permission of the publisher.

P. S. Wells, *The Barbarians Speak: How the Conquered Peoples Shaped Roman Europe*, pp. 99–121. © 1999 by Princeton University Press. Reprinted by permission of the publisher.

Chapter 5

E. N. Luttwak, *The Grand Strategy of the Roman Empire: From the First Century* AD *to the Third* (Johns Hopkins University Press, 1976), pp. 1–5. Reprinted by permission of the publisher.

Benjamin Isaac, "Frontier Policy: Grand Strategy," from *The Limits of Empire: The Roman Army in the East* (Oxford University Press, 1990), pp. 377–87. Reprinted by permission of the publisher.

Every effort has been made to trace copyright holders and to obtain their permission for the use of copyright material. The authors and publishers will gladly receive any information enabling them to rectify any error or omission in subsequent editions.

Introduction: The Study of Roman Imperialism

Craige B. Champion and Arthur M. Eckstein

This book is intended as a student's introduction to some of the problems and controversies in the modern study of Roman imperialism. It is a selection of essays and primary source material that can make no claims to being a comprehensive treatment of the subject. The selections are eclectic, and topics have been chosen with an eye to issues that teaching experience has indicated are of great interest to students.

To be sure, constraints of space and the editor's interests, expertise, and limitations of competence have been decisive influences on the shape the book has taken, but even so there were difficult decisions to make. The student will not find here treatment of some vitally important dimensions of Roman imperial power, and it is necessary to note a few of the crucial aspects of Roman imperialism which this collection does not directly address and to provide bibliographic suggestions for further study in these areas. The Roman army itself is ever present in the chapters that follow, but this is not a book about technical aspects of the Roman military, though many such exist.[1] Another important aspect of Roman imperialism that is treated only tangentially in this volume is the detailed workings and mechanisms of Roman imperial administration.[2] The relationship between the urban centers and their rural hinterlands in the Roman world is yet another important topic in the study of Roman imperialism, and Roman civilization generally. Scholars have viewed the ancient city itself as a vehicle for domination and control, as an exploitative parasite feeding on the agricultural produce of the countryside. But this relationship of town and country in the Roman world is only cursorily touched upon in these readings (e.g., by Hopkins and Brunt).[3] To give these topics the careful attention they deserve in any complete consideration of Roman imperialism would require a multivolume work. The focus of this book, instead, is upon the nature of Rome's relations with foreign states and peoples in the great age of the expansion and consolidation of Roman interstate power.

The ancient Romans themselves had a concept, *imperium*, which was vitally important to them (and indeed it is from this word that we have derived the word 'imperialism'): *imperare* means "to command," and *imperium* means the power to command and, by extension, the geographical area where such a command would be obeyed.[1] But the Romans had no word that corresponds to the modern term 'imperialism'.[5] Even if they had had such a term, we would still have to be wary of assuming that the word meant the same thing to them as it does to us.[6] Indeed, the word 'imperialism' is itself a modern coinage, which only began to gain currency after 1870. Lord Carnarvon in 1878 could write that 'imperialism', as such, was a newly coined word to him.[7] This situation compounds the difficulties in understanding just what we moderns mean when we speak of Roman imperialism.

Thus two of the most important figures in the study of modern imperialism, J. A. Hobson and V. I. Lenin, saw imperialism as a phenomenon of international politics after the industrial revolution of the eighteenth and nineteenth centuries, indeed caused by the capitalistic mode of production, which led to the search – backed by governments – for new territories for products and new fields for capitalist investment.[8] On such a view, of course, it would be anachronistic to speak of imperialism in the ancient Roman world, for it existed with an overwhelmingly agrarian and pre-capitalist economy: few industrial products that needed markets and little capital available for investment (what capital was available was for the most part reinvested in land). The economic dynamics of the modern term, therefore, would not apply.

But another major thinker who has profoundly influenced theories of imperialism, the economist J. A. Schumpeter, opposed Lenin's and Hobson's view that imperialism was an aspect of industrial-capitalist economies; rather, he thought that the modern imperialism of great states was, precisely, a primitive holdover from the aggressive, militarized social structures of pre-industrial times. Imperialism for Schumpeter was in fact something that is antithetical to capitalism and modern societal progress. In a celebrated turn of phrase, Schumpeter defined imperialism as "the objectless disposition on the part of a state to unlimited forcible expansion."[9] His comments on the Egyptian New Kingdom in the aftermath of the Hyksos invasion encapsulate his views on aggressive, ancient empires:

> This new social and political organization was essentially a war machine. It was motivated by warlike instincts and interests. Only in war could it find an outlet and maintain its domestic position. Without continual passages at arms it would necessarily have collapsed. Its external orientation was war, and war alone. Thus war became the normal condition, alone conducive to the well-being of the organs of the body social that now existed. To take the field was a matter of course, the reasons for doing so were of subordinate importance. *Created by wars that required it, the machine now created the wars it required.* A will for broad conquest without tangible limits, for the capture of positions that were manifestly untenable – this was typical imperialism.[10]

When we commonly speak of Roman imperialism, we assume that it is something rather close to Schumpeter's definition. But, as we shall see, the Roman case does not always conform to the Schumpeterian primitive "war machine." The form of Roman republican imperialism, for example, was often hegemonial rather than annexationist,[11] and there were periods during the Republic when the Roman military was surprisingly inactive (see Rich in this volume). Moreover, as Edward Gibbon noted: "The principal conquests of the Romans were achieved under the republic; and the emperors, for the most part, were satisfied with preserving those dominions which had been acquired by the policy of the senate, the active emulation of the consuls, and the martial enthusiasm of the people."[12] After Augustus, although martial ideologies of imperial expansion persisted, the goal of the Empire, in comparison with the period from roughly 200 to 50 BCE, was one of maintenance and control rather than of expansion. In fact, the *pax Romana* had already begun under the Republic in many regions of the Mediterranean – by about 150 BCE.[13] Whatever the nature of their "Schumpeterian war machine," the implication is that the Romans stopped their warfare when powerful, threatening enemies no longer existed. But if the "Schumpeterian war machine" model does not always work, how then do we account for Rome's enormously successful imperial expansion?

Thus 'imperialism', much like the words 'ethnicity' and 'culture', is both a modern term and one that is so widely and disparately employed that its very use may engender misunderstandings of an ancient world profoundly different from ours. And there is a further complication. Because the term 'imperialism' arose as an intellectual response to the expansion of the European powers into what we now call the Third World, its use inevitably involves the emotions evoked by that world-shaking process. The intellectual response was at first positive, but – pioneered by Hobson and Lenin and especially after World War I – it began to change, and in twentieth-century discourse 'imperialism' in fact often assumed highly negative connotations. The assumption is that empires are especially evil structures, and 'imperialism' a very evil process, because it is simply morally wrong to hold others in political subjection. Opposition to racism – racism which was an important aspect of the modern European empires but a little-known phenomenon in Mediterranean antiquity – also enters into this moral judgment.[14] Because of all this, one must be careful when talking about *Roman* imperialism. We wish this to be an analytical term, but it is a term that has become ideologically and emotionally loaded.

For our purposes we can say that imperialism is an unequal power relationship between two states in which the dominant state exercises various forms of control, often forcibly, over the weaker state. But within such a broad definition, we can speak of many different imperialisms, such as ones based on military conquest, economic exploitation, territorial acquisition, and direct annexation, as well as looser forms of control such as those which superordinate powers have often exercised over nominally independent client states, and even more indirect forms of control or influence, such as the seductive allure of the cultural productions of the imperial center on the periphery. Some scholars would prefer to dissociate these more indirect forms of control or influence from imperialism, calling them hegemony.[15]

It is the aim of this volume to allow for this sort of multivalence in our survey of work on imperialism in the ancient Roman world. This goal is reflected in the rubrics into which the book is divided: (1) growth of empire and imperial motivations; (2) political, economic, and social consequences of empire; (3) Roman imperial ideologies; (4) "Romanization" and cultural assimilation, hybridization, and resistance; and (5) imperial frontiers and strategies of defense. The volume focuses on the period of Rome's greatest period of military expansion. In other words, it is oriented towards Rome as an expansionist imperial republic (roughly from about 250 to 50 BCE) rather than as a relatively stable empire of maintenance, even though the latter phase comprises a significant period of Roman history. This is particularly true of the first two chapters dealing with the growth of empire and its political, economic, and social consequences. The chapters on ideology, Romanization, and the frontier allow for a more diachronic treatment and better representation of the age of Augustus and beyond.

To return to how modern theory can conceptually help the study of Roman imperialism, we may consider three of its basic but differing analytical emphases. One focuses on the imperial center (the metropole) and seeks historical explanation for imperial expansion almost solely from the study of the institutional structures and social characteristics of the conquering power. In a tradition going back to Hobson, Lenin, and Schumpeter, it is in particular the alleged distortions within the society, economy, and/or politics of the imperial power that in this view lead to large imperial expansion. A second approach takes an almost diametrically opposite view and emphasizes the historical influence upon the imperial process exercised by the people who eventually become subordinated (the periphery as opposed to the metropole). But, as before, the emphasis is on the internal distortions of the societies involved. The argument is that here on the 'periphery' one finds situations that practically invite the intervention of a powerful center and the extension of its power. These 'invitations' may take different forms: (1) weak states asking for protection from other external threats; (2) weak states divided politically, with one side or another asking for intervention from the metropole; (3) relatively strong states that are not, however, as strong as they think, and by aggression invite a vigorous response from the center.[16] The result is – not by the planning of the metropole – an empire. Moreover, the extent to which such an empire endures is determined to a considerable degree not by the power of the metropole but by the amount of collaboration (or non-collaboration) the subordinate peoples are willing to offer.[17] Finally, a third analytical approach shifts away from either the conqueror or the subject, or both, attempting to understand imperialism in a more comprehensive, holistic way by viewing a broader canvas encompassing both the conquering imperialist and the conquered subordinate within a wide and complex interstate system. Here the emphasis is on the fierce competition among states for power and security in a world with little international law. The brutal, competitive structure of international relations itself is employed as the ultimate cause for the rise of empires. Some states (for whatever reason) are more capable of success in this harsh environment than others, and they end up greatly expanding their power and influence. But the stress is not on special evil (as with the first approach) but on general tragedy (the conflictual structure of interstate relations). These three different approaches have been called metrocentric, pericentric, and systemic, respectively.[18]

The modern study of Roman imperialism offers examples of all these various approaches. For a long time the metrocentric approach held the field, and to a great extent it still does. Within it, two opposed interpretations of events have competed. In the mid-nineteenth century the great scholar of ancient Rome Theodor Mommsen argued that the expansion of Roman power was the result of outside threats and pressures, but Rome itself remained the center of attention. The Romans, according to Mommsen, acted defensively against powerful and aggressive neighbors. Their unique adjustments and responses to these external challenges resulted in empire. Mommsen's well-deserved authority ensured that his interpretation would have followers, and in the early twentieth century the American scholar Tenney Frank expounded the idea of Roman 'defensive imperialism'.[19] Italian scholars, the towering figure of Gaetano De Sanctis foremost among them, led the opposition in the early twentieth century, maintaining that Rome was a militaristic state driven by an insatiable will to power (*à la* Schumpeter). William V. Harris, in the article reprinted in this volume and in his magisterial *War and Imperialism in Republican Rome*, has most forcefully argued for a Schumpeterian, bellicose Rome. Harris's is probably the single most influential study of the rise of Roman power in the last 30 years, and many contemporary scholars accept his Schumpeterian analysis.[20]

These influential scholarly interpretations of Roman imperialism, however, are all constrained to a significant degree by a metrocentric paradigm; that is, they all assume that the answer to the historical phenomenon of Roman imperialism lies within Roman culture and society. Roman imperialism is to be explained by a close examination of Roman political, military, and social institutions.[21] The readings in chapter 1 (Harris, Gruen, Rich) and chapter 3 (Brunt, Mattern) are exemplary illustrations of this approach. We certainly need to understand that Rome in the period of its imperial expansion was an intensely militarized state, in a way almost inconceivable to moderns (though not inconceivable to ancients). But a pericentric approach also offers rich dividends. There is massive evidence to suggest, for instance, that the Celtic tribes of the Po valley were not hapless victims of Roman expansion: after all, they sacked and burned Rome itself around 390 BCE, and they periodically invaded central Italy for the next 200 years. One simply cannot understand Roman determination to control these tribes unless one accepts the Celts' own aggressive and large-scale violence. Again, it was not Roman initiative that led to Roman intervention in the Greek East in 200 BCE, forever changing its balance of power: medium-sized Greek states, under great pressure from the expansionist Greek monarchs Philip V of Macedon and Antiochus III of Syria, sent ambassadors to Rome in 202–200 BCE warning the Romans of the dangerous nature of these kings and begging for Roman intervention to protect them. We might call this "empire by invitation."[22] The readings in chapter 4 (MacMullen, Woolf, Wells) stress the periphery and subordinates' strategies of collaboration or non-collaboration in the cultural ramifications of Roman imperial expansion.

Finally, systemic approaches to empire eschew explanations based on dispositions of individual states. Scholars in this tradition – who call themselves "Realists" – point rather to the harsh characteristics of the international system as a whole, arguing that in such a system wars and empires are simply natural international events.

Realist theoreticians argue that the explanation for much of the international behavior of states lies in their understandable self-seeking within a *general* condition of violence and potential violence. This general condition is the consequence of international anarchy – that is, the absence of international law and/or a central authority or effective means to enforce such a law, which would place recognized limits on state behavior. All states need security (a sense of stable self-preservation), but in an anarchy security is scarce, often threatened – and can *only* be achieved by a state's individual accumulation of power and influence. Bluntly stated, the international world is a "self-help" system.

Hence every state is on its own, and competition to achieve both power and security is intense and ruthless. The specific conflicts of interest that arise between states competing for scarce power and security are serious and real – not the result of "misunderstanding." The situation of "self-help" leads to power-maximizing behavior by *every* state in the anarchy, for under these harsh conditions this is the only way to create an immediate environment as secure and congenial as possible: "State behavior is induced by the system: regardless of culture or ideology, all states act similarly, selfishly seeking to increase their own power."[23] States that do not act in this way risk being subordinated or (in rare cases) even destroyed. Because of the serious conflicts of interest that thus arise among multiple, brutally self-seeking states, and in the absence of international institutions that can encourage (or enforce) peace, militarism is unfortunately all too natural, since it is a central way to gain power, and war is in fact *normal* – that is, a normative way of settling serious disputes. The occurrence of war needs no special explanation, but is inherent in any anarchic interstate system. Individual states have little control over these basic facts of life. On the contrary: "States must meet the needs of the political ecosystem or risk annihilation."[24] Rome found a way to meet the needs of its brutal political "ecosystem" superbly.

One way to think about this "systemic" approach is that it employs the basic insights of *sociology* – the study of society (in this case the society of states) as a functioning system, in which the system is quite determinative of individual conduct, in that it strongly encourages some kinds of behavior (e.g., militarism) and discourages other kinds. By contrast, we may compare metrocentric and pericentric theories of imperialism to the study of individual psychology.[25]

The surprisingly peaceful and cooperative end of the Cold War led to the Realist approach being attacked as too pessimistic a view of world affairs. Some theorists now argue that the existence of modern international institutions, such as the United Nations, that foster peaceful resolutions of interstate conflicts, and the existence of quick and continual interstate communications, greatly ameliorate conflicts between states.[26] But during this essay's composition, we have seen massive terrorist attacks, nuclear rearmament in North Korea, and the President of the United States pushing for war against Iraq, who has at times run roughshod over international peacekeeping institutions. This is a sobering current event, indeed, but the reader is invited to make up his or her own mind concerning neo-liberal optimism about the modern world. In any case the world of the ancient Mediterranean states, the world in which Rome existed, seems to fulfill the grimmest paradigms of state behavior proposed by international-systems theoreticians.

There was little international law in this world – certainly none that was very effective – and wars were almost continual. This was true whether one considers monarchies, federal states, or aristocratic and democratic polities. Within this anarchic interstate structure every major state, every medium-sized state, and even many small states were highly militarized societies, habituated to employing violence and threats to achieve their aims.[27] Rome, in other words, was an intensely militaristic society – but not, in its world, exceptional in its militarism. The competition for power and security was intense; serious, objective clashes of interest occurred frequently; the stakes were high because (unlike in the modern world) polities quite frequently were destroyed.[28]

Moreover, as we have remarked, institutions of diplomacy were primitive. Ancient states did not send out permanent ambassadors to other states to keep abreast of their actions and perhaps give early warning to both sides of problems that might arise, heading them off while they could still perhaps be resolved – the type of activity moderns consider to be an essential process of conflict reduction. On the contrary, ancient ambassadors were sent out to other states only when relations had already reached crisis point, and most often what then occurred were harsh mutual demands made in public fora. Such "compellence diplomacy" often actually had a negative impact on the chances for peace. No one was willing to back down in public; and no one was bluffing. This came from a widespread belief that a fierce reputation for upholding one's rights and one's "honor" helped ensure real security, for then others would fear to interfere with your interests. Rome was guilty of such primitive behavior – and so was everyone else.[29]

The question, then, is not why the Romans fought wars continually, since the same can be said for almost every major ancient state. That was a function of the system. The real question is the one with which we began: why was Rome so successful in its imperial expansion, eventually rising to hegemony over the ancient Mediterranean world? "States are alike in the tasks they face, though not in their ability to perform them."[30] One must understand that the process of Roman expansion was not easy: the Romans suffered *90* severe defeats on the battlefield under the Republic. This gives one an idea of the fierce competitors and competition the Romans faced.[31]

Part of the answer may indeed have to do with a unique aspect of Roman culture: not its stern militarism (which was widely shared), but its special political skill and its inclusiveness (recognized long ago by Mommsen and Frank). From the mid-fourth century BCE Rome developed a system of managing subordinate allies so that they acquiesced in Roman imperial leadership, which was institutionally very easy on them (no taxes or garrisons, as in the Athenian Empire) – and backed by great force. At the same time the Romans developed a conception of citizenship that was based not on ethnicity or language, nor on geographical location, but on pure legal status.[32] This enabled the widespread inclusion of "deserving" non-Roman individuals (and occasionally even entire communities) into the Roman citizen-body, with part or even full rights. The result was that by the mid-220s BCE the number of Roman male citizens was enormous (well over 200,000). Not only was this unique for any ancient city-state, but such numbers gave Rome great resiliency in its contests for power and security against the other fierce states it faced. It may be that it was the large scale and intensity of its ability to mobilize resources – and not the intensity of its expansionist and militarist desires, although we do not wish to underestimate this factor – that was the secret to Rome's success in the militarized anarchic international system in which it existed.[33] This is to return somewhat to a metrocentric approach, but now with a different question: what were the *strengths* that allowed Rome to survive and then prevail in its harsh environment? Intriguingly, this is just the sort of question ancient intellectuals asked about successful imperial states: not what were the social pathologies, but rather what were the special internal strengths.[34]

Of the approaches surveyed here, the systemic one may well be promising for future work on Roman imperialism. In the present volume, the selections in chapter 2 (Crawford, Hopkins) and in chapter 5 (Luttwak Isaac) to some extent see Rome as part of a larger international system of states, but it must be said that research employing this approach has just begun.

Though much ancient writing on the rise of Rome and on its eventual empire has been lost, the amount that survives is still huge; we can offer here only a selection. The amount of good and interesting work by modern scholars is also huge, and we can only present some of it. It is our hope that the following selection of modern scholarly analyses, translated ancient documents, and notes with suggestions for further reading (for practical reasons restricted for the most part to publications in English) will give students a good understanding of the historical development of Roman imperialism. What are stressed are the motivations which led the Romans to acquire an extensive empire, the sorts of ideological justifications and rationalizations the Romans used for their exercise of imperial domination, and the complex political, economic, social, and cultural interactions that came to exist among Romans, allies, and subjected peoples.

A NOTE ON SOURCES AND READINGS

Appended to the readings for each chapter are sections containing primary sources in translation. In making these translations from the original Latin and Greek texts, I have consulted the editions in the Loeb Classical Library and the Penguin Classics. These translated passages allow the student to test the arguments of the modern scholars represented here against the primary source material. After each excerpt the source citation is given, with its approximate or exact date, when it is known, in square brackets. In cases where the author's name is enclosed in square brackets, the student should understand that the passage in question has been attributed to this author, but that there is reason to doubt the authenticity of authorship. Terms marked by an asterisk (the first few times they occur in a chapter) are to be found in the Glossary.

For abbreviations of ancient sources in the readings, see S. Hornblower and A. Spawforth (eds.), *The Oxford Classical Dictionary*, 3rd edn. (Oxford, 1996), pp. xxix–liv. For a guide to abbreviations used in classical scholarship, see Jean Susorney Wellington, *Dictionary of Bibliographic Abbreviations found in the Scholarship of Classical Studies and Related Disciplines* (Westport, Conn., and London, 1983).

NOTES

1   For a beginning, students may consult the following: G. R. Watson, *The Roman Soldier* (Ithaca, NY, 1969); R. E. Smith, *Service in the Post-Marian Roman Army* (Manchester, 1958); A. K. Goldsworthy, *The Roman Army at War, 100 BC–200 AD* (Oxford, 1996); L. Keppie, *The Making of the Roman Army: From Republic to Empire* (Totowa, NJ, 1984); J. B. Campbell, *The Emperor and the Roman Army, 31 BC–AD 235* (New York, 1984); Y. Le Bohec, *The Imperial Roman Army*, trans. R. Bate (London and New York, 2000); H. Elton, *Warfare in Roman Europe, AD 350–425* (Oxford, 1996); A. Ferrill, *The Fall of the Roman Empire: The Military Explanation* (London, 1986).

2   See generally A. W. Lintott, *Imperium Romanum: Politics and Administration* (London and New York, 1993). For the Republican period, see G. H. Stevenson, *Roman Provincial Administration till the Age of the Antonines* (New York, 1939); E. Badian, *Publicans and Sinners: Private Enterprise in the Service of the Roman Republic* (Ithaca, NY, 1972); E. S. Gruen, *The Hellenistic World and the Coming of Rome* (Berkeley, Los Angeles, and London, 1984); for the High Empire, see F. G. B. Millar, *The Roman Empire and its Neighbors*, 2nd edn. (New York, 1981); *idem*, *The Emperor in the Roman World, 31 BC–AD 337*, 2nd edn. (London, 1992); P. Garnsey and R. Saller, *The Roman Empire: Economy, Society, and Culture* (Berkeley and Los Angeles, 1987); see also the excellent sourcebook, B. Levick, *The Government of the Roman Empire: A Sourcebook*, 2nd edn. (London and New York, 2000).

3   This parasitic relationship of urban exploitation of the countryside was the key theme in
    M. Rostovtzeff's classic work on Roman imperial society and economy, *The Social and
    Economic History of the Roman Empire*, 2nd edn. (Oxford, 1957). On the relationship
    between urban and rural sectors in classical antiquity, see M. I. Finley, "The Ancient City:
    From Fustel de Coulanges to Max Weber and Beyond," in *Economy and Society in Ancient
    Greece*, ed. B. D. Shaw and R. P. Saller (New York, 1981), pp. 3–23.
4   On this extension, see J. S. Richardson, "*Imperium Romanum*: Empire and the Language
    of Power," *Journal of Roman Studies*, 81 (1991), pp. 1–9.
5   Cf. A. W. Lintott, "What was the 'Imperium Romanum'?," *Greece and Rome*, 28 (1981),
    pp. 53–67.
6   Cf. J. A. Schumpeter, *Imperialism and Social Classes*, trans. H. Norden (New York, 1951),
    p. 142: "One difficulty...we must face. Unless specifically proven, it is an erroneous
    assumption that social phenomena to which the same name has been applied over
    thousands of years are always the same things, merely in different form."
7   On the development of the modern word 'imperialism', see R. Koebner and
    H. D. Schmidt, *Imperialism* (Cambridge, 1964), pp. 107–65.
8   For example, see V. I. Lenin, *Imperialism: The Highest Stage of Capitalism* (New York,
    1920, repr. 1985), p. 89: "Imperialism is capitalism in that stage of development in which
    the dominance of monopolies and finance capital has established itself; in which the export
    of capital has acquired pronounced importance; in which the division of the world among
    the international trusts has begun; in which the division of all territories of the globe
    among the great capitalist powers has been completed"; J. A. Hobson, *Imperialism:
    A Study* (London, 1902), p. 55: "Aggressive Imperialism, which costs the taxpayer so
    dear, which is of so little value to the manufacturer and trader, which is fraught with such
    grave incalculable peril to the citizen, is a source of great gain to the investor who cannot
    find at home the profitable use he seeks for his capital, and insists that his Government
    should help him to profitable and secure investments abroad."
9   Schumpeter, *Imperialism and Social Classes*, p. 7.
10 Ibid., p. 33; emphasis original.
11 On this, see E. Badian, *Roman Imperialism in the Late Republic* (Oxford, 1968), ch. 3.
12 E. Gibbon, *The Decline and Fall of the Roman Empire*, vol. 1, new edn. (London, 1807),
    p. 2; conveniently in *The Portable Gibbon*, ed. D. A. Saunders (New York, 1963), pp. 27–8.
13 See T. J. Cornell, "The End of Roman Imperial Expansion," in *War and Society in the
    Roman World*, ed. J. Rich and G. Shipley (London, 1993), pp. 139–70.
14 On the relative absence of racial prejudice in Mediterranean antiquity, see F. M. Snowden,
    Blacks in Antiquity: Ethiopians in the Greco-Roman Experience (Cambridge, Mass., 1970);
    idem, Before Color Prejudice: The Ancient View of Blacks (Cambridge, Mass., and London,
    1983); L. A. Thompson, *Romans and Blacks* (Norman, Okla., and London, 1989).
15 For a definition delimited to direct political control, see, e.g., M. W. Doyle, *Empires*
    (Ithaca, NY, and London, 1986), p. 12: "One subject with which empire can easily be
    confused is international inequality...To name two important examples of international
    inequality, a *hegemonic* power, as opposed to a metropole, controls much or all of the
    external, but little or none of the internal, policy of other states, and a *dependent* state, as
    opposed to an imperialized periphery, is a state subject to limited constraints on its
    economic, social, and (indirectly) political autonomy" (emphasis original). In our view,
    the term 'hegemony', widely and disparately used under the influence of the work of
    Antonio Gramsci, simply introduces another term without descriptive precision. We prefer
    the relative simplicity of allowing for multivalence in the use of the term 'imperialism'.
16 Modern examples (in order): South Vietnam; El Salvador and Nicaragua; Iraq.
17 The founding document of periphery-centered explanations of the rise of imperial powers
    is J. Robinson and R. Gallagher, *Africa and the Victorians* (London, 1961); and on

'collaboration' by the subordinate as the crucial explanation for the stability or disinte-
gration of empires, see J. Robinson, "The Non-European Foundations of European
Imperialism: Sketch for a Theory of Collaboration," in *Studies in the Theory of Imperialism*, ed. E. R. J. Owen and R. Sutcliffe (London, 1972), pp. 117–40.

18   See Doyle, *Empires*, pp. 22–30.

19   T. Frank, *Roman Imperialism* (New York, 1914). Another classic statement of this
position was provided in 1921 by M. Holleaux, *Rome, la Grèce, et les monarchies hellénistiques au IIIe siècle avant J.-C., 273–205* (repr. New York and Hildesheim, 1969). Unfortunately this brilliant study has never been translated into English.

20   W. V. Harris, *War and Imperialism in Republican Rome, 327–70 BC* (Oxford, 1979). For
a concise and valuable account of modern scholarly interpretations of Roman imperialism,
with bibliography, see Gruen, *Hellenistic World*, pp. 5–7. The great influence of Harris:
see, e.g., K. A. Raaflaub, "Born to be Wolves?," in *Transitions to Empire: Essays in Greco-
Roman History, 360–146 BC, in Honor of E. Badian*, ed. R. W. Wallace and E. M. Harris
(Norman, Okla., 1996), pp. 273–324.

21   In a classic work, E. Badian thus argued that a key to understanding Roman imperialism is
the Roman social institution of patronage: *Foreign Clientelae, 264–70 BC* (Oxford, 1958).

22   The phrase is that of G. Lundestad, "Empire by Invitation? The United States and
Western Europe, 1945–1952," *Journal of Peace Research*, 23 (1986), pp. 263–77,
expanded in *The American "Empire" and Other Studies of U.S. Foreign Policy in Comparative Perspective* (London, 1990), ch. 2 – discussing the crucial role of the European states,
not the USA, in the creation of NATO.

23   T. Taylor, "Power Politics," in *Approaches and Theory in International Politics*, ed.
T. Taylor (London and New York, 1978), p. 130.

24   R. W. Sterling, *Macropolitics: International Security in a Global Society* (New York, 1974),
p. 336.

25   K. Waltz has provided the most influential work of this "sociological" approach to
understanding interstate conflict; see his *Theory of International Politics* (New York,
1979).

26   See, e.g., *Controversies in International Relations Theory: Realism and the Neo-liberal
Challenge*, ed. C. W. Kegley, Jr (New York, 1995); cf. M. Walzer, *Just and Unjust Wars:
A Moral Argument with Historical Illustrations*, 3rd edn. (New York, 2000), pp. 3–20.

27   On this point, see the brilliant article by J. Ma, "Fighting Poleis of the Hellenistic World,"
in *War and Violence in Ancient Greece*, ed. H. Van Wees (London, 2000), pp. 337–76.

28   Thucydides alone lists more than 30 city-states destroyed during the fifth century BCE.

29   On the primitive nature of ancient diplomacy, see A. M. Eckstein, *Senate and General:
Individual Decision-Making and Roman Foreign Relations in the Middle Republic,
264–194 BC* (Berkeley and Los Angeles, 1987), pp. xviii–xix. On the negative impact of
"compellence diplomacy," see, e.g., D. S. Stevenson, *The Outbreak of the First World War:
1914 in Perspective* (London and New York, 1997), esp. pp. 134–5.

30   Waltz, *Theory of International Politics*, p. 96.

31   Roman defeats: see the list in N. Rosenstein, *Imperatores Victi: Military Defeat and
Aristocratic Competition in the Middle and Late Republic* (Berkeley and Los Angeles,
1990), pp. 179–204.

32   See A. N. Sherwin-White, *The Roman Citizenship*, 2nd edn. (Oxford, 1973).

33   A good short analysis of this aspect of Rome as unique among ancient states is B. S. Strauss,
"The Art of Alliance and the Peloponnesian War," in *Polis and Polemos: Essays on Politics,
War and History in Ancient Greece in Honor of Donald Kagan*, ed. C. D. Hamilton and
P. Krenz (Claremont, Calif, 1997), pp. 128–39.

34   See J. DeRomilly, *The Rise and Fall of States According to Greek Authors* (Ann Arbor,
1977), ch. 2.

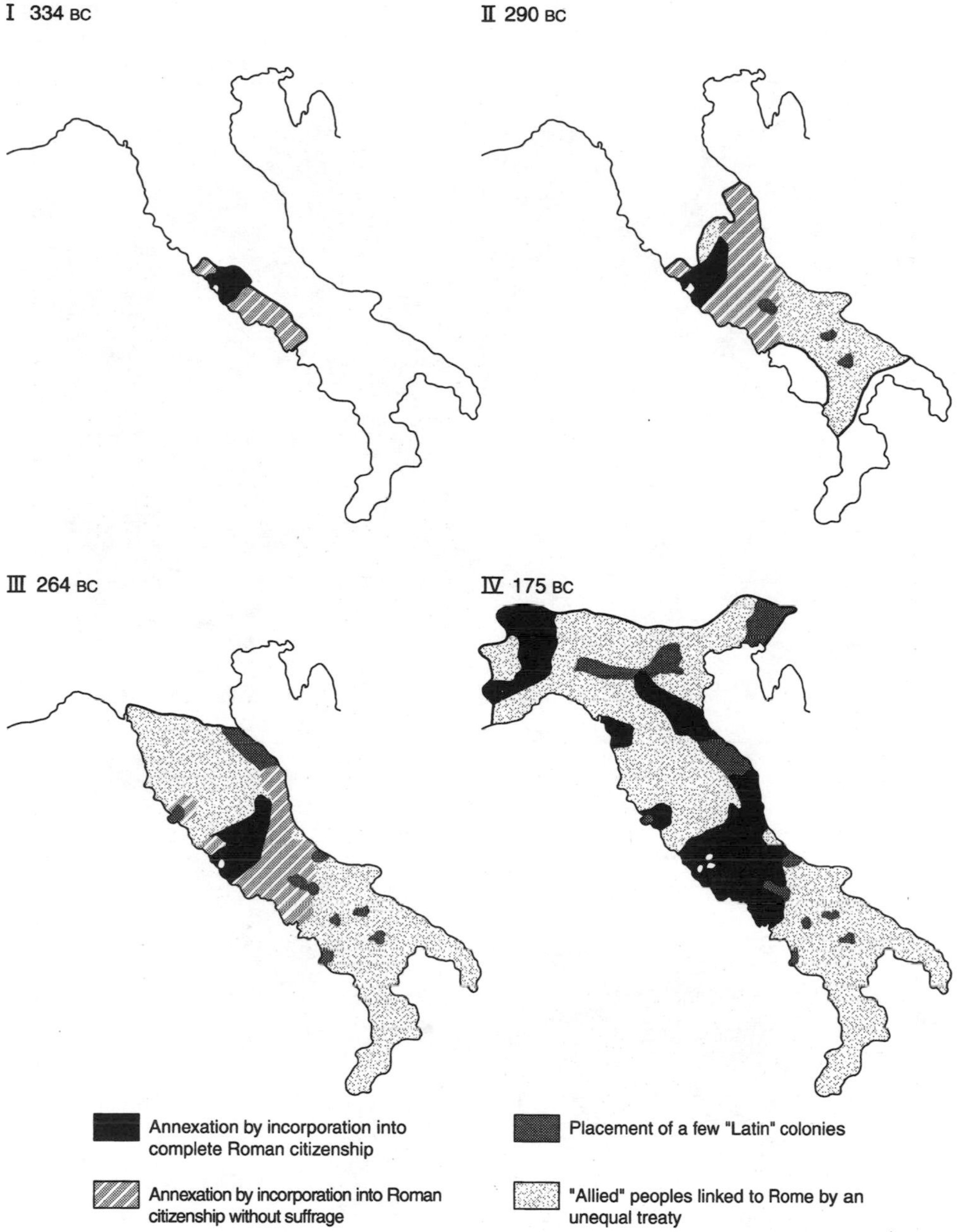

I 334 BC

II 290 BC

III 264 BC

IV 175 BC

■ Annexation by incorporation into complete Roman citizenship	▨ Placement of a few "Latin" colonies
▨ Annexation by incorporation into Roman citizenship without suffrage	▨ "Allied" peoples linked to Rome by an unequal treaty

Map 1 *The conquest of Italy and organization of territories. From M. Humbert,* Institutions politiques et sociales de l'Antiquite *(Dalloz, 1989).*

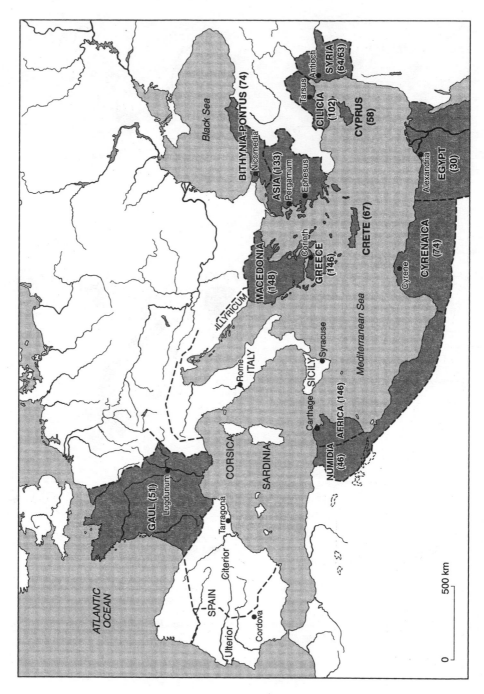

Map 2   *Roman conquests, 148–30* BC.

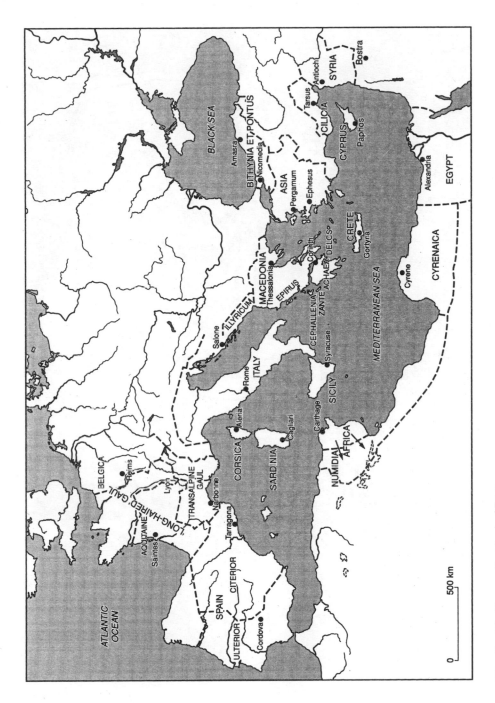

Map 3 *The Roman Empire in 27* BC.

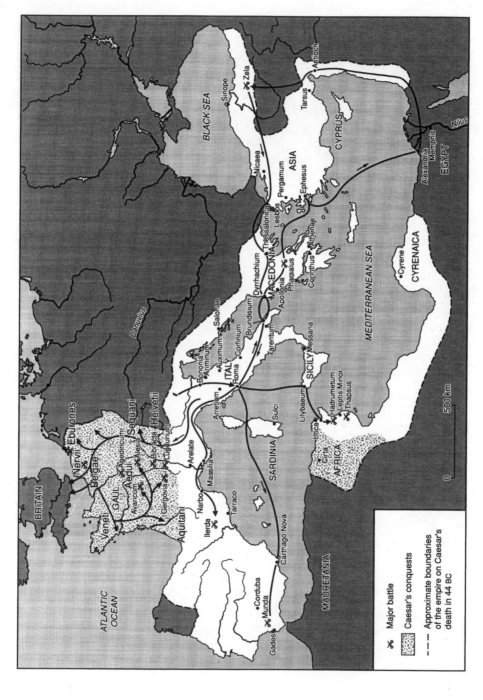

Map 4 *Caesar's conquests.*

ATLANTIC
OCEAN

BRITAIN

Veneti
Nervii Eburones
GAUL Belgae
Aedui / Sequani
Aquitani Bibracte Helvetii
Avaricum Alesia
Cenabum
Gergovia

Ilerda
Tarraco
Carthago Nova
Corduba
Munda
Gades

Narbo
Massilia
Arelate
Arretium

BLACK SEA

Sinope
Zela

Nicaea
Pergamum
Lesbos
Thessalonica
Ephesus
ASIA
Tarsus
Antioch

CYPRUS

Athenae
Corinthus

Dyrrhachium
Apollonia
MACEDONIA
Phasalus

Salonae
Bononia
Auximum
Ariminum
Corfinium
ITALY
Roma
Brundisium
Tarentum

Sulci

SARDINIA

Lilybaeum
Messana
SICILY

Utica
Cirta
AFRICA
Hadrumetum
Leptis Minor
Thapsus

Cyrene
CYRENAICA

MEDITERRANEAN SEA

Danubius

Alexandria
Memphis
EGYPT
Nilus

MAURETANIA

0   500 km

✗ Major battle

   Caesar's conquests

-- - Approximate boundaries
     of the empire on Caesar's
     death in 44 BC

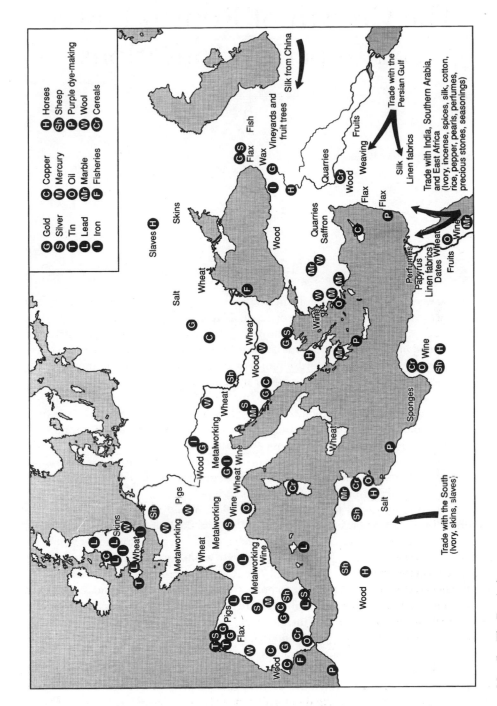

Map 5 *The Empire's resources.*

1

The Growth of Roman Power and Imperial Motivations

Introduction

These essays explore Roman imperial motivations. They all employ a metrocentric paradigm; that is, they seek to explain Roman imperial expansion by focusing almost exclusively on the structures of Roman society, on the particular disposition of the Roman state. Ernst Badian argued in several influential studies that Roman ideas of glory, virtue, honor, and deference, and hegemonial overlordship of weaker states are all far more important than crass economic drives in understanding Roman imperialism.

Harris reacts to Badian's dismissal of economic motivation as a prime causal factor in Roman imperial expansion. He points out that, first of all, our ancient sources are for the most part apologetic, and therefore they serve to conceal base Roman motivations. He further argues that while we cannot posit "mercantilist or commercial" motives, which were "generally of very slight importance for Roman imperialism in the second century [BCE]," desire for other economic advantages (e.g., public finance, plunder) was nevertheless important in the formulation of Roman foreign policy.

Gruen returns somewhat to the position of Badian. While acknowledging that military victories "brought tangible benefits" and that "prospect of loot could entice generals and stimulate recruiting," Gruen maintains that such motives were not paramount in senatorial deliberations on war making. The treasury and state economy, according to him, were not dependent on the plunder of other states. The Roman government was not controlled by the business sector, which could hope to profit from wartime contracts and other financial opportunities afforded by war, and the Roman Senate looked to political considerations rather than financial ones in its interstate behavior. It was concerned primarily with maintaining and preserving a stable international order, the allegiance of its allies, and Roman international honor and reputation.

Rich believes that Harris's work has demolished the old view of Roman "defensive imperialism," but he is concerned that Harris's thesis may share a basic weakness with the earlier position that it has rendered untenable: namely, that Harris's bellicose, "Schumpeterian" Rome is too simplistic, and his explanation for Roman imperial expansion is too monocausal. Rich eschews any monocausal explanation, arguing that due consideration must be given to three crucially important Roman concerns: fear and distrust of powerful competitors; lust for plunder and economic gain; and Roman aristocratic notions of military renown and glory, for both the individual Roman commander and the Roman state. He concludes: "Roman warfare and imperialism were complex phenomena, for which no monocausal explanation will be adequate. Any attempt to provide a more satisfactory account must take the measure of this complexity. In such an account fear, greed and glory will all play their part."

On War and Greed in the Second Century BC[i]

W. V. Harris

The problem of the possible economic motives of Roman imperialism has rightly seemed to nonspecialists one of the most important in the history of the Roman Republic, but it has for a long time received relatively little attention from specialists.[1] One kind of economic explanation, in terms of markets and opportunities for investment, was attacked long ago by Tenney Frank in what remains the classic discussion;[2] his arguments were later improved by others, and, as far as most Roman acts of expansion are concerned, explanations of this type have today little support among Roman historians. For a long time there were no extended discussions of the possible economic motives for Roman imperialism in the second century B.C.,[3] but recently a leading student of the external relations of republican Rome, Professor E. Badian, returned to the problem, and he came to decisive conclusions. In his view, "no such motives can be seen, on the whole, in Roman policy"; "strange as it may seem to a generation nourished on Marx, Rome sought no major economic benefits"; "the whole myth of economic motives in Rome's foreign policy at this time [the second century] is a figment of modern anachronism, based on ancient anachronism."[4] It is emphatically denied that desire for economic gain, public or private, was a motive that influenced Roman decisions to go to war, and those who have denied this are dismissed, not without justification, as having imposed doctrinaire views of imperialism on a set of facts that they do not fit. It can be said more generally that competent ancient historians are nowadays acutely aware of the dangers of anachronism in explaining imperialistic behavior in the ancient world; one notes the strictures of Professor K. J. Dover on those who have tried to find the "real motives" for the Athenian expedition to Sicily in 415 outside the pages of Thucydides.[5]

In the Roman case some contemporaries of the events certainly seemed to think that there were some motives that can be called "economic." When in 88 B.C. King Mithridates of Pontus captured a Roman general and exconsul, Manius Aquillius, he gave a startling demonstration of what some of their more vigorous opponents thought of the Roman imperialists: Aquillius, who had perhaps offered special provocation, was put to death in a symbolically appropriate manner, by having molten gold poured down his throat.[ii] Thus was greed rewarded. It is probable in fact that Roman greed by this time played an important part in the propaganda of the Hellenistic enemies of Rome. It may of course be the case that such accusations were completely unfair[6] or resulted from effects of Roman expansion that were purely incidental.

Again, no one doubts that by the sixties of the first century B.C. the desire of senatorial politicians to pay off their debts and to enrich themselves was an important motive and possibly the main motive of the bellicose attitude of Rome toward some foreign states. We have much less firsthand information about Roman politics and finance in the second century. Conditions were different then – but how different?

The purpose of this article is to argue that while modern scholars have succeeded in showing that certain kinds of economic motives, which can be roughly classified as mercantilist or commercial, were generally of very slight importance for Roman imperialism in the second century, they have failed to pay sufficient attention to other economic advantages that accrued to those Romans who decided what foreign policy would be. Desire for these other economic advantages was, it will be argued, an important motive in the formation of Roman policy.

We should admit straightaway that since we can only speculate about the unconscious reasons why Roman senators behaved as they did, there can never be any completely satisfying explanation of their behavior. If we restrict ourselves to more or less conscious motives, we shall still have a difficult time with the evidence. There were reasons to distort in public what may have been the real motives for action. When the Romans went to war they almost invariably felt that it was necessary to satisfy the formal requirements of the fetial law, according to which war could properly be fought only for *res repetitae*, to obtain compensation for wrongs suffered.[iii] It is clear too that the high regard felt for certain virtues, particularly *fides* ("good faith") may also have seriously distorted stated reasons for going to war. Polybius in fact tells us explicitly that when they went to war the Romans were careful to find a pretext that would appeal to foreign, that is to say mainly Greek, opinion.[7] Further, the restraints sometimes suggested by *fides*, and perhaps even those of the fetial law, may have had a real effect on policy. It is rash to assume that religious and moral beliefs of this kind are only camouflage. Evidently in the time of Polybius some, if not all, members of the Roman Senate were quite cynical about the fetial law, but it would be wrong to assume that it had no effect in determining the occasions on which Rome went to war. Finally, the character of the Roman political system made it difficult for ancient writers, and now makes it difficult for us, to know what arguments were used in favor of, or against, any particular decision to make war. Cassius Dio tells us that it was difficult to write the history of Rome under the Empire partly because the most important decisions were made in private,[8] and (whatever Dio thought) it was not much easier to write the history of the Republic. Serious discussions about foreign policy did take place in the Senate (not that any official record of the proceedings was made in the second century), and the will of the plebs, or at least part of it, could sometimes make itself felt even in matters of foreign policy (see below) – but in general, as is universally agreed, decisions of foreign policy were effectively in the hands of a rather small number of influential senior senators who had no need to broadcast full and candid accounts of their reasoning.

None of our main sources attempts to assess the possible economic motives of Roman imperialism. Polybius' generally favorable attitude toward Rome appears at its strongest (at its most defensive, some might say) on the subject of financial probity – with at least one demonstrable exaggeration as a result. He knew that the Romans had sometimes done more plundering than was required by their assumed aim of obtaining political domination over the whole world; we are prevented by textual gaps from knowing whether he had any explanation of the fact. Later on in the writing of his history, however, even Polybius came to think that the financial probity of the Romans had declined since they had begun to fight "overseas wars."[9] Later writers about the second century were almost all believers in theories of a moral decline, marked by *luxuria* ("self-indulgence") and *avaritia* ("greed"), which was supposed to have invaded the Roman state from various dates, mostly in the period 187–146. The intellectual and political history of this outlook is a matter of great interest, but it cannot be pursued here; it is enough to point out that *avaritia*, which was in the view of some later Roman writers the great charge that could be leveled against Roman imperialism, was schematically excluded from explanations of the earlier phases of Roman imperialism. Such motives were thought by, for example, Cicero and Sallust to have been foreign to the Roman aristocracy before certain dates (it is possible of course that they were right); the scheme was pervasive, and it was not thought necessary to produce evidence.[iv]

What economic effects of war were visible to second-century senators? I will deal first with public finance. It is very difficult to reach any satisfactory estimates of the actual effects of war – on the one side indemnities, booty, real property (including mines) acquired by the state, and provincial taxation; on the other side primarily the expenses of maintaining military forces. Some scholars, notably Tenney Frank, have attempted to calculate the public expenditure and income of Rome in this period.[10] The results are inevitably inconclusive – even for the period down to 167, for which Livy provides much relevant information – mainly because certain items of income, for instance provincial taxation, booty from some sources, and the income from the Spanish mines, cannot be worked out within useful limits. We do not, incidentally, have any evidence to justify the common assertion that Sicily was the only province that "paid its way" before 133. Nor can any conclusion about the proportion of public income to public expenditure be drawn from the information, provided by the elder Pliny, that in 157 the treasury contained gold, silver, and coin to the substantial but not spectacular value of 104 million sesterces, for there would have been little point in building up a reserve significantly larger than that.[11] Unfortunately the figures that Pliny gave in the same passage for the state of the treasury in 91 are not properly transmitted in the manuscripts; it certainly looks as if they showed an immense accumulation since 157, but no safe conclusion can be drawn.

There are, however, two points that can usefully be made about public finance in the second century. First, its whole scale was much greater than it had been before the Second Punic War, so that even if income exceeded essential expenditure by only a fairly small percentage (as Frank concluded – on insufficient evidence – for the period 200–157), much larger sums were now available for nonessential purposes. Second – and this is particularly important since it was evidently noticed by senators, as the precise effects of empire on the treasury may not have been – the Romans were able in the second century to afford some public luxuries unimaginable in the third century. No one will suggest that the Romans fought wars primarily to free themselves from their light burden of direct taxation, but the fact remains that in 167, when Aemilius Paullus brought home from Macedon booty to the value of some 120 million sesterces (or quite possibly a much larger sum) and Macedonian taxation began to flow into the Roman treasury, direct taxation of Roman citizens ceased. Equally, no one will suggest that the Romans fought wars in the second century primarily to provide themselves with public works that they could not have afforded before, but the fact remains that by previous standards it was a time of immense expenditure on such things. After a period of understandable restraint in the first three censorships after the Second Punic War, there began with the censorship of the elder Cato and L. Valerius Flaccus in 184 a period of vigorous activity. Frank collected most of the details,[12] and they need not be repeated here, but since so little attention is usually given to the financial implications of these activities, I will mention some important instances. As a preliminary it may be helpful to point out with all due reserve some indications of the scale of Roman public finance in this period. According to the best estimate, the ordinary annual income from direct taxation of property of Roman citizens (the *tributum simplex*) did not in the period of the Second Punic War exceed 3.6 million sesterces, and may have been even less.[13] The cost of the pay of a single legion for one year was nominally about 2.4 million sesterces (but many legions were not kept in service for a full twelve months, and deductions from cash pay were made for food and equipment). In their censorship Cato and Valerius Flaccus probably spent 6 million sesterces (exactly the amount that King Antiochus was paying in indemnity each year) on a single project, the improvement of the sewage system. Livy provides a long list of other projects, as he does for the censorships of 179 and 174. The censors of 174 undertook building not only in the city of Rome, the normal practice, but in colonies as well; it has been suggested that this was done at the expense of the colonies themselves,[14] but it is fairly clear from Livy's account that the expense was borne by the central treasury.[15] In 144–140 the Aqua Marcia, the greatest of the Roman aqueducts up to that time, was constructed at a cost of 180 million sesterces. It was also a great period of road building: not to mention roads in Macedon and Spain that had not been needed before, most of the great trunk roads of Italy were constructed in the second century, as is now becoming increasingly clear.[16] Building styles were also becoming more luxurious. In 146 the first marble buildings in Rome – the temples of Juno and Jupiter vowed by Q. Caecilius Metellus, the conqueror of Macedon, and paid for from his spoils – were erected, and the first gilded ceiling was constructed in the Capitolium in 142–141.

Scholars have often been puzzled by the emphasis that Polybius in his description of the Roman political system places on the importance to the *demos* of the state contracts for building and revenue collecting – almost everyone, he says, was involved in them.[17] That was not of course literally true, but the statement is only intelligible if we pay attention to the enormous growth of public building activity in the second century, growth which was in effect financed by war and conquest.

There were still further public luxuries: while Gaius Gracchus' grain-subsidy law of 123 would have been inconceivable for other reasons in the third century, it could not in any case have been afforded then. There had been selling of grain below the market price at least once in the third century (in 251), but for a regular scheme the treasury had to be as affluent as it was in the second century. We do not know at all reliably what the average market price of grain was at Rome in the time of Gaius Gracchus, or how many people benefited from his scheme (some three hundred and twenty thousand people eventually seem to have benefited from the later scheme of Clodius);

but it can be estimated that for every ten thousand beneficiaries the state expended in an average year from seven to eight hundred thousand sesterces. Right-wing persons later claimed that Gaius Gracchus' law exhausted the treasury, which was quite untrue; but the expense was considerable and again, in effect, financed by war and conquest.

These facts are known to the scholars who deny that economic motives were of any importance in leading Rome into war. They generally argue that Rome did not put much effort into exploiting her overseas power for public revenue. Much attention is paid to the fact that under the terms of the Roman settlement in Macedon in 167 Rome collected taxes at somewhat less than half the rate of the taxation of the Macedonian kings.[v] This is not, however, to be explained by a lack of will to exploit on the part of the Romans. It may very well have been the case that the Senate estimated that no higher rate could be exacted without the presence of a Roman governor and a regular garrison (Macedon had not been annexed), which was undesirable for other reasons.[18] There is no reason to think that the total burden of taxation paid by the Macedonians was lightened, for although they no longer had to pay for King Perseus and his army, they did have to pay (after they had suffered the devastation and pillaging of war) for the governments of four republics and, in three of them, for some military forces. Nor should we suppose that because the Senate decided to close the Macedonian mines in 167 and forego the revenue from them it was indifferent to this revenue; relations between the Senate and the *publicani* who might have organized the collection of revenue were bad at this time, and it would obviously have been dangerous to leave collection in local hands; in any case the mines were reopened in 158. It begs the question, I think, to say that increased revenues were merely an incidental result of war. Rome is said to have continued to collect revenues in the provinces "as much from inertia as from conscious choice,"[19] a phrase that I confess I do not understand. The decision to collect revenues was indeed utterly unsurprising, but there is no reason to suppose that it was anything other than entirely conscious.

Roman wars were wars of plunder, at least in the sense that plundering was a normal part of them.[20] If prisoners were lucky enough to survive, as a general rule they had to be ransomed or sold into slavery. Moveable private property – very widely defined – came into the possession of the victorious army, and, whatever the precise legal status of such booty was, a share was seldom in practice refused to the soldiers. About the effects of this on ordinary soldiers I shall have more to say later. Officers, including those of senatorial rank, received a proportionately larger share. What army commanders took for themselves is, rather oddly, less clear. There were some famous instances of self-restraint, but they help to prove that self-restraint was not the normal practice of victorious commanders.[21] When the elder Cato commanded in Spain in 195–194 his army acquired a large amount of booty, but, says Plutarch, Cato himself took none of it, except what he ate and drank. Plutarch attributes a characteristic saying to him: "I do not blame those who seek to profit from such things, but I wish rather to strive in bravery with the bravest than in wealth with the wealthiest or in greed with the greediest."[22] (For Cato's business interests, see below.) Polybius mentions two cases of such self-restraint: after the battle of Pydna in 168 the whole kingdom of Macedon and its treasury came into the power of the Roman commander Aemilius Paullus, but, says Polybius, he did not desire any of this booty or even wish to look upon it. After the capture of Carthage in 146 his son Scipio Aemilianus took nothing for himself.[23] But there were different levels of self-restraint. It was quite a common practice for victorious generals to spend at least part of their own share of booty on temples or other public purposes, with obvious benefit to themselves. Cicero praises L. Mummius, the commander of the Roman army that performed one of the most predatory and barbaric acts of late republican history, the sack of Corinth in 146, for his self-restraint with regard to booty. In this case it can be seen how self-restraint could be shrewdly combined with self-promotion: Mummius did not take booty for himself, but he "adorned" Italy and the provinces with it, as inscriptions commemorating his gifts to various towns also attest.[24] It is evident in fact that army commanders normally took a substantial share of booty for themselves, though a commander with other ends in view, renown or popularity, might abstain in a particular case or use the whole of his personal share for pseudopublic purposes.

After provinces were annexed governors had large opportunities for profiteering, and the opportunities were sometimes, perhaps regularly, taken. Attempts were made by the Senate, or at least with the Senate's approval, to limit this kind of exploitation, but the restraints were never at all strong, and there is no means of knowing what the Senate regarded as the reasonable limit of exploitation. In 171 envoys from some allies in the Spanish provinces complained to the Senate about the greed and cruelty of some Roman magistrates. Judges were appointed to hear charges against three officials, and the affair ended in one acquittal and the voluntary and not very arduous exile of two of the defendants in Latium. Evidently no money was recovered by the Spaniards. The contents list of the lost forty-seventh book of Livy indicates that it contained an account of how in the period 159–154 several praetors were accused by provincials of *avaritia* and condemned. L. Cornelius Lentulus Lupus, consul in 156, was convicted of a *repetundae* (extortion) charge, and in 149 an unsuccessful attempt was made in a famous case to convict Ser. Sulpicius Galba, a former governor of Spain, of the same charge. There followed in the same year the *Lex Calpurnia*, which set up a permanent court, with a senatorial jury, to deal with such charges, an action that has recently been interpreted, convincingly in my opinion, as an attempt to take such proceedings into the gentle hands of fellow-senators rather than as evidence of increased concern for the interests of provincials.[25] The *Lex Calpurnia* probably did have a restraining effect on provincial governors, but known convictions that genuinely arose from the economic exploitation of the provincials were rare. Such convictions could be obtained only in very exceptional circumstances, and in general the sole controls over a governor's behavior in this respect were the informal disapproval of his peers and his own conscience. Even though the egregious Verres showed such remarkable energy in exploiting Sicily when he governed it that the consuls of 72 tried to restrain him, he afterward had his governorship renewed by the Senate. No one familiar with the more detailed evidence about the behavior of governors in the first century B.C. can be confident that in the second century more than a handful of governors ever conformed to Cicero's idealistic maxim, according to which a good man should bring back from abroad one thing only – good repute.[26]

It is impossible to judge the extent of the business interests of second-century senators. Most scholars seem to think that senators had few such interests beyond those that arose directly from their ownership of land, and I do not want to press the small amount of evidence to the contrary. The *Lex Claudia* of 218, which limited the size of ships that a senator or a senator's son could use in trade, was apparently forced on a reluctant Senate. It turned out to be possible to evade it. The maritime loans of the elder Cato are often thought to have been exceptional and a mark of a "new man" in the Senate,[27] but it is hard to be confident that the rigid moralist Cato was less strict in abstaining from commercial activities than the generality of other senators. Senators were also excluded from direct participation in state contracts,[28] and thus from one means of profiting from war and empire; whether this rule too was evaded we do not know. Most of their wealth probably was in fact in the form of land. (It is likely that senators were already beginning to acquire estates in some of the provinces in the second century, but it cannot be proved.)

Did Roman governments pursue particular foreign policies designed to benefit large-scale Roman landowners? The ban that was placed on the growing of olives and vines in Transalpine Gaul, probably in 154,[29] has sometimes been cited as an instance of such a policy. It is now usually interpreted instead as a favor to Rome's allies at Marseilles, but even if that interpretation is correct, some landowners in Italy may also have benefited in an appreciable way. In one respect, however, all senators, like other men of property, benefited from victorious wars and cannot have helped noticing the fact. Such wars greatly increased the supply of slaves, the best sort of labor for farming and many other purposes. It is of course the error of Marxist theoreticians, as it was also J. A. Hobson's,[30] to single out the slave supply as the one factor that really mattered, a belief for which there is no evidence whatsoever. There certainly was a tremendous influx of slaves, so great that it indirectly threatened to disrupt the whole Roman social and political system. There are no statistics for the slave population, but the market (dominated by Roman buyers, though not confined to them), which could absorb one hundred and fifty thousand slaves from Epirus at a single time in 167, was enormous.[31] It is important to state also that the enslavement of the Epirotes was a gratuitous act – there does not seem to have been any political reason for it. Even Tenney Frank had to admit that this act "might support an inference that the Senate was eager to provide cheap labor in Italy."[32] Appian describes the situation in Italy: the rich built up their *latifundia* and used slaves on them as farm laborers and herdsmen, since free labor would have been drawn off from farming into the army. At the same time the ownership of slaves brought them great profit because of the fertility of the slaves [this is questionable]. Thus the powerful became extremely rich and the race of slaves multiplied throughout the country, while the Italians declined.... The land was held by the rich, who used slaves instead of free men on the farms.[33] As everyone in the Senate (and outside it for that matter) must have been well aware, this great supply of slaves was a direct result of Roman foreign policy.

It might be possible to argue that the moral principles or social ethos of the Roman aristocracy made it indifferent or almost indifferent to private economic gain of the kinds that I have been describing. Some such view seems to be behind a number of the arguments that have been used against economic interpretations of Roman imperialism. The moral principles and social ethos of the Roman aristocracy before the first century are obscure subjects, still in need of a comprehensive scholarly treatment. The evidence is difficult, all the more so since even in the Roman aristocracy there might be quite a variety of outlooks. The qualities that were most admired by the highest aristocracy – high birth and *virtus*, an untranslatable quality that was

best exemplified in an aristocrat's military successes and holding of offices – had
nothing to do with self-enrichment. But there is no good reason to believe that the
second-century aristocracy despised wealth or even the acquisition of wealth, and
there is not even any reason to believe that they paid little attention to the acquisition
of wealth.[34] A recent writer on the subject referred to the "old principle 'omnis
quaestus patribus indecorus visus'"[35] (all financial gain was thought unsuitable for
senators). The phrase comes from Livy's brief description of the passing of the *Lex
Claudia* in 218; it serves him as an explanation of the law, but it is obviously crude –
the *Lex Claudia* was not intended to deprive senators of "all financial gain." Some,
but not all, forms of financial gain were regarded as unsuitable for senators. Livy's
phrase is without historical value for 218,[36] and for the second century as well. Some
much better evidence about the attitude of the aristocracy toward the acquisition
of wealth in the period of the *Lex Claudia* can be found in the funeral eulogy of
L. Caecilius Metellus, *pontifex maximus* and twice consul, delivered by his son in 221.
He had achieved ten great and excellent things, in obtaining which wise men spent
their lives: he was an outstanding warrior, an excellent orator, and a mighty general;
under his command great deeds had been done; he reached the highest honors; he
had great wisdom; he was regarded as a leading senator; he acquired great wealth by
honorable means (*pecuniam magnam bono modo invenire*); he left behind many
children; and he enjoyed a great reputation in the state.[37] These ambitions are so
conventional that we should assume that "acquiring great wealth by honorable
means" was conventional as well. According to some, the only honorable means by
which such a man as Metellus could have acquired great wealth was inheritance,[38] but
this is mere supposition, and *invenire* is quite the wrong verb for inheriting.

Some forms of financial gain were naturally looked down upon by second-century
aristocrats: when the elder Cato stated that usury was not *honestum*, morally respectable,[39] he was probably expressing the general opinion of his class. Its attitude toward
what Cato calls *mercatura*, or trading (he is thinking of fairly large-scale maritime
trading), is not so clear: Cato's only explicit objection to *mercatura* is not that it is
morally unrespectable, but that it is dangerous. The *Lex Claudia*, though it was
passed without the support of the Senate, suggests that two generations earlier there
was some general feeling that senators ought not to engage in some forms of large-
scale trading – but even the *Lex Claudia* allowed the use of smaller ships for
transporting crops to market. We should assume that, with the exception of usury
and some banausic activities that are so obviously excluded that they do not need to
be mentioned and with the doubtful exception of some forms of maritime trade,
other means of self-enrichment were approved by second-century aristocrats. It
would surely be very paradoxical if the immediate profits of war were regarded by
the aristocracy as a less than honorable way of acquiring wealth. Furthermore, in
order to achieve some of their other ambitions, particularly obtaining the highest
political honors (on which the *virtus* of an aristocrat depended), they will have found
money of great importance,[40] and it is unlikely that the income from estates long in
the possession of their families was sufficient.

Did Roman aristocrats as a matter of fact enrich themselves very much by means of
war and empire? That there was an immense growth of luxury is evident from
contemporary evidence and needs no arguing. No second-century Roman can have
possessed wealth on the scale of the fortunes of Pompey or Crassus, but such figures

as we have are almost useless because they do not refer to the size of incomes. When Aemilius Paullus died in 160 he left the sum of sixty talents (1.44 million sesterces), according to Polybius, not really a very large sum; but, as Polybius himself says, Paullus was not at all well off[41] – indeed he cannot have been regarded as such in his own circle, since Polybius says that the sort of lavish gladiatorial games that were given to honor his death would cost as much as thirty talents. Similarly Scipio Aemilianus was, he says, a man of moderate property, for a Roman.[42] This at least shows us that by the standards of the Greek world Polybius considered the Romans of his time to be rich. According to Polybius, Alexander the Isian, who was the richest man in Greece, possessed a little over 200 talents, 4.8 million sesterces in Roman terms. It is likely that there were a number of Roman fortunes of this size by Polybius' time.

Now it may be the case that in spite of all this the Roman aristocracy did not allow any wish for economic gain, either public or private, to impinge on those decisions that concerned war. If the views set out above are correct, it must certainly have been quite difficult for them to prevent such considerations from having some effect, all the more so because military success was so assured. Wars always had their dangers of course, but Roman arms were virtually invincible and everyone knew it, particularly after the battle of Pydna. If one survived, self-enrichment was almost automatic.

Roman foreign policy in the second century was, within certain limits of prudence, generally aggressive and interventionist. As has already been mentioned, there were certain other restraints besides prudence, and they had their effect, mainly in relations with the Greek world before the Third Macedonian War (171–167). The aggressive and interventionist character of Roman policy has not always been clearly perceived, partly because of failure to make the distinction, introduced into ancient history by Rostovtzeff and recently emphasized by Badian, between hegemonial and annexationist imperialism – it is generally believed that there was a certain added caution about annexation.[43] (Annexation was not in any case necessarily the most rewarding method of economic exploitation.) Various factors can be seen to have contributed to this aggressiveness and interventionism: the desire of aristocrats for the psychological and political rewards of military success itself, an irrational degree of fear concerning some foreign states, and probably a constant tendency to believe, as well as to state, that the defense of the Empire required the obedience of foreigners to Rome's will in matters that were really of slight or no importance for Roman security. Some distinctions are difficult to make – the desire for the glory of celebrating a triumph might merge into the desire for economic benefits. I know of only one case in which an ancient writer states it as his own view that a second-century Roman general made war for the sake of plunder – characteristically in Spain, where, according to Appian, L. Licinius Lucullus, the consul of 151, attacked a tribe "out of a desire for glory and out of a need for money." Appian says that Lucullus was poor, but he seems to mention these motives not because they were unusual, but in order to explain the fact that Lucullus made his attack illegally, without the authority of the Senate.[44] Since it is plain that senators must have recognized the economic advantages to the state and to themselves of the foreign policy that was pursued, and since we have no reason to think that they regarded such things as unimportant – quite the reverse – economic motives must be taken to have had a considerable effect. Economic exploitation was not confined to activities that were the incidental side-effects of military victory, as is most clearly shown by the enslavement of the one hundred and fifty thousand Epirotes in 167 and by a similar act of enslavement carried out on a vast scale in Sardinia in 177.[45] For reasons that have been explained, the presence of economic motives is not excluded by the fact that the stated reasons for war were of a quite different kind. It can be added that if everyone in the Senate recognized the economic advantages of the general policy, they did not have to be debated at length. Of course there may have been some senators who were utterly indifferent to private economic gain. (Were there any who were indifferent to public economic gain?) I am not denying the existence of, or even attributing secondary importance to, motives that can be classified as "political." Perhaps the best formulation that is possible on the surviving evidence is to say that desire for economic gain was an important factor predisposing senators to take aggressive and interventionist decisions in foreign policy, and there is no reason to doubt that at least on some occasions it played a more immediate part in leading to such decisions.

Little has been said so far about the private economic interests of those outside the Senate. Nonsenatorial businessmen were obviously not indifferent to the economic advantages of war. The sort of businessmen who could expect to receive contracts like the ones allotted by a praetor in 169 for six thousand togas and thirty thousand tunics for the army in Macedon were probably sympathetic to the policies that led to there being a Roman army in Macedon. And there certainly were some occasions when Roman businessmen benefited directly from Rome's ability to have her will obeyed in more and more parts of the world, and from the willingness of Roman governments to secure privileges for businessmen, such as the freedom from port dues obtained for Roman citizens and Latins from Ambracia in 187 and the free harbor established at Delos in 167. (Both Romans and non-Roman Italians benefited from this, and the latter have for a long time been supposed to have been much more numerous than the former among Delian businessmen, but some recent research tends to reverse this conclusion.[46]) From 123 the contracts for the collection of taxes in the province of Asia were given out by the censors at Rome, and Roman businessmen profited considerably. It may be the case that the Jugurthine War was imposed on a reluctant Senate by business interests. But in general it can be agreed that nonsenatorial businessmen were not powerful enough in the second century to get particular decisions about foreign policy from the Senate, and they were certainly not powerful enough to impose a whole outlook on the Senate. They failed to get many of the economic privileges that they would presumably have liked, in particular the right to collect the taxes of Sicily, which remained in the hands of Sicilians, and those of Spain, where the taxes were collected by the quaestors. It has been suggested that Roman business interests were not in fact happy to see the commercial cities of Corinth and Carthage destroyed in 146;[47] by our lights, that would have been the rational reaction. Insofar as businessmen in general did have any influence on such matters, its total effect was surely in favor of aggressive and interventionist policies, but Tenney Frank and his followers were correct to play down the influence of nonsenatorial business interests on foreign policy.

One other group of Romans needs to be considered, in addition to senators and nonsenatorial businessmen, namely the body of those Roman citizens who were liable for military service. It is not at all fashionable to suppose that there was much exercise of popular sovereignty at Rome in the second century, least of all in foreign affairs. There was, however, one way in which the popular will must have had some effect from time to time, and that was in regard to war. There was a recurrent and increasing difficulty in recruiting soldiers for the Roman army, and this difficulty eventually became a serious crisis. The reduction of the minimum census of the fifth class from eleven thousand to four thousand *asses*, an action designed to increase the number of citizens eligible for military service, which was probably taken at some date between 200 and 150, and the eventual "proletarianization" of the Roman army by Marius in 107 were consequences of this problem. The nature of these difficulties is, one may suspect, somewhat veiled by the sources; Livy preferred to spend time retelling a story, no doubt very pleasing to his readers, about the centurion Spurius Ligustinus, who in 171 set an example to his fellow ex-centurions by doing his duty and agreeing to serve at whatever rank was assigned to him. That was how Roman soldiers were meant to behave. It seems to have become particularly difficult to find sufficient recruits for the Third Macedonian War. The Spanish wars of 153–133 intensified the problem to such an extent that, even from our very scanty sources for the period, we know that in 151 and in 138 the consuls were imprisoned by the tribunes of the plebs (whose responsibility it was to protect citizens from the unjust operation of the levy), and the government was forced to ease the conditions of military service. Solving this problem was probably among the aims of Tiberius Gracchus' radical program in 133. We do not, it is true, have any specific evidence that the Senate's deliberations were influenced by all this, but the nature of the sources makes that unsurprising.

What determined the attitudes of potential soldiers toward war and toward particular wars? It was a duty to serve, and that might have been that. There will naturally have been plenty of enthusiasm for defeating such obvious national enemies as Hannibal – not that many of Rome's enemies in the second century fell into this category. But we are not dealing with 1914 Europeans, ignorant of war and therefore eager for it. It is clear that the prospects of danger and discomfort will often have been weighed against the prospect of booty, and that when armies had been raised the most common threat to discipline was conflict over booty. We can get a view of an authentically nonaristocratic attitude toward war from Plautus. When the slave Epidicus needs to raise money quickly, he says: "ego de re argentaria / iam senatum convocabo in corde consiliarium, / quoi potissimum indicatur bellum, unde argentum auferam."[48] (I shall now summon a meeting of my mental Senate to take counsel on financial questions, against whom it is best to declare war, and where to steal some money.) Comic poets are notoriously treacherous material for historians, but this is not merely a translation from Plautus' Greek original, as the concepts and terminology show,[49] and it seems reasonable to draw from it the inference that war was regarded (as well it might be) as a means of making money. Thus we can add some further economic motives to the more effective ones that have already been attributed to the Senate.

To conclude: while no attempt should be made to revive "mercantilist" explanations of Roman imperialism in the second century, some economic motives can be detected. Combinations and conjectures can be fatal flaws in this type of explanation, but given the nature of the evidence, most of which is apologetic and, except for Polybius, far removed in date from the events, some combinations and conjectures are justified.

NOTES

1 I use the term "imperialism" here to mean expansion of power in general, not only annexationist expansion; cf. below, p. 25. In this article I have kept footnotes and discussion of the numerous peripheral controversies to a minimum.

2 *Roman Imperialism* (New York, 1914), especially 277–97. This is mostly repeated from his "Mercantilism and Rome's Foreign Policy," *AHR* [*American Historical Review*], 18 (1912–13): 233–52.

3 Filippo Cassola, *I gruppi politici romani nel III secolo a.C.* (Trieste, 1962), especially 50–83, 393–404, made some interesting remarks about the third century, and also about the second. For a critique see especially the review by John Briscoe, *Classical Review*, n.s. 13 (1963): 322–3.

4 *Roman Imperialism in the Late Republic* (2d ed.; Oxford, 1968), 17, 18, 20.

5 A. W. Gomme, A. Andrews, and K. J. Dover, *A Historical Commentary on Thucydides*, 4 (Oxford, 1970), 229–30.

6 Not that such views were restricted to those foreigners who were hostile to Rome; cf. 1 Maccabees 8:3.

7 Polybius 36.2.

8 Cassius Dio 53.19.3

9 On financial probity see Polybius 6.56.1–5 – but we know of no one who was put to death for electoral bribery. On the excessive plundering of Syracuse in 211, see Polybius 9.10. Polybius' later views are in 18.35.1–2; cf. 31.25.

10 *An Economic Survey of Ancient Rome* (hereafter *ESAR*), 1, *Rome and Italy of the Republic* (Baltimore, 1933), 126–46, 222–31.

11 Pliny *Naturalis Historia* 33.55.

12 Frank, *ESAR*, 1:183–7.

13 See Gaetano De Sanctis, *Storia dei romani*, vol. 3, pt. 2 (Turin, 1916), 623–31.

14 Frank, *ESAR*, 1:186.

15 Livy 41.27.10–13. (On the text, compare Will Richter, "Zum Bauprogramm der Censoren des Jahres 174 v. Chr. [Livius 41, 27, 5–12]," *Rheinisches Museum für Philologie*, n.s. 104 (1961): 257–69).

16 Compare my *Rome in Etruria and Umbria* (Oxford, 1971), 161–9.

17 Polybius 6.17.3–4.

18 I shall be dealing elsewhere with the Senate's supposed reluctance to annex territory in the second century, which is heavily emphasized by Badian, *Roman Imperialism*.

19 Badian, *Roman Imperialism*, 18.

20 The essential discussion of Roman law and practice concerning plunder is that of K. H. Vogel in Pauly-Wissowa, *Real-Encyclopädie*, s.v. *praeda* (1953), cols 1200–13. André Aymard, "Le Partage des profits de la guerre dans les traités d'alliance antiques," *Revue historique*, 217 (1957): 233–49, reprinted in his *Etudes d'histoire ancienne* (Paris, 1967), 499–512, is also important.

21 Note particularly Polybius 31.22.3.

22 Plutarch *Cato Maior* 10.

23 Polybius 18.35.4–5 and 31.22 (Aemilius Paullus): 18.35.9–12 (Aemilianus).

24 See Attilio Degrassi, ed., *Inscriptiones Latinae Liberae Rei Publicae*, 1 (2d ed.; Florence, 1965): nos 327–31.

25 E. S. Gruen, *Roman Politics and the Criminal Courts, 149–78 B.C.* (Cambridge, Mass., 1968), 13–15.

26 Cicero *De Legibus* 3.8.18.

27 Our information comes from Plutarch *Cato Maior* 21.

28 Theodor Mommsen, *Römisches Staatsrecht*, 3 (Leipzig, 1887), 509–10.
29 Cicero *De Republica* 3.16.
30 *Imperialism, A Study* (London, 1938), 247–8.
31 On the facts see N. G. L. Hammond, *Epirus* (Oxford, 1967), 634–5.
32 Frank, *ESAR*, 1: 188.
33 Appian *Civil Wars* 1.7.29–31.
34 M. I. Finley, "Technical Innovation and Economic Progress in the Ancient World," *Economic History Review*, 18 (1965): 31, states that there were "no subconscious guilt feelings" about wealth in the ancient world; but for second-century Rome the proliferation of sumptuary laws may suggest that this generalization goes too far.
35 P. A. Brunt, "The Equites in the Late Republic," *Second International Conference of Economic History* (Aix-en-Provence, 1962; Paris and The Hague, 1965), 1:126, referring to Livy 21.63.4.
36 Compare Adolf Lippold, *Consules, Untersuchungen zur Geschichte des römischen Konsulates von 264 bis 201 v. Chr.* (Bonn, 1963), 93–5.
37 Pliny *Naturalis Historia* 8.140, also printed in Enrica Malcovati, ed., *Oratorum Romanorum Fragmenta* (3d ed.; Turin, 1967), no. 6, fr. 2. On the importance of this passage see Lippold, *Consules*, 74–84.
38 Compare D. C. Earl, *The Moral and Political Tradition of Rome* (London, 1967), 32.
39 Cato *De Agri Cultura* preface.
40 See H. H. Scullard, *Roman Politics, 220–150 B.C.* (Oxford, 1951), especially 23–5, on the growing importance of various forms of bribery in second-century politics.
41 Polybius 18.35.5; compare 31.22.
42 Polybius 18.35.10. For the correct interpretation of this passage. see F. W. Walbank, *A Historical Commentary on Polybius*, 2 (Oxford, 1967), 597.
43 For this distinction see M. I. Rostovtzeff, *The Social and Economic History of the Hellenistic World* (Oxford, 1941), 70–1; and Badian, *Roman Imperialism*, 4.
44 Appian *Spanish Wars* 51.
45 Livy 41.28.7–9.
46 A. J. N. Wilson, *Emigration from Italy in the Republican Age of Rome* (Manchester, 1966), 105–11.
47 For example, by Cassola, *I gruppi politici romani*, 55–6; and Badian. *Roman Imperialism*, 20–1.
48 Plautus *Epidicus* 158–60.
49 Compare Eduard Fraenkel, *Plautinisches im Plautus* (Berlin, 1922), 234; E. J. Bikerman, "Notes sur Polybe, III. Initia belli Macedonici," *Revue des Etudes Grecques*, 66 (1953): 482.

EDITOR'S NOTES

i This article introduced themes which Harris expanded in his later influential study, *War and Imperialism in Republican Rome, 327–70* BC, revised edn. (Oxford, 2000); see especially pp. 54–104 on economic motives and the important review article by J. A. North, "The Development of Roman Imperialism," *Journal of Roman Studies*, 71/2 (1981/2), pp. 1–9.
ii For the sources on the dramatic episode involving M'. Aquillius and Mithridates VI of Pontus in 88 BCE, see T. R. S. Broughton, *The Magistrates of the Roman Republic*, vol. 2 (repr. Chico, Calif., 1984), p. 43; vol. 3, pp. 24–5.
iii On the fetial priesthood, see Glossary.

iv The theme of Roman decline from ancestral virtue and the debilitating effects of the
    invasion of avarice and luxury as a result of imperial success became a literary commonplace
    by the late Republic; see A. W. Lintott, "Imperial Expansion and Moral Decline in the
    Roman Republic," *Historia*, 21 (1972), pp. 626–38.
v   Livy 45.18.3–8, 29.10–11.

Material Rewards and the Drive for Empire

Erich S. Gruen

Conquest brought tangible benefits. The laws of war in antiquity assured and legit-
imized them. Expropriation of land, seizure of movable goods, imposition of monetary penalties, enslavement of the enemy went unquestioned as earned emoluments of
the victor. Romans certainly never questioned them. A society persistently primed for
war, most of whose adult males could expect to see active military duty, appreciated
both the risks and the rewards of battle. Only the naive or myopic will deny that
Romans perceived, indeed welcomed the economic advantages of conquest. The
proposition seems self-evident. But what does it tell us? Does the desire for gain
entail a drive for empire? To what extent did the acquisition of material benefits
depend upon the practice of imperialism, i.e. the deliberate and systematic exploitation of other states' resources and the control of their policies and personnel?

The subject, of course, is vast and complex. A short treatment cannot pretend to do
it justice. Limitations of time and space require focus on selective matters. For present
purposes, the study concentrates upon the early stages of Roman overseas expansion,
the critical stages of the 3rd and 2nd centuries B.C., with particular attention to
Rome and the Greek east.

A growing body of scholarly literature finds war and greed tantamount to imperialism.[1] The equation may be too simple. Distinctions need to be made and emphasized. The prospect of loot could entice generals and stimulate recruiting – which is
not the same as determining a senatorial decision to make war. The carrying off of
spoils and the exaction of indemnity might enrich the state, but would not necessarily
impel it toward an enduring system of regulation and exploitation. Enslavement or
sale of defeated enemies helped stock the plantations of rural Italy; yet nothing shows
that this either inspired Roman expansion or dictated imperial control. The leaps of
logic too easily distort and mislead.

Romans had concrete expectations from war. Soldiers enrolled eagerly for the first
conflict with Carthage, says Polybius, when commanders pointed out the prospects
for plunder. A century later, the same enticements seduced recruits for the Third
Macedonian War: they glimpsed the wealthy life-styles of veterans of previous eastern
wars and swiftly filled up the ranks.[2] In neither case, however, did the motives of
milites coincide with the reasons of state.[3] The alliance with Aetolia in 212 or 211
specified distribution of the fruits of victory: Aetolians to get all conquered territory,
farms, fields, and buildings, the Romans to get all movable booty. A clue to Rome's
motivation? Hardly. Aetolia held the upper hand in that alliance and the terms were

probably hers, leaving to Rome what (for the Aetolians) was of secondary interest. Indeed, an earlier Roman treaty with Carthage conceded to the Punic power all booty from captured towns in Latium, so long as the towns would be yielded up. Plunder did not occupy a central place in the making of policy.[4]

War meant booty. The conjunction was taken for granted, unquestioned and undebated. The Roman army even had routine, established procedures for the collection and distribution of loot.[5][i] The prayer of Scipio Africanus before embarking for Africa in 204 asked for punishment of the enemy, safe return, triumph – and plunder.[6] The contemporary comedies of Plautus regularly link warfare with enrichment, the greed of the soldier a common theme and the connection of victory and spoils an automatic one.[7] Eastern victories, of course, produced spoils in spectacular quantities. The triumphs of T. Flamininus, M'. Acilius Glabrio, L. Scipio, M. Fulvius Nobilior, and Cn. Manlius Vulso in the period 194–187 dazzled Rome with their brilliance, vast treasures on display, statues of marble and bronze, coined and uncoined gold and silver, precious art objects, and captured prizes of every description.[8] Equally majestic was the triumph of L. Aemilius Paullus twenty years later, rivaling theirs in splendor and fortune.[9] The repute of the generals soared at such demonstrations; the more so when they utilized the cash to finance lavish games, make dedications at shrines, build public monuments and bestow handsome gifts.

To what extent were these spoils sought in order to buttress the economic power of the state? The public coffers benefited, to be sure. But not in any regular or predictable way. The state economy can hardly have depended upon transmission of plunder. Commanders, in fact, had considerable leeway in the matter of booty. Distribution to the soldiers was essential; morale and politics demanded it. Occasionally all the loot was disposed of in this fashion. Otherwise, the *imperator* had broad scope; no laws compelled him to deliver specific sums or percentages to the *aerarium*. He made his own determination, often enriching friends and officers to put his generosity on show. Cato sternly stood above the practice: he would pocket no loot and play no favorites with his disbursements. Aemilius Paullus too, we are told, refrained from touching the booty of Pydna; and his son Scipio Aemilianus was equally conscientious after the fall of Carthage. The cases are, of course, exceptional, that very fact preserving the tales for posterity. They point up by contrast what the norm was or was expected to be. And even Cato did not take the position that plunder from war belonged exclusively to the treasury: the men who had first claim on the booty were the soldiers who captured it.[10] That principle was axiomatic. It also has certain interesting implications. The spoils of war belonged to the warriors; the men who issued commands also issued the proceeds. Material rewards, as well as renown and an opportunity for beneficence, accrued to victorious generals. The state got a share sometimes, though not always. It did not receive first consideration in the matter of *praeda*. Even when, as in the case of the eastern victories, the spoils were of colossal magnitude, that principle held. The practice underscores Roman avarice; who could ever have denied that characteristic? But far from providing a link between the prizes of conquest and a policy of imperialism, it points in the opposite direction. The profits of plunder meant private gains for officers and men, but did not and were not meant to supply steady income for the treasury or provide a basis on which to build the state economy.[ii]

To be sure, members of the ruling class were principal beneficiaries of these acquisitions – the very men whose *auctoritas* guided the decisions of state. A distinction between individual profits and public advantage, it could be argued, is artificial. But a more fundamental distinction bears notice here. The corporate interest of the ruling class occasionally required the disciplining of individual members, most especially when their enrichment in war threatened to elevate them above their peers. That collective concern manifested itself, for example, in charges of peculation and illicit gains levelled against men like M. Fulvius, Cn. Manlius, and the Scipio brothers in the 180s.[11] In the matter of booty, the interests of commanders and those of the state were not identical.

Indemnity payments would bring in higher sums and more regular ones.[12] Eastern kings and states that fell to Roman might have to pay dearly for their failures. The Illyrians were first to experience it across the Adriatic: Queen Teuta agreed to any exaction the Romans demanded in 228, and the Republic was still collecting cash from her successor Pinnes more than a decade later.[13] A *senatus consultum* in 196 demanded one thousand talents from Philip V, five hundred of it on the spot, the rest to be paid in ten annual installments.[14] Nabis' defeat in 195 cost him five hundred talents, one fifth of it immediately, the remainder at a rate of fifty *per annum*.[15] The vanquished Aetolians in 189 were saddled with a two hundred talent indemnity, plus another three hundred due over a six year period.[16] From Antiochus the Great Rome exacted a far larger sum in 188: a down payment of five hundred talents, twenty-five hundred more upon ratification of the peace, then twelve annual payments of one thousand talents each.[17] Manlius Vulso demanded six hundred talents from Ariarathes of Cappadocia, who had collaborated with Antiochus and now showed himself belatedly repentant.[18] After Perseus' defeat in 168, Rome presented a hefty bill to the Macedonians: they would have to pay to the Republic half the taxes normally paid to the monarchy. A similar burden fell upon the former subjects of Genthius in Illyria.[19]

The combined revenues from these sources added up to an impressive sum. Enough to constitute a motive? One cannot readily put price tags on motives. Approach from that direction may be altogether erroneous anyway. A closer look at these exactions suggests that economic considerations do not supply the principal ingredient.

Longstanding Roman policy held that the costs of war should be reimbursed by the defeated foe.[20] The principle is implicit in every insistence upon indemnity. It becomes explicit in negotiations with Antiochus the Great. The Seleucid king offered to pay half the expenses incurred by Rome in the course of her war with him. L. Scipio the consul and his *consilium* dismissed that proposal out of hand: Antiochus would pay it all. He had started the war and he was liable for its costs.[21] Roman negotiators operated with consistency on that principle. Which is not to say that figures were calculated precisely to cover the outlays of the previous conflict. The round sums belie any rigid bookkeeping of that sort. Indemnities penalized as well as reimbursed. They underlined the power of the victor and the submission of the vanquished.[22]

Politics rather than economics took central place. The senate canceled Philip's reparation payments in 190 when he proved cooperative and valuable – just as they had done, under like circumstances, with Hiero II of Syracuse more than a half-century earlier.[23] The use of monetary demands as a diplomatic posture gets clear illustration in Roman dealings with Aetolia in 191–189. Again and again, the

Republic's representatives demanded unconditional surrender and a staggering indemnity of one thousand talents, unyielding in their severity – until the Aetolians submitted. Then the consul suddenly proved amenable to persuasion: the indemnity demand was reduced by fifty percent.[24] Cash as enrichment of the public coffers evidently did not hold first importance for the Romans. In similar fashion, Manlius Vulso bullied Ariarathes of Cappadocia, stipulating six hundred talents as price for a peaceful settlement with Rome. It took only the intervention of Eumenes, however, to get that fine also cut in half.[25] The Galatians, against whom Manlius had waged ruthless warfare and from whom he carried off considerable plunder, escaped any indemnity. The *aerarium* would get no steady income from that source.

The political character of these payments stands out. Rome looked to her prestige and her international position. In the midst of the Hannibalic war, the senate gave pointed reminder to Pinnes of Illyria about an overdue bill. The act served as a clear demonstration: Rome still held sway in the Adriatic, a message to Hannibal and the Illyrians alike. It was surely not the cash that mattered.[26] More than forty years later, the *patres* were unperturbed when Antiochus IV failed to meet the deadline for his indemnity payment.[27] An incident outside the eastern context shines the brightest light on Roman attitudes. Carthaginian envoys in 191 proposed to pay off their entire indemnity. Terms of the treaty after the Hannibalic war had obliged them to remit ten thousand talents in a payment schedule that stretched over fifty years. Now, only a decade or so after the agreement, Carthage showed herself ready to discharge her obligation in a single lump sum. The *patres*, however, rejected the offer with alacrity. They would accept not a coin before the date it fell due.[28] There can be but one explanation for that sharp retort. Continuous, long-term payments emphasized the submission of the former enemy and gave repeated reminder of her defeat, a lesson to other powers who might be recalcitrant or belligerent. The economic benefit was incidental.

Of course Rome welcomed the revenue. The first two-thirds of the 2nd century witnessed large-scale expenditures, major building projects and public works, construction of the great highways in Italy.[29] Pliny reports a vast surplus in the *aerarium* for the year 157 B.C., one of its best years, of over one hundred million HS.[30] Substantial public wealth marks this era; and the connection with receipts from overseas is undeniable. But a pattern of planned and deliberate exploitation aimed at public enrichment is missing. Windfall profits were utilized, naturally. Booty from Manlius Vulso's triumph in 187 wiped out the arrears of a public debt.[31] The loot that Aemilius Paullus deposited with the treasury after Pydna was so sizable that the government could dispense with direct taxation of Roman citizens.[32] A national budget, however, could hardly depend on the proceeds of occasional plunder, even when spectacular. And indemnity payments were subject to the vagaries of international politics, retained, reduced, or canceled in accordance with the diplomatic circumstances, not the public economy. Insofar as regular, steady, and long-term income flowed from abroad, the west rather than the east supplied it. The fifty year indemnity from Carthage was only a part. Receipts from the Spanish mines brought in about thirty-six million HS annually, so Polybius attests.[33]

Nothing like this regularity featured in the profits that came out of the east, though the gains from particular conflicts could be phenomenal. The senate refrained for a remarkably long time from instituting a permanent tribute in any Hellenic state. Even the assessments levied upon the Macedonians in 167 seem to represent an arrangement whereby the new republics could pay reparations for a war provoked (from the Roman point of view) by the now deposed monarchy.[34] Systematic impositions in Macedonia began no earlier than 148, after the fall of Andriscus, when Rome at last accepted responsibility for military supervision of the state, a supervision that needed to be paid for.[35] The Macedonian mines too were treated differently from those in Spain. Rome shut them down after the fall of Perseus, unwilling to let *publicani* reap the profits and distrustful of Macedonian management.[36] The rich revenues of Asia Minor came on the initiative of Attalus III, not on the prompting of Roman policy; and installation of a tax system waited still a decade after Attalus III's death, until the tribunate of C. Gracchus.[37] In the case of Greece proper, Rome probably fixed no tribute for yet another century, in the era of Augustus.[38] Of course, neither abstinence nor altruism guided this restraint. The Republic, its leaders and its representatives had rewarded themselves handsomely with spoils from the Greek east. But until they were ready to accept the chore of policing and administering that area, they never regarded it as a steady resource for the state economy.

The business and financial communities in Rome begin to impose themselves upon public attention in this era. Evidence discloses the *publicani*, bidders on government contracts, already active and well established by the later 3rd century.[39] Their activities soon expanded and diversified. The censors let contracts for a salt tax beginning in 204. Harbor dues were collected by the *publicani* at least by 199. And they gained responsibility too for the *scriptura* or pasturage tax.[40] The contractors continued to manage the organization of supplies for Rome's armies during the 2nd century, a task that grew in magnitude and augmented their influence.[41] More lucrative still was the operation of the Spanish mines, very probably in the hands of *publicani* since 195.[42]

Publicani were not alone among the rising tide of business interests. The *lex Claudia* of 218 forbade any senator or son of a senator from owning a sea-going vessel that could carry more than three hundred *amphorae*. Whatever the political meaning of this measure, it implies at least that there were men outside the senate who *did* engage in maritime commerce on rather a handsome scale.[43] Money-lenders were much in evidence by the early 2nd century, so much so that the government had to take action against usury and to close loopholes allowing for evasion of maximum interest rates.[44] Cato, with typical self-righteousness, unceremoniously expelled the money-lenders he found in Sardinia in 198.[45] The profession, however, certainly persisted. So long as loans for transactions, whether agricultural or commercial, were in demand, the *faenerator* would be around. The comedies of Plautus regularly mock bankers and loan sharks. Before the middle of the 2nd century Scipio Aemilianus had his own personal banker to handle his financial obligations.[46] Merchants and profiteers followed the armies abroad in war-time, ready brokers of military spoils, who often made a nuisance of themselves.[47]

Business activities plainly proliferated in the late 3rd and early 2nd centuries. The *publicanus* makes appearance in the Plautine plays.[48] And from the activities of the *publicani*, many profited: censorial contracts for public works of every kind benefited shareholders, employees, agents, and a host of persons who capitalized on business arising out of the contracts.[49]

What impact did these developments have upon Roman policy in the east? Most of the information gathered above, in fact, applies to Italy and the west. Activities of the *publicani* and their concomitant beneficiaries in the Hellenic world had to await the era of Rome's occupation and permanent installations.

Lesser businessmen, to be sure, *negotiatores* and *mercatores*, moved east much earlier. No need for them to hold back and calculate military conquest or annexation. Scattered epigraphical and literary allusions disclose Italians in Hellenic lands even in the early and middle 3rd century. A certain L. Folius (or Olius) made dedication to Athena on the Acropolis at Rhodian Lindos, a bilingual offering, some time in the first half of that century.[50] Not much later, an Aetolian proxeny decree named among its honorants a Roman, Olceus son of Lucius.[51] In 252, as it happens, an incidental notice in Plutarch's *Life of Aratus* makes reference to a Roman merchant vessel bound for Syria.[52] Before the end of the century we learn of a certain Lucius, son of Gaius, in the king's service, an official in the bureaucracy of Ptolemy IV Philopator.[53] The random character of our data makes it unlikely that these are isolated examples. But they are individual examples. Nothing in that evidence suggests that Rome, rather than particular Romans and Italians, enjoyed trade relations with Rhodes, Aetolia, Syria, or Egypt.[54]

In addition, numerous inscriptions attest the presence of Romans and Italians in the Greek east during the 2nd century B.C., most of them proxeny decrees revealing little about the persons except their presence. The vast majority, however, were clearly traders, financiers, or small businessmen. Through most of the century they are to be found primarily in Greece proper and in the Cyclades. Only toward the end of the century, as might be expected, do they begin to turn up in Asia Minor, and later still further east. The best evidence comes from the island of Delos, where communities of Ῥωμαῖοι [the Romans] appear in increasing numbers not long after Delos became a free port in 166, then considerably augmented by those who migrated there following the destruction of Corinth in 146.[55] The appeal of the Hellenic east had worked its allure among steadily swelling numbers of Ῥωμαῖοι, traders and tradesmen, bankers and pilgrims, visitors and settlers.[56]

A surge in business activities and a migration of Italians to the east in this era command attention. Yet the formidable question still confronts us: what reason is there to believe that increased commercial and banking activities and the movement of private individuals to Hellenic lands helped determine senatorial policy on the east?[57]

The influence of financiers and contractors on decisions of state would be most difficult to document. And some potent evidence to the contrary stands in the way. As noted already, the senate three times at least during the early 2nd century sponsored enactments to crack down on usurious practices and to curb money-lenders.[58] The aediles of 192 were so assiduous in imposing fines upon the *faeneratores* that they collected enough capital to set up rich dedications in the Capitol and finance the building of a portico.[59] The *lex Marcia*, probably of the 180s, in a stunning reversal of previous practice, even permitted debtors to seize upon the persons of their creditors and hold them until the excessive interest that had been exacted was repaid.[60]

More interesting still are the government's relations with the companies of *publicani*. The insurance scandal engineered by two of these contractors during the dark days of the Hannibalic war hardly promoted cordiality between government and business. When the fraudulence came to light, an explosive political battle erupted,

ending in firm government action against the offending *publicani*.[61] The censors of
184 came into sharp conflict with business contractors and, despite some dissent in
the senate, eventually prevailed, with the *patres'* compliance.[62] Still another clash
burst into the open during the censorship of 169. Heated passions even provoked
criminal proceedings. The aims of the *publicani* were once again thwarted.[63] The
storm aroused in that year soured more senators on the activities of the business
community. Resentment and annoyance received outlet in 167 when the senate
refused to let contracts for the lucrative gold and silver mines and the royal estates
of Macedonia, in order to keep those profits out of the hands of the *publicani*.[64] The
mines were then shut down, to be reopened nearly a decade later – and then quite
possibly turned over to the Macedonians rather than to the *publicani*.[65]

The upshot of this testimony is clear enough. Roman senators, far from making
policy at the behest of the business communities, often found themselves in conflict
with financiers, money-lenders, and contractors. Those intermittent clashes should
not be taken to imply a fundamental and consistent divergence of interests. But the
patres plainly took their decisions on affairs of state for reasons other than the aims
and profits of *negotiatores*. A noteworthy fact needs to be underscored: the absence of
the Roman *denarius* as currency in Greek lands anywhere during the Republic.[66] The
senate did not act to ripen Hellas for plucking by businessmen.

Businessmen apart, were not senators themselves interested in gain? The very
passage of the *lex Claudia* makes sense only if some senators had engaged in shipping
on a fairly large scale; and the bill provoked substantial opposition in the *curia*.
Moreover, it was honored more in the breach than in the observance.[67] The venerable Cato himself lent out cash for maritime enterprises and invested capital in various
agricultural and business operations that brought in handsome profits.[68] Cato found
no inconsistency here with his fulminations against usury and *faeneratores*. Rightly so:
it was one thing to pursue the dubious profession as a livelihood, quite another – and
entirely acceptable – for a landed aristocrat to add to his assets by lending cash on the
side.[69] Cato, after all, wrote a book on capitalist agriculture, a venture he found
perfectly in accord with the traditional virtues of a peasant farmer.[70] Avarice *per se*, of
course, was deplorable, beneath the contempt of respectable *nobiles*. But the increase
of wealth – so long as it was done in honorable and estimable fashion – could stand as
a mark of prestige. The funeral *laudatio* delivered by Q. Metellus for his father in 221
listed among his proudest aspirations the aim to acquire great wealth *bono modo*.[71]
Cato counseled his son in similar fashion: increase of property shows the measure of a
man, indeed godlike qualities attach to him who added more to his holdings than he
inherited.[72] Polybius observed the ethos and reported it: Romans condemn illicit
gains with as much vehemence as they applaud honest money-making.[73] Sallust drew
the same distinction a century later in commending Romans of an earlier day: glory
and praise motivated them, but also "wealth acquired honorably".[74] The combined
testimony forms a clear picture. Senatorial aristocrats might affect scorn for petty
tradesmen and abhor business dealings as an occupation, but they had no disdain, in
practice or principle, for the acquisition of capital.[75]

That many Roman senators had economic interests outside the possession of land
in Italy ought never to have been doubted. It is a very long stride, however, from
acknowledgment of this rather obvious fact to the speculative surmise that senators'
economic enterprises determined or strongly influenced the decisions of state. The

patres indeed seem to have been careful to avoid even the appearance of a conflict of interest along these lines. In the late Republic, senators were barred by law from membership or share holding in the companies of contractors for public services, an exclusion that surely dates back to the 3rd and 2nd centuries.[76] Such scrupulousness in the official posture makes it most unlikely that any senator gave voice in *curia* or *contio* for economic considerations as grounds for determining foreign policy.[77] Those who reckon material advantages as a principal aim of empire get small comfort from the contemporary observations of Polybius. The Greek historian saw a connection but reversed it. In Polybius' view, accumulation of wealth had as its purpose the advance of imperialism.[78] It evidently never occurred to him that the means and ends might be the other way around.

Did the state protect financial and commercial interests in its dealings with eastern powers? The evidence allows a cautious answer: rarely, if at all, and without consistency.

The Pyrrhic war put Rome in intimate contact with communities of southern Italy, especially Greek cities in the area, heavily engaged in traffic across the Adriatic. Rome herself had no commercial stake in the region; but her own suzerainty in Italy depended on compliance and cooperation of key cities in Magna Graecia. Considerations of that sort help to explain Roman threats and then action against the Illyrians in 230 and 229: Italian traders had been harassed, and the growing Illyrian power suddenly turned into a major menace in the Adriatic. Rome was by then well acquainted with the region. Envoys from Apollonia had sought her out after the Pyrrhic war, and the senate had dispatched a Latin colony to Brundisium in 244. Interconnections between Hellenic cities on both sides of the straits of Otranto had an impact. Rome sent her forces against Illyria, it might be noted, when Epidamnus was under assault.[79] The *patres* knew well the importance of commercial exchange in the Ionian Gulf, as they appreciated the crucial situation of the straits of Messina. Insofar as such matters played a role in decisions to intervene, however, they represented the claims of Rome's allies and *amici*, not the promotion of a Roman mercantile interest.[80] The political implications of maintaining a hold on the Italian "confederacy", rather than direct economic advantage, prevailed in those decisions.

One famous senatorial action would seem to support the economic hypothesis. In 187 the *patres* passed a decree awarding Ambracia the privilege of imposing whatever harbor dues she wished – so long as Romans and Latins were exempt from payment.[81] On the face of it, economic aims furthered by the government in this instance appear incontrovertible. Depending on one's viewpoint and argument, the episode is either a cornerstone or an embarrassment, either exemplary or exceptional.[82] The matter can benefit from closer scrutiny than it has received. No parallels exist, as is often pointed out, in other Roman treaties. One can go further. This provision is not contained in a treaty at all. The relevant pact with Aetolia had been concluded two years before. A *senatus consultum* is at issue here. Political circumstances called it forth, as Livy's account makes abundantly clear. Charges surfaced against M. Fulvius Nobilior for ruthless ravaging of Ambracia. Fulvius' embittered political foe, M. Lepidus, twice thwarted by him in consular elections, engineered the accusations and coached Ambraciote representatives in their testimony.[83] Out of this acrimonious exchange came the senatorial resolution, a direct and deliberate slap at

Fulvius. The decree declared Ambracia free and self-governing, authorized recovery of all property by her citizens, and ordered restoration of all art objects plundered from the land. The allowance of port dues was but one provision in that omnibus measure.[84] Its passage plainly directed a rebuke at Fulvius and sought to make amends to the Ambraciotes. Permission of unlimited harbor tolls showed senatorial favor in a gesture meant to rehabilitate the state's finances. It was only logical and proper for the benefactors to be exempt from paying the revenues authorized by their benefaction. The measure's purpose had nothing to do with enriching Rome's commercial classes.

The Ambracia incident is a special case. Hence, no surprise that similar provisions are absent in known treaties, and no reason to postulate their presence in unknown ones.[85] The peculiar circumstances operative here preclude its citation as symptomatic of a general Roman policy. If a parallel be sought, it might indeed be found in a precisely contemporary Roman treaty – but one not to the advantage of Roman traders. The peace of Apamea in 188 contained a clause allowing Rhodes to seek any reparations due her from the Seleucid kingdom, and which guaranteed that Rhodian goods would be free of duty.[86] We may be certain whence the initiative for that provision came. Rhodes had enjoyed the privilege before in Seleucid lands and wished to continue or revive it.[87] Rome simply indulged her ally.

Two decades later, when the Republic had reason to make an example of Rhodes, she emphasized economic means again. This time, in 166, she turned Delos into a free port and put the island under the authority of Athens. Rhodian revenues dropped precipitately, as the attractions of a toll-free harbor diverted commercial traffic to Delos.[88] Roman and Italian *negotiatores* gradually began to establish themselves in the island, a development that might not have been beyond the powers of the *patres* to foresee. Nonetheless, that motive can hardly serve as explanation. The advantages of the Delian mart were open equally to merchants of all nationalities. Greeks and easterners predominated, in fact, prior to 167 and might have been expected to become chief beneficiaries. Just when the Ῥωμαῖοι became a majority on Delos is undemonstrable; it certainly did not happen overnight. Strabo's evidence places the heyday of Delian prosperity after the destruction of Corinth.[89] The senate's decision in 166 must have had reasons other than filling the pocketbooks of Italian traders. The humiliation of Rhodes stood foremost as purpose. And, it might be noticed, delivery of Delos to Athenian overlordship came at the request of Athens; the island's prosperity would be a boon for Athens, still another opportunity for Rome to supply a *beneficium*. It is no accident that the Athenian *stephanephoros*, the so-called "New Style Attic coinage", now begins to reign supreme in the Aegean and gains widespread acceptance in Euboea, Thessaly, Macedonia, and the Thracian coast. Athens rather than Rome seems the principal economic beneficiary.[90]

So much for state action to promote private business enterprise in the east. No other instance can be cited down to the late 2nd century. In wartime the government could indeed curtail such enterprise.[91] Taken singly or together, the examples do little to buttress any idea of official protection or advancement of profit-making activity in the Hellenistic world.[92] Insofar as specific steps were taken, they seem directed to the advantage of other states and peoples, rather than of the Romans: south Italian traders, Rhodians, or Athenians, as circumstances determined. Of course, unselfish philanthropy did not provide the stimulus. Rome had her own ends very much in view: the loyalty of Italian states and the value of eastern allies in maintaining a stable order that could relieve the Republic of responsibility. The direct economic gains of Rome's business and commercial communities or, for that matter, of her senatorial order, find no clear reflection in the decisions of state.

NOTES

1 See, e.g., L. Perelli, *Imperialismo, capitalismo e rivoluzione culturale nella prima metà del II secolo a.C.*, I (Torino, 1975), 130–53; W. V. Harris, *AHR* 76 (1971): 1371–85; idem, *War and Imperialism in Republican Rome, 327–70 B.C.* (Oxford, 1979), 54–104; M. H. Crawford, *Economic History Review*, 30 (1977), 42–52; K. Hopkins, *Conquerors and Slaves* (Cambridge, 1978), 25–47; D. Musti, *Polibio e l'imperialismo romano* (Napoli, 1978), 88–124. M. I. Finley, *Greece and Rome*, 25 (1978), 6, draws the proper distinction: "particular wars and single campaigns often produced much booty without leading to a permanent exploitation of the defeated, and without the latter there is no empire". But Finley's brief and general treatment passes from the conquest of Italy to the "rise of the provincial system", thus begging the question on Roman attitudes and aspirations in the middle Republic.

2 The First Punic War: Polyb. 1.11.2; cf. 1.20.1, 1.49.5. The Third Macedonian War: Livy, 42.32.6.

3 They are afterthoughts, useful for recruiting but not determinants of war-declarations which had already taken place. Observe the circumstances prior to the outbreak of the Second Macedonian War. The *comitia centuriata* first rejected, then accepted war. A consular speech helped reverse the verdict, according to Livy: in his composition, that speech contained not a word about plunder and gain; Livy, 31.6.1–31.8.1.

4 The Aetolian treaty: *SEG*, 13, 382; Livy, 26.24.8–13; note that it was Rome who sought the alliance with Aetolia; Polyb. 5.105.8; Livy 25.23.9; 26.24.1–8. The treaty with Carthage: Polyb. 3.24.5. How much truth lies in the claim, fostered by Cato, that some Roman leaders wished to war on Rhodes in 167 in order to seize her wealth, cannot be known; Gellius, 6.3.7. The war, in any case, was never undertaken.

5 Polyb. 10.16.2–9.

6 Livy, 29.27.1–4: "salvos incolumesque victis perduellibus victores, spoliis decoratos, praeda onustos triumphantesque mecum domos reduces sistatis". C. Duilius' column proudly detailed the spoils taken from Carthage after the First Punic War, *CIL*, I^2, 25 = *ILLRP*, I, # 319. The acquisition of booty from Sardinia was inscribed on Ti. Gracchus' dedication in 174; Livy, 41.28.8–9.

7 Plautus, *Epid.* 158–60; *Amph.* 193–4; *Bacch.* 1068–71; *Poen.* 802–3; *Pseud.* 583–9; *Truc.* 508; *Most.* 312. Rightly noted by Harris, *War and Imperialism*, 102–3.

8 Sources in T. R. S. Broughton, *The Magistrates of the Roman Republic* [hereafter *MRR*] (New York, 1951–2), I:344, 357, 362, 369.

9 Broughton, *MRR*, I:433–4; cf. also the triumph of L. Anicius, lesser in character because earned against Illyrians, but Anicius turned it into a memorable event; *MRR*, I:434.

10 On the whole question of the general's authority in distribution of spoils, see I. Shatzman, *Historia*, 21 (1972): 177–205, with extensive references. Cato's speeches on the subject: Plut. *Cato*, 10.4; Cato, *ORF*, fr. 98, 173, 203, 224–6. See, especially, fr. 173: "numquam ego praedam neque quod de hostibus captum esset neque manubias inter pauculos amicos meos divisi, ut illis eriperem qui cepissent". Aemilius Paullus: Polyb. 18.35.4–5, 31.22. Scipio Aemilianus: Polyb. 18.35.9–12; cf. Val. Max. 4.3.13.

11 The attacks on Fulvius: Livy, 38.42–4, 39.4–5; the opposition to Manlius: Livy, 38.42.9–13, 38.44.9–11, 38.45–50. Evidence on the trials of the Scipios is extensive and complex; for recent discussion of the testimony, see G. Bandinelli, *Index*, 3 (1972): 304–42; a summary of scholarship in F. W. Walbank, *A Historical Commentary on Polybius* (Oxford, 1979) III: 242–7.

12 Much but not all the evidence in T. Frank, *An Economic Survey of Ancient Rome* [hereafter *ESAR*] (Baltimore, 1933), I:127–38, who combines testimony on both booty and indemnities.

13 Polyb. 2.12.3; Livy, 22.33.5. The sum is not reported.

14 Polyb. 18.44.7; Livy, 33.30.7; Plut., *Flam.* 9.5; Appian, *Mac.* 9.3. Alternative and less reliable figures reported by Valerius Antias and Claudius Quadrigarius: Livy, 33.30.8.

15. Livy, 34.35.11.

16. Polyb. 21.32.8–9; Livy, 38.11.8.

17. Polyb. 21.17.4–5, 21.41.8, 21.43.19; Livy, 37.45.14, 38.37.9, 38.38.13; Appian, *Syr.* 38; Diod. 29.10.

18 Polyb. 21.41.7; Livy, 38.37.5–6.

19 Livy, 45.18.7, 45.26.14, 45.29.4; Diod. 31.18.3; Plut., *Aem. Paull.* 28.3.

20 Cf. Livy, 10.46.12 – 293 B.C.

21 Polyb. 21.14.1–7: ἔδοξε τῷ συνεδρίῳ τὸν στρατηγὸν ἀποκριθῆναι διότι τῆς μὲν δαπάνης οὐ τὴν ἡμίσειαν, ἀλλὰ πᾶσαν δίκαιόν ἐστιν Ἀντίοχον ἀποδοῦναι · φῦναι γὰρ τὸν πόλεμον ἐξ ἀρχῆς οὐ δι᾽ αὐτούς, ἀλλὰ δι᾽ ἐχεῖνον; Livy, 37.35.1–10; Appian, *Syr.* 29. And see Polyb. 21.17.4.

22 Cic., *Verr.* 2.3.12: "quasi victoriae praemium ac poena belli". Cf. the thirty talents demanded of Boeotia in 196, after the murder of Roman soldiers: a "fine", says Livy, 33.29.12: "multae nomine triginta conferre talenta".

23 On the cancellation of Philip's indemnity: Polyb. 21.3.3, 21.11.9; Livy, 37.25.12; Appian, *Mac.* 9.5; *Syr.* 23; Plut., *Flam.* 14.2. The treaty with Hiero in 263 imposed a payment of one hundred talents, according to Polyb. 1.16.9. Late Latin writers preserve a figure of two hundred talents, a less likely sum: Eutrop. 2.19.1; Oros. 4.7.3. Diodorus, 23.4.1, gives (the equivalent of) twenty-five talents, which may be a down payment; so H. Berve, *König Hieron II, AbhMünch*, 47 (1959): 36. The obligation, in any case, was cancelled in 248 when Rome framed a φιλία ἀΐδιος with Hiero; Zon. 8.16. Nothing in the evidence sanctions Harris' assertion, *War and Imperialism*, 64, that Hiero paid an annual tax in addition to an indemnity.

24 Polyb. 21.2.3–6, 21.4–5, 21.29.9–21.30.2, 21.32.8–9; Livy, 37.1.5–6, 37.6.4–37.7.6, 37.49, 38.8.1–38.9.2, 38.9.8–38.11.1, 38.11.8.

25 Polyb. 21.41.7, 21.45; Livy, 38.37.5–6, 38.39.5–6; cf. Strabo, 13.4.2 = C624.

26 In fact, Rome offered the alternative of a further postponement of the indemnity, if Pinnes were willing to provide hostages; Livy, 22.33.5.

27 Livy, 42.6.6–11; cf. II Macc. 8:10.

28 Livy, 36.4.5–9: "de pecunia item responsum, nullam ante diem accepturos".

29 Most of the references conveniently collected in Frank, *ESAR*, I:183–7; cf. Crawford, *Roman Republican Coinage* [hereafter *RRC*] (Cambridge, 1974), II:633–7, with table at 696–707; and see F. Coarelli, *AbhGött*, 97.1 (1976): 21–32; idem., *PBSR* 32 (1977): 1–23.

30 Pliny, *NH*, 33:55–6; cf. Crawford, *RRC*, II: 635.

31 Livy, 39.7.5.

32 Cic., *De Off.* 2.76; Pliny, *NH*, 33.56; Plut., *Aem. Paull.* 38.1: Val. Max. 4.3.8. This did not mean that the state could count on a permanent abolition of *tributum*; see C. Nicolet, *Tributum* (Bonn, 1976), 1–5, 79–80.

33 Polyb. 34.9.9 – as reported by Strabo, 3.2.10 = C148. Revenues from the Spanish mines have received considerable recent discussion: E. Badian, *Publicans and Sinners* (Ithaca, 1972), 31–4; J. S. Richardson, *JRS* 66 (1976): 140–7; R. C. Knapp, *Aspects of the Roman Experience in Iberia* (Vittoria, 1977), 171–3: G. Calboli, *Marci Porci Catonis, Oratio Pro Rhodiensibus* (Bologna, 1978), 156–65.

34 Livy, 45.18.7, 45.26.13–14, 45.29.4; Diod. 31.8.3; Plut., *Aem. Paull.* 28.3; see Frank, *Roman Imperialism* (New York, 1914), 209–10; Badian, *Roman Imperialism in the Late Republic* (Oxford, 1968), 18–19; W. Dahlheim, *Gewalt und Herrschaft: Das provinziale Herrschaftssystem der römischen Republik* (Berlin, 1977), 259–61.

35 Porphyry, *FGH* 260, 3, 19; Eusebius, *Chron.* 424c (Helm): Ῥωμαῖοι Μακεδόνας ὑποφόρους ἐποιήσαντο ἀναιρεθέντος τοῦ Ψευδοφιλίππου; Jerome, *Chron.* 143 (Helm): "Romani interfecto Pseudophilippo Macedonas tributarios faciunt".

36 Livy, 45.18.3–5; Diod. 31.8.7; Cassiodorus, *Chron.* s.v. 158 B.C. Cf. E. S. Gruen, "Macedonia and the Settlement of 167 B.C.", in W. L. Adams and E. N. Borza, *Philip II, Alexander the Great, and the Macedonian Heritage* (1982), 262–4.

37 Attalus III bequeathed his kingdom to Rome, probably to frustrate the designs of his challengers in Pergamum. Sources on the bequest are collected by G. Cardinali, *Saggi di storia antica e di archeologia in onore di G. Beloch* (1910), 274–6. An indirect reference in a contemporary document: *OGIS*, 338, lines 5–7. C. Gracchus instituted the *censoria locatio* in Asia ten years later: Cic., *Verr.* 2.3.12; Schol. Bob. 157, Stangl; Fronto, *Ep. ad Verum*, 2.1.17; cf. Appian, *BC* 5.4.

38 Only Corinth became subject to Roman taxation in 146 B.C. Cf. Cic., *De Leg. Agrar.* 1.5; *FIRA*, I, #8, lines 96–101, Strabo, 8.623 = C381; Zon. 9.31. See the arguments of H. Hill, *CP* 41 (1946): 35–42. Pausanias, 7.16.9–10, is plainly confused.

39 Livy, 23.48.4–23.49.4, 24.18.10–11, 25.3.8–25.5.1; Val. Max. 5.6.8; cf. Badian, *Publicans and Sinners*, 16–21. The government also borrowed money from a host of citizens outside the business community; Livy, 26.36, 29.16.1–3, 31.13, 33.42.2–4.

40 Salt tax: Livy, 29.27.3–4; Dio, 57.70–1; cf. Gellius 2.22.29. Harbor dues: Livy, 32.7.3; extended after 179 Livy, 40.51.4; cf. S. J. De Laet, *Portorium* (Bruges, 1949), 55–63. Pasturage tax: Plautus, *Truc.* 143–51; cf. Appian, *BC*, 1.7; Pliny, *NH*, 18.11.

41 See, e.g., Livy, 44.16.4 (169 B.C.). Rightly, Badian, *Publicans and Sinners*, 27–9, against Frank, *ESAR*, I: 148–50, and A. J. Toynbee, *Hannibal's Legacy* (Oxford, 1967), II:356.

42 Livy, 34.21.7, affirms that Cato arranged for collection of revenues from the iron and silver mines in that year. The evidence of Polybius speaks to the handsome income derived from that source: twenty-five thousand *denarii* a day; Polyb. 34.9.8–11; Strabo, 3.2.10 = C147–8. Frank's view, *ESAR*, I:154–5, that the Roman government supervised the mines directly until 179, has been adequately refuted; see P. A. Brunt, in R. Seager, *The Crisis of the Roman Republic* (1969), 104–7; Badian, *Publicans and Sinners*, 31–3; F. Cassola, *I gruppi politici romani nel III secolo a.C.* (Trieste, 1962), 74–7. *Publicani* do not receive express mention. Hence, Richardson, *JRS* 66 (1976): 140–7, argues that the mines were let to small-scale lessees, rather than to the major companies of *publicani* – a suggestion buttressed by Diodorus' reference to a multitude of Italians who enriched themselves through the Spanish mines; 5.36.2: πλῆθος Ἰταλῶν ἐπεπόλασε τοῖς μετάλλοις, καὶ μεγάλους ἀνεφέροντο πλούτους διὰ τὴν φιλοκερδίαν; cf. Strabo, 3.2.10 = C147. However, these persons may well have been employees or agents for the *publicani*, rather than independent small contractors. Cf. Livy, 45.18.4, on the Macedonian mines in 167: "nam neque sine publicano exerceri posse"; and see Calboli, *Catonis Oratio Pro Rhodiensibus*, 156–65.

43 Livy, 21.63.3–4. Livy's assertion that all senators except C. Flaminius opposed the bill must be exaggerated. The assembly did pass it, and hardly over unanimous senatorial objection. Cf. A. Lippold, *Consules. Untersuchungen zur Geschichte des*

römischen Konsulates von 264 bis 201 v. Chr. (Bonn, 1963), 93–5. Conventional opinion holds that the bill represents an effort by the commercial classes to exclude senators from maritime traffic. If so, it had little effect and could easily be skirted by using front men and agents; cf. Plut., *Cato*, 21.5–6; Cic., *Verr.* 2.5.45. A long register of scholarly viewpoints is summarized by Cassola, *I gruppi politici*, 216–17, who turns the theory on its head and argues that the *lex Claudia* was meant to exclude the commercial and business classes from the senate. That idea fails to account for the extensive senatorial opposition. Moralistic posturing rather than economic advantage may be the principal element. Cf. now Nicolet, *Annales*, 5 (1980): 878–82; J. H. D'Arms, *Commerce and Social Standing in Ancient Rome* (Cambridge, Mass., 1981), 31–3.

44   Livy, 35.7.2–5, 35.41.9–10 – very likely unenforceable. In any case, a *lex Junia de feneratione* was proposed not much later, containing provisions which did not find favor with M. Cato; *ORF*, fr. 56–7. The reasons for Cato's opposition have given rise to much conjecture, unverifiable and unimportant for our purposes; the most recent, with reference to previous discussions, by A. E. Astin, *Cato the Censor* (Oxford, 1978), 321–3. Still another measure, the *lex Marcia*, perhaps in the 180s, endeavored to strengthen regulations against excessive interest charges: Gaius, *Inst.* 4.23.

45   Livy, 32.27.3–4. These *faeneratores* were surely Romans or Italians, not Carthaginians: as Frank, *ESAR*, I: 208; see J. Briscoe, *A Commentary on Livy, Books XXXI–XXXIII* (Oxford, 1973), 219–20. For Cato's attitude on usury, see further, Cato, *RR, praef.* 1; Cic., *De Off.*, 2.89.

46   Polyb. 31.27. Among Plautine references to financiers and money-lenders – surely not altogether limited to Greek experience – see *Curc.* 371–9, 480, 506–11, 558–9, 618, 679–85, 721–2; *Asin.* 438–40; *Persa*, 434–7; *Pseud.* 286–7; *Epid.* 53–4, 114–15, 252; *Most.* 532–40, 560–1, 621–31, 657–8, 916–17, 1140, 1160–1; *Men.* 582–4; *Capt.* 192–3; *Aul.* 527–30; *Trin.* 425–426a; *Truc.* 66–73. See J. Andreau, *MEFRA* 80 (1968): 461–526 – who endeavors to isolate the Greek and the Latin elements in Plautus' remarks on the subject.

47   Polyb. 14.7.2–3 (Scipio's African campaign in the Hannibalic war); Livy, 34.9.12 (Cato's campaign in Spain in 195); Appian, *Pun.* 115 (the Third Punic War). A much earlier example in Italy in Livy, 10.17.3.

48   Plautus, *Truc.* 143–51; cf. *Trin.* 794; *Men.* 117–18.

49   Polyb. 6.17.1–4: καὶ σχεδὸν ὡς ἔπος εἰπεῖν πάντος ἐνδεδέσθαι ταῖς ὠναῖς καὶ ταῖς ἐργασίαις ταῖς ἐκ τούτων. See the excellent discussion by Badian, *Publicans and Sinners*, 45–7. Add also Diod. 5.36.2, quoted above, n. 42.

50   *ILLRP*, I, # 245; cf. Cassola, *PP* 15 (1960): 385–93.

51   *IG*, IX, 1², 17a, line 51.

52   Plut., *Arat.* 12.4.

53   *IC*, III, 4. 18. Other individuals, Roman or Italian, receive mention on Delian inscriptions of the 3rd century: *IG*, XI, 2, 115, line 25; *IG*, XI, 2, 287A, line 58; *IG*, XI, 4, 642. See further F. Cordano, *Settima miscellanea greca e romana* (1980), 255–70.

54   *Contra*: Cassola, *I gruppi politici*, 31–2 – who offers no arguments.

55   Most of the evidence on the Italians at Delos is collected in the classic work of J. Hatzfeld, *BCH* 36 (1912): 5–218; see further P. Roussel, *Délos, colonie athénienne* (Paris, 1916), 75–84; W. A. Laidlaw, *A History of Delos* (Oxford, 1933), 201–10; cf. A. Donati, *Epigraphica*, 27 (1965): 3–59, on Romans in the Aegean generally. Hatzfeld's broader study treats Italian traders and emigrants all over the east: *Les Trafiquants italiens dans l'Orient hellénique* (Paris, 1919), *passim*, especially 17–51. His view, ibid., 238–56, that most of the emigrants were Italians from the south, with very few Roman citizens, held the field for a long time; accepted, e.g., without question by Toynbee, *Hannibal's Legacy*, II: 363–9. The evidence, when reconsidered, however, seems to point in the opposite

direction; see A. J. N. Wilson, *Emigration from Italy in the Republican Age of Rome* (Manchester, 1966), 88–93, 105–11 (Delos); 152–5 (elsewhere in Greece – the evidence much thinner and most of it later than the 2nd century). Cf. also Cassola, *DialArch*, 4–5 (1970–1): 317, who estimates an even larger proportion of Roman citizens.

56 Discussion of their activities, unfortunately marred by excessive speculation, in Hatzfeld, *Les Trafiquants*, 193–237; briefer and more cautious is Wilson, *Emigration*, 156–64. Too little of the evidence on this matter, however, can be nailed down to the 2nd century. As example, note Sex. Orfidienus in Chyretiae in the late 190s; *ISE*, II, # 95.

57 As maintained, e.g., by Cassola, *I gruppi politici*, 56–71; Perelli, *Imperialismo*, 145–53.

58 The evidence is cited above, nn. 44–5.

59 Livy, 35.41.9–10.

60 Gaius, *Inst.* 4.23.

61 Livy, 25.3.8–25.5.1. The analysis by Toynbee, *Hannibal's Legacy*, II: 351–5, is unreliable. See Badian's discussion, *Publicans and Sinners*, 17–20.

62 Livy, 39.44.5–9; Plut. *Cato*, 19.1–2; *Flam.* 19.3. Cato plainly was not at variance with the senate here in any serious sense; rightly, D. Kienast, *Cato der Zensor* (Heidelberg, 1954), 79–87; Calboli, *Catonis Oratio Pro Rhodiensibus*, 169–73. The relative impotence and lack of solidarity among the *publicani* is stressed by Badian, *Publicans and Sinners*, 35–8.

63 Livy, 43.16.2–16.

64 Livy, 45.18.3–4: "metalli quoque Macedonici, quod ingens vectigal erat, locationes praediorumque rusticorum tolli placebat; nam neque sine publicano exerceri posse et, ubi publicanus esset, ibi aut ius publicum vanum aut libertatem sociis nullam esse"; cf. Diod. 31.8.7. In view of the episodes discussed above, there is no reason to regard Livy's language as reflecting only attitudes of the late Republic. Connection between the affairs of 169 and the senatorial decision of 167 is correctly affirmed by Badian, *Publicans and Sinners*, 40–3. But he goes too far in seeing the senate as frightened by a serious challenge to its authority on the part of the *publicani*. Nothing of this in the sources. The near conviction of one of the censors in 169 came on a very different issue: censorial interference with *tribunicia potestas*; Livy, 43.16.8–16.

65 Livy, 45.29.11; Cassiodorus, *Chron.*, s.v. 158 B.C. Who ran them subsequently is unknown. But no good reason exists to assume it was the *publicani*, as Badian, *Publicans and Sinners*, 44. Cf. Perelli, *RivFilol*, 103 (1975): 408–9.

66 See, most recently, Giovannini, *Rome et la circulation monétaire en Grèce au IIe siècle avant Jésus-Christ* (Basel, 1978), 24–35, with reference to earlier literature.

67 See above, n. 43.

68 Plut. *Cato*, 21.5–6. Note also the activity of Cato's contemporary M. Aemilius Lepidus in 179: Livy, 40.51.2.

69 See the analysis by Astin, *Cato the Censor*, 319–20; cf. Calboli, *Catonis Oratio Pro Rhodiensibus*, 192–5, and n. 45.

70 Cf. Astin, *Cato the Censor*, 249–58.

71 Pliny, *NH*, 7.139–40 = *ORF*, 6, fr. 2: "pecuniam magnam bono modo invenire".

72 Plut., *Cato*, 21.8. Cf. Cato, *ORF*, fr. 167.

73 Polyb. 6.56.3: καθ' ὅσον γὰρ ἐν καλῷ τίθενται τὸν ἀπὸ τοῦ κρατίστου χρηματισμόν, κατὰ τοσοῦτο πάλιν ἐν ὀνείδει ποιοῦνται τὴν ἐκ τῶν ἀπειρημένων πλεονεξίαν.

74 Sallust, *Cat.* 7.6: *divitias honestas*; cf. Cic., *De Off.* 1.92.

75 The point is made, most recently, by Harris, *War and Imperialism*, 56–8, 65–7, 86–93; cf. E. Gabba, *MAAR* 36 (1980): 91–102; D'Arms, *Commerce and Social Standing*, 33–9. Obvious enough once stated, but too frequently unacknowledged. Even scorn for tradesmen, laborers, and merchants had its limitations. Petty operations earned little respect, but large-scale commerce, if one takes Cicero as guide, could win admiration, especially if profits were invested in land: Cic., *De Off.*, 1.150–1; cf. Finley, *The Ancient Economy*

(Berkeley and Los Angeles, 1973), 41–56; D'Arms, *op. cit.*, 20–31. Whether this same attitude held in the middle Republic is not demonstrable.

76 Paulus, Leyden fr. 3, in G. G. Archi, *Pauli sententiarum fragmentum leidense* (Leyden, 1965), 13; Asconius, 93, Clark; Dio, 55.10.4–5; cf. Badian, *Publicans and Sinners*, 120, n. 16; Harris, *War and Imperialism*, 90–1. Nicolet, *Annales*, 5 (1980): 879–80, dates the ban, too confidently, to C. Gracchus' tribunate.

77 Cato alleged in 167 that advocates of war on Rhodes hoped to strip her of resources and make her wealth their own; Gellius, 6.3.7, 6.3.52. But no one surely argued for war openly on that basis. Indeed, if Sallust is right, the senate rejected war precisely to avoid the stigma of undertaking it for purpose of enrichment; Sallust, *Cat.* 51.5: "ne quis divitiarum magis quam iniuriae causa bellum inceptum diceret".

78 Polyb. 9.10.11: τὸ μὲν οὖν τὸν χρυσὸν καὶ τὸν ἄργυρον ἀθροίζειν πρὸς αὑτοὺς ἴσως ἔχει τινὰ λόγον · οὐ γὰρ οἷόν τε τῶν καθόλου πραγμάτων ἀντιποιήσασθαι μὴ οὐ τοῖς μὲν ἄλλοις ἀδυναμίαν ἐνεργασαμένους, σφίσι δὲ τὴν τοιούτην δύναμιν ἑτοιμάσαντας.

79 Rome as advocating the cause of Italian traders: Polyb. 2.8.2–3. Dispatch of troops during the siege of Epidamnus: Polyb. 2.10.9–2.11.1. The visit from Apollonians: Livy, *Per.* 15; Zon. 8.7; Val. Max. 6.6.5. Colony at Brundisium: Vell. Pat. 1.14.8; Cic., *Ad Att.* 4.1.4; cf. Livy, *Per.* 19. Similarly, Rome's decision to forge an alliance with Aetolia in 212 or 211 and enter the First Macedonian War probably came after Philip V's capture of Lissus, which made him a direct threat to the cities of the southern Adriatic; Polyb. 8.14; Livy, 26.24.8.

80 The senate did take up the cause of traders from Italy captured by Carthage during the Mercenary War in the 230s. Swift negotiation secured their release; Polyb. 1.83.7–10, 3.28.3; cf. Zon. 8.17; Val. Max. 5.1.1a; Eutrop. 2.27. These merchants too were probably Italians for the most part, rather than Roman citizens. Cicero obscures the distinction; *Verr.* 2.5.149; *Imp. Pomp.* 11.

81 Livy, 38.44.4: "portoria quae vellent terra marique caperent, dum eorum immunes Romani ac socii nominis Latini essent".

82 So, Frank, *Roman Imperialism*, 279–80: "an exceptional rather than a normal stipulation". By contrast, Harris, *War and Imperialism*, 94: "likely to have been extended later to some other places". M. Holleaux, *Études d'épigraphie et d'histoire grecque* (Paris, 1938–68), V: 430, n. 4, finds it irrelevant. Cassola, *I gruppi politici*, 63–4, takes it as proof of economic motivation. Badian, *Roman Imperialism*, 17, passes over the event hurriedly; it does not suit his thesis.

83 Livy, 38.43.1–2: "Inimicitiae inter M. Fulvium et M. Aemilium consulem erant, et super cetera Aemilius serius biennio se consulem factum M. Fulvii opera ducebat. Itaque ad invidiam ei faciendam legatos Ambracienses in senatum subornatos criminibus introduxit".

84 Livy, 38.44.3–6.

85 As Frank, *Roman Imperialism*, 280, observed, the *lex Antonia de Termessibus* of 71 B.C. exempts *publicani* specifically from harbor tolls – thereby implying that others were not so privileged; *FIRA*, I, # 11, *ad fin.*

86 Polyb. 18.43.16–17. The latter clause is omitted by Livy, 38.38.12.

87 Polyb. 5.88.7 – in the 220s.

88 Polyb. 30.20.1–9, 30.31.9–12.

89 Strabo, 10.5.4 = C486. For Cassola, *I gruppi politici*, 62–3, Rome foresaw all the commercial consequences and future advantages for her trading classes. So also H. H. Schmitt, *Rom und Rhodos* (Munich, 1957), 166; J.-L. Ferrary, in Nicolet, *Rome et la conquête du monde méditerranéen* (Paris, 1978), II: 783–4. Similarly, but more cautiously, Harris, *War and Imperialism*, 94. The idea is rejected by, e.g. Hatzfeld,

Les Trafiquants, 374; Frank, *Roman Imperialism*, 284–5; Wilson, *Emigration*, 1; Badian, *Roman Imperialism*, 17–18; Finley, *Greece and Rome*, 25 (1978): 11–12.

90 The date proposed for the origin of New Style Attic coinage, ca. 196, by M. Thompson, *ANSMN* 5 (1952): 25–33, and idem, *The New Style Silver Coinage of Athens* (New York, 1961), *passim*, is now almost universally rejected. A time around 164, shortly after Delos came under Athenian control, seems preferable. See the arguments of D. M. Lewis, *NC* 2 (1962): 275–300; followed and expanded by, e.g., H. B. Mattingly, *NC* 9 (1969): 327–30; C. Boehringer, *Zur Chronologie mittelhellenistischer Münzserien, 220–160 v. Chr.* (Berlin, 1972), 22–38. Further bibliography in C. Habicht, *Chiron*, 6 (1976): 130, n. 17. Note the famed Amphictyonic decree that directs all Greeks to accept the Athenian tetradrachm for four drachmas of silver; *Syll.*[3] 729 = *FDelphes*, III, 2, 139. Giovannini, *Rome et la circulation monétaire*, 64–72, proposes a date of ca. 165 to coincide with the introduction of New Style coinage. Whether the date is right or wrong, his further conclusion that this came as a *Roman* directive and represents "a decisive step in the history of Roman imperialism", ibid., 95–102, lacks all foundation and plausibility. Giovannini argues that the disappearance of the Alexander and Lysimachus coinage in the Greek world after Pydna signals a Roman desire to wipe out the vestiges of Macedonian royal influence. An unnecessary hypothesis. The Antigonid monies quite naturally vanished in Greece after Pydna, as did the Seleucid coinage in Asia Minor after Magnesia. There is no reason to postulate Roman pressure, however popular Perseus may have been in Greece before, though a Hellenic desire to appease the victor may have influenced the hurrying of previous coinage out of circulation. Rome certainly did not adopt any general anti-monarchical posture in the Greek world. It may be at this time that Eumenes began production of the Pergamene *cistophori*; cf. F. S. Kleiner – S. P. Noe, *The Early Cistophoric Coinage* (New York, 1977), 10–18. Even if its origins follow the defeat of Antiochus III in 190, however, as Boehringer, *op. cit.* 40–6, the *cistophori* continue unaffected by the Roman victory at Pydna. More recent discussion by O. Mørkholm, *ANSMN* 24 (1979): 50–62, who opts for a date ca. 175; and a reply by Kleiner, *ANSMN* 25 (1980): 45–52.

91 As when the senate prevented shipment of goods and arms to the Messenians in the late 180s; Polyb. 23.9.12, 23.17.3. Note also the senate's control over Sicilian grain exports during the Third Macedonian War: Polyb. 28.2.2, 28.2.5; cf. Frank, *Roman Imperialism*, 281–2.

92 On the closing of the Macedonian mines to thwart the *publicani* in 167, see above, n. 36. When reopened they may well have been placed in Macedonian hands. The ban on importation of salt and cutting of ship timbers in Macedonia in the same year had political reasons, irrelevant to the Roman economy: Livy, 45.29.11, 45.29.14; see Frank, *Roman Imperialism*, 281. Harris' suggestion, *War and Imperialism*, 99, that the destruction of Corinth in 146 stemmed in part from hostility toward the city by businessmen in Delos, is unconvincing.

Economic considerations may – or may not – have played a larger role in Roman decisions in the west. The evidence is inadequate and requires no extended discussion here. The demolition of Carthage in 146 and the prohibition of any further settlement within ten miles of the sea obviously aimed to eliminate her as a maritime power; Livy, *Per.* 49; Appian, *Pun.* 81; Diod. 32.6.3; Zon. 9.26. Whether Italian businessmen were the intended beneficiaries, however, is beyond knowing. The fact that some Italians were in North Africa before the Third Punic War does not prove it; Polyb. 36.7.5; Appian, *Pun.* 92; cf. Plautus, *Poen.* 79–82; Frank, *ESAR*, I:202–3. Cicero has no doubt that strategic and political reasons dictated the crushing of Corinth and Carthage: *De Leg. Agrar.* 2.87.

The notorious ban on vine and olive cultivation among Transalpine tribes continues to generate discussion. Cicero, *De Rep.* 3.16, claims it was designed to protect and enhance

Italian agriculture. The dramatic date of the dialogue would set the measure some time before 129 B.C. Perhaps a reference to 154 when Romans last fought in Transalpine Gaul, at the behest of Massilia – thus an economic measure to benefit the Massiliotes rather than the Romans? So, Frank, *Roman Imperialism*, 280–1; followed by Badian, *Roman Imperialism*, 19–20; G. Clemente, *I Romani nella Gallia meridionale* (Bologna, 1974), 18–19, 132–3. That is speculation and unverifiable. A. Aymard, *Études d'histoire ancienne* (Paris, 1967), 585–600, set the measure late in the 2nd century at the time of formation of the Roman province; similarly, B. Van Rinsveld, *Latomus*, 40 (1981): 280–91. A 1st century date too has been proposed by M. Clavel, *Béziers et son territoire dans l'Antiquité* (Paris, 1970), 310–16. J. Paterson, *CQ* 28 (1978): 452–8, offers the novel suggestion that Cicero refers to the Galli Transalpini who migrated to Italy and were expelled in 183 Livy, 39.22.6–7, 39.45.6–7, 39.54.2–13; L. Piso, *HRR*, fr. 35 (Peter). On this view, Cicero's language is metaphorical and no ban on cultivation existed. That is not the most obvious reading of the text. In any case, chronological uncertainty and the absence of known parallels forbid the building of any hypotheses about Roman economic policy on the basis of this passage. Clemente, *op. cit.*, 21–71, has compiled an impressive array of evidence for Italian commerical connections with southern Gaul, beginning in the 3rd century. But none of it establishes his claim, ibid., 75, that Roman senators took an interest in promoting this activity – at least not before the late Republic; cf. T. P. Wiseman, *LCM* 1 (1976): 21–2.

EDITOR'S NOTES

i   On the Roman sacking of cities, see A. Ziolkowski, "*Urbs direpta*, or How the Romans Sacked Cities," in *War and Society in the Roman World*, ed. J. Rich and G. Shipley (London and New York, 1993), pp. 69–91.
ii On the autonomy of the Roman general in the field of command, see A. M. Eckstein, *Senate and General: Individual Decision-Making and Roman Foreign Relations, 264–194 BC* (Berkeley and Los Angeles, 1987).

Fear, Greed, and Glory: The Causes of Roman War Making in the Middle Republic

John Rich

THE MODERN DEBATE

Down to the middle of the fourth century Rome was a power of merely local significance. The Romans had fought a great many wars against their neighbours, but for most of their history they had been merely one of the more prominent of the cities in the plain of Latium.[i] Quite suddenly, from about 343,[1] all this changed, and in a period of just over seventy years the Romans fought their way to a position of mastery over the whole of Italy south of the Po valley. This success was followed by great wars, first against Carthage, and then against various Hellenistic kings. From all of these the Romans emerged victorious, and by the middle of the second century, contemporaries like Polybius recognized them as the undisputed masters of the Mediterranean world. They now ruled a number of overseas territories directly, as provinces, and elsewhere they exercised an informal hegemony. Over the next two centuries, down to the reign of Augustus, the first emperor, the Romans continued on the same path of warfare and expansion. In the late Republic, the drive to expansion was largely fuelled by the ambitions of powerful individuals, like Pompey and Caesar. But down to the outbreak of the Social War, in 91, the political system remained relatively stable. Why did the Romans fight so many wars, and expand their power so widely?

Until recently, the dominant view among scholars was that Roman imperialism was essentially defensive. The principal factor which led the Romans to undertake their wars was, it was held, the fear of powerful neighbours, a fear which was in some cases well-founded, in others mistaken. Some writers also stressed the importance of accident and misunderstanding. However, it was thought that the prospect of economic gain did not play an important part in bringing about the wars, and that the Romans' territorial expansion was largely unsought. This doctrine originated with Mommsen (1877–80), and early in this century found notable exponents in Frank (1914) and Holleaux (1921). More recent statements of the case include those of Badian (1958, 1968), Walbank (1963) and Errington (1971).

From time to time various writers expressed dissent from this view, in this country notably Finley (1978) and Hopkins (1978, 25–37). However, the first full-scale attack was mounted in 1979 by William Harris in his important book *War and Imperialism in Republican Rome 327–70* BC. Harris laid stress on the fact that the Romans had become habituated to continuous warfare, and argued that the most important of the factors which brought about the wars was the Romans' desire for the glory and economic benefits which successful warfare conferred.[2] He conceded that defensive considerations played a part in some wars, but in general sought to minimize this element. The core of his case is made in the first two chapters, where he gives a structural account of the role of war in Roman life, the attitudes both of the Roman élite and of ordinary citizens to war, and the economic benefits which Romans derived from war. He follows this up in the fifth and final chapter with a survey of the origins of individual wars, designed to show that they conform to his theory. Chapters 3 and 4 are devoted to Roman expansion: here he argues that expansion was a Roman aim, and that the Romans generally welcomed opportunities to annex territory except when special circumstances decided them against doing so.

Harris's book has aroused much interest. It was, for example, accorded the unique distinction of receiving, in effect, two reviews in successive numbers of the *Journal of Roman Studies*, by Sherwin-White (1980) and North (1981). Harris himself has returned to the fray several times (Harris ed. 1984, with responses to his critics at pp. 13–34, 89–113; Harris 1989, 1990). Since his book appeared, there has been a wealth of publications on various aspects of Roman Republican imperialism: notable instances are the books by Gruen (1984), Sherwin-White (1984), Dyson (1985), Richardson (1986), Eckstein (1987), Ferrary (1988) and Rosenstein (1990).[3] All these works address in various ways the questions posed by Harris. The continuing vitality of the debate is shown by the diversity of views expressed in the present volume [see S. Oakley, "The Roman Conquest of Italy," and T. Cornell, "The End of Roman Imperial Expansion," in *War and Society in the Roman World*, ed. J. Rich and G. Shipley (New York and London, 1993), pp. 9–37 and 139–70 respectively].

A number of these recent writers have persisted in maintaining some form of the 'defensive imperialism' view, notably Gruen, Sherwin-White, Dyson and Eckstein.[4] These and other critics of Harris who share their position have made some telling points. However, none of them has fully taken the measure of Harris's objections to the 'defensive imperialism' view. In my judgement, no one has succeeded in producing a coherent and convincing restatement of that doctrine, and I do not believe that such a restatement could be produced.

Richardson, in his excellent study of the development of Roman rule in Spain, is in general in sympathy with Harris, but provides an important corrective to Harris's views on the annexation and exploitation of territory. He makes a good case for supposing that the Romans were rather slower to exploit their conquests by taxation, mining, and so on than Harris claimed. He rightly insists that to declare a region as a *provincia* originally meant just that it was marked out as an area of military responsibility, and that the development from this practice to the fully-fledged system of provincial administration was a long drawn out process. As to the question of whether it was better to assign conquered territory to Roman commanders as their province or to leave it to the inhabitants to administer it for themselves, the Roman government seems to have had no general preference but to have considered each case on its merits. In any case, as Harris himself recognized (Harris 1979, 133–6), the choice was not between maintaining or abandoning control, but between different forms of control.[5]

For many readers Harris's view of the causes of Roman warfare and imperialism has powerful appeal. There are, I think, two reasons for this. One is that it seems to accord with common sense. The 'defensive imperialism' view propounded a paradox. The Romans valued military achievements above all others and their strongly militaristic culture was displayed in such institutions as the triumph. They fought wars almost continuously and on the whole successfully, and as a result acquired both empire and great economic gains. Yet the 'defensive imperialism' doctrine requires us to believe that this warfare and expansion was not of the Romans' seeking, and was the product largely of fear. After reading Harris's trenchant attack on this position, most people tend to feel, rightly in my view, that the paradox can no longer be sustained.

The second reason why the view that the Romans were the aggressive power is so compelling is that it fits our contemporary attitudes and preconceptions. The intellectual background to the 'defensive imperialism' hypothesis has recently been explored by Linderski.[6] He shows that Mommsen's interpretation of Roman expansion derived from his German nationalist beliefs (for him the Romans' true destiny was to unite the Italian *Volk* and their overseas conquests were a historical error forced on them by circumstances). As for Holleaux and Frank, their willingness to acquit Rome of seeking expansion was not unconnected, Linderski argues, with the claims made for France and the USA in their own day. It is obvious that Harris's book, too, is a product of its time. Although the great European empires came to an end only a generation ago, most people now regard imperialism as something to be deplored and find it hard to comprehend the attitude of mind, not so long ago commonplace, which regarded empire as something noble and glorious. Harris, an Englishman living in the USA, wrote his book as the Vietnam conflict was being played out.

However, the very seductiveness of Harris's interpretation should put us on our guard. The old 'defensive imperialism' thesis was too crude, too monocausal. May not Harris's alternative suffer from the same fault? John North's criticisms of Harris are pertinent here. North holds that Harris's refutation of the 'defensive imperialism' theory is conclusive: Harris has, he says, settled 'once for all the question of whether Rome's wars were aggressive or defensive' (North 1981, 9). However, he complains that Harris focuses too much on specifics at the expense of general issues, that he concentrates too much on the Romans' conscious decision-making and not enough on the structures in Roman society which made for war and expansion. At times, North over-simplifies Harris's views, but he has put his finger on a major weakness of the book. Harris is at his most compelling in his first two chapters when he discusses the structural role of Roman warfare. He is least convincing in his last chapter when he yields to the polemicist's temptation to overstate his case and seeks to show that the principal factors behind all of Rome's individual war decisions were the need to keep fighting wars and the desire for glory and economic gain. Here North's comments are just. 'Wars begin from complex situations, in which aggression, mutual fear, confusion, accident, bad communications, personal and political ambitions and many other factors play a part' (ibid. 2). 'The argument from structure cannot explain the specific, only the long-term trend' (ibid. 7).

Harris's account of the structural role of Roman warfare is partial. He devotes much space to some aspects like the part played by military success in the aristocratic ethos. Yet, to take the two examples adduced by North, he is brief and equivocal on slavery and omits altogether the Italian alliance, whose importance in this regard was first stressed by Momigliano.[7] War generated a supply of slaves, whose availability transformed Italian agriculture and so created a continuing demand for cheap slaves which only war could adequately supply. The Romans exploited their Italian allies not by taxing them, but by demanding troops, and so, if they were to continue to profit from the alliance, they had to keep finding ways of employing Italian soldiers. Moreover, the opportunity to serve in and share some of the profits of Rome's wars may actually have helped to secure Italian loyalty, for, until their conquest by Rome, continuous warfare had been as much a part of the experience of some of the other peoples of Italy as it was for the Romans. It is Harris's preoccupation with motivation and decision-making which accounts for his partial treatment. He is rightly reluctant to assert that the need to maintain the slave supply or to keep the Italians occupied directly influenced the Roman government's war decisions. However, factors of this kind could, without the Romans' being aware of it, play their part in circumscribing their range of choices, and help to explain their continuing willingness to fight wars.

North concludes (ibid. 7–8) that

> Harris is working with an unrealistic model of the senate's freedom of action.... The senate, in the end, had little freedom except to organize the details of the year's campaigning.... There were of course moments when more weighty issues arose; these were the beginnings of the major wars.... Even at those moments, the debates were about where to invest this year's resources or whether to defer action against a major

enemy for a year or even two. . . . The senate's freedom of action lay in matters of detail, of timing, of organization.

In his view, since Harris has demonstrated that Rome's wars were aggressive, 'the focus of debate can now be shifted towards the far deeper problems of the origins, significance and eventual disappearance of the expansion-bearing structures in Roman society and organization' (ibid. 9).

Thus, while North regards Harris's interpretation of the origins of individual wars as too simplistic, he himself holds that the underlying structures were all working in the same direction, towards continuing war and expansion. In my view, this is mistaken. Whatever the differences between them, Harris and North are essentially in agreement on a one-sided view of Roman warfare and imperialism, which seems to me in its way almost as misleading as the old 'defensive imperialism' view.[8] Roman expansion was not a continuous process, maintained at a constant rate. Whether at the level of conscious decision-making or of underlying structures, the determining factors were many and complex and did not all pull in the same direction.

TRENDS AND FLUCTUATIONS IN ROMAN WAR AND EXPANSION

The habit of constant war was as old as the Republic. There were very few years in the Republic's history when its forces saw no fighting (Harris 1979, 9–10; Oakley, ["Roman Conquest"], pp. 14–16). Yet the character of that warfare and the military commitment that it required underwent great changes during the Republic's history.

In the period down to 264, when the Romans' military activity was confined to Italy, their warfare had an annual rhythm. For the most part it was restricted to the summer campaigning season. An army was levied, marched out to fight for a few months, and then returned to be discharged. The command was normally held by the chief magistrates of the state – usually the consuls, but sometimes instead consular tribunes or a dictator. Sometimes they campaigned separately, but often they combined their forces.

The First Punic War (264–241) brought some important changes. During the war the Romans had to maintain a permanent military presence in Sicily all the year round, and for the first time they mobilized large war fleets. After their victory, the Carthaginians ceded Sicily (241) and Sardinia (238). What initial arrangements the Romans made for the control of these territories is uncertain, but from 227 two additional praetors were elected annually for this purpose.

The Second Punic War (218–201) made unprecedented demands. Casualties were very heavy, particularly in the opening years: on a conservative estimate, some 50,000 citizens may have been lost in 218–215 – one-sixth of all adult males and over 5 per cent of the citizen population.[9] The war was conducted in several theatres – Italy, Spain, Sicily, Illyria and Greece, and eventually Africa – and in some of these the Romans had to deploy a number of armies. Thus in total the Romans mobilized far greater forces than they had ever done before, as the detailed information given by Livy shows. From 214 to 206, twenty or more legions were in service. Many of the legions were kept in being for long periods.[10] Numerous additional commanders were required besides the two annually elected consuls. This need was met by using praetors, by proroguing magistrates after the end of their term of office (a device which had been employed occasionally since 326, and from now on was to be commonplace), and by electing private citizens to special commands (*privati cum imperio* – a new expedient, which after 199 was hardly used again until the late Republic).

In the first third of the second century, the Romans' military commitments, although less than they had been during the Second Punic War, were still much greater than before that war. The period saw three great wars against eastern kings: Philip V of Macedon (200–196), Antiochus III (191–188) and Philip's son Perseus (171–168). There was also much warfare in northern Italy: it was in this period that Rome completed the conquest of the peninsula up to the foot of the Alps. The victory over Carthage had left Rome with another permanent commitment overseas, in Spain, where Rome controlled the Baetis valley and the Mediterranean coastal strip. Maintaining and extending their control in Spain involved much fighting during these years, but by 178 the Romans had succeeded in extending their authority over the central plains. Once again Livy supplies us with detailed information on legionary deployment. The average number of legions in service in 200–168 was 8.75; in twelve of these years ten or more legions were deployed (Afzelius 1944, 34–61; Brunt 1971, 422–6; fig. 1). Those who fought in northern Italy might serve for just one or two campaigns, but for the eastern wars service was for the duration, and in Spain legions were kept in post for long periods, with individual soldiers being gradually replaced. Some evidence suggests that six years' service in Spain became accepted as entitling a man to discharge (Brunt 1971, 400–1). As always down to the Social War, contingents of Italian allies served alongside the legions; in this period the ratio of allied to Roman troops varied from 2:1 to parity (Afzelius 1944, 62–79; Brunt 1971, 681–4). The main commands in the East and in northern Italy went to the consuls. From 197 the two Spanish commands were normally assigned to praetors (increased then to six per year).

After 167 we lack Livy's full narrative, but it is clear that the years from 167 to 154 were comparatively peaceful. Spain still had permanent legionary garrisons and in

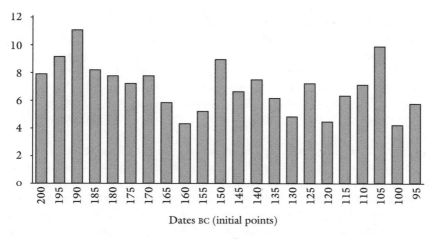

Figure 1   *Legions in service by five-year periods, 100–91* BC. *Source: Brunt 1971, pp. 422–34.*

most (if not all) years legions were deployed in northern Italy, but both regions saw little fighting. Elsewhere there were minor wars, in Corsica and Sardinia (163–2), Dalmatia (156–5) and Transalpine Gaul (154). According to Polybius (32.13.6–7), one factor which led to the Dalmatian war was the Romans' concern lest 'the Italians should be made effeminate by the long peace, it being now the twelfth year since the war with Perseus'.

Serious warfare broke out again in Spain from 153, and in 149–146 the Romans found themselves fighting major wars on a number of other fronts as well – against Carthage (ending with the destruction of the city in 146) and in Macedonia and Greece. These wars led to the creation of two new provinces, Africa and Macedonia. From now on a legionary garrison was maintained in Macedonia to defend the province against the neighbouring tribes, but it saw little action until the late second century. Heavy fighting (much of it unsuccessful for the Romans) continued in Spain until 133, but thereafter the Spanish garrisons were comparatively inactive. The later years of the second century saw a number of wars in various regions, two of which led to the creation of new provinces (Asia after the war against Aristonicus in 133–129, and Transalpine Gaul after the wars of the late 120s). However, it was not until the closing years of the century that Rome was again involved in major wars on a number of fronts, most notably against the Cimbri and their allies.

Without Livy, we lack detailed information on legions from 166, but Brunt has made a plausible reconstruction of the annual deployment of legions (Brunt 1971, 426–34; see fig. 1).[11] It is clear that by and large the Romans' military commitment in this period was rather lower than in the early years of the second century. The overall annual average for 167–91 is 6.48. Only in seven or eight of these years were there ten or more legions in service.

Harris and North present us with a model of the Roman social system as geared to continuous war and requiring for its smooth working that a regular flow of the opportunities and profits of war should be maintained. The reality, as briefly sketched above, is rather more complex. It is true that there were few years when Rome was nowhere at war. However, the levels of Roman belligerence fluctuated very greatly. Periods of intense warfare, often on several fronts, alternated with comparatively peaceful periods with only a few minor campaigns, and sometimes, as in 167–154, these peaceful interludes were quite extended. Warfare had once been the consuls' summer activity, but by the second century most commands lasted longer, and every year the Romans deployed forces in a number of regions, some of which they were committed to garrisoning permanently. In some periods these garrison forces were involved in heavy fighting, but in others they remained comparatively inactive (as in Spain from 178 to 154 and after 133). Overall, the years 167–91 saw a rather lower level of military activity and required somewhat lower force levels than the preceding period.

The momentum of Roman expansion was by no means constant. In the Greek East, the Romans preferred to maintain indirect hegemony and avoided permanent military commitments as long as possible. They were constantly embroiled in the affairs of the cities and kingdoms, but it was only very rarely that a problem became so critical that they deemed it necessary to despatch an armed force. Normally they limited themselves to what they could achieve by diplomatic means and by the weight of their authority. In the resultant game of brinkmanship, some eastern powers succeeded in defying Roman orders without adverse consequences. Thus Ptolemy VI Philometor ignored Roman instructions that he should hand over Cyprus to his brother, and Antiochus V Epiphanes flagrantly disregarded his treaty obligations not to maintain a fleet or keep elephants.[ii] After Antiochus' death, when the kingdom was weak, a Roman embassy had the ships burnt and the elephants hamstrung, but, when the head of the embassy was murdered, no punishment was exacted, although in the Romans' eyes there was no more fitting ground for war than offences against embassies.[12]

Even in the West, the Roman advance was in some respects surprisingly patchy. The subjugation of northern Italy was largely completed by about 170, but the Alps and their foothills remained outside Roman control. Although troops were frequently stationed in northern Italy thereafter, they seem to have engaged in little fighting and for the most part Rome left the Alpine tribes alone until Augustus undertook and rapidly completed their conquest. The provincial boundaries established for Trans-alpine Gaul after the wars of the late 120s remained unaltered until Caesar's ambition to rival Pompey led him to undertake the conquest of the rest of Gaul. Although at least two legions were always maintained in Spain, expansion there virtually ceased after 133, and the conquest of the north of the Iberian peninsula was left to Augustus.

It is not the case that the benefits of successful war were maintained in constant supply. The most conspicuous disruption was the ending of land settlement. The two chief benefits which ordinary Roman citizens got from warfare were booty and land. From the fifth century the Roman government had confiscated land from defeated states in Italy, and much of that land had been distributed in land allotments. This practice played an important part in ending the social conflicts which troubled the early Republic and maintaining political stability thereafter. However, once the conquest of Italy was complete, the confiscation of land ceased, and as a result land allotment also ceased, about 170. The result was that an unsatisfied demand for land built up which in due course was met by tribunes and generals in spite of senatorial opposition. All this could have been avoided if the Roman government had been willing to make land allotments overseas, but they would not contemplate this solution, and stoutly opposed the few proposals of this kind which were made, notably Gaius Gracchus' attempt to refound Carthage. It was not until the dictatorship of Caesar that a large-scale programme of overseas settlement was undertaken.

Although none of the élite's benefits ceased altogether, a level flow was not maintained, as the record of triumphs shows. Information on triumphs is provided both by ancient historical writers and by the *Fasti Triumphales*, an inscribed list of triumphs set up at Rome under Augustus (Degrassi, ed., 1947, 64–87, 534–71). The data for the early centuries are of doubtful authenticity, and a lacuna in the *Fasti* for 155–129 means that some uncertainty subsists about those years.[13] However, it is clear that there were two peaks, in the late fourth and early third century, and in the first thirty or so years of the second century (fig. 2). The first peak starts with the period of the conquest of Italy and extends into the first part of the First Punic War. The second peak corresponds to the years of heavy and largely successful warfare in northern Italy, Spain and the Greek East. The decline in the level of military activity in the rest of the second century, which we have already noticed, is matched by a sharp drop in the number of triumphs: 39 triumphs were celebrated in the years 200–167,

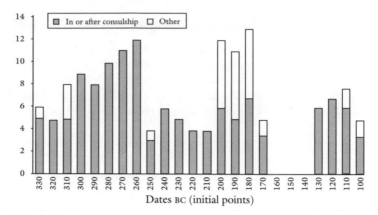

Figure 2   *Triumphs and ovations per decade, 330–91 BC.*

an average of 1.15 per year, whereas in 166–91 only 46 triumphs were celebrated, an annual average of 0.6.

Closer inspection reveals significant differences between the two peak periods. In the first period, most triumphs were held in or following consulships, and the rest were celebrated by dictators. In the second, the number of consular triumphs was not much higher than later in the century. The high total in the period 200–167 was the result of an exceptionally large number of non-consular celebrations – eighteen in, or following, praetorships, and two by men who had commanded in Spain as *privati cum imperio*. Before 200 only one praetor had earned a triumph (in 241). The new, wider range of Rome's commitments brought unprecedented opportunities to win glory at this earlier stage of the political career, particularly in Spain, where twelve of the praetorian triumphs were earned. It is true that the two *privati* and seven of the Spanish praetors were awarded not a full curule triumph but the lesser honour of an *ovatio* (in which the victor entered the city on foot or on horseback, rather than in a chariot), and a joke in Plautus suggests that there may have been some contemporary cynicism about the frequency of triumphs.[14] Nonetheless, the value placed on these honours is confirmed by the success of those who won them in subsequent elections to the consulship (Harris 1979, 32, 262–3; Richardson 1986, 105–6).

After 167, praetors' opportunities for triumphs were sharply reduced. In the period 166–91 only six men are known to have triumphed after their praetorship.[15] [iii] This change is related to the overall downturn in military activity in this period, and in particular to a shift in the way in which the consuls themselves were deployed (fig. 3).[16] In the period 200–168 the consuls normally campaigned in northern Italy. The great eastern wars were conducted by consuls, but otherwise only two consuls were sent overseas in those years (Cato to Spain in 195 and Tiberius Gracchus to Sardinia in 177). The completion of the conquest of northern Italy led to a change in practice. The loss of Livy means that our information on consular provinces is defective, but it is clear that it became much commoner for consuls to be sent overseas: 57 consuls are attested as holding overseas provinces in the period 167–91. Consuls sent overseas normally engaged in warfare.[17] The senate's usual practice seems to have been to send one of the consuls to wherever the main overseas

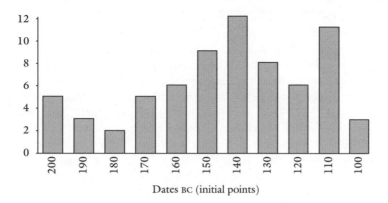

Figure 3   *Consuls assigned overseas provinces per decade, 200–91* BC.

trouble spot happened to be. Thus in fourteen of the years between 153 and 133, when Spain saw continued heavy fighting, one of the Spanish provinces was assigned to a consul. So in most years the best opportunities for winning glory went to consuls, and it was only exceptionally fortunate praetors who had the chance of a triumph.[18]

The consuls who were sent overseas went out to perform the traditional task of a consul, command in war. But the majority of consuls in this period still stayed behind in Italy. Although presence in Italy is positively attested for only about thirty, we can assume that most of those whose province is unrecorded also stayed in Italy, since some record is likely to survive of overseas activity. Yet only eleven triumphs were won in northern Italy in that period,[19] and only two other consuls are attested as having campaigned there.[20] Some consuls are known to have engaged in road-building (Wiseman 1970), and some appear to have spent all their year of office in Rome (for example, Scaevola in 133, Fannius in 122 and Marius and Valerius Flaccus in 100). How the rest spent their time is a matter of conjecture, but it seems likely that most spent some time in northern Italy in effect on garrison duty, commanding an army but not fighting. This inactivity of the consuls in Italy is all the more remarkable in view of the fact that opportunities for war lay ready to hand in the as yet unconquered Alps.[21]

Thus the picture presented by Harris and North of irresistible pressures impelling the Romans to constant warfare and expansion is too simple. The levels of Roman belligerence fluctuated; fundamental changes took place in the nature of their military commitments; and in the later second century at least, opportunities for war and expansion were often missed and many consuls did not engage in warfare at all. Roman expansion was a patchy, untidy business, and we must take full account of this when seeking to explain the processes which were at work. The benefits of successful war were real enough and undoubtedly do help to explain the Romans' readiness to resort to war so often. However, there were also countervailing factors, which may in part account for the patchiness which we have observed. Two such factors were pointed out by Sherwin-White in his critiques of Harris: manpower limitations and aristocratic rivalry (Sherwin-White 1980, 178–9; 1984, 13).

The Romans' ability to call on vast reserves of citizen and allied manpower was a factor of fundamental importance in their success. It was this that enabled them to survive the crisis of the Hannibalic War. Their manpower commitments in the second century were less than those that had been required in that war, but still very heavy.[22] It would have been only prudent for the senate to seek to conserve manpower and to hesitate before undertaking new long-term manpower commitments. As Harris himself noted (1979, 144–5), this may help to explain why Macedonia was not made a province in 167, immediately after the overthrowing of the monarchy. It is commonly supposed that the maintenance of a property qualification for legionary service led to a manpower crisis in the later second century as more and more citizens fell below the qualifying level. If this were true, it could have played an important part in bringing about the lower level of belligerence which we have observed in this period.[23] However, I have argued elsewhere that there is no reason to suppose that the numbers of qualified men declined steeply enough to lead to a shortage (Rich 1983).[24] There is, though, evidence of contemporary concern, not about the property qualification, but about whether the peasantry were bearing and rearing enough children.[25] Such fears were exaggerated, but they may have had some effect on decisions about wars and expansion.

As Harris has admirably shown, the traditions of their class drove Roman aristocrats to seek success and glory, and military achievements were the most highly prized. However, those same traditions would ensure that aristocrats would do all they could to prevent their rivals stealing a march on them. In the second century on average about ten senators may have become eligible every year for the six praetorships, and probably only about one in five of those senators who survived to the requisite age attained the consulship (cf. Hopkins and Burton 1983, 47–8). In that century only about one in four consuls celebrated a triumph during or after their year of office, and, as we have seen, after the early years of the century those who drew Italy in the ballot for provinces stood a much lower chance. Only a minority of praetorian provinces involved the command of an army,[26] and, as we have seen, except in the period 200–170 praetorian triumphs were a rarity. Common sense suggests that the majority who stood to be disappointed of the highest prizes would not make it easy for the minority to win them, and this presumption is confirmed by the sources. Livy and other writers are full of stories of controversies in the senate over, for example, whether a commander should have his term extended or be granted a triumph. It is reasonable to suppose that this factor also operated as a brake on the initiation of war.[27]

THE DECISION-MAKING PROCESS

In theory Roman wars could not be begun unless authorized by the assembly of the people. In practice, however, only a minority of wars were submitted to the assembly for approval. Only about eight war votes by the assembly are known in the period from the First Punic War to the end of the Republic. There may have been some others of which no record has survived, but probably not many. Rome fought many wars in the period 218–167, but Livy records only four popular war votes in those years; since he takes scrupulous note of these, it is unlikely that he passed over others. A glance at the list of those wars for which popular votes are attested suggests that it was normally only before wars against major powers, such as Carthage and the Hellenistic kings, that the assembly was consulted (Rich 1976, 13–17; cf. Harris 1979, 41–2, 263).

Proposals for war were generally only put to the assembly after they had been approved in the senate.[28] Only once do we hear of objections being raised in the assembly, namely against the Second Macedonian War in 200. On that occasion the tribune Q. Baebius induced the people, weary after the Second Punic War, to vote against the proposal, but a stern speech from the consul soon persuaded them to reverse their decision (Livy, 31.6.1–8. 1; Rich 1976, 79–80).

The readiness of the Roman people to give their consent to wars when it was sought and to acquiesce in wars being begun without their being consulted is not a mark of their political impotence, but shows rather that they were generally not averse to war.[29] On one occasion, if Polybius is to be believed, they proved more bellicose than the senate. In an account probably deriving from the Roman annalist Fabius Pictor, he tells us that in 264 the senate could not make up its mind whether to send help to Messana, but that the people decided to do so, thus initiating the train of events which led directly to the First Punic War.[30]

If Polybius is right, the First Punic War is a unique instance of the crucial decision leading to war being taken in the assembly. For other wars the real decision was taken elsewhere, either in the senate or by the commanders in the field.

War decisions which were reached when a Roman army was already in the field were generally taken by the army commander. This sometimes happened even in areas not permanently garrisoned by Rome. Thus Flamininus, after defeating Philip, went on to fight a war against Nabis of Sparta in 195, and, when Manlius Vulso arrived in 189 to take over the command against Antiochus only to find that the king had already made peace, he proceeded to campaign against the Galatians. Both decisions were essentially taken by the commanders, although the senate seems to have given some sort of authorization to Flamininus (Livy, 33.45.3; 34.22.5) and perhaps also to Manlius (see below). In areas where armies were permanently stationed, like Spain from the late third century and Macedonia from 148, war decisions were commonly taken by the commander alone, although occasionally the senate too might be involved, as with the negotiations with the Spanish city Segeda in 154 (App. *Hisp.* 44; Diod. 31.39).

It might be expected that the desire to win glory and booty would have played a particularly important part in bringing about those wars which commanders began at their own discretion. Some commanders were criticized at the time for beginning war without due cause, and the fiction that wars required the consent of the people was sometimes exploited to add to their discomfiture. Enemies of Manlius Vulso unsuccessfully opposed his triumph, and one of the arguments they used was that his Galatian campaign was unauthorized (Livy, 38.45–6). In 178, two tribunes attacked A. Manlius for launching a campaign in Histria from his province in Cisalpine Gaul without authorization (Livy, 41.7.7–8). M. Popillius in 173 is said to have launched an unprovoked attack on the Ligurian Statellates and then to have enslaved them after accepting their surrender; the senate ordered their restitution to freedom, and after his return Popillius was put on trial, although his family's influence ensured that the proceedings were not brought to a conclusion (Livy, 42.7–10, 21–2). M. Aemilius Lepidus Porcina, proconsul in Hither Spain in 136, began war on the Vaccaei and persisted despite express instructions from the senate to stop; his campaign was

unsuccessful, and he was stripped of his command and fined on his return (App. *Hisp.*
80–3; Oros. 5.5.13). M. Iunius Silanus was prosecuted unsuccessfully in connection
with the defeat which he had suffered at the hands of the Cimbri in 109; the case
against him included the charge that he had made war on the Cimbri without the
approval of the people (Asc. 80C). A number of other second-century commanders,
against whom no action was taken at Rome, are alleged by our sources to have started
wars without provocation out of desire for booty and/or a triumph, namely
L. Licinius Lucullus against the Vaccaei in 151 (App. *Hisp.* 51–5), Ap. Claudius
Pulcher against the Salassi in 143 (Dio fr. 74),[31] and L. Caecilius Metellus against the
Dalmatians (App. *Ill.* 11). Not all these allegations may have been fully justified. Thus
Manlius Vulso could point out that the Galatians had not only been a long-standing
menace to peace in Asia, but had fought on Antiochus' side (Livy, 38.47–8), and a
notice in Livy (37.51.10) suggests that the senate envisaged the possibility of a
Galatian campaign before Manlius left Rome. Both Lucullus and Lepidus made
allegations against the Vaccaei in justification of their attacks, and there may have
been some substance in their claims (Richardson 1986, 149–50). However, we need
not doubt that at least some of these commanders began their wars chiefly or wholly
in order to win glory and booty, and that the same took place on other occasions
which have attracted no comment in our sources.

Harris regards the personal advantages which commanders derived from success in
war as one of the main causes of Roman war-making, and Richardson has put this
factor at the centre of his interpretation of Roman expansion in Spain, which he
regards as a process of 'peripheral imperialism' (Richardson 1986, 177), with the men
on the spot making the running and the government in Rome generally showing little
interest. For Richardson, Roman warfare in the region conveys the appearance of 'an
unsystematic hunt for peoples to defeat and booty to carry home' (ibid. 98).[32] Such
views seem to me to take insufficient account of the patchiness of Roman warfare
which we noted in the previous section. As we have seen, there was relatively little
warfare in Spain in the years from 178 to 154 and again after 133. In the periods
when there was heavy fighting in Spain, most of it took place in areas which the
Romans already claimed to control, and those campaigns which did extend Roman
authority further afield were probably at least partly motivated by the wish to ensure
the security of the territory already held. While some of those consuls who held
command in northern Italy in the later second century did undertake campaigns with
questionable justification, like Claudius in 143 and Metellus in 119, the majority, as
we have seen, seem to have done no fighting at all.

It seems then that simple triumph-hunting was the exception, not the rule. Why
was this? At least part of the answer must, I think, be that unscrupulous triumph-
hunting was politically risky. Richardson holds that at least in the early second century
the senate regarded the commander's job as being to win victories and did not care
how they were come by (ibid. 108–9, 125). This seems to me mistaken. It was public
policy that wars should not be begun without due cause. As the cases cited above
show, commanders who flouted this might provoke an outcry at Rome. Senatorial
vigilance in such matters was no doubt partly inspired by principle, but an important
part was, of course, also played by personal rivalries, as in the case of Manlius Vulso.
Another significant factor may have been ties of patronage between senators and
subject communities. It is true that generally the penalties were not heavy. Only

Lepidus was convicted, and his case was very exceptional: he had defied an express order by the senate, which was itself an extraordinary measure, prompted by a string of recent disasters in Spain. Although the senatorial consensus was firmly against Popillius, he was able to avoid conviction, and went on to hold the censorship in 159.[33] Others, like Lucullus, were never called to account. Nonetheless, any proconsul who was tempted to attack a tribe in the hope of winning booty and a triumph had to reckon with the possibility that, even if his campaign went well, he might face a scandal, or worse, when he returned to Rome. It may be for this reason that so many proconsuls played safe and took no military action during their term of office.

When starting a war involved despatching an army to a region where the Romans did not maintain a permanent presence, the decision to initiate the war was normally taken in the senate. Because of the relative ease of communications, the senate also played a much greater part in such decisions in northern Italy than it did in the overseas provinces. North, as we have seen (above, pp. 49–50), holds that the senate's freedom of action was in reality always very restricted. In my view, the senate had a good deal more freedom of choice than he allows. The way in which senatorial war decisions were taken varied widely. At the beginning of every year the senate assigned provinces and armies. These arrangements often implied that a war would be begun in a particular region, and for many minor wars the senate took the decision to begin the war simply by decreeing the region as a province. However, that does not justify us in saying, with North, that all that the senate did was to 'organize the details of the year's campaigning'. The senate never began a war without reasons, just because it had to have a war somewhere.

For major wars, like those against Carthage and Hellenistic kings, the decision-making process was more complex. Such wars, as we know from Livy, were begun with due formality; in the year when war was to be begun, the consuls, on entering office, were instructed to sacrifice for the successful outcome of the war and to seek the approval of the popular assembly (Rich 1976, 13). In most cases the senate's real decision for war had already been taken months earlier (ibid. 18–55). Sometimes we can pinpoint precisely the moment when the decision was taken, as, for example, with the Second Macedonian War: the senate committed itself to this war when, in the autumn of 201, it agreed to the appeals of Attalus and the Rhodians for help. In other cases the matter is more complex: the senate took steps which were not at the time clear decisions for war, but which committed them to a course of action which turned out to lead unavoidably to war. The Second Punic War is an example. In 220 the senate warned Hannibal not to attack Saguntum. Hannibal responded by doing just that. In my view, when it learnt of his attack, the senate was unanimous that Hannibal's disregard of the Roman warning must be treated as grounds for war (ibid. 28–44). Another instance is afforded by the war with Antiochus. In 196 the senate presented Antiochus with various demands which were unacceptable to him. Both sides were prepared to make some compromises, but neither was willing to concede enough to bridge the gap. As a result war was inevitable, although it did not actually begin until 191.[34] The complexity of the decision-making process should not obscure the fact that the senate did have a real choice, which was not just confined, as North claims, to matters of timing and organization. It could have decided not to warn Hannibal off Saguntum, not to agree to the appeal of Attalus and the Rhodians, not to present its demands to Antiochus.

The senate's decisions were reached after debate. We are very poorly informed about what was said in the debates relating to wars (Harris 1979, 6–7, 255). Only on a few occasions are we told anything about them, and the value of this information is often doubtful. We have substantial fragments of just one speech, that made by Cato in 167 against the proposal (which in the event was rejected) for war against Rhodes (Gell. *NA* 6.3 = *ORF*, frs. 163–71). However, although we know so little about individual debates, it is not difficult to get an idea from the voluminous tradition about Rome's wars of the kinds of arguments which were deployed in debates on issues of war. Moral arguments will, of course, have bulked large: the enemy's unjust acts, the Romans' obligation to help their allies and humble the arrogant, and so on. Almost all belligerents, ancient and modern, have convinced themselves that they were in the right, and the Romans' concern with such questions was fortified by the tradition of the *ius fetiale*. Nor was their conscience indefinitely elastic: at least one war, the Third Punic War, may have been delayed by scruples about the justice of the Roman cause.[35] Alongside such moral considerations, prudential arguments will have been deployed, arguments about what was in the interest of the Roman people. Often moral and prudential arguments will have been intertwined, as they are in Cato's Rhodian speech (Astin 1978, 276–81). Prominent among such prudential arguments will have been defensive considerations, such as claims that, unless Rome went to war against some power, it would menace the Roman people and its interests. Our sources frequently report the use of such arguments, and, although in many individual cases their historicity is doubtful, we cannot doubt that they were a prominent part of the repertory of debate.

A much less prominent part was probably played, at least in senatorial debates, by arguments from the personal advantage, material and otherwise, which participants stood to derive from prospective wars. If speakers in the senate used this argument to advance the case for a war, they probably chose their words with care. For, in the Roman view, while it was not dishonourable to profit from war, wars should not be begun for this reason alone. Part of Cato's case against the proposed Rhodian war was that its proponents wanted to grab the wealth of Rhodes for themselves (Gell. *NA* 6.3.7, 52). I referred above (p. 57) to Polybius' account, probably drawn from Fabius Pictor, of how the Romans decided to help the Mamertines of Messana in 264. Whatever its historicity, it is good evidence for the value which a third-century senator put on the various possible arguments. The senate could not make up its mind, because morality told against sending help in view of the Mamertines' shameful past but prudence told in favour in view of the threat to Rome's interests if Carthage got possession of Messana. The deadlock was resolved in the assembly, in part because the consuls pointed out to the people the profits to be derived from the war. Fabius, it would seem, regarded this as an argument more appropriate for the assembly than the senate and as disreputable.

Of course, the arguments which senators deployed in debate would be a very imperfect guide to their motives for voting for a war. Defensive arguments might often be employed disingenuously, as they were by the Roman government in 238 when it claimed that the preparations being made by the Carthaginians to resume their legitimate control of Sardinia were directed against Rome (Polyb. 1.88.10), by Caesar to justify his campaigns against the Helvetii and the Belgae (Caes. *BGall.* 1.10.2; 2.1) and by Augustus to justify his advance against Maroboduus

(Vell. Pat. 2.109). Many senators' votes in favour of war were undoubtedly coloured by their expectation of profit for themselves or their friends. However, at each such meeting there will have been more senators who did not stand to profit personally from the decision, and some for whom it would mean the advancement of their personal enemies. It therefore seems to me likely that in most decisions which led directly or indirectly to war most senators' votes were determined less by the hope of personal advantage than by their judgement of what was right and/or in the public interest.

Why did senators so frequently judge that justice and the public interest required Rome to embark on yet another war? Much of the answer to this question is, of course, supplied by the structural elements stressed by Harris and North. The Romans' possession of a magnificent fighting machine, their habituation to war and their extraordinary record of success in it, the benefits that that success brought them and the continuing demand for more of the same that it generated – it is these factors, above all, which made the Romans so ready to discern and take up occasions for war. However, other factors too played their part, and there is one in particular which must not be neglected. The Romans were not always successful in their wars and some enemies – the Gauls, Pyrrhus, Hannibal – threatened the very survival of the Republic. Memories of those dangers were real enough, and in my judgement the fear of powerful neighbours, although not, as used to be supposed, the key to Roman imperialism, must remain an important factor in accounting for it.[36] Striking testimony to the potency of such fears is afforded by the human sacrifices performed at Rome in 228, 216 and 114/13, whose purpose, as recent studies have shown, was to ward off external threats (Eckstein 1982; Bellen 1985, 12–15, 21, 36–8). Brunt once remarked that 'Roman reactions to the possibility of a threat resembled those of a nervous tiger, disturbed when feeding' (1978, 177 = 1990, 307). The image seems to me apt enough, not least because it does not dispute that the tiger was frightened.

Polybius quite often explains Roman actions in terms of fear. Thus, as we have seen, he claims that one factor in the Roman decision to help Messana was the fear that, if they stood aside, the Carthaginians would get control of Sicily and would be 'excessively vexatious and dangerous neighbours' (1.10.6). Fear of growing Carthaginian power reappears as the reason for the conclusion of the Ebro treaty (2.13.3). Polybius' account of the Gallic invasion of 225 is dominated by references to the Gallic threat and the fear it evoked at Rome (e.g. 2.23.7; 31.7). The decision to retain both consuls in Italy in 197 is attributed to 'the threat from the Gauls' (18.11.2). In the famous passage in which, without indicating his own view, he reports Greek opinions about the destruction of Carthage, Polybius represents Greeks favourable to Rome as approving of the destruction because Carthage was a threat (36.9.4)[37] Polybius could, of course, err in his explanation of individual Roman actions. However, these passages do have a cumulative force.[38] We should not lightly disregard the belief of such a well-placed and perceptive contemporary observer that fear of other nations was at times a significant factor in Roman policy-making.

The Third Punic War is in fact a crucial case. Our sources – including the Polybian passage just cited – show that the Roman government gave as the reason for its actions that it had come to believe that Roman security required the destruction of the city of Carthage. If this is what the Romans really believed, they were in the grips of an irrational fear. Attempts to represent it as rational founder on the fact that such resurgent power as Carthage had shown had already been destroyed by Masinissa in the war which provided the pretext for the Romans' own war declaration.[39] Not surprisingly, many modern writers have tried to provide alternative explanations. Harris himself is the most recent contender. For him, Carthage, having once again attracted Roman attention, fell victim to the Romans' constant need for new wars, glory and booty (Harris 1979, 234–40; 1989, 153–6). This is a banal and implausible explanation of the Romans' terrible and extraordinary decision, and is made all the more unlikely by the fact that they had heavy military commitments elsewhere at the time. The Romans, who at the Second Punic War had accepted the survival of Carthage, now declared that the city must be destroyed. In my view, we must accept that, strange as it may seem, they did so because they had become convinced that the city was a threat which must be extirpated.

CONCLUSION

Harris and his followers have exploded the old doctrine of 'defensive imperialism', but what they have offered in its place is also too one-sided. It is true that the Romans fought a war somewhere in almost every year, but at least by the second century there was no need for them to seek wars out: their far-flung imperial commitments ensured that there was generally no shortage of wars for them to fight.[40] Moreover, as we have seen, the pattern of Roman warfare and expansion was a good deal patchier than Harris' simple model implies: the nature of the Romans' military activity and commitments changed greatly over time, and in many regions there were long periods which saw few wars and little or no expansion. The wealth and prestige which success in war conferred certainly help to explain the Romans' readiness to fight, but there were countervailing factors. In particular, the ethos of aristocratic competition had more complex consequences than Harris allows. The likely participants and their friends might be impelled towards war by the prospect of the booty and glory to be won, but this same prospect might impel their rivals to thwart them. Due attention must be paid also to the workings of the decision-making process. Until the age of Caesar, the most important wars, which marked the crucial stages in Rome's advance, were the product of decisions taken in the senate, a body which on such matters is likely to have been swayed more by considerations of morality and the public interest than by personal advantage.

Roman warfare and imperialism were complex phenomena, for which no mono-causal explanation will be adequate. Any attempt to provide a more satisfactory account must take the measure of this complexity. In such an account fear, greed and glory will all play their part.[41]

NOTES

1   All dates are BC.
2   In insisting on the importance of these factors Harris stands in an old and distinguished tradition. See, for example, Montesquieu 1734, ch. 1 (pp. 7 and 9 of Jullian's edition):

La république ayant des chefs qui changeaient tous les ans, et qui cherchaient à signaler leur magistrature pour en obtenir de nouvelles, il n'y avait pas un moment de perdu pour l'ambition; ils engageaient le sénat à proposer au peuple la guerre, et lui montraient tous les jours de nouveaux ennemis.... Or la guerre était presque toujours agréable au peuple, parce que, par la sage distribution du butin, on avait trouvé le moyen de la lui rendre utile.... Les consuls, ne pouvant obtenir l'honneur du triomphe que par une conquête ou une victoire, faisaient la guerre avec une impétuosité extrême: on allait droit à l'ennemi, et la force décidait d'abord. Rome était donc dans une guerre éternelle et toujours violente.

[Since the Republic had leaders who changed every year and sought to single out their year in office by some remarkable action, there was not a moment lost for their ambition; they engaged the Senate to propose war to the commons, and they constantly showed to them new enemies.... Warfare was nearly always agreeable to the people, because, by the wise distribution of war booty, a way was found to make it profitable for them.... The consuls, only being able to obtain the honor of a triumph by conquest or victory, made war with an extreme impetuosity: one would go straight at the enemy, and force decided the issue. Rome was therefore in war, eternal and always violent.]

3 I have discussed a number of these works in reviews: Rich 1985a, 1985b, 1988a, 1988b, 1991.

4 For criticisms of Harris in these works see especially Gruen 1984, chs 8–9; Sherwin-White 1984, 11–17; Eckstein 1987, xiv–xvi.

5 Richardson 1986, especially chs. 1 and 8. See also Lintott 1981.

6 Linderski 1984. See also Frézouls 1983; Hermon 1989.

7 Momigliano 1975, 45–6. Harris's discussion of the topic at Harris (ed.) 1984, 89–113, is unsatisfactory. See further Cornell 1989, 385–9, and Oakley's remarks, ["Roman Conquest"], pp. 16–18.

8 Cf. Doyle 1986, especially chs. 1 and 6, on the inadequacy of what he classifies as 'dispositional, metrocentric theories' of imperialism, which seek to explain it simply in terms of internal drives to expansion within the dominant 'metropoles'. His principal instances of such theories are Hobson, Lenin and Schumpeter, but he cites Harris as a more recent example (p. 24).

9 Cf. Brunt 1971, 54, 419–20. Compare the First World War: for the seven original belligerent nations, soldiers killed and dying of wounds during the war amounted to 2 per cent of the total population (Wright 1965, 664).

10 For numbers of legions and length of service see Toynbee 1965, ii.79–80, 647–51; Brunt 1971, 400, 417–22.

11 Brunt arbitrarily assumes that two legions were deployed in Northern Italy every year down to 135, but thereafter only when a military presence is explicitly attested there. This may mean that some of his estimates are too high for years before 135 and too low thereafter.

12 For the events see Gruen 1984, 655–65 and 699–702, with my comments at Rich 1985a, 96.

13 The lacuna, which is about 33 lines long, probably listed fourteen or fifteen triumphs, of which seven are known from other sources (Degrassi 1947, 557–9). Over the period 160–131 triumphs probably averaged six per decade.

14 Plautus, *Bacchides*, 1067–75. The slave Chrysalus represents himself metaphorically as bringing an army home loaded with booty, and then adds: 'But, audience, don't be surprised if I don't hold a triumph: it's so common, it's not worth it'.

15 The names of a few more are probably lost in the lacuna for 155–129.

16 The data are collected in *MRR* [*Magistrates of the Roman Republic*].
17 A possible exception is M. Porcius Cato in 118: he may have been assigned to Africa to carry out a diplomatic mission, the settlement of Numidia after Micipsa's death.
18 Richardson 1975 clearly sets out the changing patterns in triumph-holding, but unnecessarily posits a stricter policy in the senate on granting triumphs to explain the drop in praetorian celebrations. The law passed between 180 and 143 requiring 5,000 enemy killed may have been the initiative of the tribune who proposed it rather than senatorial policy (as Richardson supposes), and, since most commanders would probably have had no scruples about claiming so many dead, it need not have had any significant effect on the frequency of triumphs.
19 In Liguria: 166 (two), 158, 155. Against the Salassi: 143 (unauthorized: see below n. 31). In and beyond the Julian Alps: 129, 117 (two), 115. Against the invading Cimbri: 101 (two).
20 [Cn.] Papirius Carbo was defeated by the Cimbri in 113 (*MRR* i.535). L. Licinius Crassus defeated raiders in 95 and claimed a triumph, but his colleague vetoed it on the grounds that his achievements were too insignificant (*MRR* ii.11).
21 Consular inactivity in Italy is stressed as an objection to Harris by Sherwin-White 1980, 178; 1984, 12.
22 For estimates of numbers of citizens serving and of the proportion of the citizen body in arms in 218–91, see Brunt 1971, 416–34; Hopkins 1978, 33.
23 Cf. Harris 1979, 49–50. Here and at pp. 36–8 he does show some recognition of the decline in belligerence in the course of the second century, but he fails to recognize the importance of the phenomenon or offer an adequate explanation.
24 There is no foundation for the widely accepted view that the qualification was progressively reduced in response to the supposed shortage: Rich 1983, 305–16.
25 Rich 1983, 299–305. The decline in the numbers registered at the census between 164/3 and 136/5 may have lent colour to such fears.
26 Every year one or two praetors were retained at Rome. After the Hannibalic War Sicily and Sardinia were normally garrisoned only with allied troops, if at all, and the same was true of the new provinces of Africa from 146 and Asia from 129.
27 North replies to this objection as follows (North 1981, 6):

> In the middle republic, if one faction failed to gain a particular command or opportunity, there was always next year to hope for better things. It must have been far more important to all factions to keep a regular flow of opportunities and profits, than to attempt to exclude rivals from command.

This seems to me to disregard the strongly individualistic nature of Roman political culture, and recalls the misguided view of Roman politics as dominated by factions which North himself has recently dubbed the 'frozen waste' theory (North 1990).
28 Apart from the First Punic War (see below), when the issue was strictly not whether war should be declared but whether help should be sent to Messana, the only recorded exception is a not very serious proposal for war against Rhodes in 167 (Livy, 45.21).
29 On popular attitudes to war see Harris 1979, 41–53. Millar 1984 rightly insists on the political importance of the assemblies in the middle Republic.
30 Polyb. 1.10.3–11.3. Hoyos 1984 shows that Polybius must mean that the decision was taken in the assembly, not the senate.
31 Claudius was denied a triumph and celebrated one on his own authority, but the refusal seems to have been based on the inadequacy of his military achievements rather than doubts about the justice of the war (Oros. 5.4.7).
32 For criticism of Richardson's views see Cornell 1987; Rich 1988a.

33   Compare Ser. Sulpicius Galba, who massacred surrendered Lusitanians in 150, was acquitted in a celebrated trial, and went on to hold the consulship in 144 (*MRR* i.456–7, 470).

34   Cf. Briscoe 1981, 30–3, rightly rejecting the view of Badian 1959 that the war came about through a series of accidents and even in 192 could still have been avoided.

35   Polyb. 36.2; Livy, *Per.* 48–9. On Nasica's opposition to this war see especially Astin 1967, 276–80; Bellen 1985, 4–8.

36   Bellen 1985 is an interesting recent study of the topic.

37   Polybius goes on to say that those who took the opposite view saw it as part of a policy of ruthless extermination. Scholars differ about which view Polybius himself favoured: see e.g. Harris 1979, 271–2; Walbank 1985, 168–72, 286–9; Ferrary 1988, 327–43. Possibly Polybius presented the question in this way because his sympathies were torn and he felt unable to make up his mind.

38   This is ignored by Harris 1979, who treats these passages dismissively and in isolation (e.g. pp. 186, 198, 205). By contrast, he sets great store by Polybius' judgement when it supports his case. He is far too impressed (ibid. 107–17) by Polybius' notion that from some point the Romans consciously set out to conquer the world. That doctrine is Polybius at his worst: schematic theorizing, contradicted by his own detailed statements (Walbank 1963, not refuted by Derow 1979).

39   *Contra* Astin 1967, 274–5; 1978, 285–6. However, Astin 1967, 48–54, 270–81, remains the best account of the preliminaries of the war.

40   The frequency with which the Romans fought wars is in itself not so very remarkable. As Finley remarks (1985, 67), 'Athens . . . was at war on average more than two years out of every three between the Persian wars and the defeat . . . at Chaeronea in 338 BC, and . . . it never enjoyed ten consecutive years of peace in all that period.' The history of several major powers in modern times shows a high frequency of wars, and there is a clear correlation between states' political importance and their proneness to war (Wright 1965, 220–2, 650–5; Singer and Small 1972, 258–87).

41   This chapter has profited greatly from the observations of those who attended the original seminar [held in Leicester and Nottingham between 1998 and 1990] and from Tim Cornell's comments on a later draft.

EDITOR'S NOTES

i   On Roman republican warfare to 350 BCE, see T. J. Cornell, *The Beginnings of Rome: Italy and Rome from the Bronze Age to the Punic Wars* (*c. 1000–264* BC) (London and New York, 1995), pp. 293–326.

ii   Read "Antiochus IV Epiphanes" for "Antiochus V Epiphanes."

iii On the Roman praetorship, see now T. Corey Brennan, *The Praetorship of the Roman Republic*, 2 vols. (Oxford and New York, 2000).

REFERENCES

Afzelius, A. (1944), *Die römische Kriegsmacht während der Auseinandersetzung mit den hellenistischen Grossmächten* (Copenhagen).

Astin, A. E. (1967), *Scipio Aemilianus* (Oxford).

—— (1978), *Cato the Censor* (Oxford).

Badian, E. (1958), *Foreign Clientelae (264–70 BC)* (Oxford).
—— (1959), 'Rome and Antiochus the Great: a study in cold war', *CP* 54: 81–99; = *Studies in Greek and Roman History* (Oxford, 1964), 112–39.
—— (1968), *Roman Imperialism in the Late Republic* (2nd edn.; Oxford).
Bellen, H. (1985), *Metus Gallicus – Metus Punicus* (Stuttgart).
Briscoe, J. (1981), *A Commentary on Livy Books XXXIV–XXXVII* (Oxford).
Brunt, P. A. (1971), *Italian Manpower 225 BC–AD 14* (Oxford).
—— (1978), 'Laus imperii', in P. D. A. Garnsey and C. R. Whittaker (eds.), *Imperialism in the Ancient World* (Cambridge), ch. 8 (pp. 159–91); = *Roman Imperial Themes* (Oxford, 1990), ch. 14 (pp. 288–323).
Cornell, T. J. (1987), review of Richardson 1986, *TLS* 21 August, p. 906.
—— (1989), 'The conquest of Italy', in *CAH*² vii. 2, ch. 8 (pp. 351–419).
Degrassi, A. (ed. 1947), *Inscriptiones Italiae*, xiii. 1 (Rome).
Derow, P. S. (1979), 'Polybius, Rome and the East', *JRS* 69: 1–15.
Doyle, M. W. (1986), *Empires* (Ithaca).
Dyson, S. L. (1985), *The Creation of the Roman Frontier* (Princeton).
Eckstein, A. M. (1982), 'Human sacrifice and fear of military disaster in Republican Rome', *American Journal of Ancient History*, 7 (1): 69–95.
—— (1987), *Senate and General: Individual Decision-making and Roman Foreign Relations, 264–194 BC* (Berkeley, Los Angeles and London).
Errington, R. M. (1971), *The Dawn of Empire: Rome's Rise to World Power* (London).
Ferrary, J.-L. (1988), *Philhellénisme et impérialisme: aspects idéologiques de la conquête romaine du monde hellénistique, de la seconde guerre de Macédoine à la guerre contre Mithridate* (Rome).
Finley, M. I. (1978), 'Empire in the Graeco-Roman world', *Greece and Rome*, 25: 1–15.
—— (1985), *Ancient History: Evidence and Models* (London).
Frank, T. (1914), *Roman Imperialism* (New York).
Frézouls, E. (1983), 'Sur l'historiographie de l'impérialisme romain', *Ktema*, 8: 141–62.
Gruen, E. S. (1984), *The Hellenistic World and the Coming of Rome* (Berkeley, Los Angeles and London).
Harris, W. V. (1979), *War and Imperialism in Republican Rome 327–70 BC* (Oxford).
—— (ed. 1984), *The Imperialism of Mid-Republican Rome* (Rome).
—— (1989), 'Roman expansion in the west', in *CAH*² viii, ch. 5 (pp. 107–62).
—— (1990), 'Roman warfare in the economic and social context of the fourth century BC', in W. Eder (ed.), *Staat und Staatlichkeit in der frühen römischen Republik* (Stuttgart), pp. 494–510.
Hermon, E. (1989), 'L'Impérialisme romain républicain: approaches historiographiques et approaches d'analyse', *Athenaeum*, 67: 407–16.
Holleaux, M. (1921), *Rome, la Grèce et les monarchies hellénistiques au III siècle avant J.-C. (273–205)* (Paris).
Hopkins, K. (1978), *Conquerors and Slaves* (Cambridge).
—— and Burton, G. P. (1983), 'Political succession in the late Republic (249–50 BC)', in K. Hopkins, *Death and Renewal* (Cambridge), ch. 2 (pp. 31–119).
Hoyos, B. D. (1984), 'Polybius' Roman *hoi polloi* in 264', *LCM* 9: 88–93.
Linderski, J. (1984), '*Si vis pacem, para bellum*: concepts of defensive imperialism', in W. V. Harris (ed.), pp. 133–64.
Lintott, A. W. (1981), 'What was the "Imperium Romanum"?', *Greece and Rome*, 28: 53–67.
Millar, F. G. B. (1984), 'The political character of the classical Roman Republic, 200–151 BC', *JRS* 74: 1–19.
Momigliano, A. D. (1975), *Alien Wisdom* (Cambridge).
Mommsen, T. (1877–80), *The History of Rome*, trans. W. P. Dickson, (London).

Montesquieu, L. (1734), *Considérations sur les causes de la grandeur des romains et de leur decadence*, ed. C. Jullian (Paris, 1900).

North, J. A. (1981), 'The development of Roman imperialism', *JRS* 71: 1–9.

——(1990), 'Democratic politics in Republican Rome', *Past and Present*, 126: 3–21.

Rich, J. W. (1976), *Declaring War in the Roman Republic in the Period of Transmarine Expansion* (Collection Latomus, 149; Brussels).

——(1983), 'The supposed Roman manpower shortage of the later second century BC', *Historia*, 32: 287–331.

——(1985a), review of Gruen 1984, *LCM* 10: 90–6.

——(1985b), review of Dyson 1985, *LCM* 11: 29–31.

——(1988a), review of Richardson 1986, *JRS* 78: 212–14.

——(1988b), review of Eckstein 1987, *CR* 38: 315–17.

——(1991), review of Rosenstein 1990, *CR* 41: 401–4.

Richardson, J. S. (1975), 'The triumph, the praetors and the senate in the early second century', *JRS* 65: 50–63.

——(1986), *Hispaniae: Spain and the Development of Roman Imperialism, 219–82 BC* (Cambridge).

Rosenstein, N. S. (1990), *Imperatores Victi: Military Defeat and Aristocratic Competition in the Middle and Late Republic* (Berkeley, Los Angeles and London).

Sherwin-White, A. N. (1980), 'Rome the aggressor?', review of Harris 1979, *JRS* 70: 177–81.

——(1984), *Roman Foreign Policy in the East 168 BC to AD 1* (London).

Singer, J. D., and Small, M. (1972), *The Wages of War 1816–1965: A Statistical Handbook* (New York).

Toynbee, A. J. (1965), *Hannibal's Legacy* (London).

Walbank, F. W. (1963), 'Polybius and Rome's eastern policy', *JRS* 53: 1–13; = Walbank 1985, 138–56.

——(1985), *Selected Papers* (Cambridge).

Wiseman, T. P. (1970), 'Roman Republican road-building', *PBSR* 38: 122–52; = *Roman Studies* (Liverpool, 1987), 126–56.

Wright, Q. (1965), *A Study of War* (2nd edn.; Chicago and London).

Sources

Roman imperial expansion

The greatest period of Roman imperial expansion roughly coincides with the period of the Roman Republic (traditional dates, 509–31 BCE), and in its most accelerated phase, with the period of the Middle Republic (traditional dates, 264–133 BCE). The period commonly referred to as the Principate, the rule of the Roman emperors (traditional dates, 27 BCE–284 CE), was by contrast generally an empire of consolidation and maintenance;[1] this phase of Rome's imperial history is represented in subsequent chapters concerning social and economic consequences of empire, imperial ideology and government, cultural ramifications of empire, and imperial strategies of defense.

Who could be so worthless or slothful as not to want to know by what means and under what system of polity the Romans in less than 53 years [220–167 BCE] have succeeded in subjecting nearly the whole inhabited world to their sole government – a thing unique in history? Or who could there be so passionately devoted to other attractions or studies as to regard anything as of greater importance than the acquisition of this knowledge?

> Polybius, *Histories*, 1.1.5–6 [ca. 150 BCE]

[Comparison with other empires] confirms the claim I made in the beginning that the Romans' advance was not due to chance and was not involuntary, as some Greeks choose to think, but that by schooling themselves in such vast and perilous enterprises it was perfectly natural that they not only gained the courage to strive for universal dominion, but attained their aim.

> Polybius, *Histories*, 1.63.9 [ca. 150 BCE]

But if anyone wants greater things, and thinks it finer and more glorious to be the leader of many men and to dominate many and have the eyes of all the world turned to him, it must be admitted that from this point of view the Spartan constitution is defective, while that of Rome is superior and better constructed for getting power, as is indeed clear from the actual course of events. For when the Spartans tried to obtain supremacy in Greece, they very soon ran the risk of losing their own freedom; whereas the Romans, who had aimed merely at the subjection of Italy, in a short time brought the whole world under their sway, the abundance of supplies they had at their command conducing in no small measure to this result.

> Polybius, *Histories*, 6.50.3–6 [ca. 150 BCE]

The Roman legions

But to speak more precisely, let us take the conduct of war as an example. The Carthaginians naturally are superior at sea both in efficiency and equipment, because naval proficiency has long been their national business, and they concern themselves with the sea more than any other people; but the Roman military is much more efficient on land. They expend their whole energies on this, whereas the Carthaginians entirely neglect their infantry, though they do pay some slight attention to their cavalry. This is because the troops they employ are foreign and mercenary, whereas those of the Romans are natives and citizens. So that in this respect also we must pronounce the political system of Rome to be superior to that of Carthage, the Carthaginians continuing to depend for the maintenance of their freedom on the courage of a mercenary force but the Romans on their own bravery and on the help of their allies. Consequently even if they happen to be beaten at the outset, the Romans redeem defeat by final success, while it is the opposite with the Carthaginians. For the Romans, fighting as they are for their country and their children, never can relax their fury but continue to throw their whole hearts into the struggle until they get the better of their enemies. . . . Now not only do Italians in general naturally excel Phoenicians and Africans in bodily strength and personal courage, but by their institutions also they do much to foster a spirit of bravery in the young men.

Polybius, *Histories*, 6.52.1–10 [ca. 150 BCE]

In this famous passage the Greek historian Polybius explains the reasons that the Roman infantry formation is superior to the tightly-packed Macedonian formation of pikemen, the phalanx[*].

Such being in general and in detail the nature of the phalanx, I have now, for comparison, to speak of the distinct qualities of the Roman equipment and system of formation and the differences in both. Each Roman soldier with his arms occupies a space of three feet in breadth, but as in their way of fighting each man must move separately, as he has to cover his person with his long shield, turning to meet each expected blow, and as he uses his sword both for cutting and thrusting it is obvious that a looser order is required, and each man must be at a distance of at least three feet from the man next to him in the same rank and those in front of and behind him, if they are to be effective. Consequently one Roman must stand opposite two men in the first rank of the phalanx, so that he has to face and encounter ten pikes, and a single man cannot cut through them all in time once they are at close quarters and it is by no means easy to force their points away, as the rear ranks can be of no help to the front rank either in thus forcing the pikes away or in the use of the sword. So obviously, as I said at the beginning, nothing can withstand the charge of the phalanx as long as it preserves its characteristic formation and force.

How then did the Romans defeat the phalanx? It is because in war the time and place of action is uncertain and the phalanx has only one time and one place in which it can perform. Now, if the enemy were obliged to adapt themselves to the times and places required by the phalanx when a decisive battle was looming, those who use the phalanx would in all probability, for reasons stated above, always get the better of their enemies; but if it is not only possible but easy to avoid its onset why should one any longer dread its attack? . . . Now in all these matters the Macedonian formation is at times of little use and at times completely useless, because the phalanx soldier can be of service neither in detachments nor singly, while the Roman formation is efficient. For every Roman soldier, once he is armed and sets about his business, can adapt himself equally well to every place and time and can meet any attack. He is also equally prepared and equally in condition whether he has to fight together with the whole army or with a part of it or in maniples[*] or singly. So since in all particulars the Romans are much more serviceable, Roman plans are much more likely to result in success than those of others.

Polybius, *Histories*, 18.30.5–31.4, 32.9–13 [ca. 150 BCE]

In an extended speculation (*History of Rome*, 9.17.1–19.17), Livy discusses what would have happened had Alexander the Great (356–323 BCE) turned his attention to the West and invaded Italy and Rome.

We must compare the forces on both sides, whether for numbers, or types of soldiers, or size of their contingents of auxiliaries. The records from that time put the [Roman] population at 250,000.... In those years frequently four and five armies at a time were in operation, in Eturia, in Umbria (where they also fought the Gauls), in Samnium, and in Lucania. Later on Alexander would have found all Latium, with the Sabines, the Volsci and the Aequi, all Campania, and a portion of Umbria and Etruria, the Picentes and the Marsi and the Paeligni, the Vestini and the Apulians, together with the whole coast of the lower sea, held by the Greeks, from Thurii as far as Naples and Cumae, and from there all the way to Antium and Ostia – all these, I say, he would have found either powerful allies of the Romans or their defeated enemies.... Add to this, that the Romans would have had ready recruits, but Alexander, as happened afterwards to Hannibal, would have found his army wear away, while he fought in a foreign land. His men would have been armed with targets and spears; the Romans with an oblong shield, affording more protection to the body, and the Roman javelin, which strikes, on being thrown, with a much harder impact than the lance. Both armies were formed of heavy troops, keeping to their ranks; but their phalanx was immobile and consisted of one kind of soldier; the Roman line was more open and comprised more separate units; it was easy to divide, wherever necessary, and easy to unite. Moreover, what soldier can match the Roman in entrenching? Who is better at enduring toil?

Livy, History of Rome, 9.19.1–9 [ca. 25 BCE]

First steps towards empire and some early reverses[2]

From the foundation of the Republic, Rome had been embroiled in wars with local powers: the neighboring Latin and Etruscan cities, as well as the nearby mountain tribesmen who supplemented their pas-toral economy with raiding of the fertile lowlands. There were also sporadic marauding invasions of Celtic peoples that kept Romans in constant dread.

An early example of unconditional surrender to Roman power

Collatia, and what land the Sabines had on the nearer side of Collatia, was taken from them.... The surrender of the Collatini took place...in accordance with this formula: the king [Tarquinius Priscus, reigned 616–578 BCE] asked, "Are you the legates and spokesmen sent by the people of Collatia to surrender yourselves and the people of Collatia?" "We are." "Is the people of Collatia its own master?" "It is." "Do you surrender yourselves and the people of Collatia, city, lands, water, boundary marks, shrines, utensils, all appurtenances, divine and human, into my power and that of the Roman people?" "We do." "I receive the surrender." Upon the conclusion of the Sabine War Tarquinius returned to Rome and triumphed. He then made war against the ancient Latins.

Livy, History of Rome, 1.38.1–4 [ca. 25 BCE]

The siege and conquest of Etruscan Veii (406–396 BCE)

The Augustan historian Livy, writing around 25 BCE, is our fullest source for the regal period (traditional dates, 753–510 BCE) and the early Republic (510–264 BCE). He records local Roman expansion under several of the quasi-historical kings in the area of Latium. The Romans of the early Republic struggled against Latins, Etruscans, and hill tribes such as the Aequi, Volsci, and Hernici. A significant event in this period was the ten-year-long siege and conquest of the nearby Etruscan city of Veii, which gave the Romans control of the Tiber river and its salt flats. The conquest also roughly doubled the extent of Roman territory. In this passage Livy describes the fall of Veii.

The air was filled with shouting; discordant threats of the besiegers and despairing cries of the defenders were blended with wailing of women and children. Suddenly armed soldiers were everywhere hurled from walls, and gates thrown open. Some Romans poured through them in a body, others scaled deserted walls; the city was overrun with enemies; the battle raged in every quarter; then, when there already had been great slaughter, the fighting began to wane, and the dictator* ordered the heralds proclaim that those without arms should be spared. This ended the slaughter. The unarmed began to give themselves up, and the Romans scattered, with the dictator's permission, in quest of booty. When this was brought before him, and he saw that it was considerably larger and of greater value than he had hoped or thought, he reportedly raised his hands to heaven and prayed that if any god or man deemed his good fortune and that of the Roman people to be excessive, it might be granted him to appease that envy with the least harm to his own private interests and to the public welfare of the Roman People.... On the following day the dictator sold the free-born inhabitants into slavery.... Such was the fall of Veii, the richest city of the Etruscans, which gave evidence of its greatness even in its final overthrow; since after a blockade of ten continuous summers and winters, during which time it had inflicted considerably heavier losses than it had sustained, it yet was ultimately taken, when at last even destiny fought against it, by siege-works and not by force.

Livy, *History of Rome*, 5.21.11–22.8 [ca. 25 BCE]

Rome and Latium

The Cassian treaty (*foedus Cassianum*) of 493 BCE is named after the plebeian* consul* who negotiated it, Spurius Cassius Vecellinus. It was still extant in Cicero's day (*In Defense of Balbus*, 53). An important document in the history of Roman imperi-alism, this bilateral agreement established peace between Rome and the federated Latin-speaking communities of Latium*, making provision for a common defensive army. But frictions later arose that led to the great Latin War and the Roman subjection of the Latin cities in 338 BCE. Thereafter Latin cities could enter only singly, but no longer as a bloc, into treaties with Rome, and they were required to supply an annual quota of troops to the Roman military.

A new treaty of peace and friendship was made with all the Latin cities, and confirmed by oaths, since [the Latins] had not attempted to create any disturbance during the sedition [the secession of the plebeians in 494 BCE], had openly celebrated the return of the populace, and seemed to have been swift in assisting the Romans against those who had revolted. The provisions of the treaty were as follows: "Let there be peace between the Romans and all the Latin cities as long as heaven and earth remain where they are. Let them neither make war upon one another themselves nor bring in foreign enemies nor grant a safe passage to those who shall make war upon either. Let them assist one another, when warred upon, with all their forces, and let each have an equal share of the spoils and booty taken in their common enterprises. Let suits relating to private contracts be determined within ten days, and in the nation where the contract was made. And let it not be allowed to add anything to, or take anything away from, these treaties except by the consent both of the Romans and of all the Latins." This was the treaty entered into by the Romans and the Latins and confirmed by their oaths sworn over sacrificial victims.

Dionysius of Halicarnassus, *Roman Antiquities*, 6.95 [ca. 10 BCE][3]

The consuls then decided [338 BCE] ... to proceed with their victorious army to the complete conquest of the Latins; nor did they rest until, by storming every city or receiving its surrender, they had brought all Latium* under their dominion. Then, distributing garrisons amongst the recovered towns, they departed for Rome, to enjoy the triumph* awarded them by general consent. ... The leading senators ... said that ... the consuls [should] introduce proposals concerning the several [Latin] peoples by name, as each should seem to merit. They were therefore taken up and disposed of separately.

Livy, *History of Rome*, 8.13.8–9, 14.1–2 [ca. 25 BCE]

Rome and the Gauls

In the fourth and third centuries BCE, Gallic-Celtic tribesmen posed serious threats to Roman security. Around 386 BCE the Gauls captured and sacked the city of Rome itself, and the Romans were forced to ransom their own city. The Roman victory in the battle at Telamon (225 BCE) eliminated the Gauls as a serious threat to Rome's existence, and Caesar's Gallic wars (50s BCE) prepared the way for the pacification and Romanization of the Gauls. The following three passages describe the earlier life-and-death struggle and the Gallic sack of Rome; the fourth the decisive Roman victory of the 220s BCE.

The Romans, after making a truce on conditions satisfactory to the Gauls [ca. 386 BCE] and being thus unexpectedly returned to their homes and now started, so to speak, on the road of aggrandizement, continued in following years to wage war on their neighbors. After subduing all the Latins by their valor and the chances of war, they fought first against the Etruscans, then against the Celts, and next against the Samnites, whose territory was coterminous with that of the Latins on the east and north. Afterwards the Tarentines, fearing the consequences of their insolence to Roman envoys, begged Pyrrhus for intervention. . . . The Romans had earlier subdued the Etruscans and Samnites and had crushed the Italian Celts in many battles, and they now for the first time attacked the rest of Italy not as if it were a foreign country, but as if it rightfully belonged to them. Their struggle with the Samnites and Celts had made them true masters in the art of war, and after bravely supporting this war with Pyrrhus [280–275 BCE] and finally expelling him and his army from Italy, they continued to fight with and subdue those who had sided with him.

Polybius, Histories, 1.6.3–8 [ca. 150 BCE]

The Celts, being close neighbors of the Etruscans* and having much contact with them, lusted after their beautiful country and, on a small pretext, suddenly attacked them with a large army and, driving them from the plain of the Po, took it themselves. . . . They lived in unwalled villages, without superfluous adornments; for as they slept on beds of leaves and ate meat and were exclusively occupied with war and agriculture, their lives were very simple, and they had no knowledge of any art or science. Their possessions were cattle and gold, because these were the only things they could carry about with them everywhere and shift where they chose. They treated comradeship as of the greatest importance, those among them being the most feared and most powerful who were thought to have the largest number of attendants and associates.

On their first invasion they not only conquered this country but reduced to subjection many of the neighboring peoples, terrorizing them by their audacity. Not long afterwards they defeated the Romans and their allies in a pitched battle [the battle at the Allia river, ca. 390 BCE], and pursuing the fugitives, occupied, three days after the battle, the whole of Rome with the exception of the Capitol.

Polybius, Histories, 2.17.3–18.3 [ca. 150 BCE]

The Senate met and instructed the tribunes of the soldiers to arrange peace terms. Then, at a conference between Quintus Sulpicius, the tribune, and the Gallic chieftain Brennus, the affair was settled and a thousand pounds of gold was agreed on as the price of a people who would rule the world as their destiny. The business was a foul disgrace in itself, but an insult was added: the weights brought by the Gauls were dishonest and, on the tribune objecting, the insolent Gaul added his sword to the weight, and a saying intolerable to Roman ears was heard – "Woe to the conquered!"

Livy, History of Rome, 5.48.8–9 [ca. 25 BCE]

Such was the end of the wars [of the 220s BCE] against the Celts, a war which, if we look to the desperation and daring of the combatants and the numbers who took part and perished in the battles, is second to no war in history.

Polybius, Histories, 2.35.2–3 [ca. 150 BCE]

The conquest of Italy

The Samnite wars[4]

Events in the mid-fourth century BCE drew Rome into a larger international orbit, when the peoples of Campania in southern Italy appealed to Rome for assistance against loosely confederated, rugged highlanders of the central-southern Apennine mountains, the Samnites. Three wars were fought, the second of which was particularly harrowing for Roman fortunes. The Samnite wars brought the extension of Roman power to central and southern Italy. The Samnites posed a serious challenge to the Romans for control of Campania and Italian hegemony in the fourth century BCE. By the time the Romans had finally subjected the Samnites early in the third century BCE, the last serious opposition to Roman power in Italy had been eliminated. The tradition reports three Samnite wars (343–341, 327–304, 298–290 BCE). The Roman defeat by the Samnites at the Caudine Forks between Capua and Beneventum in 321 was a disaster of the same magnitude as the Gallic victory at the Allia earlier in the century. Once the Samnite wars were over, Rome had welded the peoples of Italy into an Italian confederation, organized through bilateral treaties with individual cities ranging from defensive alliances to full incorporation into the Roman state; and by 300 BCE, this confederation, whose primary function from a Roman standpoint was to allow Rome to utilize the enormous military manpower reserves of Italy, stood poised to increase Roman power across the seas.

I now come to relate wars of greater magnitude, in respect both of the forces of our enemies and of the remoteness of their countries and the long periods of time involved. For in that year [343 BCE] war arose against the Samnites, a people powerful in arms and in resources; and right after the Samnite war, waged with varying success, came war with Pyrrhus, and after that with the Carthaginians. How vast a series of events! How often we came to the brink, in order that our empire might be exalted to its present greatness, hardly to be maintained! Now the cause of the war between the Romans and the Samnites, who had been united in friendship and alliance, was of external origin and not owing to themselves. The Samnites had unjustly attacked the Sidicini, because they happened to be more powerful than they, and the Sidicini, driven in their need to appeal to a more wealthy nation, had attached themselves to the Campanians. The Campanians had brought reputation rather than real strength to the defense of their allies; worn out by luxury, they had encountered a people made hardy by the use of arms, and being defeated in the territory of the Sidicini, had then drawn down the full force of the war upon themselves. For the Samnites, disregarding the Sidicini and attacking the Campanians – the very stronghold of their neighbors – from whom they would gain an easy victory and more plunder and renown, had seized and with a strong force occupied Tifata – a range of hills looking down on Capua – and from there had descended in battle order into the plain that lies between. There a second battle had been fought, and the

Campanians, being worsted, had been shut up within their walls; and having no chance for relief, after the loss of their best troops, had been driven to seek assistance from the Romans.

Livy, History of Rome, 7.29.1–7 [ca. 25 BCE]

The disaster of the Caudine Forks (321 BCE)

First the consuls,* little better than half naked, were sent under the yoke, then their subordinates were humbled, each in the order of his rank; and then, one after another, the several legions. The enemy under arms stood on either side, reviling them and mocking them; many they actually threatened with the sword, and some, whose resentment of the outrage showing too plainly in their faces gave their conquerors offense, they wounded or slew outright.

Livy, History of Rome, 9.6.1–2 [ca. 25 BCE]

The decisive battle at Sentinum (295 BCE)

In the war with the Etruscans,* Gauls, Samnites, and the other allies, the Romans slew 100,000 men [clearly exaggerated] in the consulship of Fabius [Q. Fabius Maximus Rullianus, 295 BCE], according to Duris.

Something similar is told by Duris, Diodorus, and Dio: that when the Samnites, Etruscans, and the other nations were at war with the Romans, Decius [P. Decius Mus], the Roman consul . . . devoted himself to the enemy, and on that day 100,000 of the enemy were slain.

Diodorus of Sicily, Universal History, 21.6.1–2 [ca. 30 BCE]

Twenty-five thousand of the enemy were slain that day, and 8,000 were captured. Nor was it a bloodless victory; for of the army of Publius Decius 7,000 were slain and 1,700 of the army of Fabius. Fabius sent out men to search for the body of his consular colleague, and, piling up the spoils of the enemy, burned them in sacrifice to Jupiter the Victor.

Livy, History of Rome, 10.29.17–19 [ca. 25 BCE]

The Pyrrhic War (280–275 BCE)

King Pyrrhus of Epirus was a minor Hellenistic king in search of glory and renown. He accepted an invitation by the Greek city of Tarentum to help check the growth of Roman power. Pyrrhus brought to Italy a mercenary force which was superior to the Roman army in terms of equipment and tactics, and he inflicted several serious defeats upon the Romans in the "Pyrrhic War." This was the first time that the Romans had encountered the war-elephant, and it took them some time to adjust to this formidable creature. But in the end, the strength of Rome's Italian confederation with its superior manpower reserves won the war of attrition, and Pyrrhus returned to Greek lands.

Pyrrhus...was forced to fight another battle. After replenishing his army he decamped and engaged the Romans near Asculum [279 BCE]....The Romans, unable to maneuver backward and forward as previously, had to fight man to man on level ground; and being anxious to drive back the infantry before the elephants could come up, they fought fiercely with swords among the Macedonian spears, not sparing themselves and looking only to wound and kill, without regard to what they suffered. It is reported that the Romans first yielded ground, after long fighting, in the sector where Pyrrhus himself was leading the attack. But the overwhelming force of the elephants caused the greatest rout, since the Romans, unable to make use of their valor, thought it necessary to yield as if before an advancing flood or a crushing earthquake and not to stand their ground and die in vain, suffering all that is most grievous without gaining the least advantage....The armies separated; and Pyrrhus reportedly said to one who rejoiced with him in his victory, "If we win one more battle against the Romans, we shall be completely ruined." For he had lost a great part of the force he had brought with him and almost all his friends and commanders. There were no others he could summon from home, and he saw his allies in Italy losing enthusiasm while, as from a fountain continually flowing out of the city, the Roman army was quickly and plentifully filled up with fresh men who did not lose courage because of their defeats, but who even from their very anger gained new force and determination to go on with the war.

Plutarch, Life of Pyrrhus, 21.5–10 [ca. 115 CE]

Overseas conquests and extra-Italian expansion

The Punic wars (264–241, 218–201, 149–146 BCE)

By around 300 BCE, Rome controlled peninsular Italy south of the Po river through an Italian confederation of various sorts of treaties and alliances with Italian states. Sometime around 290 BCE Campanian Roman mercenaries, the Mamertines*, seized and held the city of Messana on the northeastern tip of Sicily and sought to control the strait between Sicily and Italy. Some two decades later Hiero II, the king of Sicilian Syracuse, attempted to expel them. The Mamertines first called in the north African coastal power of Carthage for assistance, and later the Romans.

Roman involvement was a decisive step on the road to empire, as it was Rome's first overseas venture; and it led to war with Carthage, which had had longstanding interests in Sicily. After a 24-year-long war of attrition (264–241 BCE), the Romans emerged triumphant. They assumed *de facto* hegemony in Sicily and imposed a heavy war indemnity on the Carthaginians; and when the Carthaginians became embroiled in a war with their discharged mercenaries, the Romans took the opportunity to move into Corsica and Sardinia and to increase Carthage's indemnity.

The First Punic War[5]

When the news of what had happened at Agrigentum reached the Roman Senate [262 BCE], in their joy and elation they no longer kept to their original designs and were no longer satisfied with having saved the Mamertines and with what they had gained in the war itself, but, hoping that it would be possible to drive the Carthaginians entirely out of the island and that if this were done their own power would be much increased, they concentrated their attention on this project and on plans that would serve their purpose.

Polybius, *Histories*, 1.20.1–2 [ca. 150 BCE]

Lutatius readily agreed to negotiate [after the Roman victory off the Aegates islands in 241 BCE] . . . and he succeeded in putting an end to the war by a treaty more or less as follows. "There shall be friendship between the Carthaginians and Romans on the following terms if approved by the Roman people. The Carthaginians to evacuate the whole of Sicily and not to make war on Hiero [king of Syracuse] or bear arms against the Syracusans or the allies of the Syracusans. The Carthaginians to give up to the Romans all prisoners without ransom. The Carthaginians to pay to the Romans by installments in 20 years 2,200 Euboean talents*." But when these terms were brought back to Rome, the people did not accept the treaty, but sent ten commissioners to examine the matter. On their arrival they made no substantial changes in the terms, but only slight modifications rendering them more severe for Carthage: for they reduced the term of payment by one half, added 1,000 talents to the indemnity, and demanded the evacuation by the Carthaginians of all islands lying between Sicily and Italy.

Such . . . was the end of the war between the Romans and the Carthaginians for the possession of Sicily, and such were the terms of the peace. It had lasted without interruption for 24 years [264–241 BCE], and is the longest, most constant, and greatest war on record.

Polybius, *Histories*, 1.62.7–63.5 [ca. 150 BCE]

While . . . the Roman crossing to Sicily was not contrary to treaty, for the second war, that in which they made the treaty about Sardinia [ca. 238 BCE], it is impossible to find any reasonable pretext or cause. In this case everyone would agree that the Carthaginians, contrary to all justice, and merely because the occasion permitted it, were forced to evacuate Sardinia and pay the additional sum I mentioned.

Polybius, *Histories*, 3.28.1–3 [ca. 150 BCE]

The Second Punic War[6]

In the sequel to the First Punic War, the Carthaginians regrouped under the leadership of the Barcid clan, rebuilding their power base in Spain. The precipitating cause of the second war was Hannibal's siege of recalcitrant Saguntum, which, incidentally, was well within the Iberian Carthaginian sphere of influence as recognized by a Romano-Carthaginian treaty of ca. 226 BCE. Hannibal was a brilliant field commander who surprised the Romans with a lightning march from Spain over the Pyrenees and the Alps into Italy. He inflicted several defeats upon the Romans, the most serious of which occurred at Cannae in Apulia, where there may have been as many as 70,000 Roman casualties. But Hannibal's overall plan was a calculated gamble that the Italian allies would defect *en masse* after Rome lost several battles.

This failed to materialize, and in the end Rome, with its superior manpower resources, won the war of attrition. The Roman commander P. Cornelius Scipio (Africanus) delivered the death blow, as he transferred the war to African soil and defeated Hannibal at the Battle of Zama in 202 BCE. Rome was now well on the way to supremacy in the Mediterranean.

Hannibal's passage across the Alps (218 BCE)

On the ninth day they arrived at the summit of the Alps, having come for the most part over trackless wastes and by tortuous routes, owing either to the perfidy of their guides, or – when they would not trust the guides – to their blindly entering some valley, guessing at the way. For two days they lay encamped on the summit. The soldiers, worn out with work and fighting, were allowed to rest; and a number of baggage animals which had fallen among the rocks made their way to the camp by following the tracks of the army. Exhausted and discouraged as the soldiers were by many hardships, a snow-storm – for the constellation of the Pleiades was now setting [late October] – threw them into consternation. The ground was everywhere covered with a deep snow when at dawn they began to march, and as the column moved slowly on, dejection and despair were to be seen on every face. Then Hannibal, who had gone on ahead of the main body of his troops, made the army halt on a certain promontory which commanded an extensive prospect, and pointing out Italy to them, and just under the Alps the plains about the Po river, he told them that they were now scaling the ramparts not only of Italy, but of Rome itself; the rest of the way would be level or downhill; and after one, or, at the most, two battles, they would have in their hands and in their power the citadel and capital of Italy.

Livy, *History of Rome*, 21.35.4–9 [ca. 25 BCE]

The Roman disaster at Cannae (216 BCE)

In this famous battle, Hannibal utilized the terrain of the site to hide the disposition of his forces and employed the double envelopment tactic, whereby he allowed the Roman center to break through his own but won the battle on the flanks; he then turned in upon the Roman center in an outflanking maneuver and annihilated it.

The Romans as long as they could turn and present a front on every side to the enemy, held out, but as the outer ranks kept falling, and the rest were slowly huddled in and surrounded, they finally all were killed where they stood, among them Marcus and Gnaeus, the consuls of the preceding year, who had carried themselves in the battle like brave men worthy of Rome. While this murderous combat was going on, the Numidians following up the flying cavalry killed most of them and unseated others. A few escaped to Venusia, among them the consul Gaius Terentius, who disgraced himself by flight and in his tenure of office had been useless to his country.

Such was the outcome of the battle at Cannae between the Romans and the Carthaginians, a battle in which both the winners and the losers displayed conspicuous bravery, as the facts showed. For of the 6,000 cavalry, 70 escaped to Venusia with

Terentius, and about 300 of the allied horse reached different cities in scattered groups. Of the infantry about 10,000 were captured fighting but not in the actual battle, while only perhaps 3,000 escaped from the field to neighboring towns. All the rest, numbering about 70,000, died bravely.

Polybius, *Histories*, 3.116.10–117.4 [ca. 150 BCE]

Roman resolve in the aftermath of Cannae

Some wanted to ransom the prisoners at public expense; others would have the state expend no money, but would not prohibit ransoming at the expense of individuals.... Though most of the senators, too, had relatives who were prisoners, yet, besides the example of a state which had always shown the scantiest consideration for prisoners of war, they were also moved by the great amount required, not wishing either to exhaust the treasury, on which they had already made a heavy draft to purchase slaves and arm them for service, or to furnish Hannibal with money – the one thing of which he was rumored to stand most in need. When the stern reply, that the prisoners would not be ransomed, had been given, and fresh sorrow had been added to the old at the loss of so many of their fellow citizens, the crowd attended the envoys to the gate with many tears and lamentations. One of them departed to his home, pretending to have freed himself from his oath when he deceitfully returned to the enemy's camp. As soon as this became known and was reported to the senators, they voted unanimously to arrest him and appointed guards to conduct him back to Hannibal.

Livy, *History of Rome*, 22.60.3–4, 61.1–4 [ca. 25 BCE][7]

The Roman hegemony over Greece

In this famous passage, the Aetolian Greek ambassador Agelaus urges the Macedonian king Philip V to make peace in Greece at a conference at Naupactus in 217 BCE. His plea is based on the idea that only a unified Greece will stand a chance against the ultimate victor of the Hannibalic War, Rome or Carthage.

I would advise you now at least to agree together and to take appropriate measures for your safety, seeing the vast armaments now in the field and the greatness of this war in the west. For it is clear even to those of us who pay little attention to affairs of state, that whether the Carthaginians or the Romans win this war, it is not in the least likely that the victors will be content with the sovereignty of Italy and Sicily, but they are sure to come here and extend their ambitions unjustly.... But put aside your differences with the Greeks and your wars here until you have leisure enough for such matters, and give your whole attention now to the more urgent question, so that the power may still be yours of making war or peace with them at your pleasure. For if once you wait for these clouds that loom in the west to settle on Greece, I am very much afraid that we may all find these truces and wars and games at which we now play, so rudely interrupted that we shall have to pray to the gods to give us still the

power of fighting with each other and making peace when we will, the power, in a
word, of deciding our differences for ourselves.

Polybius, *Histories*, 5.104.2–4, 9–11 [ca. 150 BCE]

Rome became involved in affairs east of the Adriatic as a result of Illyrian raiding on Italian maritime commerce in 229/8 BCE (see Polybius, *Histories*, 2.2–12). This brief conflict, the First Illyrian War, as well as further Roman punitive action against the marauding activities of the Illyrian dynast Demetrius of Pharos about a decade later, may well have raised the suspicions of the Macedonian monarchy, who would have viewed Rome's action in Illyria as an encroachment upon a traditional Macedonian sphere of influence. In any event, the Macedonian king Philip V struck an alliance with Rome's enemy Hannibal in 215 when it looked as if he had the upper hand in his war against the Romans (Polybius, *Histories*, 7.9), and in 212/11 Rome made a pact with Macedonia's inveterate enemy, the Aetolian confederation (Livy, *History of Rome*, 36.24). Rome declared outright war against Macedonia in 200, once it was relieved of the struggle against Carthage. The war ended with the decisive victory of the Roman maniple* over the Macedonian phalanx* at Cynoscephalae ("Dog's Head") in 197. At the Isthmian Games at Corinth in 196 the Roman commander Titus Quinctius Flamininus proclaimed the non-annexationist policy of the Romans and declared "the freedom of the Greeks."[8]

They had taken their places at the games and the herald with the trumpeter, as is customary, had come forth into the middle of the arena, where the games regularly begin with a ritual chant, and proclaiming silence with a trumpet call, the herald read the decree: "The Roman Senate, and Titus Quinctius the commander, having conquered King Philip and the Macedonians, declare to be free, independent, and subject to their own laws, the Corinthians, the Phocians, all the Locrians, the island of Euboea, the Magnesians, the Thessalians, the Perrhaebians, and the Phthiotic Achaeans." These were all the states which had once been subject to Philip. When the herald's voice was heard there was rejoicing greater than men could grasp in its entirety. They could hardly believe that they had heard correctly, and they looked at one another marveling as at the empty vision of a dream; they asked their neighbors what concerned each one, unwilling to trust the evidence of their own ears. The herald was recalled, each one wanting not only to hear but to see the man who brought news of his freedom, and again the herald read the same decree. Then, when the ground for their joy was certain, such a storm of applause began and was so often repeated that it was easily apparent that of all blessings none pleases a throng more than freedom.

Livy, *History of Rome*, 33.32.4–10 [ca. 25 BCE]

The Antiochene War (192–189 BCE)

In the 190s the Aetolian confederation grew restive, disgruntled over the Roman settlement in Greece following the war against Philip V. The Aetolians had expected to incorporate states into their confederation which the Romans declared to be free. Meanwhile Antiochus III, king of Seleucid Syria,[9] had returned from his famous campaign in the east, the anabasis to the "Upper Satrapies," and began reclaiming territories in Thrace (197/6 BCE). Following Roman remonstrances and Aetolian invitations, Antiochus invaded Greece, posing as its liberator, and brought on war with Rome. He was defeated at Thermopylae in Greece and Magnesia in Asia Minor. A peace treaty was signed at Apamea on the Orontes river; now two of the great Hellenistic monarchies had fallen to the Roman Republic.

Cause of the Antiochene War

It is clear that the cause of the war between Antiochus and Rome was the Aetolians' anger, who (as I above stated) looking upon themselves as having been cheated in many ways by the Romans as regards their share in bringing the war with Philip to an end, not only invited Antiochus over, but were ready to do and suffer anything owing to the anger they conceived. But the liberation of Greece, which they announced in defiance of reason and truth going round with Antiochus from city to city, we must consider to be the pretext of this war, and its beginning the landing of Antiochus at Demetrias.

Polybius, Histories, 3.7.1–3 [ca. 150 BCE]

Treaty terms at Apamea (188 BCE)

There shall be friendship between King Antiochus and the Romans on these conditions and terms: the king shall permit no army intending to wage war with the Roman people or its allies to march through the territories of his kingdom or of his allies, and he shall not aid them with grain or with any other form of assistance; the Romans and their allies shall guarantee the same to Antiochus and to those who are under his control. Antiochus shall have no right to wage war upon those peoples who inhabit the islands nor to cross to Europe. He shall withdraw from the cities, lands, villages, and strongholds on this side of the Taurus mountain as far as the Halys river and from the valley as far as the ridges of Taurus where it slopes down into Lycaonia.... He shall give up all his elephants and acquire no more. He shall surrender also his warships and their rigging, and he shall have not more than ten decked ships nor more than ten merchant vessels, nor shall any of these be propelled by more than 30 oars, nor shall he have a ship of one bank for a war in which he himself shall be the aggressor.... He shall pay 12,000 Attic talents[*] of tested silver within 12 years in equal instalments...and 540,000 modii[*] of wheat.

Livy, History of Rome, 38.38.2–14 [ca. 25 BCE][10]

Imperial motivations

Plans for universal empire?

Because of their defeat of the Carthaginians in the Hannibalic War [218–201 BCE] the Romans, feeling that the main and most necessary step in their scheme of universal aggression had now been taken, were first emboldened to reach out their hands to grasp the rest and to cross with an army to Greece and the continent of Asia.

> Polybius, *Histories*, 1.3.6 [ca. 150 BCE]

War as a way of life: a Schumpeterian "war machine"?

In the consulship of Lucius Genucius and Servius Cornelius [303 BCE] there was in general a break from foreign wars . . . Nevertheless, that their year might not go by without any war whatever, the consuls made a little expedition into Umbria, because of a report that armed men issuing from a certain cave were making raids upon the farms.

> Livy, *History of Rome*, 10.1.1–5 [ca. 25 BCE]

The Senate heard [the accusations] with much attention and were outraged at the Dalmatians' obstinacy and rudeness; but their chief motive for action was that for several reasons they thought the time right for making war on the Dalmatians [157/6 BCE]. First of all they had never entered those parts of Illyria which face the Adriatic since they expelled Demetrius of Pharos [219 BCE], and next they did not at all want the Italians to become effeminate owing to the long peace, it being now 12 years since the war with Perseus and their campaigns in Macedonia. They therefore determined to recreate, as it were, the spirit and zeal of their own troops by undertaking a war against the Dalmatians, and by striking terror into the Illyrians to compel them to obey their commands. These, then, were the reasons why the Romans went to war with the Dalmatians, but to the world at large they gave out that they had decided on war owing to the insult to their ambassadors.

> Polybius, *Histories*, 32.13.4–9 [ca. 150 BCE]

The following poetic fragment is from the second-century BCE poet Ennius as it is preserved by Aulus Gellius. It is of interest because it seems to cut against the grain of the idea of middle republican Rome as a Schumpeterian "war machine." Ennius enjoyed the patronage of powerful Romans and wrote at the time of the beginning of Rome's great imperial expansion, the period in which some historians have seen the Romans at their most bellicose. Does the fragment merely demonstrate the separation of literature from politics, showing the poet doing little more than following an anti-war convention of his Hellenistic Greek literary prototypes?[11]

[When] wars are announced, wisdom is driven from their midst, matters waged by force; the good speaker is shunned, the rude soldier loved. Not contending with erudition, nor plaguing one another with curses, they carry on vendettas; not by process of law to pursue claims, but rather with violence they seek property and mastery, proceeding by brute force.

> Aulus Gellius, *Attic Nights*, 20.10.4 [ca. 180 CE]

Defensive imperialism[12]

Rome's first overseas crossing

For a long time before this [ca. 230 BCE] [the Illyrians] had been used to maltreating ships sailing from Italy, and now while they were at Phoenice, some of them detached themselves from the fleet and robbed or killed many Italian traders, seizing and carrying off many prisoners. The Romans had up to now ignored complaints made against the Illyrians, but now when many approached the Senate on the subject, they appointed two envoys, Gaius and Lucius Coruncanius, to proceed to Illyria, and investigate the matter.

Polybius, *Histories*, 2.8.1–4 [ca. 150 BCE]

Roman deliberations on the eve of the First Punic War

[The Romans] ... saw that not only was Libya reduced to subjection by the Carthaginians, but also much of Spain besides, and that Carthage controlled all the islands in the Sardinian and Tyrrhenian seas. They were therefore in fear that, if they also became masters of Sicily, they would be most troublesome and dangerous neighbors, closing them in on all sides and threatening every part of Italy. That they would be masters of Sicily, if the Mamertines* were not helped, was evident; for once Messene had fallen into their hands, they would shortly subdue Syracuse also, as they were absolute lords of almost all the rest of Sicily. The Romans, foreseeing this and thinking it necessary not to abandon Messene and thus allow the Carthaginians as it were to build a bridge for crossing over to Italy, debated the matter for long, and, even in the end, the Senate did not sanction the proposal for the reason given above, considering that the inconsistency of their behavior was equal in weight to the advantages of intervention.[13] The commons ... listened eagerly to the commanders who ... pointed out the great plunder which each and every one would evidently derive from it. They were therefore in favor of sending help; and when the people passed the measure they appointed to the command one of the consuls, Appius Claudius, who was ordered to cross to Messene [264 BCE].

Polybius, *Histories*, 1.10.5–11.5 [ca. 150 BCE]

The Romans now [ca. 238 BCE], on the invitation of the Sardinian mercenaries who had defected to them, undertook an expedition to that island. When the Carthaginians objected because the sovereignty of Sardinia was rather their own than Rome's, and began preparations for punishing those who were the cause of its revolt, the Romans made this the pretext of declaring war on them, alleging that the preparations were not against Sardinia, but against themselves. The Carthaginians, who had barely escaped destruction in this last war [the First Punic War, 264–241 BCE], were completely unprepared at this moment to resume hostilities with Rome. Yielding therefore to circumstances, they not only gave up Sardinia, but agreed to pay a further sum of 1,200 talents* to the Romans to avoid going to war for the present.

Polybius, *Histories*, 1.88.8–12 [ca. 150 BCE]

The Macedonian king Philip V's lust for universal dominion

[Philip] immediately set out with his army to recover as soon as possible the rebellious cities, and decided to make war all around on [the Illyrian dynast] Scerdelaïdas, considering it most essential for his other projects and for his anticipated crossing to Italy to arrange matters to his satisfaction. For [Philip's courtier] Demetrius continued to inflame the king's hopes and ambitions with such assiduity that Philip in his sleep dreamt of nothing else than this, and was full of his new schemes.

Polybius, *Histories*, 5.108.3–6[14]

Roman remonstrances against the aggressive designs of Antiochus the Great (196 BCE)

After the Isthmian Games Quinctius [Flamininus] and the ten [Roman] commissioners received the embassies from the kings and states. Representatives of King Antiochus were summoned first. Since they made about the same deceptive speech that they had previously made at Rome, no ambiguous answer was now given, as on the former occasion, when the future was uncertain and Philip was unconquered, but clear warning was given him, to withdraw from the cities in Asia which had belonged to King Philip or King Ptolemy, to keep his hands off the free states and molest none of them in war: all the Greek cities everywhere must enjoy both peace and freedom. Before all, he was warned not to cross to Europe in person nor to send troops there.

Livy, *History of Rome*, 33.34.15 [ca. 25 BCE][15]

Julius Caesar and defensive imperialism

Caesar received news [58 BCE] that the Helvetians planned to march through the land of the Sequanians and the Aeduians into the borders of the Santones, which are not far removed from the borders of the Tolosates, a state in the [Roman] province [of Gallia Narbonensis]. He realized that this event would greatly endanger the province; for it would have a warlike tribe, unfriendly to the Roman people, as neighbors to a district which was at once unprotected and agriculturally rich. He therefore sent Titus Labienus, lieutenant-general, in command of the fortification which he had made, and himself hurried by forced marches into Italy. He enrolled two legions in Italy, and brought out of winter quarters three that were wintering near Aquileia; and with these five legions he hurried by the shortest route to Further Gaul, over the Alps. . . . In the first place, he could see that the Aeduians, often hailed by the Senate as brothers and kinsmen, were held in slavery and subjection by the Germans, and he knew that their hostages were with Ariovistus and the Sequanians [58 BCE]. This, considering the greatness of the Roman Empire, he considered an utter disgrace to himself and to the state. Next, he could see that the Germans were getting used to crossing the Rhine, and that the arrival of masses of them in Gaul was dangerous for the Roman people. Nor did he suppose that barbarians so fierce would stop short after seizing the whole of Gaul; but rather, like the Cimbri and Teutones before them, they would break forth into the province, and push on from there into

Italy, especially as there was only the Rhone to separate the Sequanians from the Roman province.

Caesar, Gallic War, 1.10, 33 [ca. 50 BCE]

While Caesar was spending the winter in Nearer Gaul [57 BCE]...he received frequent rumors, and Labienus also informed him, that all the Belgians...were conspiring against Rome and giving hostages to each other. The causes of their conspiracy, it was said, were as follows. First, they feared that when all Gaul was pacified they might themselves be brought face to face with a Roman army; second, they were being stirred up by certain Gauls, who had either been unwilling that the Germans should stay longer in Gaul, and were now no less distressed that a Roman army should winter and establish itself in Gaul, or who for sheer fickleness and inconstancy were committed to a change of rule; in certain cases, too, agitation was due to the fact that in Gaul the more powerful chiefs, and such as had the means to hire men, commonly endeavored to make themselves kings, and this they could not so readily effect under our empire.

Caesar, Gallic War, 2.1 [ca. 50 BCE]

The guards protecting Maroboduus' kingdom, brought almost to the Roman standard of discipline by constant drill, soon made him a threat even to our empire. His policy toward Rome was to avoid provoking war, but at the same time to make it clear that, if he were provoked by us, he had in reserve the power and the will to resist. The envoys whom he sent to the Caesars sometimes commended him to them as a suppliant and sometimes spoke as though they represented an equal. Races and individuals who rebelled against us found refuge with him, and in all respects, with but little concealment, he played the part of a rival. His army, which he had brought up to the number of 70,000 foot and 4,000 horse, he was steadily preparing, by exercising it in constant wars against his neighbors, for some greater task than that which he had in hand. He was also feared on this account, that, having Germany at the left and in front of his settlements, Pannonia on the right, and Noricum in the rear of them, he was feared by all as one who might at any moment attack all. Nor did he permit Italy to be free from concern as regards his growing power, since the summits of the Alps which mark its boundary were not more than 200 miles distant from his boundary line. Such was the man and such the region that Tiberius Caesar resolved to attack from opposite directions in the coming year [6 CE].

Velleius Paterculus, Roman Histories, 2.109.1–5 [30 CE]

Economic motivations[16]

And so the power of the state increased by diligence and justice. Powerful kings were vanquished, savage tribes and huge nations were brought down; and when Carthage, Rome's imperial rival, had been destroyed, every land and sea lay open to Rome. It was then that fortune turned unkind and confounded all of the Roman's enterprises. To the men who had so easily endured toil and peril, anxiety and adversity, the leisure and riches which are generally regarded as so desirable proved a burden and a curse. Growing avarice, and the lust for power which followed it, gave birth to every kind of evil. Avarice destroyed honor, integrity, and every other virtue, and instead taught men to be proud and cruel, to neglect religion, and to hold nothing too sacred to sell.

Sallust, *The Conspiracy of Catiline*, 10 [ca. 42 BCE]

On the following day [after the capture of the Etruscan city of Veii in 396 BCE after a ten-year-long siege] the dictator sold the free-born inhabitants into slavery. This was the only money that went into the state treasury...Such was the fate of Veii, the wealthiest city of the Etruscan race.

Livy, *History of Rome*, 5.22.1, 8 [ca. 25 BCE]

[L. Papirius Cursor in 293 BCE] was granted a triumph* by unanimous consent when he came to Rome. He celebrated it, while still holding office, in a style which, for those times, was magnificent. Foot-soldiers and horsemen marched or rode past the crowds adorned with decorations; many civic crowns were seen, and many that had been won in the siege. Men inspected spoils he had taken from the Samnites, and compared them for splendor and beauty with those his father had won, which were familiar to them from being often used in decorating public places. Some noble captives, famous for their own and their fathers' deeds, were led in procession. Of heavy bronze there were carried past 2,533,000 pounds. This bronze had been collected, it was said, by the sale of captives. Of silver which had been taken from the cities there were 1,830 pounds. All the bronze and silver was placed in the treasury; none of the booty was given to the soldiers. The resentment which this gave rise to in the plebs was increased by the gathering of a war-tax to pay the troops, since, if the consul had foregone the glory of depositing the captured money in the treasury, the booty would then have afforded the soldiers a donative, as well as providing their pay.

Livy, *History of Rome*, 10.46.2–7 [ca. 25 BCE]

The senators also hated [Gaius Flaminius] because of an unprecedented law which Quintus Claudius the tribune of the plebs had introduced [218 BCE], despite the Senate's opposition, with the backing of Gaius Flaminius alone of all that body, providing that no senator or senator's son should own a sea-going ship of more than 300 amphoras burden – this was reckoned to be sufficient to transport the crops from one's fields, and all money making was held unseemly in a senator.[17]

Livy, *History of Rome*, 21.63.3–4 [ca. 25 BCE]

The Gauls are exceedingly addicted to wine and fill themselves with wine brought by merchants, drinking it unmixed, and since they drink without moderation because of their craving for it, when they are drunken they fall into a stupor or a state of madness. Consequently many Italian traders, induced by the love of money which characterizes them, believe that the Gauls' love of wine is their own godsend. For these transport the wine on the navigable rivers by means of boats and through the level plain on wagons, and get an incredible price for it; for in exchange for a jar of wine they receive a slave, getting a servant in return for the drink.

Diodorus of Sicily, *Universal History*, 5.26.3 [ca. 30 BCE]

Now [215 BCE] that the siege of Cumae was raised, Tiberius Sempronius, surnamed Longus, also fought successfully in Lucania, near Grumentum, with Hanno the

Carthaginian. He slew above 2,000 men, and captured 280 soldiers and some 41 military standards.... And three towns of the Hirpini, Vercellium, Vescellium, and Sicilinum, which had revolted against the Roman people, were forcibly recovered by Marcus Valerius, the praetor*, and those who had advised revolt were beheaded. Over 5,000 captives were sold at auction; the rest of the booty was given over to the soldiers, and the army was led back to Luceria.

Livy, *History of Rome*, 23.37.10–13 [ca. 25 BCE]

Treaty between Rome and Aetolia (212/11 BCE)

If any cities . . . are seized by force by the Romans, the Roman people agrees that the Aetolians may take possession of those cities and their territories; whatever [movable] property the Romans capture the Romans shall possess. If the Romans and Aetolians capture any cities together, the Roman people agrees that the Aetolians may take possession of those cities and their territories; the Romans and the Aetolians shall share equally whatever else they capture. If any city capitulates or surrenders [without resistance] to the Romans or to the Aetolians, the Roman people agrees that those men and those cities and their territories may be admitted into the Aetolian Confederation.

Supplementum Epigraphicum Graecum, vol. 13, no. 382[18]

The prayer of P. Cornelius Scipio Africanus (204 BCE)

At dawn Scipio was on his flagship, and after the herald had secured silence, he prayed: "Gods and goddesses who inhabit seas and lands, I pray and beg you that whatever under my authority has been done, is being done, and will be done, may prosper for me, for the Roman people, for the allies and Latins who by land, by sea, and by rivers follow the lead, authority, and auspices of the Roman people and of myself; and that you lend your beneficent aid to all these acts and make them successful; that when the enemy has been defeated, you bring the victors home with me safe and sound, adorned with spoils, laden with booty, and in triumph."

Livy, *History of Rome*, 29.27.1–3 [ca. 25 BCE]

Triumph of Cn. Manlius Vulso (187 BCE)

In his triumph* Gnaeus Manlius carried 212 golden crowns, 22,000 pounds of silver, 2,103 pounds of gold, of Attic four-drachma pieces 127,000, of *cistophori* 250,000, of gold *Philippei* 16,320; also arms and many Gallic spoils carried in carts, and 52 leaders of the enemy led before his car. To the soldiers he gave 42 denarii* each, twice that amount to each centurion* and three times the amount to each cavalryman, and he gave them also double pay. . . . But Manlius' friends curried favor with the people as well; at their insistence the Senate passed a decree that, with regard to the tax which the people had paid into the treasury, whatever portion of this was in arrears should be paid out of the money carried in the triumph. The city quaestors, displaying fidelity and diligence, paid 25.5 asses* each per thousand asses.

Livy, *History of Rome*, 39.7.1–5 [ca. 25 BCE]

[T]he Senate passed a decree [187 BCE] that the Ambraciots should regain all their property; that they should be free and autonomous; that they should collect port duties at their pleasure . . . provided that Romans and allies of the Latin confederacy should be exempt from paying them.

Livy, *History of Rome*, 38.44.4–5 [ca. 25 BCE]

L. Aemilius Paullus and the settlement of conquered Macedonia (167 BCE)

The consuls were carrying out the levy [for the war against Perseus] with more painstaking care than usual. Licinius was also enrolling the veteran soldiers and centurions; likewise many enlisted voluntarily, because they saw that those who had served in the former Macedonian campaign or against Antiochus in Asia had become rich.

Livy, *History of Rome*, 42.32.6 [ca. 25 BCE]

When . . . Perseus was defeated and taken captive [168 BCE], the Rhodians were in great apprehension because of what had been said and done on many occasions in the popular assemblies; and they sent envoys to Rome, to apologize for the hastiness of some of their fellow citizens and vindicate their loyalty as a community. When the envoys reached Rome and were admitted to the Senate, after having humbly put their case they left the House, and the senators gave their opinions. When some of the senators complained of the Rhodians, declaring that they had been disloyal, and recommended that war be declared against them, Marcus Cato arose. He tried to defend and save our very good and faithful allies, to whom many of the most distinguished senators were hostile through a desire to plunder and possess their wealth; and he delivered that famous speech entitled *For the Rhodians*, which is included in the fifth book of his *Origins* and is also in circulation as a separate publication.

Aulus Gellius, *Attic Nights*, 6.3.5–7 [ca. 180 CE]

Lucullus being greedy of fame and needing money, because he was in straitened circumstances, invaded the territory of the Vaccaei [in Spain, 151 BCE], another Celtiberian tribe, neighbors of the Arevaci, although he had no warrant from the Senate, nor had they ever attacked the Romans, or offended Lucullus himself.

Appian, *Spanish Wars*, 51 [ca. 160 CE]

As he ended this speech [ca. 150 BCE] it is said that Cato shook out the folds of his toga and contrived to drop some Libyan figs on the floor of the Senate house, and when the senators admired their size and beauty he remarked that the country which produced them [Carthage] was only three days' sail from Rome.

Plutarch, *Life of Cato the Elder*, 27.1–2 [ca. 115 CE]

So Athens experienced horrors [86 BCE]. Sulla put a guard around the Acropolis, to whom Aristion [the leader of Athens' rebellion] and his company were soon forced by hunger and thirst to surrender. He inflicted the death penalty on Aristion and his bodyguard, and upon all who had any authority or who had done anything at all contrary to the rules laid down for them after the first capture of Greece by the

Romans. The rest he pardoned and gave to all of them substantially the same laws that had previously been established for them by the Romans. About 40 pounds of gold and 600 pounds of silver were obtained from the Acropolis – but these events at the Acropolis took place somewhat later.

Appian, Mithridatic Wars, 39 [ca. 160 CE]

But when Lucullus simply ravaged the country [in his campaign in Bithynia and Galatia, 73 BCE] with cavalry incursions, which penetrated to Themiscyra and the plains of the river Thermidon, his soldiers blamed him because he brought all the cities over to him by peaceable measures; he had not taken a single one by storm, they said, nor given them a chance to enrich themselves by plunder.

Plutarch, Life of Lucullus, 14.2–3 [ca. 115 CE]

Warfare as a palliative for internal socio-economic unrest

The next year [455 BCE] was unsettled with great events. For the tribunes again stirred up internal struggles, which seemed to have died down; and some foreign wars arose, which were unable to harm the state, but which contributed to eliminating these struggles. For a long time the city had grown accustomed to being harmonious in times of war and to be in internal conflict in times of peace. Those who assumed the consulship therefore considered the appearance of a new war as an answer to a prayer. They themselves invented pretexts and grievances for war when the enemy were quiet, since they saw that wars made the state great and prosperous, while internal sedition made it humble and weak. Having come to this same conclusion, the consuls of that year determined to lead an expedition against the enemy, apprehensive that idle and poor men might, because of peace, raise disturbances.[19]

Dionysius of Halicarnassus, Roman Antiquities, 10.33 [ca. 10 BCE]

Military glory and public service

The Roman state stands upon ancient morals and men.
Ennius, Annales, fragment 156 Skutsch [ca. 185 BCE]

Single-handed combat of champions (361 BCE)

The two armies were separated by a bridge, and neither side wished to break it down because that would look like an indication of fear. There were frequent contests for possession of the bridge, but as the strength of both forces was unknown, it was uncertain who would take it. Then an enormous Gaul advanced on to the empty bridge and shouted as loudly as he could: "Let the bravest Roman come on and fight, so that the two of us can show which race is superior in war!" ...When they took their stand between the two armies, the hearts of everyone standing round them oscillated between hope and fear. The huge Gaul towered over the Roman; holding his shield in his left arm in front of himself he brought his sword down with a slashing stroke, which made a thunderous noise without harm. The Roman, with the point of his weapon raised, struck up his adversary's shield with a blow from his own against its lower edge; and slipping in between the man's sword and his body, so close that his own body was protected, he gave one thrust and then immediately another, and gashing the groin and belly of his enemy brought him down, where he lay stretched out over a monstrous space. He offered no other indignity to the Gaul than to strip his body of one thing – a chain necklace or torque which, splattered with blood, he put around his own neck. The Gauls were struck by fear and awe, while the Romans, quitting their station, ran eagerly to meet their champion and brought him with praise and congratulations to the dictator. Amidst the rude banter thrown out by the soldiers in a kind of verse was heard the appellation "Torquatus," and thereafter this was given currency as an honored surname, used even by descendants of the family. The dictator gave him, besides, a golden chaplet and delivered a splendid eulogy of his heroics.

Livy, *History of Rome*, 7.9.7–10.14 [ca. 25 BCE]

P. Decius Mus and the award of the civic crown (343 BCE)

In the course of the First Samnite War, the military tribune P. Decius Mus heroically rescued the consul A. Cornelius Cossus Arva and his army from a trap and received the *corona civica*, a wreath of grass, as the highest award of civic valor.

With the issue of the battle successful, the consul called an assembly, and praised Decius, in which he rehearsed, in addition to his former services, the fresh glories his bravery had achieved. Besides other military gifts, he presented him with a golden chaplet and 100 oxen, and one choice white one, fat and with gilded horns. The soldiers who had been on the hill with him were rewarded with a double ration for the rest of their lives, and for the present an ox apiece and two tunics. Following the consul's award, the legions, accompanying the gift with cheers, placed on Decius' head a wreath of grass, to signify his rescuing them from a siege; and his own detachment crowned him with a second wreath, indicative of the same honor.

Livy, *History of Rome*, 7.37.1–2 [ca. 25 BCE]

An aristocratic epitaph (Scipio Barbatus, consul 298 BCE)

Cornelius Lucius Scipio Barbatus, son of Gnaeus, a brave and wise man – whose physical form was equal to his virtue – he was consul*, censor*, aedile* among you – he stormed Taurasia and Cisauna in Samnium; he subjugated all Lucania and led off war captives.

Inscriptiones Latinae Liberae Rei Publicae,
ed. A. Degrassi (Florence, 1957) no. 309

Because of these achievements, the consul [L. Postumius Megellus, consul 294 BCE] requested a triumph from the Senate, more as a matter of custom than with any hope of obtaining his request. When he perceived that some were for denying him on the ground of his tardiness in leaving the city, and others because he had gone over without the authorization of the Senate from Samnium into Etruria – a part of these critics being his personal enemies, and the rest friends of his colleague, who were minded to console the latter for his rebuff by denying a triumph to Postumius also – seeing, I say, how matters stood, he spoke as follows: "I shall not be so respectful, conscript fathers, of your dignity as to forget that I am consul. In virtue of the same authority with which I conducted my wars, I intend, now that those wars are happily concluded with the defeat of Samnium and Etruria and the winning of victory and peace, to celebrate a triumph." So saying he left the Senate.

Livy, *History of Rome*, 10.37.6–9 [ca. 25 BCE]

He [Cato the Elder] says that he never wore a garment which cost more than 100 drachmas[*], that even when he was a praetor or consul he drank the same wine as his slaves, that he bought the fish or meat for his dinner at the public market and never paid more than 30 asses for it, and that he allowed himself this indulgence for the public good in order to strengthen his body for military service.

Plutarch, *Life of Cato the Elder*, 4.4–5 [ca. 115 CE]

A Roman aristocratic funeral [20]

Whenever any famous man dies, he is brought at his funeral into the forum to the so-called rostra[*], sometimes conspicuous in an upright posture and more rarely lying down. Here with all the people standing round, an adult son, if he has left one who happens to be present, or if not some other relative mounts the rostra and praises the virtues and successful achievements of the deceased. Consequently the multitude, and not only those who had a part in these achievements, but those also who had none, when the facts are brought to their minds and before their eyes, are moved to such sympathy that the loss seems to be not confined to the mourners, but a public one affecting the whole people. Next after the burial and the performance of the usual ceremonies, they place the image of the deceased in the most conspicuous position in the house, enclosed in a wooden shrine. This image is a mask reproducing with remarkable accuracy both the features and complexion of the dead man. At public sacrifices they display these images, and decorate them with great care, and when any distinguished member of the family dies they take them to the funeral, putting them on men who seem to bear the closest resemblance to the original in stature and carriage. These representatives wear togas, with a purple border if the deceased was a consul or praetor, whole purple if he was a censor, and embroidered with gold if he had celebrated a triumph or achieved anything similar. They all ride in chariots preceded by the fasces[*], axes, and other insignia by which the different magistrates are accompanied according to the respective dignity of the offices of state each held during his life; and when they arrive at the rostra they all sit in a row on ivory chairs. There could not easily be a more ennobling spectacle for a young man who aspires to fame and virtue.

Polybius, *Histories*, 6.53.1–10 [ca. 150 BCE]

The triumph [21]

The celebration of a military victory called a triumph[*] was somewhat as follows. When any great victory worthy of a triumph had been won, the soldiers immediately hailed the general as imperator[*], and he would bind sprigs of laurel upon the fasces and deliver them to the messengers who announced the victory to the city.... In triumphal dress and wearing armlets, with a laurel crown on his head, and holding a branch in his right hand, he called together the people. After praising collectively the troops who had served with him, and some of them individually, he presented them with money and honored them also with decorations. To some he gave armlets and spears without iron; to others he gave crowns, sometimes of gold, sometimes of silver, bearing the name of each man and the representation of his particular feat.... After these ceremonies the triumphant general would mount his chariot. Now this chariot did not resemble one used in games or in war, but was fashioned in the shape of a round tower. And he would not be alone in the chariot, but if he had children or relatives, he would make the girls and the infant male children get up beside him in it and place the older ones upon the horses.... A public slave ... rode with the victor in the chariot itself, holding over him a golden crown with precious stones, and kept saying to him, "Look behind!," warning him to consider the future and events yet to come, and not to become haughty and arrogant because of present events.

John Zonaras, *Epitome*, 7.21 [twelfth century CE]

After the defeat of King Perseus [168 BCE] Paullus [L. Aemilius Paullus]... made his own house no richer, thinking himself well rewarded in that others took money from that victory but he took the glory. Q. Fabius Gurges, N. Fabius Pictor, and Q. Ogulnius subscribed to this view of his. Sent as envoys to King Ptolemy, they put all the gifts they had received from him privately into the treasury, and that before they reported on their mission to the Senate. Evidently they held that nobody should gain anything from public service except praise for well-performed duty.

Valerius Maximus, *Memorable Deeds and Sayings*, 4.3.8–9 [ca. 30 CE]

Calendar of triumphs in the 40s BCE

45: Quintus Fabius Maximus, son of Quintus, grandson of Quintus, consul year 708 over Spain; three days before the Ides of October.

45: Quintus Pedius, son of Marcus, proconsul[*]; year 708 over Spain; Ides of December.

44: Gaius Julius Caesar, son of Gaius, grandson of Gaius, hailed imperator[*] for the sixth time, dictator for the fourth year; year 709 ovatio[*] from the Alban Mount; seven days before the Kalends of February.

43: Lucius Munatius Plancus, son of Lucius, grandson of Lucius, proconsul year 710 over Gaul; four days before the Kalends of January.

43: Marcus Aemilius Lepidus, son of Marcus, grandson of Quintus, hailed imperator for the second time, triumvir for re-establishing the state, proconsul year 710 over Spain; day before the Kalends of January.

42: Publius Vatinius, son of Publius, proconsul year 711 over Illyria; day before the Kalends of Sextius.

41: Lucius Antonius, son of Marcus, grandson of Marcus, consul year 712 over the peoples of the Alps; Kalends of January.

40: Imperator Caesar [Octavian], son of a god, grandson of Gaius, triumvir for reestablishing the state; year 713 ovatio because he had made peace with Marcus Antonius . . .

40: Marcus Antonius, son of Marcus, grandson of Marcus, triumvir for reestablishing the state; year 713 ovatio because he had made peace with Imperator Caesar [Octavian] . . .

Inscriptiones Italiae, vol. 13.1, p. 87

[I]n the case of Crassus a new desire, in addition to his habitual greed, began to show itself. The glorious exploits of Caesar made Crassus also long for trophies and triumphs – the one field of activity in which he was not, he considered, Caesar's superior. This passion of his gave him no rest or peace until it ended in a shameful death and a national disaster [at Carrhae in 53 BCE].

Plutarch, *Life of Crassus*, 14.5–6 [ca. 115 CE]

EDITOR'S NOTES

1 Cf. J. A. Schumpeter, *Imperialism and Social Classes*, trans. H. Norden (New York, 1951), pp. 65–6: "the policy of the [Roman] Empire was directed only toward its preservation . . . True, there was almost continuous warfare, because the existing situation could be maintained only by military means. Individual emperors . . . might wage war for its own sake, in keeping with our definition, but neither the Senate nor the emperors were generally inclined toward new conquests. Even Augustus did no more than secure the frontiers. After Germanicus had been recalled, Tiberius tried to put into effect a policy of peace toward the Germans. And even Trajan's conquests can be explained from a desire to render the empire more tenable. Most of the emperors tried to solve the problem by concessions and appeasement. But from the Punic Wars to Augustus there was undoubtedly an imperialist period, a time of unbounded will to conquest."

2 For the earliest phases of Roman imperialism to the Roman consolidation of peninsular Italy, see the monumental study of T. J. Cornell, *The Beginnings of Rome: Italy and Rome from the Bronze Age to the Punic Wars* (London and New York, 1995).

3 Cf. Livy, *History of Rome*, 2.33.4 [ca. 25 BCE].

4 See E. T. Salmon, *Samnium and the Samnites* (Cambridge, 1967).

5 On this war, see J. F. Lazenby, *The First Punic War: A Military History* (Stanford, Calif., 1996).

6 See now S. Lancel, *Hannibal*, trans. A. Nevill (Oxford and Malden, Mass., 1998).

7 See also Polybius, *Histories*, 6.58.2–13.

8 For Hellenistic Greek propaganda conventions that served as background for the Isthmian Proclamation, see E. S. Gruen, *The Hellenistic World and the Coming of Rome* (Berkeley, Los Angeles, and London, 1984), pp. 132–57.

9 For the nature and administration of the Seleucid realm, see S. Sherwin-White and A. Kuhrt, *From Samarkhand to Sardis: A New Approach to the Seleucid Empire* (Berkeley and Los Angeles, 1993); and for Antiochus III's administration of Greek cities, see now John Ma, *Antiochos III and the Cities of Western Asia Minor* (Oxford and New York, 1999).

10 Cf. Polybius, *Histories*, 21.42.1–43.3 [ca. 150 BCE].

11 For further discussion, see D. Cloud, "Roman Poetry and Anti-Militarism," in *War and Society in the Roman World* (London and New York, 1993), pp. 113–38, at pp. 126–36.

12 For the classic formulation of Roman defensive imperialism, see T. Frank, *Roman Imperialism* (New York, 1914).

13 The Romans had punished their mercenaries who had seized Rhegium in Italy; their mercenaries in Sicilian Messene, like those in Italian Rhegium, had unlawfully seized an independent city. Roman aid to the Mamertines would thus be inconsistent.

14 See also Polybius, 15.24.6 [ca. 150 BCE].

15 Cf. Polybius, *Histories*, 18.45.10–12 [ca. 150 BCE].

16 For a catalogue of Rome's income and expenditures in the period of its greatest imperial expansion, ca. 200–150 BCE, see T. Frank, *An Economic Survey of Ancient Rome*, vol. 1 (Baltimore, 1933), pp. 126–46.

17 For a comparative study of aversion to commerce in traditional aristocracies, see J. H. Kautsky, *The Politics of Aristocratic Empires* (Chapel Hill, 1982), pp. 28–48.

18 Cf. Livy, *History of Rome*, 26.24.1–15 [ca. 25 BCE].

19 See Livy, *History of Rome*, book 2, for a recurrent pattern of internal sedition being alleviated in war time, and exacerbated in peace time.

20 See the excellent study of H. I. Flower, *Ancestor Masks and Aristocratic Power in Roman Culture* (Oxford, 1996).

21 On the Roman triumph, see the exhaustive study of H. S. Versnel, *Triumphus: An Inquiry into the Origin, Development, and Meaning of the Roman Triumph* (Leiden, 1970).

2

Political, Economic, and Social Consequences of Empire

Introduction

The essays in this chapter consider political, economic, and social consequences of Roman imperial expansion. Crawford considers the case of Greece, and this is an important case study, because some ancient Roman sources would lead us to believe that Greece enjoyed a favored status and a privileged position among states subservient to Roman power. Cicero, for example, calls Greece the birthplace of civilization itself (*Letters to Brother Quintus*, 1.1.27). Crawford argues that Rome in the second century BCE was militaristic and interventionist, and that much of Roman policy-making can best be described as cynical. Roman tribute extracted from Greece partially found its way back, but the overall process was debilitating to the Greeks, serving "to remove from the east to Italy moveable objects such as works of art, that constituted together with coin and plate (largely removed as booty) the inherited capital of the Greek East; and to place Romans and Italians as large-scale landowners in the eastern provinces."

Hopkins takes a more expansive view of the Roman imperial process, with an eye to the ramifications of Roman imperial success on the economy and society of Roman Italy. He sketches the interrelationships (conveniently set out in a flow-chart illustration) of increasing elite wealth, impoverishment of free peasants, and burgeoning of towns and cities in Italy. Roman wars of conquest led to profound socio-economic dislocation in Roman Italy: hard-pressed rank-and-file soldiers returned from wars abroad only to find run-down, neglected small farms; many of them gravitated to urban centers, swelling the urban proletariat; socio-economic elites appropriated the public land (*ager publicus*), and they imported slaves on a massive scale to work their large estates. And these developments led to a seemingly paradoxical result: Roman imperial success caused profound political, economic, and social crises for the Roman state. As Hopkins notes, "The mass eviction of the poor by the rich underlay the political conflicts and civil wars of the last century of the Roman Republic."

Rome and the Greek World: Economic Relationships[1]

Michael H. Crawford

It is well known that in the course of the second century B.C. the Roman state acquired financial resources far greater than any available previously, though the extent of these resources has perhaps not been fully appreciated; and that at the same time the wealth of prominent individuals increased enormously, though again the increase is hard to quantify. It is also generally accepted that in some measure Rome's gain was the loss of Greece and the Hellenistic Kingdoms (also of Spain and Africa); it is furthermore widely believed that Rome was not led to conquer by motives of greed and was not systematic in the exploitation of that which she came to control.[2] This article attempts two things: to show that Roman exploitation of the Greek East was from a relatively early date a conscious policy, and to add some precision to our picture of this exploitation and of its economic consequences. Vague generalizations about economic ruin are not very useful unless we have a precise idea about what we mean by the term, and can point to specific evidence of its occurrence.[i]

It is necessary to begin by indicating the broad outlines of the view taken in this article of the nature of Roman imperialism and of the cynicism of Roman policy-making. In the first place, Roman society can be seen as deeply militaristic from top to bottom, in a way and to an extent that is not true of any Greek state, not even Sparta.[ii] One may cite what Prof. Nicolet has sensitively described as "la guerre – institution, qui revient avec une necessité quasi biologique avec chaque printemps" ["the institution of war, which returned with an almost biological necessity every spring"];[3] one may cite Polybius's observation, correct even if for the wrong reasons, that Rome was of all states the best suited for conquest and domination.[4] It is Polybius also who recalls that Roman institutions encouraged a fighting spirit.[5]

At the same time, the structure of Roman society at the very least encouraged intervention beyond the frontiers of Rome and even beyond what might reasonably be taken as her sphere of influence. Internal struggles within the Roman oligarchy found expression in involvement with the internal affairs of the royal house of Macedon, or in support for one Syrian princeling against another, or in the affairs of Pergamum.[6] And this same urge to intervene can be found in the activities of the state as a whole, whether in Spain in the case of Saguntum or in Asia against Antiochus III. The attitude of mind involved is summed up perfectly in a speech of Flamininus, the authority for which is ultimately Polybius; if Antiochus does not do what the Romans wish, Rome can contract new friendships in Asia, the territory of the King.[7] Finally, on the question of imperialism, out of the enormous bibliography on the origins of the Second Macedonian War, the conclusion of Prof. Will stands out: "on en arrive finalement à penser que les causes de la guerre . . . sont à chercher à Rome même, et que la vrai raison doit, en définitive, être appelée par son nom: l'impérialisme romain" ["one finally comes to think that the causes of war . . . are to be sought for in Rome itself, and the true reason ought to be called by its proper name, Roman imperialism"][8].

The cynicism of Roman policy-making was already clear to Polybius. According to him, the Senate refused to receive Eumenes of Pergamum in 167/6 in order to humiliate his allies and strengthen the Gauls of Asia Minor against him.[9] In 164/3 the Senate preferred the weak son of Antiochus IV to Demetrius as king of Syria, clearly in their own interests;[10] in 163/2 Rome arbitrated in Egyptian affairs to advance her own interests; "many Roman decisions are now of this kind; profiting by others' mistakes they effectively increase and build up their own power, simultaneously doing a favour and appearing to confer a benefit on the guilty party."[11]

In order to substantiate the argument that Rome from a relatively early date deliberately used the resources of the Greek East to finance her own activities, the settlements of Macedonia and Illyria by L. Aemilius Paullus in 167, and the decisions taken then and later with regard to the Macedonian silver mines, may be considered in some detail. In her dealings with foreign powers Rome had for some time taken the convenient view that since wars were always the fault of the other party, the other party should re-imburse Rome for the outlay she had been forced to undertake. Thus indemnities were imposed on Hiero of Syracuse, Carthage after the First Punic War, Illyria after both wars, Carthage after the Second Punic War, Macedonia, Boeotia and Sparta after the Second Macedonian War, Syria and her Aetolian ally after the First Syrian War.[12] This attitude of Rome resulted from the combined operation of several factors; the increasing need to fight long wars (sometimes far from Rome) led to the institution of pay for the army;[13] since traditional sources of revenue were inadequate, it was necessary to levy *tributum* from the citizens of Rome;[14] this levy, however, was apparently regarded as more in the nature of a loan to be repaid if possible;[15] what more natural than to impose an indemnity on the enemy to ensure that repayment was possible?[16]

But in 167 Roman policy underwent a change; for the first time in an eastern context Rome imposed a money tribute, on Macedonia and Illyria, to be levied in perpetuity,[17] the treatment hitherto reserved for Spaniards (already in any case a dependency of Carthage) was now extended to the Greek East.[18] In the same year *tributum* was suspended, not to be revived until the period of the Second Civil War. The act is linked in the sources with the booty brought back by Paullus;[19] but a single windfall can hardly be regarded as a satisfactory reason for a suspension of *tributum* lasting over a hundred years. The correlation with the beginning of a process by which the whole of the Greek East was made tributary to Rome is far more significant.[20] It is remarkable that the first book of the Maccabees, in talking of Roman power, emphasizes above all the imposition of tribute.[21]

The decisions taken with regard to the Macedonian silver mines are even more remarkable. The Senate originally wished to close the mines in Macedonia, apparently without exception;[22] in the event the gold and silver mines were closed, the iron and copper mines allowed to continue working;[23] complementary reasons are given for this policy adopted by the Senate, that to allow *publicani* to manage the mines would lead to oppression of the inhabitants of the province, to allow Macedonia to do the job would lead to quarrels and disturbances. The first reason given is redolent of the disapproval of *publicani* commonly found in first-century sources, and I am not sure how authentic it is; even if it is authentic, it is worth drawing attention to a parallel to the final arrangement whereby iron and copper mines were allowed to continue working and gold and silver mines were closed; a year or two before 167 the Senate decided to suspend the production of silver coinage and concentrate as far as possible on bronze coinage.[24] The measure is not unlike a sumptuary law, but aimed at the state instead of at individuals, and smacks of nostalgia for a simpler past and of disapproval of the growth of luxury. I suspect the closing of the Macedonian precious metal mines to be at any rate in part a product of the same climate of opinion.

The closure of the mines seems not to have remained in force for very long. Under the year 158 Cassiodorus records the fact that *metalla in Macedonia reperta*. Taken literally, this passage records the discovery of mines in Macedonia, but it has always been taken without hesitation to refer to the re-opening of the mines closed in 167. So far the conventional view is, I think, right. But it has not been realised that the re-opening of the mines is to be connected with the fiscal requirements of the Roman state. The year 157 saw the resumption of silver coinage at Rome, on a scale far greater than before; the decision the year before to re-open the Macedonian mines was surely taken in order to ensure a steady supply of bullion.[25] With this decision the Senators clearly indicated, if they had not already done so, that in their view the resources of the Empire were theirs for Rome to use; the stage was set for the unhesitating use by Tiberius Gracchus of the legacy of Attalus of Pergamum in order to finance his agrarian programme and for the handing over by C. Gracchus to the *publicani* of the contract for the collection of the tribute of Asia, doubtless in the interests of efficiency. The protest against exploitation transmitted to us by Cicero went unheeded.[26]

The imposition of tribute directly affected the finances of the Greek cities, documenting in the process the relationship between Rome and the upper classes in the cities. The practice early became established whereby the revenues which accrued normally in a city, from local monopolies, dues of one sort or another, public lands, were used to pay part of the tax obligations of the citizens to the Roman state.[27] It does not require a great deal of imagination to argue that the upper classes of the cities of the East, firmly in control of the governments of their cities, thus relieved the burdens on themselves rather than those on the lower classes. The link between resentment at Roman levies and hostility to the upper classes perhaps emerges in the disturbances at the Achaean city of Dyme in the late second century, put down by the Romans; the object of the conspirators was the cancellation of debts and the method they chose to adopt was the burning of the town hall and the *public* records;[28] it is hard not to suppose that the indebtedness of the lower classes resulted in part from inability to meet obligations to Rome.[29]

The use of city revenues to pay tribute to the Romans was, it can be argued, responsible for the end of the cities as independent fiscal units, a state of affairs which brought with it the end of the silver coinages of the cities. A large number of mints in Greece went on striking silver until the Caesarian age, at least Dyrrhachium and Apollonia in the west, the Thessalian League, and Athens.[30] It is clear that Roman rule involved no prohibition on coinage in silver; this was, however, both an integral part of the fiscal administration of a city of any size and a symbol of the cities' fiscal autonomy; as the cities' finances came to be subservient to those of Rome, their revenues used to pay tribute to the Romans, so their coinages ceased.

But what were the economic consequences of the regular and continuous flow of cash tribute from the Greek East to Rome, not to mention the frequent, but irregular exactions of provincial governors? There is an important distinction between this phenomenon and the imposition of short-term levies. It was a simple matter to denude an area of *all* the stored treasure and cash which was available and this was an approach which was consciously practised in antiquity; when in 39 it looked as if the Peloponnese might be handed over to Sex. Pompeius, M. Antonius attempted to denude the area of its liquid resources;[31] earlier, Mithridates had stripped Asia of funds when he realized that he would be forced to abandon it to the Romans once more.[32] Levies of this kind, large and small, were imposed at various times on the Greek East; but their effect on an economy whose basis was subsistence agriculture (except insofar as they led to *indebtedness*) would have been negligible. The rest of this article is concerned with the implications for such an economy of a permanent arrangement whereby it was forced to transfer an annual cash tribute to what was effectively a foreign state.[33] Before the arrival of Rome in the Greek East, the surplus produced for the community by the economy of a Greek city had of course for the most part been spent and circulated locally; even in the case of one of the Hellenistic monarchies, monies raised circulated for the most part within the state concerned.

It should be clear at once that much of the annual tribute to Rome must in the long run have come back to the provinces concerned with the same regularity with which it left them; the alternative would be to suppose (once available stocks of coin and bullion had been removed) continuous new production by the mines in the tax-paying provinces of enough metal to pay the annual tribute, and at the same time replace the metal lost by hoarding, etc. It should be equally clear that the tribute must have come back in return for goods and services of one sort or another; financial gifts to the provinces are almost exclusively an imperial phenomenon.[34]

There are two possible means by which the Roman state may have returned the annual tribute to the Greek East, either by itself purchasing goods and services or by distributing its revenues to Romans so that they could buy goods and services from the provincials. Of these two possibilities, it seems that the second is what actually happened. There are no traces under the Republic of large-scale state purchases from the Greek world nor is there any likelihood that these occurred.[35] On the other hand, it can be shown that the amount of coinage issued by the Republic year by year from 157 down to Sulla corresponds with what can be argued on other grounds to have been the expenditure of the Republic on three main items, army stipends, official salaries and public works;[36] it seems reasonable to argue that during the period in question, no doubt for accounting purposes, Rome paid all her expenses in new coin. It follows that the surplus tribute of the Greek East to Rome, which was not necessary for the pay of soldiers and officials in the East, was returned to the countries in which it originated via the pockets of Roman citizens and their Italian associates, many of them no doubt engaged in the execution of public works.[37]

Perhaps the most obvious way to return to the East the cash which had been removed in the form of tribute was by making loans to provincial communities or needy individuals; but all that this achieved was to increase the flow of cash to Rome. The best-known example of this process is to be found in what happened as a result of the indemnity levied by Sulla from the province of Asia; the provincial communities borrowed the sum needed from the *publicani* and found themselves paying to the limit of their capacity each year without ever managing to pay all the interest charges due,[38] an example of a short-term levy transformed into a standing obligation.

What then were the goods which Romans and Italians acquired in exchange for cash which returned to the eastern provinces so that they could pay the next round of tribute, gubernatorial exactions, fees to *publicani* and interest charges? Three categories seem to be particularly relevant. I list them in ascending order of importance: works of art, land, and slaves.

The Romans, of course, in the process of conquering, simply took a great many works of art from Greece and Asia back to Italy; but their wealth also generated in the last century of the Republic a substantial trade in works of art. The great Asinius Pollio had an art collection that would do credit to a modern museum of classical sculpture;[39] even more revealing is the network of dealers to which Cicero had access through his friend Atticus when he wanted to decorate his villa at Tusculum;[40] Q. Hortensius paid 36,000 denarii for a single picture, a sixth of the tribute paid by the wealthy city of Tralles.[41]

Acquisition of land in the provinces was perhaps even more widespread and certainly more sinister in its imperial implications. The process occurred at every level of society, from the soldier at one end of the social scale to the financial magnate at the other.[42] It was in the late Republic common for soldiers to be discharged at the end of their term of service in the eastern provinces, in which they had served, and some at least must have acquired property.[43] Of greater interest, because of the scale of the operations involved, is the acquisition of estates like those of Atticus in Epirus.[44]

That there was a demand for land in the east from Romans and that this demand was sometimes resisted by the Greek cities, with their traditions of reserving land-holding to citizens,[45] emerges with great clarity from a letter of Cicero from Cilicia to Q. Minucius Thermus, governor of Asia;[46] this latter is to use his authority to ensure that one L. Genucilius Curvus is allowed to hold land in the city of Parium on the Hellespont; the city is presumably contesting his claim and one may well doubt Cicero's protestations that permission had been legally granted and taken up without controversy. The problems of C. Curtius Mithres over his *fundus* in Colophon, about which Cicero also wrote to the governor of Asia, perhaps arose likewise from an attempt of the city of Colophon to dispute his title.[47] The lengths to which a Roman would go to acquire land in Asia are exemplified by the manoeuvres of Decianus at Apollonis, involving seduction, fraud and violence.[48] It is remarkable to find that just as the Athenian Empire made possible the illegal acquisition of land by Athenians in the cities which Athens ruled, so the power of the Roman government was used to support those Romans who wished to invest in land in the provinces against the wishes of the community concerned.[49]

Finally, slaves. Many of these of course came to Italy as booty; of those sold in the east, as after the sack of Corinth, some may have been bought in the first instance by Greek slave-traders for transmission to Italy; in this case the profit of the traders will have involved a flow of cash back to the east. But it is clear that the largest sums went back to the east in return for slaves captured in slave-raids and put on the slave-market. The slaves who rebelled in Sicily in the First Slave War included a large group of Syrians, the leader of the slaves in the First War was a Syrian, Eunus, a subsidiary leader in the First War and another in the Second War were Cilicians, Cleon and

Athenio; yet Rome had never fought wars of conquest against Cilicia or Syria. I see no reason to doubt the substantial truth of the complaint of Nicomedes of Bithynia that his country had been denuded of its population by slave-traders.[50] It is also fairly clear that the men and women who were transferred to the west as slaves were free persons enslaved, not already slaves in their country of origin. This emerges not only from the structure of the slave-movements in Sicily,[51] but also from the fact that slaves never existed in such large numbers in the east as in the west during the Republic; for the first century it is explicitly stated that children were sold into slavery to raise the money due to the *publicani* as interest on the money loaned to the province of Asia in order to pay the indemnity of Sulla.[52]

Roman complicity in the slave-trade has long been suspected;[53] this is not surprising, with a people whose record as far back as 173 includes the casual enslavement of a Ligurian tribe (whatever the prime motive of Laenas may have been in his action against the Statielli). But it is worth emphasising that two powerful economic forces were pushing the Republic in the direction of acquiring more and more slaves; in the first place, the cash coming in from the east had to be returned somehow and slaves were clearly a readily available commodity to acquire in exchange; secondly, slaves were what the upper classes needed, to exploit the increasing areas of the Italian Peninsula that were coming under their control, as lands taken from foreign conquered peoples were let out at a nominal rent and as peasants were dispossessed of their land. *En passant*, I should be tempted to suggest that some cases of purchase of Italian land by members of the upper classes provided the working capital for the Italians who are so active as businessmen in the eastern Mediterranean in the second and first centuries B.C. If I am right, this will have been yet another way in which cash flowed back to the east.

Slavery also provides a context in which it is possible to document the alliance between the Romans and the upper classes in the provinces. Plutarch[54] records that men of wealth and high birth took to slave-raiding and slave-trading, and his generalization can be substantiated with particular examples: Zenicetes of Olympus or Athenodorus in the early first century.[55] Strabo recounts that the slave-raiders on the north coast of Asia Minor maintained good relations with local city governments.[56]

What of the effects of the flow of cash to the east in return for land and slaves? The basic structure of the economy, of course, remained unchanged, with peasants producing what they needed to feed themselves together with a surplus to support the cities and the upper classes and, ultimately, part of the structure of the Roman government; one must assume that they sold part of their corn to those who were the recipients of cash from sales to Romans and Italians. But if I am right to argue that one of the things sold on a large scale was human beings, we should expect evidence of substantial depopulation.[57] Of this there is a great deal of talk; early Imperial writers on Greece state or imply that the country was depopulated and given over to herding.[58] But it is clear that behind their remarks lies primarily a refusal to believe that cities as small as Greek cities could have achieved the glorious deeds about which they read in Herodotus and Thucydides; unfortunately there is little hard evidence to suggest that depopulation had occurred. For Greece, there is only the isolated and useless piece of information that Pompey settled some reformed pirates at Dyme, because it was underpopulated.[59] Otherwise the result of the circular flow of tribute from the east to Rome and back again was two-fold: to remove from the east to Italy moveable objects such as works of art, that constituted together with coin and plate (largely removed as booty) the inherited capital of the Greek East; and to place Romans and Italians as large-scale landowners in the eastern provinces.

Two problems remain. I have argued that from 167 the Roman state was quite clear that as a collectivity it was entitled to use the resources of the Empire; what was the attitude of individual Romans to their own use of these resources? Second, how far did the pattern of economic relationships I have outlined change with the transition from Republic to Empire?

Extortion by provincial governors of the Republic is so notorious as to need no discussion; as early as 171 complaints were made from Spain about the conduct of Roman officials; in the same year C. Lucretius Gallus acted *superbe, avare, crudeliter* towards the inhabitants of Chalcis in Greece: haughtily, avariciously, cruelly.[60] What requires emphasis is that the desire for private enrichment, for which the provinces provided the most obvious source, was built into the system. One of the consequences of expansion was an increase in the number of junior magistracies, without any corresponding increase in the number of consuls; this led inevitably to increased competition, the growth of bribery and the need for wealth. At the same time, in a society where status was measured by, among other things, wealth,[61] once one member has acquired wealth, others must follow suit, in order not to *lose* status and hence the opportunity for social and political advancement. The pursuit of power was linked to the pursuit of wealth, and by 133 the oligarchy was conscious enough of their dependence on their wealth to object to the proposals for agrarian reform of Ti. Gracchus on the explicit grounds that they would lose from them financially. Through the second century, the oligarchy made a series of attempts to remove the link between wealth and power, passing sumptuary legislation to prevent individuals from breaking the cohesion of the group by flaunting their wealth,[62] enacting that a governor might not use his wealth to acquire a slave (except as a replacement) while actually in his province and possessed of the power to influence the price.[63] But the urge to insure oneself, as it were, by acquiring wealth was always stronger than the urge to do something about the consequences of wealth.

What happened with the end of the Republic? In the first place, the absolute amount of cash taken was reduced; the tribute of Asia was reduced by a third by Caesar, who also took its collection out of the hands of the *publicani*;[64] we have no information for Greece, but perhaps less was taken from there also; furthermore, once the Empire was established, it was in the Emperor's interest to ensure that revenues came primarily to the central treasury, rather than went into the pockets of individual members of the upper classes. At the same time money began to flow back to the east in the shape of Imperial gifts; more important than this is the fact that the establishment of the Empire brought with it the permanent stationing in Syria of four legions, together with the setting up of a network of Imperial officials; to a greater extent than before, cash will have flowed out of the eastern provinces as tribute and back as payment for an agricultural surplus used to support Roman soldiers and officials. One must postulate a certain amount of trade within the east, since Asia, for instance, produced tribute, but had no soldiers.[65]

Secondly, the Roman demand for works of art and for what one might call works of sub-art, elegant furniture etc. could not in the end be satisfied by acquiring what already existed. The demand thus stimulated a revival of artistic production and of manufacture in the eastern part of the Empire.[66] Finally, it has long been noticed that the Roman and Italian businessmen active in the east in the late Republic settled and became absorbed in the early Empire, families such as the Crepereii of Attaleia and Pisidian Antioch and the Plancii of Perge; benefactors of their adopted cities, they served to transfer back at least some of the wealth which their ancestors had removed.[67]

APPENDIX

I take it that provincial revenue from the east used to pay soldiers and officials there did not travel *via* Rome, but remained in the east, whether in the hands of Roman officials or on deposit with *publicani*; it was then spent in the form of local currency (note at the very beginning of the second century that Roman troops in Epirus marching against Philip V expected to buy provisions, presumably in local currency, Plutarch, *Flam.* 5). Only the surplus went to Rome, where it was melted down in the form of coin (the records of the contents of the treasury in Pliny show that it did not hold foreign coin and this did not circulate in Italy in the last century of the Republic; a few hoards including foreign coin from Italy of this period are exceptional and are to be regarded as comprising booty belonging to individuals, *Inventory of Greek Coin Hoards*, 2053–7). Silver bullion was then struck into denarii, gold bullion doubtless sold for silver to be coined (no gold was struck at Rome between the Second Punic War and Sulla, little before Caesar; for a rare instance of gold bullion being paid out by the treasury note the rewards paid to the killers of Flaccus and Gracchus in 121). I suspect that much of the flow of currency back from Italy to the east was in the form of gold bullion; hoards of denarii are relatively rare in the Greek world before the age of Augustus. (Given the existence of an Iberian coinage on the denarius standard struck to pay tribute and spent in Spain by Rome, the large number of denarius hoards in Spain from the last century of the Republic may be taken as an indication that Spain as a province cost more than it brought in, see my article cited above n. 18).

NOTES

1 This article owes much to discussion over a considerable period with Keith Hopkins and to comments by C. R. Whittaker on an earlier draft; it was also a great pleasure and contributed much to the improvement of the paper to read it to seminars in Paris and Warsaw. Any errors and other blemishes are my own.

2 For a critique of some recent views see W. V. Harris, 'On War and Greed in the Second Century B.C.', *American Historical Review*, LXXVI (1971), 1371.

3 In J. P. Brisson, ed. *Problèmes de la Guerre à Rome* (Paris and The Hague, 1969), p. 117.

4 Polybius vi, 50, 1–6.

5 vi, 52, II.

6 See F. W. Walbank, *Philip V of Macedon* (Cambridge, 1940), pp. 240–52 (Macedon); H. H. Scullard, *Roman Politics* (Oxford, 1973), pp. 229–30 (Syria); Polybius xxx, 1–3 (Pergamum).

7   Livy xxxiv, 58, 1–3; see also Diodorus xxviii, 15, 3 (much more favourable to Rome).

8   *Histoire Politique du Monde Hellénistique*, II (Nancy, 1967), 123.

9   Polybius xxx, 19, 1–13.

10 Polybius xxxi, 2, 1–7.

11 Polybius xxxi, 10; see in general F. W. Walbank, *Polybius* (Berkeley, 1972), pp. 168–70.

12 Polybius i, 16, 9 (Hiero – see Zonaras viii, 16, for the eventual remission of the residue of the indemnity); Polybius i, 62, 9; 63, 3 (Carthage); ii, 12, 3; Livy xxii, 33, 5 (Illyria); Polybius xv, 18, 7 with commentary of F. W. Walbank (Carthage); Polybius xviii, 44, 7; Livy xxxiii, 30, 7 (Macedon); xxxiv, 35, II (Sparta); Polybius xxi, 30, 2; Livy xxxviii, 9, 9 (Aetolia); Polybius xxi, 42, 19; Livy xxxviii, 38, 13 (Syria).

13 During the siege of Veii in 406 B.C. if Livy iv, 59, II is to be believed; see my 'The Early Roman Economy', in *Mélanges F. Heurgon* (Rome, 1976), 197–207.

14 The link between *tributum* and *stipendium* is particularly clear in Festus, s.v. *Tributorum conlationem*; Livy v, 20, 4–5; other sources in J. Marquardt, *De L'Organisation financière chez les Romains* (Paris, 1888), pp. 116, n. 3; 207, n. 2; 208, n. 2; see also Cl. Nicolet, *L'Ordre equestre*, I (Paris, 1966), pp. 38–52.

15 See the discussion in Marquardt, op. cit., pp. 209–11, emphasizing that there was no *right* to reimbursement.

16 See, for instance, Polybius i, 16, 9 (Hiero of Syracuse). In earlier times Rome confiscated land from conquered Italian communities and distributed it to her own citizens.

17 Plutarch, *Aem. Paul.* 28; Livy xlv, 18, 7; 26, 14; 29, 4 (half of the tribute paid to the Kings of Macedon, to allow for the existence of a local administrative structure).

18 Sicily, Sardinia, and Corsica paid a tithe in produce. The precise situation in Spain is unclear; I have argued ('The Financial Organisation of Republican Spain', *Numismatic Chronicle*, 7th ser. IX (1969), 82–3) that levies in money were demanded from 197 B.C. onwards, but John Richardson suggests to me that a *fixed* amount which can fairly be described as regular provincial taxation was not levied until later. Roman levies in money, whether irregular or fixed, were doubtless paid partly from accumulated wealth, partly from the produce of Spanish mines and partly from the disposal of an agricultural surplus to Roman troops in Spain. The drying-up of booty suggests that the first source had disappeared by the middle of the century; Spanish mines were doubtless coming progressively under Roman control from the time of Cato onwards (Livy xxxiv, 21, 7; see Cato, fr. 93 Peter; also the important remarks of J. S. Richardson, 'The Spanish Mines', *Journal of Roman Studies*, LXVI (1976), 139, on how the mines were exploited). For the balance of revenue from and expenditure in Spain see Appendix.

19 Listed in Marquardt, op. cit., p. 225, nn. 2–3.

20 I do not share the view of J. A. O. Larsen in T. Frank, ed., *Economic Survey of Ancient Rome* (hereafter *ESAR*), IV (Baltimore, 1938), 307–8, and H. Hill, 'Roman Revenues from Greece after 146 B.C.', *Classical Philology*, XLI (1946), 35, that the norm for Greece after 146 B.C. was not tribute.

21 Maccabees 8, 1–4.

22 Livy xlv, 18, 3.

23 Livy xlv, 29, II. We are not told whether the proposal not to exploit the royal estates was carried out or not.

24 M. H. Crawford, *Roman Republican Coinage*, 1 (Cambridge, 1974), 47–8 and 74.

25 Ibid. I, 74, and II, 635. The fact that 157 B.C. is one of the three years for which Pliny reports the contents of the *aerarium* suggests that it was a turning-point in the fiscal history of Rome. The coinage of the first Macedonian region and of Thasos in this period both doubtless used bullion from the Macedonian mines; their relationship to each other and the relationship of both to the fiscal requirements of the Roman state require study.

26 *De re p.* iv, 7; compare ii, 26; *de leg.* iii, 18; contrast Cicero's wish that Trebatius may be enriched in Gaul, *ad. fam.* vii, 13, 1–2; note also the revealing incident in Dio xliii, 47, 5, when Caesar gave a certain Basilus a large sum of money instead of a province.

27 See my remarks in Appendix iii to 'Finance, Coinage and Money from the Severans to Constantine' in H. Temporini, ed., *Aufstieg und Niedergang der römischen Welt*, II, 2 (Berlin, 1974), 592. For peculation by city officials (presumably while the poor paid their taxes) see Cicero, *ad Att.* vi, 2, 5; Plutarch, *Cic.* 36; Cicero, *ad fam.* ii, 13, 3.

28 R. K. Sherk, *Roman Documents from the Greek East* (Baltimore, 1969), no. 43. A. Fuks, 'Social Revolution in Dyme', *Scripta Hierosolymitana*, XXIII (1972), 21, is an unilluminating paraphrase of the inscription.

29 For Dyme in the third century B.C. see Polybius iv, 59–60.

30 For the western group of coinages see the recently found Albanian hoards, in M. Thompson, O. Mørkholm, C. M. Kraay, eds., *Inventory of Greek Coin Hoards* (New York, 1973), nos. 665, 666 and 667; for the coinage of Thessaly see the Aidona hoard, ibid., no. 351; the possibility of Thessalian coinage after 146 B.C. was raised by J. A. O. Larsen, *Acta Classica*, I (1958), 128. For Athens, I remark only that I share the views of those who hold that it continued after Sulla. (For the exhaustion of the mines of Laurion in the time of Strabo see ix, 399.)

31 J. A. O. Larsen, in *ESAR*, IV, 433–4 with n. 22.

32 T. R. S. Broughton, ibid., 515 with n. 77.

33 At this point it is worth giving some indication of the scale of what was involved. Athenian imperial revenue in 431 B.C. was 600 talents (Thucydides ii, 13, 3) = 3.6 million drachmae or denarii; from 157 B.C. onwards the annual *expenditure* of the Roman Republic hardly ever dipped below this figure and was often over 10 million denarii (see Table lviii in my *Roman Republic Coinage*, II, 696). In addition, we have to reckon with the sums pocketed by the *publicani* as their fee for collecting the tribute and never transmitted to the treasury at all.

34 Note the building activities of Ap. Claudius Pulcher at Eleusis (A. Degrassi, *Inscriptiones Latinae Liberae Rei Publicae*, 1 (Florence, 1957), no. 401; Cicero, *ad Att.* vi, 1, 26; 6, 2); the restoration of statues by P. Servilius Isauricus on Calymnos (W. Dittenberger, *Orientis Graeci Inscriptiones Selectae*, II (Leipzig, 1905), no. 449, n. 2; L. Robert, *Hellenica*, VI, 38, n. 4), Tenos and perhaps Aegae (*Corpus Inscriptionum Latinarum* i², nos. 784–5 = A. Degrassi, ibid., nos. 403–4).

35 For Miletus building ten ships for Rome *ex pecunia vectigali* see Cicero, *II in Verr.* i, 89; money for ships seems normally to have been an extra levy, *pro Flac.* 27–33, compare *in Pis.* 90. Lucullus refused money from Rome for a fleet in the Mithridatic War and relied wholly on the allies: Plutarch, *Luc.* 13.

36 See my *Roman Republican Coinage*, II, 617–18. The corn-dole becomes progressively more important. The amount of money involved in public contracts was large; in 179 B.C. the whole of a year's revenue was devoted to them (Livy xl, 46, 16); in 184 B.C. of the extensive works undertaken (Livy xxxix, 44, 5–7) repairs to the sewers alone apparently cost 6 million denarii (Dionysius Hal. iii, 67, 5 = Acilius fr. 6 Peter); the Aqua Marcia cost 45 million denarii; the evidence of the coinage (see n. 33) shows that the Censors of 108 B.C. spent some 14 million denarii. Note also the spate of building activity in the non-Roman areas of central Italy in the late second century B.C., from Monterinaldo via Palestrina to Pietrabbondante.

37 For the surplus of income from Asia over expenditure for Asia see Cicero, *de imp. Pomp.* 14. For the mechanics of the circular flow of money from the East to Rome and back again see Appendix.

38 Cicero, *ad. Q. fr.* i, 1, 33 with Plutarch, *Luc.* 7 and 20; Appian, *Mith.* 83, 376.

39   Pliny, *NH* xxxvi, 33. Archaeologists have discovered a number of wrecks of ships carrying
      works of art to Italy (an interim account in M. I. Rostovtzeff, *Social and Economic History
      of the Hellenistic World* (Oxford, 1941), p. 1505, n. 13).
40   Cicero, *ad. Att.* i, 5–11; 3–4; 1. See also F. Münzer, *Pauly's Real-Encyclopädie*, x, 1034,
      on Iunius Damasippus, and n. 66 below.
41   Pliny, *NH* xxxv, 130, with Cicero, *pro Flac.* 91.
42   There is a brief survey in A. J. N. Wilson, *Emigration from Italy* (Manchester, 1966),
      pp. 159–60; note the following instances of the phenomenon:

      Beroea (Augustan) – M. G. Demitsas, *He Makedonia*, no. 58, *hoi enkektemenoi Romaioi.*
      Messene – *Supplementum Epigraphicum Graecum*, xi (1940–4), nos. 1033–5 with earlier
          references, lists of amounts raised in taxation, from Romans among others, the Romans
          probably landowners.
      Cos (Augustan) – G. Lafaye, ed., *Inscriptiones Graecae ad Res Romanas Pertinentes*, iv
          (Paris, 1927), no. 1087, Romans and metics distinguished from each other, both
          enektemenoi kai georgountes.
      Chios – Appian, *Mith.* 47, 183, *ta enktemata Romaion.*
      Chersonese – Cicero, *ad Att.* vi, 1, 19 and 5, 2, interest not precisely defined in
          property.
      Asia – *ad fam.* xiii, 72, *possessiones* of Caerellia; *pro Flac.* 84–9, property of Valeria.
      Parium – *ad fam.* xiii, 53, 2, controversies over land of L. Genucilius Curvus.
      Cyme – *pro Flac.* 46, farm changes hands at Rome; G. Lafaye, ibid., no. 1302, Q. Vaccius
          Labeo bequeaths land to city (Augustan).
      Apollonis – *ad Quintum fr.* i, 2, 10–11, property of L. Octavius Naso; *pro Flac.* 70–83,
          exploits of Decianus (note the Romans in the late first century B.C. list of ephebes in L.
          Robert, *Villes d'Asie Mineure* (Paris, 1962), pp. 246–52).
      Colophon – *ad fam.* xiii, 69, 2, controversies over land of C. Curtius Mithres.
      Alabanda – *ad fam.* xiii, 56, 2, Cluvius is about to foreclose.
      Cilicia – *ad fam.* viii, 9, 4, M. Feridius owns land held in usufruct by local *civitates.*

43   P. A. Brunt, *Italian Manpower* (Oxford, 1971), pp. 219, n. 9–220, n. 3.
44   See Wilson, op. cit., 93; Cicero, *ad Att.* i, 5, 7; ii, 6, 2; Nepos, *Att.* 14, 3; Varro, *RR* Intro.
      6 – i, 2; ii, 1 and 20; v, 1.
45   J. Hatzfeld, *Les Trafiquants italiens dans l'Orient hellénique* (Paris, 1919), pp. 299–300, is
      very unsatisfactory on *enktesis.*
46   *Ad fam.* xiii, 53, 2.
47   *Ad fam.* xiii, 69, 2.
48   *Pro Flac.* 70–83.
49   It is worth remarking that Roman investment in land in the East perhaps ultimately
      increased the outflow of cash (compare the effect of foreign investment in poor nations
      today).
50   Diodorus xxxvi, 3, 1; Rostovtzeff, op. cit., pp. 782–3, saw that Nicomedes had himself
      sold his subjects into slavery; see Suetonius, *Aug.* 32; *Tib.* 8 for violent enslavement in
      Italy in the Triumviral period.
51   See M. I. Finley, *Ancient Sicily* (1968), pp. 137–47.
52   Plutarch, *Luc.* 7; compare Appian, *BC* iv, 275; Tacitus, *Ann.* iv, 72 for people selling their
      children into slavery in response to Roman exactions; note also Apollonius viii, 7, 12.
53   Hinted at by Strabo xi, 668–9. Verres as governor of Sicily simply took over those slaves
      whom he wanted from a captured pirate ship, Cicero, *II in Verr.* v, 63–79.
54   *Pomp.* 24.
55   Broughton in *ESAR*, iv, 522, n. 112.

56   xi, 496.
57   There is no relevant early evidence: Polybius xxxvi, 17, 5, talks of a decline in population because of wilful childlessness; Polybius xxxvi, 17, 13, on Macedon under Roman rule and Zonaras ix, 31, on Greece under Roman rule (both favourable) are about the advantages of *political* stability, not about economic conditions.
58   Broughton in *ESAR*, iv, 467–8.
59   Plutarch, *Pomp.* 28; the foundation of colonies in Greece by Augustus is equally useless as evidence. The reflections of Servius Sulpicius Rufus, (Cicero) *ad fam.* iv, 5, 4 are perhaps suggestive – once flourishing cities now in ruins.
60   Livy xliii, 7, 8; compare 4, 8–10 for Abdera.
61   See Pliny *NH* viii, 140 on the wealth of L. Metellus, cos. 251 and 247 B.C.; Polybius xviii, 35, 1–2; xxxi, 25.
62   See on this the brilliant remarks by D. Daube, *Aspects of Roman Law* (Edinburgh, 1969), pp. 117–28.
63   See Cicero, *II in Verr.* iv, 9; *pro Flac.* 86; *ad Att.* vi, 3, 5; 1, 6; *Digest* xviii, 1, 62; xlix, 16, 9; Lex Agraria 54 with H. B. Mattingly, *Jnl. Roman Studies*, LIX (1969), 135; Gnomon of Idios Logos 111. The story in Posidonius, fr. 265 Edelstein-Kidd = fr. 59 Jacoby shows Aemilianus going one better than the law and sending home for a replacement for a dead slave; it seems to me likely that the law prohibiting the purchase of a slave except as a replacement dates from the Lex Calpurnia of 149 B.C.
64   Broughton in *ESAR*, iv, 538, n. 17.
65   For corn going from Asia to Syria in the third century A.D. see G. Bean and T. B. Mitford, *Journeys in Rough Cilicia* (Vienna, 1970), nos. 19–21.
66   Activity in this field goes back to the second century B.C.; note the Cossutii, E. Rawson, 'Architecture and Sculpture: The Activities of the Cossutii', *Papers British School at Rome*, XLIII (1975), 36. For the first century B.C. note the Attic workshop of C. Avianius Evander, Cicero, *ad fam.* xiii, 2; compare vii, 23, 1–3. Estimates of the volume of trade passing through Asian ports, as by Broughton, in *ESAR*, iv, 565–66, are not much use, since there is no way of knowing what proportion is local trade.
67   *Exempli gratia*, see a recently published inscription (bibliography in J. and L. Robert, *Bulletin Epigraphique*, 1971, no. 342), recording the gift by Sex. Tempsonius A.f. of a building for the Agoranomoi to Acraephia.

EDITOR'S NOTES

i   See also M. Crawford, *Coinage and Money under the Roman Republic* (Berkeley, 1985), ch. 13.
ii   This statement could be contested as an overstatement; see now collected essays in H. van Wees, ed., *War and Violence in Ancient Greece* (London and Swansea, 2000).

Conquerors and Slaves: The Impact of Conquering an Empire on the Political Economy of Italy

Keith Hopkins

THE ARGUMENT

At its height, the Roman empire stretched from the north of England to the banks of the river Euphrates, from the Black Sea to the Atlantic coast of Spain. Its territory covered an area equal to more than half that of continental USA and it is now split among more than twenty nation states. The Mediterranean was the empire's own internal sea. Its population is conventionally estimated at about fifty to sixty million people in the first century AD, about one fifth or one sixth of the world population at the time.[1] Even today this would be considered a large national population, difficult to govern with the aid of modern technology. Yet the Roman empire persisted as a single political system for at least six centuries (200 BC–AD 400); its integration and preservation surely rank, with the Chinese empire, as one of the greatest political achievements of mankind.

The main subject of this chapter is the impact of acquiring an empire on the traditional political and economic institutions of the conquerors. Most of this story is well known. I shall not try to give yet another detailed chronological account. Instead I have selected certain repeatedly important elements in the process of conquest (such as the militaristic ethos of the conquerors, the economic consequences of importing two million slaves into Italy, the shortage of farming land among the free poor) and I have attempted to analyse their relationships to each other. This involves going over familiar territory, if sometimes by unfamiliar paths. Roman history can be profitably studied from several viewpoints which complement each other.

The acquisition of a huge empire in the last two centuries before Christ transformed a large sector of the traditional Italian economy. The influx of imperial profits in the form of booty and taxes changed the city of Rome from a large town to a resplendent city, capital of an empire. By the end of the last century BC, the population of the city of Rome was in the region of one million. Rome was one of the largest pre-industrial cities ever created by man.[2] It was here that aristocrats displayed their booty in triumphal processions, spent most of their income and competed with each other in ostentatious luxury. Their private expenditure, and public expenditure on building monuments, temples, roads and drains, directly and indirectly contributed to the livelihood of several hundred thousand new inhabitants. Immigration from the countryside was also encouraged by the grant of state subsidies on wheat distributed to citizens living in the city of Rome.

The growth in the population of the capital city and indeed in the population of Italy as a whole . . . , implied a transformation of the countryside. The people living in the city of Rome constituted a huge market for the purchase of food produced on Italian farms: wheat, wine, olive oil, cloth and more specialised produce. To be sure, the city of Rome was fed partly from the provinces; a tenth of the Sicilian wheat crop, for example, was extracted as tax and was often sent to Rome. But a large part of the food consumed in the city of Rome and in other prosperous towns such as Capua and Puteoli also came from estates newly formed in Italy, owned by rich Romans and cultivated by slaves.[3]

The transformation of a subsistence economy which had previously produced only a small surplus into a market economy which produced and consumed a large surplus was achieved by increasing the productivity of agricultural labour on larger farms. Fewer men produced more food. Under-employed small-holders were expelled from their plots and replaced by a smaller number of slaves.[4] The rich bought up their land, or took possession of it by violence. They reorganised small-holdings into larger and more profitable farms in order to compete with other nobles, to increase the return on their investment in land and in slaves, and to exploit their slaves more effectively. Moreover, in many parts of Italy, large land-owners changed the pattern of land-use.[5] Considerable areas of arable land were turned into pasture, perhaps so that higher value produce such as wool or meat, instead of wheat, could be sold in the city of Rome, even after the heavy transport costs had been paid. Other land was converted into olive plantations and vineyards, and the value of its produce increased. These improvements were important: they figured largely in Roman handbooks on agriculture. But their scope was limited by the size of the available market. Many peasant farms remained intact. After all, the urban poor constituted the only mass market, and they probably spent about as much on bread as on wine and olive oil together.[6] This weakness in the aggregate purchasing power of the urban sector helped insulate a sizeable sector of the Italian peasantry from the agrarian revolution which transformed working practices on larger farms.

The conquest of an empire affected the Italian countryside in several other important respects. Military campaigns all around the Mediterranean basin forced prolonged military service on tens of thousands of peasants. Throughout the last two centuries BC, there were commonly over 100,000 Italians serving in the army, that is more than ten per cent of the estimated adult male population.[7] Global numbers disguise individual suffering; we have to think what prolonged military service meant to individual peasants, what its implications were for their families and for the farms off which they lived. Many single-family farms could bear the absence of a grown-up son, even for several years; military service may even have helped by giving them some alternative employment and pay. But in some families, the conscription of the only adult male or the absence of an only son in the army overseas when his father died meant increasing poverty and debt.[8]

Over time, mass military service must have contributed to the impoverishment of many free Roman small-holders. At least we know that thousands of Roman peasants lost their land. In addition invasions by Carthaginians and Celtic tribes, slave rebellions and civil wars which were repeatedly fought on Italian soil all contributed to the destruction of traditional agricultural holdings. Even so, more Italian peasants might have survived both the demands of military service and the destruction of war but for one other factor: the massive investment by the rich of the profits derived from empire in Italian land. The rich could establish large estates in Italy only by the wholesale eviction of Italian peasants from their farms. Typically these estates were cultivated by imported slaves. The displacement of large numbers of free peasants by slaves helped transform the agricultural economy of Italy, and fomented the political conflicts of the late Republic.

The mass eviction of the poor by the rich underlay the political conflicts and civil wars of the last century of the Roman Republic. For example, the possession of public land (*ager publicus*) and its redistribution to the poor became a major political issue, and exacerbated the tensions between the rich and the poor.[9] This public land in Italy had been kept apart out of land sequestrated by the Romans from conquered tribes or rebellious allies, ostensibly for the collective benefit. It constituted a significant but minor part of all Roman land, being by modern estimates well less than a fifth of all Roman land in the mid-third century BC, and hardly more than that in the second century BC (such estimates are inevitably crude); but its maldistribution became a political *cause célèbre*. The public land was concentrated in the hands of the rich; the laws which prohibited large holdings of public land were ignored (so Cato, frag. 167 *ORF*); and the rents which should have been paid to the state were by senatorial inertia left uncollected (Livy 42.19).[10]

A narrative history of the last century of the Republic would be punctuated by conflicts over this land, by land laws and by land distributions, which were more often proposed than effected. In 133 BC for example, a young aristocratic and revolutionary tribune of the people proposed the redistribution of the public land illegally held by the rich. He was assassinated by his opponents in the senate, but the land commission which he had founded succeeded in distributing some land to poor citizens.[i] The trouble was that in spite of legal safeguards, the new settlers were as likely to be evicted as the old; the same forces were still at work. Again in the first century BC, citizen soldiers who had military power and the patronage of political generals such as Sulla, Pompey and Julius Caesar, occasionally secured small-holdings for themselves at the end of their service. But they usually took over land which was already being cultivated by other small-holders, and in addition, some of them failed to settle down on their lands, which were again bought up by the rich. Thus the successive redistribution of small-holdings probably did not significantly increase the total number of small-holders, even if it slowed down their demise.[11] The overall tendency was for poor Romans to be squeezed out of any significant share in the profits of conquest so long as they stayed in the Italian countryside.

The central place of land in Roman politics sprang from the overwhelming importance of land in the Roman economy. Land and agricultural labour remained the two most important constituents of wealth in all periods of Roman history. Manufacturing, trade and urban rents were of minor importance in comparison with agriculture. That does not mean they should be ignored; the deployment of ten to twenty per cent of the labour force in non-agricultural tasks is one of the factors which differentiates a few pre-industrial societies from the rest. In Italy at the end of the period of imperial expansion, the proportion of the population engaged in urban occupations may have risen towards thirty per cent, because the profits of empire and the economic changes, reflected in the change of occupation from country to town, from agriculture to handicrafts or to service trades, were concentrated in Italy. The city of Rome was the capital of the Mediterranean basin. In the rest of the

Roman empire, the proportion of the labour force primarily engaged in agriculture was probably in the order of ninety per cent, as it had been in Italy before the period of expansion.[12] But even in Italy at the peak of its prosperity, and at all levels of society, among nobles, bourgeois and peasants, power and wealth depended almost directly on the area and fertility of the land which each individual possessed. Land-holdings were the geographical expression of social stratification.[ii]

Among the rural population, even when slavery in Italy was at its height, free peasants probably constituted a majority of the Italian population outside the city of Rome.[13] By peasants, I mean ideally families engaged primarily in the cultivation of land, whether as free-holders or as tenants (often as both), tied to the wider society by the liens of tax and/or rent, labour dues and political obligation. The persistence of the peasantry is important; but so were the changes in the ownership and organisation of estates, and the mass emigration of free Italian peasants which made those changes in estate organisation possible.

Some indications of scale may be helpful; they are rough orders of magnitude only, though based on or derived from the careful analysis of the evidence by Brunt (1971). Rather speculatively I calculate that in two generations (80–8 BC), roughly half the peasant families of Roman Italy, over one and a half million people, were forced mostly by state intervention to move from their ancestral farms. They went either to new farms in Italy or overseas, or they migrated of their own accord to the city of Rome and other Italian towns. The main channel of their mobility was the army. In a complementary flow, but over a long period, many more than two million peasants from the conquered provinces became war captives and then slaves in Italy.[14] Changes such as these affected even those peasants who stayed secure in their ancestral farms. Indeed, the growth of markets, the import of provincial slaves and taxes, the imposition of rents and a general increase in monetisation changed the whole structure of the Roman economy. But in spite of these changes and migrations, the solid core of Italian peasants remained peasants.

In this chapter, I shall concentrate on the impact of conquest on the two most important elements in the Roman economy, land and labour. We can see their changing relationship, for example, in the acquisition of large estates by the rich and the massive import of slaves to work them; both had deep social and political repercussions. The impact of victory on the conquering society presents us with a process of extraordinary sociological interest. Rome provides one of the few well-documented examples of a pre-industrial society undergoing rapid social change in a period of technical stagnation. Military conquest served the same function as widespread technical innovation. The resources of the Mediterranean basin were heaped into Italy and split the traditional institutions asunder. The Roman government tried to absorb the new wealth, values and administration within the existing framework. It failed, just as most modern developing countries fail, to establish institutions for the allocation of new resources without violent conflict.[15]

THE INTRUSION OF SLAVES

Two aspects of the transformation of the Italian economy in the period of imperial expansion stand out: the increase in the wealth of the Roman elite and the massive growth of slavery. Let us deal with slavery first. . . . According to the best modern estimates, there were about two (or even three) million slaves in Italy by the end of the first century BC. That is about thirty-five to forty per cent of the total estimated population of Italy. Given our evidence, these figures are only guesses; they may well be too large; when slavery was at its height in the southern states of the USA, the proportion of slaves was only one third. However that may be, no one can reasonably doubt that huge numbers of slaves were imported into Italy during the last two centuries BC. Roman Italy belonged to that very small group of five societies in which slaves constituted a large proportion of the labour force.

When we compare Roman with American slavery, the growth of slavery in Roman Italy seems surprising. In the eighteenth century, slavery was used as a means of recruiting labour to cultivate newly discovered lands for which there was no adequate local labour force. Slaves by and large grew crops for sale in markets which were bolstered by the incipient industrial revolution. In Roman Italy (and to a much smaller extent in classical Athens), slaves were recruited to cultivate land which was already being cultivated by citizen peasants. We have to explain not only the import of slaves but the extrusion of citizens.

The massive import of agricultural slaves into central Italy implied a drastic re-organisation of land-holdings. Many small farms were taken over by the rich and amalgamated into larger farms so that slave-gangs could be efficiently supervised and profitably worked.[16] Even so, slavery was by no means an obvious solution to the elite's needs for agricultural labour. Many peasants had surplus labour, and free labourers worked part-time on the estates of the rich. The interdependence of rich men and of free peasants, many of whom owned some land and also worked as part tenants or as labourers on the land of the rich, is well illustrated in the following passage from the agricultural treatise of Varro (last century BC):

> All agricultural work is carried out by slaves or free men, or by both; by free men, when they cultivate the ground themselves, as many poor people do with their families, or when they work as hired labourers contracted for the heavier work of the farm, such as the harvest or haying . . . In my opinion, it is more profitable to work unhealthy land with free wage labourers than with slaves; and even in healthy places, the heavy tasks such as the storage of the harvest can best be done by free labourers. (*On Agriculture* 1.17)[17]

The extrusion of peasants from their plots increased the pool of under-employed free labourers. Why did the rich not make use of free wage-labourers, instead of buying slaves out of capital? That is always one of the problems about mass chattel slavery. I argue . . . that slaves were normally quite expensive (though the evidence is sparse); to make a profit on their investment in slaves, slave-owners had to keep their slaves at work twice as long as Roman peasants normally needed to work in order to live at the level of minimum subsistence.[18] This implies that Roman agricultural slavery could work economically only if peasant small-holdings were amalgamated into larger units and if crops were mixed so as to provide slaves with full employment, and masters with a larger product from slaves' labour than was commonly achieved with free labour on small peasant farms. Masters also had to take into account the risk that their slaves might die, and their investment might be lost; add to that the cost of supervision. The massive replacement of free citizen peasants with conquered slaves was a complex process, which is difficult to understand.

As with most sociological problems, each attempt at an explanation involves further explanations. An examination of the growth of slavery involves us in a whole network of changes which affected almost every aspect of Roman society. Why slaves? Was it the chance of greater profit which induced the rich to buy slaves, or was it rather the values of free men which inhibited them from working as the permanent dependants of other Romans? How far was the growth of slavery affected by the frequency of wars, the demand for citizens as soldiers, or the ease with which the conquered were enslaved? What was the fit between the increase in the size of farms, in the size of the surplus and of the urban markets which consumed the increased surplus? It is, of course, much easier to asks questions than to provide answers. But for the moment I want to stress the complexity of the problem and the degree to which economic changes were connected with and affected by political traditions and social values. Rather arbitrarily, I have decided to concentrate on seven processes, which in my view most affected the growth of slavery:

continuous war;
the influx of booty;
its investment in land;
the formation of large estates;
the impoverishment of peasants;
their emigration to towns and the provinces;
and the growth of urban markets.

I shall deal first with their interconnections, and then with each of the processes in turn in the later sections of this chapter; but the processes were interwoven to such an extent that neatly segregated analysis of each factor has been impracticable.

A first look at the scheme

The diagram (Figure 4) provides an overview of the connections between these seven processes. I am not sure whether the scheme is more useful as an introduction or as a summary which should be put at the end of the chapter; it is meant, rather like a passport photo or a menu, only as a guide to a complex reality, not as a replacement for it. . . .

The Romans conquered the whole of the Mediterranean basin in two centuries of almost continuous fighting. During these two centuries of conquest, a higher proportion of Roman citizens was under arms for longer than I have found in any other pre-industrial state.[19] Repeated successes in war enabled the Romans to bring back to Italy huge quantities of booty in the form of treasure, money and slaves. The accumulated treasure of the eastern Mediterranean was transferred to Rome. Booty delivered to the state treasury was soon supplemented by provincial taxes which then gradually became the chief source of state revenue. The Roman elite enhanced its status by spending this new wealth on ostentatious display in the city of Rome and other Italian towns. Such expenditure provided new forms

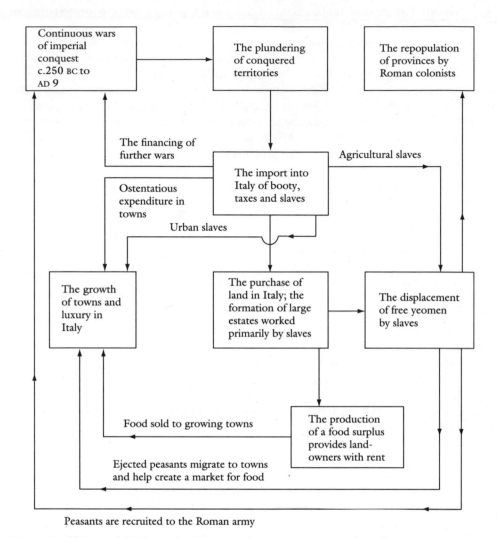

Figure 4 *The growth of slavery in Roman Italy – a scheme of interdependence.*

of employment for both free citizens and for slaves, and created a new demand
for food in towns. This increased demand for food was met partly by imports
of food raised as tax in the provinces, and partly out of a new surplus grown on Italian
farms.

The same forces created new markets and a new surplus at roughly the same time.
As members of the Roman elite grew richer, they invested a considerable part of their
wealth in agricultural land in Italy. Land was the only safe and prestigious large-scale
investment available. The rich concentrated their land-holdings and built up their
estates near home on land previously occupied by citizens. Large numbers of the
displaced citizens migrated to the city of Rome to take advantage of the increased
expenditure there, or joined the army, or migrated to the newly opened northern

Italian plain. It does not seem at all clear why the Roman land-owners so often preferred slaves to free workers. Several arguments have been advanced: the greater profitability of slaves, the cheapness of slaves (which I doubt), the liability of free small-holders to military service and their consequent unavailability as part-time labourers, and the reluctance of free citizens to work full-time as labourers on the farms of the rich. Whatever the reasons, several results seem clear. The economic situation of many free peasants deteriorated. Many of the 'conquerors of the world', as the Romans often called themselves, were ejected from their farms and displaced by peoples whom they had vanquished and enslaved.

Yet the massive import of *slaves* defined even poor *citizens* as belonging to a superior stratum (estate).[iii] The displacement of peasants had political repercussions which resulted in the reallocation of small-holdings to the landless and to ex-soldiers. These allocations temporarily alleviated but did not effectively improve the condition of poor citizens. State subsidies for food distribution to the urban poor increased the flow of migrants to the city of Rome, and, as I shall argue, further stimulated agricultural production on large estates, by underwriting the purchasing power of the urban poor. The final solution to the conflict of interests between citizen peasants and large land-owners was initiated by Julius Caesar and followed through under Augustus: the massive resettlement of Roman colonists in the provinces reduced the pressure from landless citizens and the urban poor on land in Italy; and it also allowed the further expansion of elite land-holdings in Italy.

These, in sum, are the arguments which I shall be putting forward in the rest of this chapter and which are summarised in the flow-chart (Figure 4). But I should like to add another perspective on the function of slavery in the political system. The exploitation of slaves permitted the Roman elite to expand its wealth to a level which was commensurate with its political control over the Mediterranean basin, without having to exploit the mass of free citizens overtly, except in their traditional role as soldiers. This statement may seem strange, if we consider the scale on which peasants were expelled from their lands. But it makes sense if we consider how much more obvious the exploitation would have been, if, for example, expelled peasant citizens had been reduced to working for rich Romans as domestic servants, as they were in England before and during the Industrial Revolution.

Slavery also made it possible to maintain agricultural production in Italy, in spite of the high levels of recruitment into the army and of emigration to the city of Rome. Unlike the Manchu conquerors of China in the seventeenth century, who latched on to the existing bureaucracy and became pensioners or sinecurists of the tax-system, the Roman conquering elite secured its wealth by the acquisition of land in the home country. As Max Weber saw, this process required changes in the laws governing the ownership of land so as to allow unlimited accumulation and secure tenure of public and private land.[20]

Once large urban markets had been established, land-ownership provided the elite with continuous income, whereas exploitation of the provinces did not. For under the Roman political system, aristocratic families had to seek election to political office from the plebs. The great majority of Roman aristocratic families ran the risk of not securing election to high office in each generation and the chance of provincial profit which went with it. When they did reach office, the pressure to make a profit, and to convert their booty into landed income was all the greater. Thus one of the main functions of slavery was that it allowed the elite to increase the discrepancy between rich and poor without alienating the free citizen peasantry from their willingness to fight in wars for the further expansion of the empire; slavery also allowed the rich to recruit labour to work their estates in a society which had no labour market; and it permitted ostentatious display, again without the direct exploitation of the free poor. Slavery made it unnecessary for the rich to employ the poor directly, except as soldiers.

This failure of the rich to employ the urban masses directly left the poor at the mercy of market forces. Agriculture was liable to sharp variations of production, and supplies to the city of Rome depended upon unreliable transport. Luckily for the urban poor, their power as citizen voters secured the use of state resources, through the agency of politicians who wanted their favour. The state in turn secured supplies of wheat through taxation, and supplied a substantial sector of the market with wheat (34 kg per month per citizen) first at a fixed low price and later free. I argue below that this support by the state served to underwrite the capacity of the poor to buy more wheat and oil and wine produced on the estates of the rich. But the conversion of the capital's citizens into state pensioners, while it cushioned them against poverty, also heralded the demise of their political power.

A SKETCH OF THE ECONOMY

The Roman economy in Italy and the provinces, in all periods, rested upon the backs of peasants. Let us therefore begin by examining some factors which repeatedly constrained the relationship between peasants and the elite. Afterwards we can turn our attention to the economic conditions out of which the Roman state began its territorial expansion overseas. To simplify our task, we shall make two assumptions. These assumptions, like several which follow, are obviously speculative, but they do help us gain a clearer perspective of the Roman economy. One easy check on their plausibility is to think of the consequences of alternative assumptions. First, let us assume that four fifths of the Italian and provincial labour force were primarily engaged in producing food (I think the real figure was probably higher). And second, let us assume that the *average* consumption by townsmen, most of whom were poor, was near that of peasants. We can then draw two conclusions. First, agricultural productivity was low since it took four food-producing families to feed a fifth. It was only after the agricultural revolution in England in the eighteenth century that these average proportions began radically to be changed; in the USA now (1973 figures) for example, one farm worker produces enough food for over fifty people. Secondly, *on average*, Roman peasants consumed four fifths of their own produce and supported non-peasants with the remaining fifth.

As in any self-sufficient pre-industrial economy, the bulk of the empire's labour force was primarily engaged in producing food, most of which the producers also consumed. This was the most important element of the Roman economy. We may add to this picture by assuming also that peasants individually grew most of their own food and did not exchange much produce with each other. In addition, it seems likely that handicraft workers, because of the low level of capital investment, each

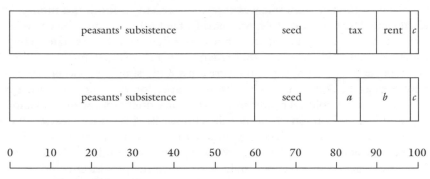

a = rent and tax paid in produce.

b = produce sold in the local market for cash to pay rent and tax in money.

c = produce sold in the market to buy goods for peasants' consumption.

Figure 5 *Peasants ate most of their own produce: a hypothetical scheme. The scheme illustrates the large subsistence sector of the economy, the small non-agricultural sector, the equivalent functions of tax and rent, the low value of money exchange between peasant and town, the low average standard of living of peasants. It is, of course, crudely hypothetical and if roughly true, only true for the population as a whole.*

produced little more than the average peasant. We can now see that an extremely large proportion of all that was produced both in Italy and in the provinces was never traded; it stood outside the market, solid and inflexible, almost untouched by the forces of money. Analysis of the Roman economy has always to take that solid unmarketed core into account.

The methods by which the elite both created and extracted the peasants' surplus produce: taxes, rent and market exchange, constituted a second important element in the structure of the Roman economy. Of these three, in the empire as a whole, taxation gradually came to be the largest in volume, and the tax on land and crops comprised a very large proportion of all taxes; however, it should be stressed that the Romans made their way rather jerkily from a tradition of plunder to a stable system of taxation. And levying taxes did not preclude officials from private profiteering both at the moment of conquest and during the subsequent administration of conquered provinces.[21] To be comprehensive, therefore, we should add plunder, including slaves, and private profiteering to taxes, rents and market exchange as common methods of extracting a surplus from primary producers.

There were wide regional differences in the incidence of taxation. Roman citizens in Italy paid no tax at all on land after 167 BC. This privilege was preserved until the end of the third century AD. Who profited from it? Immunity from tax enabled landlords to charge higher rents and so helped push up the price of Italian land. In Egypt, by contrast, peasants living off irrigated Crown land paid no rent, but regularly gave up half their produce in tax. In other provinces, the most common rate of tax seems to have been a tithe of the crop (*decuma*).[22] If we take this tenth of the crop as an average tax for the whole empire, which seems reasonable, then on our previous assumptions, land taxes brought in (or were equal in value to) about one half of the food consumed by non-peasants.

As the common use of the word tithe (*decuma*) for tax implies, a considerable volume of tax in the late Republic was extracted directly as food, not money. Wheat from Sicily and Africa, for example, was used to feed the army and the city of Rome. Even when taxes were raised in money, they were often spent by the state to buy food for Roman soldiers. The considerable reliance on taxes levied in food helped the Roman state support a large superstructure with fairly simple economic institutions and only a small market sector. The city of Rome, for example, depended for its prosperity on Roman political power and on the consequent inflow of taxes and rents; unlike pre-industrial London, it did not depend for its size on its capacity to export manufactures or on trade. It is worth noting that in so far as taxes were levied in money in the provinces and spent in Italy, they probably stimulated the import of an equal volume of goods by value into Italy, with which the provinces could, as it were, buy their money back, and pay their taxes in the next year. No doubt, it took quite a time to establish such a balance of trade and tax, so that in the early stages of conquest the provinces were impoverished and fell into debt, while some inflation occurred in Italy. Of course, this crude model of the imperial economy needs to be refined to take more factors (such as mining) into account, but even in this primitive form, it draws attention to important relationships between taxes and trade.

After taxes, rents from agricultural land were the most important method for getting the surplus produce out of the hands of peasants into the hands of the elite and into towns. For the upper classes, agricultural rents and the income from farms worked by slaves and administered by agents constituted the largest source of income. Government service (including tax-collection) came a poor second. Some rents too were collected in food not money; this practice restricted the market sector still further. In the empire as a whole, the total value of rents (including income from farms managed by agents) probably amounted to less than taxes. This was because many fewer people paid rent than paid tax, not because rent levels were lower. There was always a substantial body of independent, non-rent-paying peasants both in Italy and the provinces. Their numbers fluctuated but they never disappeared. Finally, from descriptions of peasant life in many other societies, it seems reasonable to suppose that although there was considerable variation, nevertheless most peasants in the Roman empire were poor; rent and tax took away most of their surplus; if there was anything left to spare, they were likely to eat most of it. Only a very small proportion of their gross product went on the purchase of goods manufactured (made by hand) in towns. But I do not want to exaggerate. The aggregate demands of fifty million peasants, even if most of them were poor, constitutes a significant market for urban produce.

The preponderance of tax plus rent over market exchange underlines the common view that in the Roman world the relationship between town and country was to a large extent one of exploitation.[23] The towns were 'centres of consumption', consuming the bulk of the townsmen's own produce as well as the bulk of the peasants' surplus. But it should not be forgotten that townsmen also provided services, for example of government and administration, which gave peasants a stable environment in which they could work. The price which the peasants paid for this peace was very high. As in other pre-industrial empires, it seems remarkable that they tolerated the impositions of government and landlords for so long.

The formation of large estates

The profits of empire, were the single most important factor in gradually building up the wealth of the Roman elite. A large portion of the profits taken out of the provinces was invested in land, especially in Italian land. Since the Roman upper classes got most of their regular income from land, a general increase in their wealth was necessarily accompanied by the formation of larger estates. This strong link between (1) imperial profits, (2) the increased wealth of the elite and (3) the formation of large land-holdings often seems overshadowed by... more dramatic processes... the violent acquisition of fortunes in the provinces, their ostentatious display in the city of Rome, and the manipulation of free floating cash by financiers, like Crassus and rich tax-farmers. Of course, the transfer of money from the provinces and its investment in Italian land was a gradual process; its gradualness may have contributed to its neglect. In any one year or even generation, the volume of profits brought back from the provinces was smaller than the inherited stock of capital; and once the year's profits were invested, they too became part of the common capital. Thereafter, they were redistributed through the normal channels: dowry and inheritance, supplemented by bankruptcy and confiscation. Thus at any one time, these normal channels for the transfer of property seemed of more importance to contemporaries than provincial profits.

To be sure, a significant proportion of booty was spent rather than invested. Whether invested or spent, the money was passed on to someone else. The same money could be used to pay creditors, who might buy luxuries with it; they, in turn, might buy land from peasants, who then used the same money to buy clothes and food... The concept 'the multiplier effect of money' refers to such sequences.

The high cost of maintaining status by ostentatious expenditure and of securing election to public office were important factors underlying profiteering in the provinces. Nobles, particularly in the first century BC, commonly incurred debts in the hope of paying them off afterwards with what they made out of provincial office.[24] Retainers as well as creditors had to be paid. Pompey, in 61 BC, for example, probably gave each of his lieutenants one million HS (c. 2,000 tons wheat equivalent). Huge sums were lavished on prestigious displays, silver plate, marble statues and other *objets d'art*. One indication of increasing wealth is that the finest town house in the city of Rome in 78 BC was said not to have been even in the top hundred a generation later (Pliny, *Natural History* 36.109). The senate tried to preserve traditional simplicity (and so to restrict competition from rich *arrivistes*) by a whole succession of laws restricting consumption, for example, at feasts and funerals;[25] but in vain. Senators and leading knights maintained elaborate households staffed with hundreds of slaves, including cooks, scribes, librarians, doctors, name-callers, at once a mark of their culture, and of an extravagance which enhanced their status.

This expenditure of provincial profits in the city of Rome particularly concerns us here because it considerably expanded the market for agricultural produce. Nobles kept and fed slaves, built palaces, commanded services and spent money which by its multiplier effects gave lots of people enough money to buy food. Without this expansion of the city population and market, and a similar expansion in other Italian towns, investment by nobles in Italian agricultural land would have been useless.

As in most other pre-industrial societies, land-ownership was the bedrock of wealth. Generally speaking, both senators and knights derived the bulk of their incomes from land. The richer they became, therefore, the larger their land-holdings. But good agricultural land in central and southern Italy was already cultivated, much of it by free peasants. The formation of large land-holdings inevitably involved their expropriation and expulsion. The process was gradual, and estates were enlarged piecemeal, as and when opportunity offered. This partly explains why large land-holdings in Italy during the late Republic typically comprised several scattered estates. This fragmentation of land-holdings was politically important in that it by and large precluded Roman aristocrats, unlike European feudal lords, from basing their power on the control of a particular territory.[26]

Land was the main source of wealth, and wealth was a mainspring of political power. The trouble was that the rich and poor were competing among themselves and with each other for a strictly limited resource. Conflict over the ownership of land in Italy constituted a major axis of political activity throughout the last two centuries of the Republic. The conflict was expressed, for example, in laws limiting the extent of public land which a citizen could hold, in mass confiscations of property and its redistribution to soldiers and other citizens, and in the induced migration of citizens away from their homes to distant and less populated parts of Italy. As we have seen, the changing pattern of land-ownership led to the mass importation of slaves and to the emigration of the free poor from the land to the army and to the city of Rome. The resulting evolution of a professional army (or perhaps more accurately, a core of long-service soldiers) and of an urban proletariat upset the traditional balance of power and contributed to the chaos of the last decades of the Republic. The solution to the conflict over land is interesting: the emigration of several hundred thousand citizens to the provinces, organised by Julius Caesar and Augustus, relieved the pressure of the poor on Italian land; complementarily, the advent of peace and the integration of the empire under the stable administration of the emperors enabled the Italian rich increasingly to own land in, and transfer rents from the provinces.

As usual, the evidence for many of these assertions is both fragmentary and disputed. But the main outlines seem clear enough. For example, we have no detailed information on senators' or knights' incomes, on the relative importance of agricultural and urban rents, of income from loans or tax-farming, commerce and manufacture. But it is revealing that ancient authors simply assumed that rich men were land-owners, that land was their prime source of wealth. Cicero for example, in a philosophical discussion of the very rich and the comfortably rich man noted that 'he takes 600,000 HS from his farms, I take 100,000 HS from mine' (*Paradoxes of the Stoics* 49). The minimum census qualification for senators and knights (1 million and 400,000 HS respectively) was expressed in value of property, mostly landed property, and not in terms of income. Julius Caesar's and the emperor Tiberius' laws on debt presupposed that large-scale debtors had given land as security, and seem to have required creditors to invest two thirds of rapid loans in Italian land. Two common words for wealthy (*locuples, possessor*) both imply the ownership of land.[27] Even the politically powerful minority of knights who specialised in tax-farming probably operated from a basis of land-owning. This is implied by the fact that they were required to give land as security for the performance of their contracts. It follows *a fortiori* that lesser knights, locally powerful in their Italian home towns, were primarily land-owners; indeed Cicero referred to them several times collectively as farmers, countrymen (*agricolae, rusticani*).[28] Besides, it seems obvious that in a predominantly agrarian society, without a sophisticated administrative superstructure, land would be the major source of wealth. Even if a man made a lot of money in some other way, he would achieve both high status and security by investing it in land (Cicero, *On Duties* 1.151).

The prevalence of land-owning among the Roman rich did not mean that senators and knights got their income only from land. Land-ownership was compatible with the pursuit of other financial interests. In the modern world, the specialisation of occupations tempts us to think of land-owners, bankers, financiers, tax-officials and businessmen as different people. In Rome, they were often the same people. It was common for large land-owners, for example, not to rent out all their land to free tenants, but to exploit some of it directly. Typically, a slave manager (*vilicus*) was put in charge of the day-to-day running of a rich man's farm. But it seems probable that many rich men, even nobles, took a direct and lively interest in the sale of surplus produce from their estates, though explicit evidence on this is scarce.[29] Similarly it seems probable that many rich men, even nobles, set up their slaves and ex-slaves in business, providing them with capital and in one way or another taking a share of their profits. This is one factor which would help to account for the dominance of ex-slaves in the commercial life of Rome and other Italian cities. But it is only a conjecture; we have no testimony on how closely, or whether slave-owners supervised such business activities.

The involvement of senators in trade or commerce of any sort has often been denied, and in support of this view much is usually made of a law passed in 218 BC forbidding senators the right to own large ships. They were allowed to own small ships, of under seven tonnes burden, 'enough to carry crops from the farms. All profit-making was thought demeaning for senators' (Livy 21.63). But we know that by 70 BC this law was a dead letter, and that by then senators were deeply involved in loan finance, either directly or through agents. The young noble Brutus, for example, lent money to a town in Cyprus at four per cent monthly compound interest and got the senate to pass a special decree exempting his loan from normal regulations limiting interest rates. M. Crassus had quite openly built up his fortune partly by speculation in metropolitan property.[30]

Ideally, nobles were not expected to be interested in profit-making; we find similar ideals in other pre-industrial 'high cultures'. But the ideal was both honoured and violated; indeed many ideals exist because they are generally not achieved. Ironically, Cicero approved of trade, provided it was on a large scale; only small-scale trade seemed demeaning to him (*On Duties* 1.151). Probably attitudes had changed in the course of Rome's expansion. Senators could be barred from profit-making by law in 218 BC because it was relatively unimportant. When banking, loan-financing and commerce grew in importance, I suspect that senators participated, even in violation of traditional values.

But commerce and finance were only the cream on the cake, not the cake itself. We have no Roman figures, but estimates from England in 1801 are suggestive. The average income of the top two thousand merchants and bankers was only 2,600 pounds sterling per year, compared with 8,000 pounds sterling per year for the top group of land-owners, and 3,000 pounds sterling per year for the upper gentry.[31] By that time England was much more industrialised and commercially sophisticated than Rome ever became. The ratio of agrarian to non-agrarian incomes in Rome, even in the exceptional conditions of the Republic, was almost certainly higher. The high status of large land-owners was enhanced by their huge wealth (*nihil dulcius agricultura* ["nothing is sweeter than farming"]).

Even if Roman land-owners had wanted to invest in business, they faced one difficulty which constituted a serious obstacle to economic growth. The Romans never evolved a legal form for commercial or manufacturing enterprises similar to our joint stock company, which had the advantage of limiting investors' liability, and of preserving the business as a unit beyond the death of its owner. It was only in the spheres of tax-farming and mining that the Romans devised a corporation (*societas*). The right to collect taxes in each province was auctioned every five years; the sums and the risk involved went beyond the scope of individual fortunes. To solve this, tax-farming corporations were set up which took in investments and guarantees from numerous individuals. Each corporation existed as a juridical entity, but was much more liable to dissolutlion than modern corporations. Indeed the death or withdrawal of the president (*manceps*) was apparently sufficient in some circumstances to necessitate dissolution.[32] Investment in tax-farming thus depended on success in periodic auctions, and might be intermittent as well as short-term. Perhaps the system worked, only because Roman tax-farmers, as we have seen, worked from the more stable base of land-owning.

The organisation and aggregated capital of tax-farmers were never applied to trade and manufacture; they remained very fragmented, dominated by small, single-family businesses. The largest had slave-workers, but typically employed far fewer men than large agricultural estates (*latifundia*);[33] besides, there was in trade and industry no equivalent overlord institution such as tenancy, which allowed the large-scale, coordinated exploitation of the poor by a single rich man. Perhaps a few fortunes may have been made in trade, but not many and not large fortunes. Traders, unlike tax-farmers, did not constitute a group which Q. Cicero thought worth courting in elections; while in much later times, the fortunes of prosperous merchants in the empire's chief trading city, Alexandria, were perhaps only a fraction of those of large land-owners.[34]

It was the shortage of alternative investments and the high status of land-owning which above all induced men to invest capital in land. Among senators there was an additional pressure. The opportunity to profit hugely from empire occurred infrequently. Many senators had only one or two chances in a life-time to hold government posts in the provinces, and that in a junior capacity (as *quaestor* or as governor's aide – *legatus*). A more favoured group, which varied from two to three fifths of those who entered the senate, were elected to the office of *praetor* and so became eligible for appointment as provincial governor. In theory, each official had the opportunity to govern a province for one year, since the Romans for long periods kept a balance between the number of provinces and the number of senior elected officials (praetors and consuls).[35] In fact, there were often lags and shortages, especially at the very end of the Republic, so that some officials like Verres or Cicero's brother, for example, governed a province for three years, while others, although eligible, never governed a province at all. We show [in chapter 1 of volume Two of this work] that only an extremely small number of leading families secured access to high office for one of their sons in each generation; for example, only four per cent of consuls 249–50 BC (N = 364) came from families with consuls in six successive generations; complementarily, over a quarter of the consuls came from families with only one consul in two centuries. The bulk of senators, therefore, could not be sure that either they or their sons would have another opportunity to make money out of high office. The senators who were successful therefore felt constrained to make their pile and invest it in land. It might have to support the family for generations.

NOTES

1   For estimates of world population, based on backward extrapolation and on estimates of Chinese and Roman populations of this period, see D. M. Heer, *Society and Population* (Englewood Cliffs, N.J., 1968), 2.

2   Rome was the largest city in the world and was perhaps not equalled in size before the rise of the great cities of China in the Sung dynasty. See G. Rozman, *Urban Networks in Ch'ing China and Tokugawa Japan* (Princeton, 1973), 35, and the compendious, useful but not obviously reliable T. Chandler and G. Fox, *3000 Years of Urban Growth* (New York, 1974). The population of London reached about one million in 1800 and it was then by far the largest city in Europe. In 1600, only two European cities had populations over 200,000, namely Paris and Naples.

3   There is no direct confirmation of this generalisation in the classical texts. But that does not matter. We must suppose either that large Italian landowners sold the produce of their estates to Italian townsmen, or that they got no return on the capital which they repeatedly invested both in land and in the slaves who worked it. The first generalisation seems more economical.

4   It is not possible to prove this assertion by the traditional method of selective quotation from classical sources. For example, Livy (6.12) suggested that the frequent wars in a district of central Italy in an earlier period might be explained by its high population. He noted that in his time the district produced few soldiers, and would have been deserted but for slaves. My assertion is compatible with such passages in the sources, but cannot be validated by them. Instead, I have tried to consider both the probability and the consequences of the assertion being wrong, and then to ask: What alternative assertion is more likely to be true? This procedure, based on a compatibility theory of historical truth, is used often in this book.

5   'I was the first to make shepherds give way to ploughmen on the public land', *Inscriptions Latinae liberae rei publicae*, ed. A. Degrassi (Florence, 1957–63), n° 454. This was one of the proud boasts of a consul (? of 132 BC) who had a milestone, in the genre of a market cross, set up in a southern Italian town and inscribed with his achievements. The inscription is commonly understood to refer to the distribution of public land to small-holders in accordance with the Gracchan land laws (133 BC). Varro (*On Agriculture* 2, preface 4) also wrote that latterly Romans had 'turned arable into pasture out of greed and against the law'.

From such snippets, it is difficult to prove any general change in land use. But my general impression is that the rapid expansion of pasture and vineyards was based on the conversion of arable as well as on the extension of private property over hitherto unclaimed or common lands. On the growth in volume and prestige of Italian wines, dated to the second century BC, see Pliny, *Natural History* 14.87–8; on the growth of pasture, see A. J. Toynbee, *Hannibal's Legacy* (Oxford, 1965), vol. 2, 286ff.

6   The relative size of the markets for agricultural crops is obviously an important problem.
    The ancient data are clearly insufficient. As a sighting shot, without any implication that
    the prices in Rome were of the same order and for illustration only, I looked at the single
    case of Madrid in the mid-eighteenth century. Goods entering the city (which had a
    population of about 135,000 in 1757) were checked for customs; in 1757, imports
    totalled as follows: 96,000 *arrobas* of olive oil, 500,000 *arrobas* of wine, 520,000 *fanegas*
    of wheat. I took average prices for 1753–62 for New Castile from L. J. Hamilton, *War
    and Prices in Spain 1651–1800* (New York, 1957), 229 ff, and figures on consumption
    from D. R. Ringrose, 'Transportation and economic stagnation in 18th-century Castille',
    Journal of Economic History 28 (1968), 51–79. Of the three products, wheat constituted
    46% of the total costs; wine 45%; olive oil 9%. Wheat consumption works out at about
    160 kg per person year, wine at 100 litres per adult year – which is rather low for wheat and
    high for wine. However, these figures can serve as only a very rough guide. For compari-
    son, I posited the same consumption but with prices from Marseille, 1701–10; this
    produced somewhat different ratios of cost: wheat 64%, wine 19%, oil 17%; data from
    R. Baehrel, *Une Croissance* (Paris, 1961), 530ff. In Rome wheat was probably also the
    single most important product, in volume and value, particularly for the poor.
7   P. A. Brunt, *Italian Manpower 225* BC–AD *14* (Oxford, 1971), 425, lists the size of the
    Italian armed forces for the twenty-one years between 200 and 168 BC for which we have
    full information. The average size of the army and smallish fleet was about 140,000, drawn
    from an adult male population of about one million (ibid. 59).
8   In the traditional Roman histories, folk-heroes faced similar problems; it seems likely that
    their problems reflected anxieties which persisted. For example, Cincinnatus summoned
    to be dictator while working at the plough is said to have exclaimed: 'My land will not be
    sown this year, and so we shall run the risk of not having enough to eat' (Dionysius of
    Halicarnassus, *Roman Antiquities* 10.17). Another famous general, Atilius Regulus serv-
    ing in Africa during the first war against Carthage wrote to the senate to say that the bailiff
    of his small farm had died, that a farm hand had taken the stock, and requested that a
    replacement be sent to see to its cultivation, so that his wife and children should not starve
    (Valerius Maximus 4.4.6). Poor soldiers had no such privilege.
9   Ancient commentators on the political struggles of the late Republic usually saw the main
    axis of conflict as between nobles and the people; see L. R. Taylor, *Party Politics in the Age
    of Caesar* (Berkeley, 1944). The direct opposition rich – poor is only rarely mentioned in
    historical sources of the period (see, for example, Appian, *Civil Wars* 1.10). Nevertheless,
    it seems to have underlain much social and political conflict; see the interesting discussion
    by M. I. Finley, *The Ancient Economy* (London, 1973), 35ff.
10 See Toynbee (1965): vol. 1, 166; vol. 2, 556–7. The traditional histories reflect
    this concern with the maldistribution of public land, sometimes anachronistically. Cf.
    Dionysius of Halicarnassus (*Roman Antiquities* 8.73–5; cf. 9.51) who lived in the reign
    of Augustus; he recorded a debate purportedly held in 486 BC, but it probably reflected
    typical attitudes of a much later period. A leading senator, Appius, said (73.4): 'As things
    now stand, the envy of the poor against the rich who have appropriated and continue to
    occupy the public lands is justified; it is not surprising that they demand that public
    property should be divided among all citizens instead of being held by the few...' But he
    went on to argue that splitting state-land into small lots would be troublesome to the
    poor, because they were poor; it would be better for the state to lease land in large lots:
    these would bring in large revenues, from which soldiers could be paid and fed. With some
    refinements, the suggestion was generally approved. For a long discussion of the evidence,
    see G. Tibiletti, 'Il Possesso dell' Ager Publicus', *Athenaeum* 26 (1948), 173–236.
11 Soldiers were commonly given land which was already under cultivation; 'where the
    plough and reaping hook have been', as a law of Augustus on colonies stated (Hyginus,

On the Fixing of Boundaries, ed. Lachmann (Berlin, 1848), 203). This led to repeated friction between colonists and the old inhabitants (see, for example, Granius Licinianus, p. 34F). Some ex-soldiers settled by Sulla before 80 BC were involved in the rebellion of Catiline in 63 BC; according to Sallust (*Catiline* 16): 'they had squandered their resources and remembered their former victory and booty'. This seems an inadequate basis for thinking that all ex-soldiers were bad farmers. It was always assumed in the classical world that soldiers could turn into peasants and vice versa. On all this, see Brunt (1971: 294ff).

12 Some comparative evidence may help as a guide. Bulgaria (1910), Yugoslavia (1931) had 81% and 79% of their work-force engaged in agriculture. The figures for Turkey (1927) and China in the 1940s were 82% and over 80%. See O. S. Morgan, ed., *Agricultural Systems of Middle Europe* (New York, 1933), 48 and 359; *Recensement général de la population 1927* (Ankara, 1929), 29; C. K. Yang, *A Chinese Village* (Cambridge, Mass., 1959), 23. The composition of these populations was already somewhat affected by their links with foreign, industrial markets. I think the comparable figures for the Roman empire would have been higher.

13 It is impossible to calculate the ratio of free men to slaves outside the city of Rome accurately, but we can see whether our guesses are compatible with each other and with what else we know. For present purposes, I assume a total population in Italy of 6.0 million, which is between the best guesses of Beloch (5.5 million (*Die Bevölkerung der griechisch-römischen Welt*, 436) and Brunt (7.5 million (1971: 124)). I follow Beloch in thinking that there were no more than two million slaves (see note 14 below).

   If all the rural population worked on the land, and the agricultural land constituted 40% of Italy's surface (as against 55% in 1881), then at roughly 10 million hectares, it allowed over two hectares per person, which is feasible but not generous, given (*a*) low yields, (*b*) the high proportion of adults among slaves, and (*c*) their need to produce a surplus. For similar arguments, see Beloch (1886: 417) and Brunt (1971: 126). I agree with Beloch that the estimated slave population was extremely high for Roman conditions.

14 There is no clear evidence on the number of slaves in Italy, and the best we can do is guess. Beloch (1886: 418) thought that there were less than two million slaves in Italy at the end of the first century BC; Brunt (1971: 124) thought that there were three million. The discrepancy serves as an index of the plausible margin of error.

   One discrepancy should be mentioned here. Since male slaves predominated and mortality was high, the total of slaves ever imported was higher than the number of slaves at any one time. There is therefore little point in adding up the known figures of enslaved captives, even if they were accurate.

   For a thorough discussion of the sources of slavery, see E. M. Schtaerman, *Die Blütezeit der Sklavenwirtschaft in der römischen Republik* (Wiesbaden, 1969), 36–70. She is quite right to point out how exceptional it was for Romans to enslave the conquered. But I still think that war was the most common source of slaves in the period of imperial expansion. Nor were war and trade mutually exclusive; enslaved prisoners of war were imported into Italy and distributed by traders.

15 I have dealt with some of the problems of this process in 'Structural differentiation in Rome' in I. M. Lewis, ed., *History and Social Anthropology* (London, 1968), 63–78,...more generally, see S. N. Eisenstadt, *The Political Systems of Empires* (New York, 1963), and N. J. Smelser in B. F. Hoselitz and W. E. Moore, *Industrialization and Social Change* (Paris, 1963).

16 It is useful to distinguish between holdings and farms. Rich men had huge holdings of land, commonly divided into farms; many of these were much larger than peasant family farms, but they were not *latifundia*. This is deduced from the illustrations used by the agricultural writers Cato, Varro and Columella of farms varying from 25 ha (100 *iugera*) for a vineyard to 50 ha (arable) and 60 ha (olives), worked by 16, 8–11 and 13 slaves

respectively. The recommended size of herds was 50–100 goats, 100–120 cattle, 100–150 pigs – large by peasant standards, but hardly ranching.

    For testimony, see Cato, *On Agriculture* 10–11; Columella, *On Agriculture* 2.12; and on livestock, see Varro, *On Agriculture* 2.3–5 and P. A. Brunt, *JRS* [*Journal of Roman Studies*] 62 (1972), 154.

17   See also: Cato, *On Agriculture* 5 and 144; Suetonius, *Julius Caesar* 42. The best discussion of Roman agricultural labour, although awkwardly arranged, is still W. E. Heitland, *Agricola* (Cambridge, 1921) and see also K. D. White, *Roman Farming* (London, 1970).

18   See [K. Hopkins, *Conquerors and Slaves: Sociological Studies in Roman History* (Cambridge, 1978)], ch. 11, notes 15 and 23.

19   In Prussia under Frederick William I and Frederick the Great for less than fifty years, and in France under Napoleon for less than twenty years, rates of recruitment perhaps equalled and may have surpassed average rates of recruitment in late Republican Rome. But these rates were not maintained for long compared with Rome. See *The New Cambridge Modern History*, vol. 7, ed. J. O. Lindsay (Cambridge, 1957), 179 and 305; vol. 9, ed. C. W. Crawley (Cambridge, 1965), 32 and 64. I have not considered warlike tribes such as some Red Indians or the Zulu as comparable. On the general problem of military participation ratios see S. Andreski. *Military Organization and Society* (London, 1954).

20   M. Weber, *Die römische Agrargeschichte* (Stuttgart, 1891), 67ff and 119ff. Roman law (in contrast, for example, to traditional Chinese law) was marked by the complete freedom of the head of the household to sell or testate land to whomever he wanted. Moreover, communal land was slowly transformed into privately held land (through the right of seizure, *ager occupatorius*), and the traditional limits on the amount which could be held were removed; by agrarian laws of *c.* 113–111 BC, private tenure of previously public land in Italy was confirmed. See E. G. Hardy, *Roman Laws and Charters* (Oxford, 1912), 35ff.

21   Roman nobles thought themselves judged by their victories and by the value of their booty. For example, in 182 BC, a governor returned from Spain where he had one or two minor victories, 'He entered the city with an ovation [i.e. a minor triumph]. In his procession he carried 9,320 [Roman] pounds of silver, eighty-two [Roman] pounds of gold and sixty-seven golden crowns' (Livy 40.16). This passage implies both the public record of booty and competition. Even when Roman administrators took over previous systems of taxation, as in Sicily, they were still under pressure to make a profit for themselves. Laws to protect subjects were ineffective. One exceptionally rapacious governor (Cicero, *Verrines* 1.40) boasted that one third of the profits from the province would be used to pay off his patrons and protectors in case of trial for unjust extortion, one third for the jurors, and one third to secure a comfortable living. In the civil wars of the last century BC, rivals for power extorted as much as they could from the provinces, and it was only in the High Empire that extortion was firmly controlled; it was never suppressed. See P. A. Brunt, 'Charges of provincial maladministration under the early Principate', *Historia* 10 (1961), 189–227.

22   A tithe was paid in Sicily and Sardinia. Tax was reckoned as a tithe in Asia, until the reform of Julius Caesar, but was probably often paid in money. A tax in kind was also collected in Africa (see for example *ESAR* [*Economic Survey of Ancient Rome*, ed. T. Frank (Baltimore, 1933–40)] 4.89ff). The evidence is collected by W. Schwahn in *RE sv Tributum* and A. H. M. Jones, *The Roman Economy*, ed. P. A. Brunt (Oxford, 1974), 151ff.

23   This was one of the basic perspectives in M. I. Rostovtzeff, *Social and Economic History of the Roman Empire* (Oxford², 1957). See also the evocative book by R. MacMullen, *Roman Social Relations* (New Haven, 1974), and the articles by M. I. Finley, 'The city from Fustel de Coulanges to Max Weber and beyond', *Comparative Studies in Society and History* 19 (1977), 305ff, and K. Hopkins, 'Economic growth in towns in classical

antiquity', in P. Abrams and E. A. Wrigley, eds., *Towns in Societies* (Cambridge, 1978), 35ff.

24 For a discussion of debt, see M. W. Frederiksen, 'Caesar, Cicero and the problem of debt', *JRS* 56 (1966), especially 128–30; Cicero (*Catiline* 2.18; *Offices* 2.78ff) mentioned a category of rich men, heavily in debt. For Pompey, see Pliny, *Natural History* 37.16 and *ESAR* 1.325.

25 Levels of ostentatious expenditure rose considerably after Rome's conquest of the eastern Mediterranean (see Pliny, *Natural History* 33 *passim*, but especially 138ff). On sumptuary laws, see, for example, Aulus Gellius, *Attic Nights* 2.24 and I. Sauerwein, *Die Leges Sumptuariae* (diss. Hamburg, 1970).

26 Of course, Roman aristocrats had local political connections and clients. In 83 BC. Pompey recruited troops in Picenum 'because of his father's reputation there' (Appian, *Civil Wars* 1.80), but his support there melted away in the civil war against Julius Caesar in 49 BC. See also Caesar, *Civil Wars* 1.34 and 56, and M. Gelzer, *The Roman Nobility* (Oxford, 1969), 93f. Other political connections were much more important.

27 On laws of debt, see Tacitus, *Annals* 6.17; Suetonius, *Tiberius* 48; and Frederiksen (1966), 134ff. The word *possessor* originally, and apparently still in the time of Cicero, referred to someone who held public land without full title (on this see C. Nicolet, *L'Ordre équestre à l'époque républicaine* (Paris, 1966), 301). On *locuples*, see Cicero, *de republica* 2.16; Aulus Gellius, *Attic Nights* 10.5. The prevalence of land in the estates of the rich persisted. The emperor Trajan ordered senators to have one third of their fortunes in Italian land; Olympiodorus (frag. 44) tells us that in the fourth century wealthy senators got one quarter of their incomes in the form of farm produce, the rest from rents.

28 By a swing in intellectual fashion this view of the knights has become widely accepted: the pioneering essays were: P. A. Brunt, 'The equites in the Late Republic', *Second International Conference of Economic History 1962* (Paris, 1965), vol. 1, especially 122ff, and Nicolet (1966: 285ff); see also [C.] Meier [*Res Publica Amissa* (Wiesbaden)], (1966: 64ff). The previous view that knights were primarily a class of businessmen was over-modernising.

29 Nobility does not preclude concern with money; see the very interesting study of the fortunes of English aristocrats by L. Stone, *Family and Fortune* (Oxford, 1973). We have no such information about Roman nobles; some like Cato, Varro and Pliny obviously cared about their estates. Epictetus (*Discourses* 1.10) says that the conversation of non-philosophers presumably in court circles turned on accounts, land prices and wheat prices. Senators' names survive on wine-jars and bricks, presumably made on their estates (*ESAR* 1.355 and 5.208–9); such labels are indices of involvement but not of close care. In brief, we don't know how much the predominant culture induced aristocrats typically to care for or ignore their sources of income.

30 Plutarch, *Crassus* 2; on Brutus, see [Cicero, *Letters to Atticus*, 6.1.5–6]; Cicero (*Verrines* 5.45) said that the law on ship-owning by senators was ineffectual, but it survived in a law of Julius Caesar – see the Leiden fragment of Paul's *Sententiae* (ed. G. G. Archi et al., Leiden, 1956).

31 G. Mingay, *English Landed Society in the Eighteenth Century* (London, 1963), 21 (cf. 26). The number of land-owners discussed was smaller (400 + 750), but their aggregate wealth was greater than the merchants' and bankers'.

32 Cf. [E.] Badian, [*Publicans and Sinners: Private Enterprise in the Service of the Roman Republic* (Ithaca, NY)], (1972: 67–81); G. Urögdi, *sv Publicani* in *RE*, Suppl. xi, col. 1184ff.

33 I think the largest factory we know of in the ancient world was in Athens in the fourth century BC – a shield-factory with nearly 120 men (Lysias 12.19). By contrast, Pliny's estate in Umbria, would have employed several hundred men, in different tenancies. The important texts are Pliny, *Letters* 10.8; 3.19; Columella, *On Agriculture* 2.12. For a

detailed discussion, see R. P. Duncan-Jones, *The Economy of the Roman Empire* (Cambridge, 1974), 19–20, 48–9; I agree broadly with his conclusions, but his calculations depend too much on fixed assumptions.

34   [Q. Cicero], *Guide to Electioneering (Comm. Pet.)*. On Alexandrian trade, see Jones (1964: 870–1); the evidence which Jones cites comes mostly from the sixth century AD; it is the only such evidence we have, and his conclusions are often referred to. Unfortunately, the testimony cited hardly authenticates Jones' conclusion. Nevertheless he may well be right. See also Jones, ([*The Later Roman Empire* (Oxford)], (1974: 35ff).

35   F. B. Marsh, *The Founding of the Roman Empire* (Oxford, 1927), 2ff.

EDITOR'S NOTES

i   The reference here, of course, is to Tiberius Sempronius Gracchus.

ii   Cf. P. Garnsey and R. Saller, *The Roman Empire: Economy, Society and Culture* (Berkeley and Los Angeles, 1987), pp. 43–103.

iii   This is one of the central tenets of the award-winning survey of freedom and slavery in Western civilization, O. Patterson, *Freedom in the Making of Western Culture*, vol. 1 (New York, 1991); see pp. 203–90 on Rome.

Sources

Political consequences of Empire

The politics of largesse and individual generals' distributions

The wealth that conquering generals could acquire from ca. 200 BCE onwards allowed them to win the allegiance of their soldiers in the field through the distribution of war booty and to seduce the populace at home through magnificent triumphal processions, public games, and public building projects.[1]

Then after Scipio Africanus [201 BCE] had sent the bulk of his army by sea, he himself, in making his journey through Italy, which was rejoicing in peace no less than in victory, while not only the cities rushed forth to pay their respects, but crowds of rustics crowded the roads, reached Rome and rode into the city in the most magnificent of all triumphs[*]. He delivered into the treasury 123,000 pounds of silver. To each of his soldiers he distributed 400 asses[*] out of the spoils of war.

Livy, *History of Rome*, 30.45.3–4 [ca. 25 BCE]

Marcus Porcius Cato displayed in his Spanish triumph [194 BCE] 25,000 pounds of silver bullion, 123,000 silver denarii[*], 540,000 silver Oscan coins, and 1,400 pounds of gold. From the spoils of war he gave to each of his soldiers 270 asses, and three times that amount to each of his cavalry.

Livy, *History of Rome*, 34.46.2–3 [ca. 25 BCE]

Quintus Fulvius Flaccus, one of the consuls*, celebrated a triumph over the Ligurians [179 BCE]. This triumph was certainly due to Flaccus' influence rather than his achievements. He displayed in his triumph a great mass of arms taken from the enemy, but practically no money. Yet he still distributed to each of his infantry soldiers 300 asses, twice that amount to each of his centurions*, and three times that amount to each of his cavalry.

Livy, *History of Rome*, 40.59.2–3 [ca. 25 BCE]

Manius Acilius Glabrio and the censorial elections for 189 BCE

The people favored Glabrio because he had placed a large number of voters in his debt through the distribution of many largesses. When a large number of aristocrats were outraged that a new man should be so far preferred to them, two tribunes of the people, Publius Sempronius Gracchus and Gaius Sempronius Rutilus, brought an accusation against Glabrio, that some of King Antiochus' money and much of the booty taken from his camp had neither been displayed by Glabrio in his triumph nor turned in to the state treasury. . . . M. Porcius Cato said that gold and silver vessels which he had seen in the camp along with other booty from the king had not been displayed in the triumph. . . . The proposed fine was 100,000 asses.

Livy, *History of Rome*, 37.57.11–58.1 [ca. 25 BCE]

Enormously successful individual generals threatened to disrupt the political equilibrium of the senatorial aristocracy. With the growth of the urban population at Rome, control of the electorate became increasingly difficult for the senatorial aristocracy.[2] Powerful individuals, through reputation and private expenditure, began to explore ways to harness the newly emerging complex political networks. In the decades after 200 BCE, the sources report cases of electoral bribery or *ambitus*, as well as lavish expenditures on games (*ludi*) in order to win votes. The Senate attempted to control its constituency in these areas through legislation.

Electoral bribery

The consuls, with the authority of the Senate brought before the Roman people a law to check electoral bribery [181 BCE].[3]

Livy, *History of Rome*, 40.19.11 [ca. 25 BCE]

Roman politicians of the great aristocratic houses had traditionally relied upon networks of clientage in order to monopolize the electoral process and return members of their families to the highest magistracies of state. In addition to the unwieldy growth of the urban populace, the secret ballot laws of 139 BCE threatened to disrupt the traditional game of Roman politics.

In the consulship of Gnaeus Piso and Marcus Popillius... Aulus Gabinius, who was a grandson of a domestically bred slave woman, carried a law for secret ballots in elections.

Livy, *Summaries*, 54 [ca. 25 BCE]

Senate limits expenditure on games (ludi)

The Senate decreed [in 179 BCE] that games to Jupiter Optimus Maximus should be held and that two commissioners should be appointed to negotiate the contract for the temple to Fortuna Equestris. Regarding expenditure, the Senate decreed for the games that costs not exceed what they had set as the limit for Fulvius Nobilior's games in the aftermath of the Aetolian War, and the senators also voted that Quintus Fulvius should neither invite nor exact contributions for these or do anything contrary to the provisions regarding games in the consulship of Lucius Aemilius and Gnaeus Baebius [182 BCE]. The senators had passed this decree because of the unbridled outlay which Tiberius Sempronius the aedile* had made on games, which had burdened not only Italy and the Italian allies, but outside provinces as well.

Livy, *History of Rome*, 40.44.10–11 [ca. 25 BCE]

In 180 BCE the Senate attempted, through the tribune L. Villius, to retard the meteoric rise of ambitious young politicians by imposing minimum age requirements for the various stages of the cursus honorum*.

In that year the tribune Lucius Villius proposed an unprecedented motion which would set the ages at which each magistracy might be pursued and held.

Livy, *History of Rome*, 40.44.1–2 [ca. 25 BCE]

The army and the land

In the following passage Polybius suggests that Gaius Flaminius was the originator of popular land distribution schemes in the third century BCE in Picenum.

Five years later, in the consulship of Marcus Aemilius Lepidus [232 BCE], the Romans divided the territory in Gaul known as Picenum among their citizens, from which they had ejected the Senones when they conquered them. Gaius Flaminius was the originator of this popular policy, which we must say was the first step in the demoralization of the people, as well as the cause of the war with the Gauls that followed.

Polybius, *Histories*, 2.21.7–9 [ca. 150 BCE]

The Gracchan revolution[4]

Tiberius Gracchus' tribunate in 133 BCE was a watershed in Roman republican political history. In attempting to implement his land reform, he ushered in a new style of Roman politics which threatened to weaken the Senate's traditional powers and authority. Tiberius' tactics were unorthodox, and he resuscitated the original character of the tribunate as a protector of the common people. Perhaps most galling of all to the senators was Tiberius' attempt to bypass the Senate in the use of the legacy to Rome of King Attalus III of Pergamum, which Tiberius intended to use to fund his program after the Senate had denied him sufficient resources.

Even though the rectification of injustice [of the wealthy occupying the best land in Italy and driving the poor off their small farmsteads] was extremely considerate, the people were content to let the matter rest provided that they could be safe from such wrongs in the future. But the men of great wealth and property hated Tiberius' law because of their insatiable greed, and by their anger and contentiousness they hated the lawgiver as well, and they tried to turn the people away from Tiberius' proposed reforms by charging that he was introducing a bill for land redistribution because he wanted to confuse the people and set a general revolution in motion. But they were unable to accomplish anything, because Tiberius, working to support a program both honorable and just with great eloquence, was formidable and unconquerable, whenever he mounted the speakers' platform with the people crowding around. Then he took his stand and pleaded for the poor: "There are wild beasts that roam free over Italy," he would say. "They have caves or lairs for protection; but the brave men who fight and perish for Italy enjoy only the common light and air, nothing else. Destitute and homeless they wander about with wives and children. And their commanders lie to them with their exhortations before battles to defend shrines and sepulchers from the enemy. For these men do not have any hereditary altars, these many Romans do not have ancestral tombs, but they fight and die in support of others' luxury and wealth; and although they are called the masters of the world, they do not have a clod of earth they can call their own."

Plutarch, *Life of Tiberius Gracchus*, 9.3–5 [ca. 115 CE]

But Octavius [a fellow tribune who, at the instigation of the Senate, was obstructing Tiberius' proposed land reform bill] would not relent, and so Tiberius issued an edict which prevented all office holders from conducting any public business until his proposals should either be accepted or rejected by vote.... The rich then put on clothes of mourning and went down to the forum in this pitiful and abject condition; but in secret they began to plot Tiberius' assassination, with the result that Tiberius, as everyone knew full well, wore a concealed short sword just like thugs use.

Plutarch, *Life of Tiberius Gracchus*, 10.5–7 [ca. 115 CE]

King Attalus died and Eudemus of Pergamum brought to Rome the king's will [133 BCE], in which he had made the Roman people his heir. Immediately Tiberius courted the populace by proposing a bill which provided that Attalus' legacy, when brought to Rome, should be handed over to those citizens who had received a plot of the public land, to aid them in setting up and maintaining their farms. As for the cities of Attalus' kingdom, Tiberius said that it was not the Senate's business to deliberate about them, but that he would submit a resolution concerning them directly to the people. He gave by this act more offense than ever before to the senators.

> Plutarch, *Life of Tiberius Gracchus*, 14.1–2 [ca. 115 CE]

As tribune in 123–122 BCE Gaius Gracchus continued and extended the reform program of his deceased brother Tiberius. Two weighty issues arose at this time that would prove to be of crucial importance in subsequent decades: the planting of Roman citizen colonies overseas and the question of granting Roman citizenship to the Italian allies.

Gaius Gracchus, the brother of Tiberius, who was a more gifted orator than his older brother, passed several ruinous laws during his tribunate. Among these were a law on the grain supply to the effect that grain should be sold to the common people for six and one third asses; a second law concerned the land, similar to the legislative program of his brother Tiberius...When Gaius was re-elected tribune for a second year, he passed land laws and founded several colonies in Italy and one on the site of destroyed Carthage. For this African colony he was himself appointed to the three-man board and founded the colony.

> Livy, *Summaries*, 60 [ca. 25 BCE]

Gaius proposed laws with the purpose of gratifying the populace and weakening the Senate. One of these was agrarian, and it divided the public land among the poor citizens. Another of these laws was military; it stipulated that the soldiers should be provided with clothing at public expense; that they should have nothing deducted from their pay for this; and that no one under seventeen years of age should be pressed into military service. Another law concerned the allies, and would give the Italians equal voting rights with Roman citizens. Another law related to the grain supply, lowering the market price on behalf of the poor. Yet another concerned the appointment of judges.... In his attempts to carry this law Gaius showed remarkable seriousness and zeal, and this was especially evident in the following innovation. All popular orators before him had faced the Senate house and that part of the Roman forum called the comitium*, but Gaius now set a new example by facing the other part of the forum as he addressed the people, and he continued in this fashion. By this slight change he raised large questions, and to a certain extent this act seemed to change the constitution from an aristocratic to a democratic form, since the implication of his innovation was that speakers should address themselves to the people, and not to the Senate,

> Plutarch, *Life of Gaius Gracchus*, 5.1–3 [ca. 115 CE]

Abuses of allies and provincials and their political ramifications

Abuse of provincials by Roman magistrates led to a series of ad hoc civil procedures against the offenders, with little in the way of corrective justice as a result. In 149 BCE the tribune Lucius Calpurnius Piso Frugi carried a law which established a standing court for cases of extortion.[5] Initially senators manned the juries, but the interests of the senatorial provincial governors and the businessmen who bought state contracts for tax collection in the provinces frequently were at odds. During his tribunate Gaius Gracchus transferred the composition of the courts to the equestrians (to simplify a complex problem, we may say that the equestrian class was the wealthy, non-political sector, often engaged in business; in opposition to the political class, the senatorial aristocracy). Control of the juries continued to be a contentious political issue in the decades that followed.

Spanish complaints to the Senate (171 BCE)[6]

Envoys from the two Spanish provinces were next introduced to the Senate. They complained of the greed and arrogance of Roman magistrates, and they begged the senators as suppliants that they would not allow them, their allies, to be more fouly despoiled and harassed than their enemies. Because they complained of further injustices and it was plain that money had been extorted from them, the praetor Lucius Canuleius, to whom Spain had been allotted, was given the task of assigning for each man, from whom the Spaniards were seeking to recover money, five judges of senatorial rank and to allow the Spaniards to choose advocates. The senatorial decree was read out to the Spanish envoys, who had been called to the Senate house, and they were ordered to name their advocates.

Livy, *History of Rome*, 43.2.1–5 [ca. 25 BCE]

Greek complaints to the Senate (170 BCE)

In Chalcis temples had been plundered, and Gaius Lucretius had transported the spoils in his ships to Antium; free-born people had been ushered into servitude; allied possessions had been plundered and continued to be plundered. . . . On the day of the trial the tribunes accused Gaius Lucretius before the people and proposed a fine of 1,000,000 asses. All 35 tribes voted for condemnation.

Livy, *History of Rome*, 43.7.10–11, 8.10 [ca. 25 BCE]

The criminal courts[7]

But it is most important in all public administration and service to avoid even the slightest suspicion of self-seeking. "I would," says Gaius Pontius the Samnite, "that fortune had withheld my appearance until a time when the Romans began to accept bribes, and that I had been born in those days! Then I would not be able to endure their rule." Yes, but he would have had to wait for many generations, as this plague has only recently invaded our state. And so I take delight in the fact that Pontius lived then instead of now, since he was such a powerful man! It is not yet 110 years since the enactment of Lucius Piso's bill to punish extortion; there had been no such law before. But afterwards came so many such laws, each more stringent than the other, so many men were accused and so many convicted, so horrible a war arose because of the fear of what our courts would do to still others, so frightful was the pillaging and plundering of the allies when the laws and courts were suppressed, that now we find ourselves strong not in our own strength but in others' weakness.

Cicero, *On Duties*, 2.21.75 [mid-40s BCE]

And so Gaius Sempronius Gracchus was elected as a tribune of the plebeians* for a second consecutive term [122 BCE]. After he had already bought the plebeians, so to speak, by similar political tactics, he began to woo the equestrian order, which holds a middle place in the Roman state between senators and plebeians. Gaius transferred the control of the extortion courts, which had lost all credibility because of bribery, from the senators to the equestrians. . . . The senators were exceedingly ashamed of these things, and they yielded to Gaius' law, and the people ratified it. Thus the courts were transferred from the Senate to the equestrians.

Appian, *Civil Wars*, 1.22 [ca. 160 CE]

Gaius' law curtailed the senators' powers most of all, since they alone had served as judges in criminal cases, and because of this they were formidable both to the common people and the equestrian order. Gracchus' law, however, increased the Senate's membership, which was 300, adding 300 more men from the equestrian order, and allowed the newly constituted body of 600 to serve as judges.

Plutarch, *Life of Gaius Gracchus*, 5.2–3 [ca. 115 CE]

In the following passage Tacitus reveals that the consul for 106 BCE, Q. Servilius Caepio, passed legislation that returned some sort of control of the judicial court to the Senate; it probably made provision for mixed juries of senators and equestrians.

The emperor Claudius [41–54 CE] gave over full judicial power which had so often in the past been disputed by sedition or by force – when, for example, the Sempronian laws placed the equestrian order in possession of the courts; or when the Servilian laws gave the courts back to the Senate; or when, in the times of Marius and Sulla, the question actually became the ground for hostilities.

Tacitus, *Annals*, 12.60 [ca. 115 CE]

Sulla, dictator* from 81 to 79 BCE, increased the number of senators to 600, part of the motivation for which was an extension of the system of permanent courts. The extortion court was returned to senatorial control. In his prosecution against Verres, the orator Cicero complains of the corruption of the senatorial juries as restored by Sulla.

I shall not only recall the entire story, but I shall set it out and corroborate every detail, the tale of all judicial crimes and outrages that have been perpetrated since the transfer of the courts to the Senate ten years ago. I shall instruct the Roman people how it came about that for as long as the courts were in the control of the equestrian order, nearly 50 years altogether, not the slightest suspicion rested upon one single knight, gentlemen, when serving as a judge, of taking a bribe to return a particular verdict.

Cicero, *Against Verres*, 1.13.37–8 [70 BCE]

[Caesar] restricted the right of manning the juries to the senatorial and equestrian classes, disqualifying the third group, the tribunes of the treasury.[8]

Suetonius, *Julius Caesar*, 41.2 [early second century CE]

The warlords of the Roman Republic[9]

Rome's imperial success in the second century BCE somewhat paradoxically led to profound crises for the Republic in the late second and first centuries. The senatorial aristocracy failed to respond adequately to the challenges that the acquisition of a vast empire had thrust upon it. In the 130s and 120s Tiberius and Gaius Gracchus, in the office of tribune, attempted land reforms that would have alleviated many of these problems, but the obdurate senatorial aristocrats murdered them for their efforts. The solution to socio-economic and military recruitment crises would come by another means, the rise of the great warlords. Men such as C. Marius and L. Cornelius Sulla began the process of forging the unholy alliance between charismatic general and an army loyal to him, which ultimately would destroy republican government in Rome. The greatest of the warlords were Cn. Pompeius Magnus and C. Iulius Caesar. The so-called First Triumvirate between Pompey, Caesar, and Crassus served its members' personal ambitions and undermined the collective authority of the Senate. The civil war which ultimately developed between Pompey and Caesar was in effect a struggle for personal supremacy in Rome, and Caesar's victory over Pompey in 48 BCE in effect returned Rome, after close to 500 years of republican government, to monarchical rule.

Up until this time murders, civil strife, and violence had been internal and sporadic. Afterwards the leaders of the factions attacked one another with great armies, according to the laws of war, and their own country was the prize of their contention. The beginning and origin of these struggles came about in this way right after the Social War [91–88 BCE, on which see below].

Appian, *Civil Wars*, 1.55 [ca. 160 CE]

The career of Gaius Marius (ca. 157–86 BCE)

Gaius Marius was a *novus homo*, a man without ancestors who had held the highest magistracies at Rome. He came up through the military ranks with the aid of the patronage of the powerful Metelli family. He gained unparalleled power after his heroics against the Numidian king Jugurtha (107–105 BCE) and against the Cimbri and Teutones, Germanic tribesmen (104–102 BCE); he was elected to an unprecedented number of consulships (107, 104–100, 86 BCE). Marius courted popular favor among his troops and used contacts among business elements in Rome and Africa. Either in the Jugurthine War or the Cimbric wars, Marius in effect abolished the property qualification for military service, creating a volunteer, *de facto* personal army that gave its allegiance to its commander. In this way he paved the way for the warlords who followed.

Marius' reform of the levy[10]

Gaius Marius was the first, as certain writers assert, to have enlisted those men without property into the army at the time of the wars with the Cimbri when times were most difficult for the Republic, or rather, as Sallust says, the reform took place at the time of the war against Jugurtha.

Aulus Gellius, *Attic Nights*, 16.10.14 [ca. 180 CE]

Meanwhile [during the war against Jugurtha] Marius himself enrolled soldiers, not in accordance with the property classes in the manner of the ancestors, but allowing anyone to volunteer, for the most part from those without property. According to some authorities he took this step because he did not have enough good men; others say he did it to curry favor, since these people had bestowed honor and rank upon him. It is true that for one who aspires to power the indigent man is most helpful, since he has no concern for his property, having none, and thinks anything honorable if he gets his pay.

Sallust, *Jugurthine War*, 86.2–4 [ca. 40 BCE]

Overtures to soldiery, Roman commons, and business classes

Marius was unafraid of every undertaking.... His advice and foresight distinguished him from the other officers of his rank, and he won the soldiers' affections by demonstrating his ability to live the soldier's hard life.

Plutarch, *Life of Marius*, 7.3–4 [ca. 115 CE]

Marius spared no action or statement that could win him popularity. He relaxed discipline among his soldiers in his winter quarters, and he talked about the war disdainfully and boastfully with traders and businessmen, of whom there were a great number in Utica. He said that if he were in charge of only half the army, he would have Jugurtha as prisoner within a few days. His commander [Metellus], he said, was prolonging the war on purpose, because of his extravagance and tyrannical pride, and that he delighted excessively in the exercise of power. This sort of talk strongly appealed to the traders, because the protracted war was adversely affecting their business interests, and for the greedy nothing moves quickly enough.

Sallust, *Jugurthine War*, 64.5–6 [ca. 40 BCE]

The common people at Rome believed what had been written in letters about Marius and [his commander in Africa] Metellus. The chief commander's high birth, which before this had been an honor to him, now became a reason for his unpopularity, while Marius' humble origins increased his favor. But party spirit had greater influence than the personal characters of the two men. Moreover, seditious magistrates were stirring up the emotions of the masses, charging in every assembly that Metellus had committed treason and exaggerating Marius' merits. The common people finally were so worked up that all the artisans and farmers, whose financial integrity depended on the work they did with their own hands, left their work and attended Marius, considering their own necessary labors less important than Marius' success.

Sallust, Jugurthine War, 73.3–7 [ca. 40 BCE]

The career of L. Cornelius Sulla (ca. 138–78 BCE)

L. Cornelius Sulla was of an aristocratic family that had been in obscurity. He came to prominence as a commander in the Jugurthine and Cimbric wars, and he played an important role in the war against the Italian allies. Thereafter his principal opponent was C. Marius, with his established reputation and multiple consulships. When Sulla's command against the Pontic king Mithridates VI was transferred by the tribune P. Sulpicius Rufus to Marius, Sulla marched his army on Rome and won the command by force (88 BCE). Upon his return to Rome from his eastern command, Sulla proscribed Marian supporters in a blood bath, and thereafter he exercised the powers of dictator. His reforms appear to have been intended to restore the authority of the Senate (which he enlarged from 300 to 600), and to curtail tribunician agitation. His settlement did not long survive him, but the precedents for violence and strong-arm tactics were not lost on the warlords who followed him.

After subduing Italy in this way by fire, sword, and murder, Sulla's generals went to the various cities and established garrisons at suspected locations.... Sulla himself addressed the Roman people in assembly, expatiating on his own deeds and making other threatening statements in order to instill terror. He ended his speech by saying that the changes he intended would benefit the Romans, provided that they obeyed him, but that he would spare none of his enemies, but would punish them all with the utmost severity.... After this he proscribed 40 senators and 1,600 knights. He seems to have been the first to make up a formal list of those whom he sought to punish, to offer rewards to murderers and to informers, and to threaten anyone who should protect the proscribed.... In this way Sulla became king, or tyrant, in fact, not by election, by rather by strength and force.

Appian, Civil Wars, 95, 98 [ca. 160 CE]

Aside from the proscriptions, Sulla's conduct was cause for offense. In reviving an authority that had lain dormant for 120 years, he named himself dictator. He was given immunity for all his past acts by formal decree, and for the future he was to wield the powers of life and death, the power to confiscate property, to establish colonies, to create new cities or to destroy old ones, and to remove or grant kingdoms according to his pleasure. When he sold confiscated estates seated on a raised platform, his arrogant and dictatorial manner made him more detested for his gifts than for his depredations.

Plutarch, *Life of Sulla*, 33.1–2 [ca. 115 CE]

The career of Cn. Pompeius Magnus (106–48 BCE)[11]

Cn. Pompeius Magnus represents the new type of Roman statesman of the late Republic and a progression of the warlord syndrome from the careers of Marius and Sulla. A lieutenant of Sulla's early in his career, he extorted a triumph from the aging dictator when he was not yet a member of the senatorial class (81 BCE), he gained the consulship without having gone through the cursus honorum* (70 BCE), and he obtained through tribunician proposals two extraordinary commands, against the Mediterranean pirates (by the Gabinian law of 67 BCE) and against the Pontic king Mithridates VI (by the Manilian law of 66 BCE), which gave Pompey unprecedented powers. His eastern campaign (66–62 BCE) brought him unparal- leled resources and clientage, but despite his preeminence, or perhaps because of it, he found senatorial obstruction to his schemes upon returning to Rome (61 BCE). At this juncture Pompey benefited from association with the young Caesar, who as consul in 59 BCE obtained for Pompey land grants for his veterans and ratification of his settlement of the eastern provinces. But the growth of Caesar's power in Gaul led to the estrangement of the erstwhile allies, and Pompey eventually was drawn into the command of the republican forces against Caesar. Caesar defeated Pompey's forces at Pharsalus in Thessaly (48 BCE). Pompey fled to Egypt, where he was treacherously murdered.

[W]hen some said that if Caesar should march upon Rome, they did not see any forces with which to defend it from him, with a smiling face and calm manner [Pompey] told them not to fear: "For," he said, "in whatever part of Italy I stamp upon the ground, there will spring up armies of infantry and cavalry."

Plutarch, *Life of Pompey the Great*, 57.5 [ca. 115 CE]

Pompey's eastern campaign (66–62 BCE)

Pompey, when he had accomplished what has been related, proceeded again to Pontus and after taking over the forts returned to Asia and from there to Greece and Italy. Thus he had won many battles, had brought into subjection many poten- tates and kings, some by war and some by treaty, he had colonized eight cities, had opened up many lands and sources of revenue to the Romans, and had established and organized most of the nations in the continent of Asia with their own laws and constitutions, so that even to this day they use the laws that he laid down.... He celebrated the triumph in honor of all his wars at once, including in it many trophies beautifully decked out to represent each of his achievements, even the smallest; and after them all came one huge one, decked out in costly fashion and bearing an inscription stating that it was a trophy of the inhabited world.

Cassius Dio, Roman History, 37.20.1–2, 21.2 [ca. 205 CE]

At the end of the winter Pompey distributed rewards to the army.... Then he marched to Ephesus, embarked for Italy, and hastened to Rome, having dismissed his soldiers at Brundisium to their homes, a democratic action which greatly surprised the Romans. As he approached the city he was met by successive processions, first of youths, farthest from the city, then bands of men of different ages came out as far as they severally could walk; last of all came the Senate, which was lost in wonder at his exploits, for no one had ever before vanquished so powerful an enemy, and at the same time brought so many great nations under subjection and extended the Roman rule to the Euphrates. He was awarded a triumph exceeding in brilliance any that had gone before... It occupied two successive days, and many nations were represented in the procession from Pontus, Armenia, Cappadocia, Cilicia and all Syria, besides Albanians, Heniochi, Achaeans of Scythia, and Eastern Iberians.

Appian, Mithridatic Wars, 116 [ca. 160 CE]

The career of Gaius Julius Caesar (100–44 BCE)[12]

Julius Caesar, through an extraordinary command in Gaul and Illyricum (59–50 BCE), subjugated the Transalpine Gallic peoples and created a new Roman province, thus extending the territorial extent of the Roman Empire. Caesar represents the greatest of the Roman warlords; he was perhaps the only one who realized the historical inevitability of the demise of senatorial government and the re-establishment of one-man rule at Rome. In addition to his military conquests, Caesar was important for the development of Roman imperialism in his far-sighted policy of extending Roman citizenship to the provinces of the Empire.

Of course in the matter of the constitution the right course is the same for both of us; but the constitution is not now in question. It is a struggle between two kings [Pompey and Caesar], in which defeat has overtaken the more moderate king [Pompey], the one who is more upright and honest, the one whose failure means that the very name of the Roman people must be wiped out, though if he wins the victory, he will use it after the manner and example of Sulla.

Cicero, Letters to Atticus, 10.7.1 [49 BCE]

Sincere belief in Rome's freedom died long ago, when Marius and Sulla were admitted within the walls; but now, when Pompey has been removed from the world, even the sham belief is dead.

M. Annaeus Lucanus, On the Civil War, 9.204–6 [ca. 62 CE]

Caesar's Gallic command (59 BCE)

Backed therefore by his father-in-law and son-in-law, out of all the numerous provinces he made the Gauls his choice, as the most likely to enrich him and furnish suitable material for triumphs. At first, it is true, by the bill of Vatinius he received only Cisalpine Gaul with the addition of Illyricum; but presently he was assigned Gallia Comata as well by the Senate, since the members feared that even if they should refuse it, the people would give him this also.

Suetonius, *Julius Caesar*, 22.1–2 [early second century CE]

The civil war of 49–48 BCE

In his commentaries on the civil war, Caesar argues that his hand was forced by the recalcitrance and unjust demands of Pompey and the Senate in Rome.

The demand that Caesar should leave Ariminum and return to his province while [Pompey] himself was to keep his province and legions that were not his was grossly unfair. [Pompey] desired that Caesar's legions should be disbanded while he continued to recruit soldiers. He wanted to promise that he would go to his province and not to set a time limit for his departure, in order that he not be held guilty of failing to keep his word should he still be present when Caesar's consulship expired. Finally, his refusal to give Caesar a conference and his promise that he would approach Caesar made the possibility of peace seem remote.

Caesar, *Civil Wars*, 1.11 [ca. 47 BCE]

Extension of Roman territory and Roman citizenship[13]

The foundation of Roman and allied Latin colonies secured Roman power, first in Italy, and then in the provinces. The Gracchan program had stirred up questions of the political status of the Italian allies. In the 90s BCE the issue of Roman citizenship for the Italian allies came to a head. In 91 BCE the tribune M. Livius Drusus proposed a bill for the enfranchisement of the Italians, but he was murdered in the unrest that followed, and his enfranchisement plans were scrapped by the Senate. Civil war resulted. Rome put down the insurrection, with the later rivals Marius and Sulla playing a conspicuous role against the insurrectionists, but the Italians were ultimately granted the citizenship.

Those people who possessed public lands delayed the division according to the Gracchan commission for a long time. Some of them suggested that all the Italian allies, who greatly resisted the plan, be granted Roman citizenship so that they might stop contesting the land in return for the favor. The Italians were willing to accept this, since they valued the Roman citizenship more than possession of the land. The consul and member of the three-man commission for dividing public land, Fulvius Flaccus [125 BCE], worked strenuously to bring this about, but the senators were displeased with the notion of making their subjects their equals.

Appian, Civil Wars, 1.21 [ca. 160 CE]

One of Gaius Gracchus' tribunician colleagues, Rubrius, brought in a proposal for a colony of Roman citizens upon the site of destroyed Carthage, conquered by Scipio Aemilianus, and Gaius, who obtained the task through lot, sailed off to Africa to oversee the new foundation [123 or 122 BCE].

Plutarch, Life of Gaius Gracchus, 10.2 [ca. 115 CE]

In the place where Carthage had once stood the Gracchan commissioners marked out the city for the colony (Junonia). . . . They assigned 6,000 colonists, larger than the number fixed by law, so that they might further ingratiate themselves with the populace. They invited the 6,000 from the whole of Italy upon their return from Africa.

Appian, Civil Wars, 1.24 [ca. 160 CE]

After the failure of the Gracchani, Marcus Livius Drusus, a man of exalted birth, made a promise to the Italians, who urged him on, that he would propose a bill that would grant them Roman citizenship. The Italians especially wanted this because with this they would become rulers of empire rather than subjects. In order to win plebeian support for this measure he led out to Italy and Sicily several colonies that had been voted on earlier, but not yet founded.

Appian, Civil Wars, 1.35 [ca. 160 CE]

The tribune of the plebeians, Marcus Livius Drusus, had worked in the interests of the Senate. In order to bring greater resources to this cause, he aroused the allies and the Italians with the hope of Roman citizenship. With the Italians' help he forced through laws on land and grain distributions, and in addition he pushed through a law on the courts, so that they be shared equally by senators and knights.

Livy, Summaries, 71 [ca. 25 BCE]

The Social War (91–88 BCE)

When the Italian peoples learned about the murder of Livius Drusus and of the allegations for which their other supporters had been banished from Rome, they decided that they could no longer tolerate the fact that those men who were working for their political advancement should suffer such outrages, and since they saw no other avenue for obtaining the Roman citizenship, they decided upon open rebellion, and they endeavored to make war against the Romans with all their strength. They secretly sent envoys to one another, formed a league, and exchanged hostages as pledges of their good faith.

Appian, Civil Wars, 1.38 [ca. 160 CE]

The rebellion erupted when all the neighboring peoples declared war simultaneously, the Marsi, the Paeligni, the Vestini, the Marrucini; the Picentines followed, along with the Frentani, the Hirpini, the Pompeiians, the Venusini, the Apulians, the Lucanians, and the Samnites. These had been enemies of Rome long before. . . . Ambassadors went to Rome complaining that although they had cooperated with the Romans in all ways in erecting their dominion, the Romans had been unwilling to admit their helpers to citizenship. The Senate sternly answered that they could send ambassadors only if they repented for their actions. The Italians, in despair of any way out, continued to mobilize.

Appian, *Civil Wars*, 1.39 [ca. 160 CE]

The lex Iulia of 90 BCE: *enfranchisement of the Italians* [14]

This was the course of events in the Social War, which had raged violently up to this point, until all Italy came into the Roman state, except for the Lucanians and Samnites, who later seem to have gained their objective, too. The allies were enrolled in separate tribes of their own, like those who had been granted citizenship earlier, in order that they might not, by being mixed up with the older citizens, vote them down in elections by their strength of numbers.

Appian, *Civil Wars*, 1.49 [ca. 160 CE]

The Julian law came last of all, according to which Roman citizenship was offered to the allies and Latins provided that those states which had not "given consent" should not have the citizenship. . . . Whenever the Roman people have made any law, and when this law is of a kind which is likely to give to certain states, whether bound to us by treaty or free, the option of deciding for themselves, with reference to their own needs and concerns, not ours, what legal principle they want to adopt, then we certainly should ask whether these states have or have not "given consent."

Cicero, *In Defense of Balbus*, 21 [56 BCE]

Extension of Roman colonies overseas under Caesar and Augustus [15]

The following is an excerpt from Julius Caesar's charter for the Roman colony of Genetiva Julia at Urso (modern Osuna, Spain), dated to 44 BCE. This passage relays detailed measures that attempt to prevent bribery and electoral corruption in town politics.

No candidate in the colony Genetiva . . . is to provide banquets for the purpose of winning a magistracy, or invite anyone to dinner, or hold a banquet, or knowingly and with wrongful intention arrange for someone else to hold a banquet, or invite anyone to dinner for the sake of his candidacy, except that the candidate himself, in the year in which he is seeking a magistracy, may invite up to nine men a day, and may hold a banquet, if he so wishes. . . . If anyone has acted against these regulations, he will be condemned to pay 5,000 sesterces* to the colonists of Genetiva Julia.

Corpus Inscriptionum Latinarum, vol. 1, 2nd edn., no. 594, section 132 [44 BCE]

In his autobiographical account of his political career and services to the Roman people, the emperor Augustus records his cash outlay for the foundation of Roman colonies in Italy and in the provinces.

For lands which I assigned to my soldiers in my fourth consulship [30 BCE] I paid money to the municipal towns; and afterwards in the consulships of Marcus Crassus and Gnaeus Lentulus the augur [30 and 4 BCE]. This sum was about 600,000,000 sesterces which I paid for lands in Italy, and about 260,000,000 sesterces which I paid for lands in the provinces. Of all those who established soldier colonies in Italy or in the provinces, I was the first and only one to do this within living memory.

Augustus, *Accomplishments* (*Res Gestae Divi Augusti*), 16 [14 CE]

The year 212 CE marked the culmination of the extension of Roman citizenship. In that year the emperor Caracalla granted blanket citizenship to the free inhabitants of the Empire by an edict known as the *constitutio* *Antoniniana*. Many historians take a cynical view of Caracalla's measure, viewing it as a device to simplify and extend tax collection.

The Emperor Caesar Marcus Aurelius Severus Antoninus Augustus [Caracalla] decrees . . . I grant the Roman citizenship to all my subjects throughout the world except for those who have surrendered to the Roman people, and local citizenship will remain intact. For it is just that the multitude should not only assist in carrying all burdens but should now also be included in my victory.

Giessen Papyrus, no. 40, column 1 [ca. 212 CE]

The true reason that [Caracalla] made everyone in the empire into Roman citizens was this: he pretended to be honoring them, but his real intention was to increase his income by this means, since [as non-Roman citizen inhabitants of the empire] aliens did not have to pay most of the taxes.

Cassius Dio, *Roman History*, 77.9 [ca. 205 CE]

Economic consequences of Empire

Roman wars financed by defeated foes

Supposing that Hiero II would be of great service to them, the Romans readily accepted his friendly overtures. Having made a treaty by which the king bound himself to give up his prisoners to the Romans without ransom [263 BCE], and in addition to this to pay them a hundred talents*, the Romans from that point on treated the Syracusans as allies and friends.

Polybius, *Histories*, 1.16.9–10 [ca. 150 BCE]

Rome and Carthage

"There shall be friendship between Carthaginians and Romans on the following terms if approved by the Roman people. The Carthaginians to evacuate the whole of Sicily and not to make war on Hiero II or bear arms against the Syracusans or their allies. The Carthaginians to give up to the Romans all prisoners without ransom. The Carthaginians to pay to the Romans by installments in 20 years 2,200 Euboean talents*."...[The ten commissioners made] only slight modifications rendering them more severe for Carthage: they reduced the term for payment by half, added 1,000 talents to the indemnity, and demanded the evacuation by Carthage of all islands lying between Sicily and Italy [241 BCE].

Polybius, *Histories*, 1.62.8–63.3 [ca. 150 BCE]

Roman ambassadors were also sent to King Pineus in Illyria [217 BCE], to demand a tribute that was overdue, or in the event that the king sought an extension, to take hostages.[16] So far were the Romans, although burdened by a great war, from permitting any of their concerns to escape them, in however a remote part of the world it lay.

Livy, *History of Rome*, 22.33.5–7 [ca. 25 BCE]

Scipio Africanus' terms for defeated Carthage (202 BCE)

Reparation was to be made to Rome for all unjust actions during the armistice....The Carthaginians were to supply the Roman army with sufficient grain for three months and pay the soldiers until they received word from the Romans regarding the treaty; they were to contribute 10,000 talents in 50 years, paying 200 Euboic talents every year.

Polybius, *Histories*, 15.18.1–8 [ca. 150 BCE]

Rome and the Greek world

A few days later the commissioners arrived from Rome [196 BCE], and with their approval peace was granted to [the Macedonian king] Philip [V] on these terms: that all the Greek cities in Europe or in Asia should enjoy their liberty and laws...that [Philip] should pay to the Roman people an indemnity of 1,000 talents, half at once and half in ten annual installments. Valerius Antias states that a tribute of 4,000 pounds of silver annually for ten years was imposed on the king; Claudius says that the indemnity was 4,200 pounds annually for 30 years and 20,000 pounds at once.[17]

Livy, *History of Rome*, 33.30.1–9 [ca. 25 BCE]

Quinctius [Flamininus] then summoned only his lieutenants and the tribunes of the soldiers, and wrote down the terms on which peace should be made with [Nabis, Spartan] tyrant [195 BCE]...that he should give five hostages that these conditions should be observed, such as were satisfactory to the Roman commander, and among them his son, and should pay 100 talents each year for eight years.[18]

Livy, *History of Rome*, 34.35.1–11 [ca. 25 BCE]

Marcus [Fulvius Nobilior] next agreed with the Aetolians to make peace on the following conditions [189 BCE]. They were to pay 200 Euboic talents at once and 300 more in six years in yearly installments of 50; they were to restore to the Romans in six months without ransom the prisoners and deserters who were in their hands; they were not to keep in their confederation or to accept into it any of the cities which after the crossing of Lucius Cornelius Scipio [190 BCE] had been taken by the Romans or had entered into alliance with them; the whole of the island Cephallenia was to be excluded from this treaty.

Polybius, *Histories*, 21.30.1–5 [ca. 150 BCE]

The terms in detail were as follows: "There shall be friendship between Antiochus [III, king of Syria] and the Romans for all time if he fulfills the conditions of the treaty [lengthy conditions and terms follow].... Antiochus shall pay to the Romans 12,000 talents of the best Attic money in 12 years, paying 1,000 talents a year, the talent not to weigh less than 80 Roman pounds, and 540,000 modii* of grain."

Polybius, *Histories*, 21.43.1–20 [ca. 150 BCE][19]

The Senate resolved that the Macedonians should pay half the taxes which they were accustomed to pay to their kings to the Roman people [167 BCE]. A similar mandate was given to the Illyrians. The individual arrangements were left to the discretion of the generals and commissioners themselves; the present plan was intended to lay firmer foundations for planning.

Livy, *History of Rome*, 45.18.7–8 [ca. 25 BCE]

Resources of the Empire

Now Judas heard of the fame of the Romans, that they were very strong and were well disposed toward all who made an alliance with them, that they pledged friendship to those who came to them, and that they were very strong. He had been told of their wars and of the brave deeds that they were doing among the Gauls, how they had defeated them and forced them to pay tribute, and what they had done in the land of Spain to get control of the silver and gold mines there, and how they had gained control of the whole region by their planning and patience, even though the place was far distant from them.

1 Macc. 8.1–4 [after mid-second century BCE]

The Spanish mines (195 BCE)

Having restored order in the province, [Cato the Elder] arranged for the collection of large revenues from the iron and silver mines, and as a result of the regulations made at that time the wealth of the province increased every day. By reason of these achievements in Spain the senators decreed a thanksgiving for three days.

Livy, *History of Rome*, 34.21.7–8 [ca. 25 BCE]

Polybius, in mentioning the silver mines of New Carthage [in Spain], says that they are very large; that they are distant from the city about 20 stadia* and embrace an area of 400 stadia in circuit; and that 40,000 workmen stay there, who (in his day) brought into the Roman treasury a daily revenue of 25,000 drachmae[*].

Strabo, Geography, 3.2.10 (C 148) [ca. 15 BCE][20]

Much later the Spaniards understood the peculiar qualities of silver, and they struck notable mines, receiving a huge income from working the veins of the most excellent silver in the world.... These mines are incredible in their deposits of copper, silver, and gold. Unskilled laborers have been known to take out a Euboic talent in three days' time, since the ore is filled with solid silver dust which shines forth from it.

Diodorus of Sicily, Universal History, 5.36.1–2 [ca. 30 BCE]

Inscriptions show that whereas in the past the proceeds to the state treasury from taxation were some 50,000,000 drachmae, Pompey's additions to the empire (60s BCE) were now bringing in 85,000,000; and that he was adding to the state treasury in coined money and gold and silver plate 20,000 talents, and this apart from the money he had given to his soldiers, each of whom had received at least 15,000 drachmae[*].

Plutarch, Life of Pompey the Great, 45.3–4 [ca. 115 CE]

The state of the Treasury[21]

The gold contained in the national treasury at Rome in the consulship of Sextus Julius and Lucius Aurelius [157 BCE]... amounted to 17,410 lbs, the amount of silver was 22,070 lbs, and in specie there was 6,135,400 sesterces; in the consulship of Sextus Julius and Lucius Marcius [91 BCE]... there was... [lacuna] lbs of gold and 1,620,831 lbs of silver. Gaius Julius Caesar, on first entering Rome during the civil war that bears his name [49 BCE], drew from the treasury 15,000 gold ingots, 30,000 silver ingots, and 30,000,000 sesterces in coin; at no other period was the state more wealthy.

Pliny the Elder, Natural History, 33.55–6 [ca. 75 CE]

Remission of the citizen tax in Italy

People have added an unbounded popularity with the common people to the exploits of Aemilius Paullus in Macedonia, because he brought so much money into the state treasury that the people no longer needed to pay special taxes until the times of Hirtius and Pansa, who were consuls during the first war between Marc Antony and Octavius Caesar [43 BCE].

Plutarch, Life of Aemilius Paullus, 38.1–2 [ca. 115 CE]

Aemilius Paullus also after the defeat of King Perseus [168 BCE] paid in to the treasury from the booty won in Macedonia 300 million sesterces; and from that date onward the Roman nation left off paying the citizens' property tax.

Pliny the Elder, Natural History, 33.56 [ca. 75 CE]

After the defeat of King Perseus [168 BCE] Paullus [L. Aemilius Paullus] satiated the ancient hereditary poverty of our city with the wealth of Macedonia so that the Roman people then for the first time freed itself from the burden of paying war-tax.

Valerius Maximus, *Memorable Deeds and Sayings*, 4.3.8 [ca. 30 CE]

Wealthy Roman aristocrats as art collectors

As you have advised, I have acquired the 20,400 sesterces for Lucius Cincius for the statues of Megarian marble. I have already fallen in love with those Pentelic marble statues of Hermes with bronze heads, which you wrote about. Please then send these and anything else that you think suitable for my place and for my enthusiasm for such things, and your own taste – send as many as soon as you can – especially those which you intend for the gymnasium and colonnade.

Cicero, *Letters to Atticus*, 1.8 [67 BCE]

I am impatiently waiting for the statues of Megarian marble and those of Hermes, the ones you mentioned in your letter. Please don't hesitate to send anything else of the kind that you may have, as long as it is suitable for my Academy. My bank account can handle it. This is my little vice; and I especially want things that are fit for the gymnasium. Lentulus promises his ships.

Cicero, *Letters to Atticus*, 1.9 [67 BCE]

Asinius Pollio, as he was an avid collector, was concerned that his art collection attract visitors. In his collection are *Centaurs Carrying the Nymphs* by Arcesilaus, *Muses of Helicon* by Cleomenes, *Oceanus and Jupiter* by Heniochus, *Nymphs of the Appian Water* by Stephanus, the double busts of Hermes and Eros by Tauriscus (the native of Tralles, not the celebrated worker of metal and ivory), *Jupiter the Patron of Strangers* by Papylus, Praxiteles' student, and Apollonius and Tauriscus' composition from Rhodes, that is *Zethus and Amphion*, and then Dirce and the bull with its rope, all carved from the same block of marble.

Pliny the Elder, *Natural History*, 36.33–5 [ca. 75 CE]

Among Euphranor's contemporaries was Cydias. The orator Hortensius paid 144,000 sesterces for Cydias' picture of the Argonauts, and he made a shrine to house it at his villa at Tusculum.

Pliny the Elder, *Natural History*, 35.130 [ca. 75 CE]

Roman and Italian businessmen and Roman war making

In the course of the second century BCE enterprising Romans of the non-senatorial class became increasingly wealthy through commercial activities which senators had considered to be beneath their dignity. This "commercial class" thrived on state contracts for public works and tax collection in the provinces. Its political influence, though indirect, grew steadily.[22]

Publicani* are those who . . . deal with the public property of the Roman people, for it is from this that they get their name.

> Ulpian, *Digest*, 39.4.1.1 [ca. 160 CE]

Throughout Italy there are a vast number of contracts; these the censors* give out for construction and maintenance of public buildings, and in addition duties on many other things are farmed out: navigable rivers, harbors, gardens, mines, lands, in short everything that forms a part of Roman power. The people undertake all these things, and we could almost say that everyone has an interest in these contracts and the work they bring. Certain people actually purchase the contracts from the censors, others are their partners, some stand surety for them, while others pledge their own estates for this purpose.

> Polybius, *Histories*, 6.17.2–5 [ca. 150 BCE]

Merchants and profiteers follow the Roman army

[P. Decius Mus] gathered his soldiers together and spoke: "Will this one victory or these spoils satisfy you? Will your expectations not equal your courage? All Samnite cities and the riches left behind in them belong to you, since, after defeating their legions in so many battles, you have finally thrown them out of their country. Sell these prizes and with hope of gain lure the traders on to follow your column" [296 BCE].

> Livy, *History of Rome*, 10.17.4–6 [ca. 25 BCE]

Private enterprise during the Hannibalic War (215 BCE)

In dire financial straits after crushing defeats at Trasimene (217 BCE) and Cannae (216 BCE), the Senate was in a compromised position for provisioning the army, and the business class filled the need, but clearly had the upper hand in negotiating state contracts.

Three companies of 19 men appeared in person to take the state contracts on the appointed day. They had two demands: exemption from military service for as long as they were under state contract, and that the state should underwrite their cargoes, assuming liability for any damages caused by the violence of enemies and storms. They contracted when these demands were met, and the state was carried on by private funds.

> Livy, *History of Rome*, 23.45.1–3 [ca. 25 BCE]

A publican swindle in the Hannibalic War (212 BCE)

The conduct of M. Postumius of Pyrgi interfered with the consular levy, and this almost caused a serious insurrection. This man was a tax farmer (*publicanus*), and for many years he had no rival in dishonesty and greed in the state . . . Because the Roman state had assumed liability for damages sustained from violent storms in cases of army shipments, these men fraudulently reported imaginary shipwrecks, and they caused by their own trickery even those which were correctly reported. They would put small cargoes of cheap materials in old, battered vessels and sink them at sea...This criminal behavior was reported to M. Aemilius, the praetor*, and he brought it to the attention of the Senate, but there was no senatorial decree, because the senators did not want to offend the tax farmers as a class at such a time of crisis.

Livy, *History of Rome*, 25.3.8–13 [ca. 25 BCE]

The whole of Asia was...afflicted by the accustomed ways of the Roman usurers and tax collectors [71 BCE]. Lucullus later drove these people off, harpies that they were, snatching up the people's sustenance; but then he tried merely, by reprimanding them, to make them more moderate in their exactions, and he worked to stop the disturbances in the towns, as there were hardly any that were in a peaceful condition.

Plutarch, *Life of Lucullus*, 7.5–6 [ca. 115 CE]

Do you think that a tax collector, being in this way at liberty to take from the farmers as much grain as he pleased, might now and again demand a little more than what was due to him? Would you or would you not expect this to happen, remembering that it could well happen through inadvertence as well as through greed? I say it was bound to happen, again and again. I can assure you, indeed, that every one of the tax collectors took away more, and by a great margin, than his 10 percent.

Cicero, *Against Verres*, 2.3.12 [70 BCE]

Gaul is crammed full with businessmen, full of Roman citizens. No one of the Gauls wages any business without a Roman citizen; in Gaul no debts are called in without the account books of Roman citizens.

Cicero, *In Defense of Fonteius*, 11 [69 BCE]

My dear friends, the Roman equestrians are sending me letters every day from Asia. They are concerned about the great sums of money they have invested in farming taxes for your revenues. Because of our close connection they have apprised me of the threats to the public interest and the great danger to their own personal fortunes.

Cicero, *On the Manilian Law* [66 BCE]

The equestrians have now come along with a really almost insupportable fantasy, which I have not only put up with but have even supported with my oratorical skills. The tax farmers who bought up the contract for the province of Asia from the censors have complained that in their zeal they made too high a bid, and now they want it canceled.... This request was disgraceful, a confession of recklessness. But if I turned them down altogether there would have been the danger of a complete break between the equestrian and senatorial classes.

Cicero, *Letters to Atticus*, 1.17.9 [61 BCE][23]

Now hear about the people of Salamis in Cyprus, which I see has come as a surprise for you, just as it did for me. I don't recall ever hearing [Brutus] say the money was his. Indeed I remember his memorandum stating that the Salaminians owe money to my friends M. Scaptius and P. Matinius. He recommends them to me, adding as an inducement that he has pledged surety of a large amount for them. I had made

arrangements for the debtors to pay with a 1 percent interest rate per month for...
years, the interest to be added to the principal annually. Scaptius however demanded
4 percent per month....if Brutus will think that I should have imposed an interest
rate of 4 percent when I had recognized 1 percent throughout the province and
stated this in my edict to the satisfaction of the harshest usurers...I will have to be
sorry for displeasing him, but sorrier by far to discover that he is not the man I seek.

Cicero, Letters to Atticus, 6.1.5–6 [50 BCE][24]

The Athenians...used actually to take oaths that all lands which produced olives or
grain were their own. The Gauls think it disgraceful to grow grain by manual labor;
and consequently they go forth armed and reap other men's fields. We ourselves,
indeed, the most just of men, who forbid the races beyond the Alps to plant the olive
or the vine, so that our own olive groves and vineyards may be the more valuable, are
said to act with prudence in doing so, but not with justice; so that you can easily
understand that wisdom and equity do not agree. Indeed, Lycurgus, famed as the
author of excellent [Spartan] laws and a most equitable system of justice, provided
that the lands of the rich should be cultivated by the poor as if the latter were slaves.

Cicero, On the Republic, 3.9.16 [ca. 55 BCE]

Gabinius after restoring [the Egyptian king Ptolemy] sent no word home about his
actions, so that he might not be the first to announce his own crimes [55 BCE]. But
such enormities could not be hidden, and the people immediately learned about
them. The Syrians complained loudly against him, especially because they had been
outraged by pirates when he was gone, and the tax collectors, as they were not able to
collect their taxes because of the marauders' depredations, found that their debts
were becoming enormous.

Cassius Dio, Roman History, 39.591–2 [ca. 205 CE]

When the tax collectors asked for financial relief, [Caesar] relieved them of a third
part of their obligation, and he straightforwardly warned them that when they
contracted for the taxes in the future, they should be careful not to bid too recklessly
[59 BCE].

Suetonius, Julius Caesar, 20.3 [early second century CE]

The Senate voted to stop leasing the Macedonian mines [167 BCE], which brought in
enormous revenues, and rural estates, for these could not be farmed without a
publican, and where there was a publican, there either the state's ownership lapsed,
or the allied peoples' freedom was extinguished.

Livy, History of Rome, 45.18.2–4[25]

And as Jesus sat down to dinner in the house, many tax collectors and sinners came
and were sitting with him and his disciples. When the Pharisees saw this, they said to
his disciples, "Why does your teacher eat with tax collectors and sinners?" But when
he heard this, he said, "Those who are well have no need of a physician, but those
who are sick. Go and learn what this means, 'I desire mercy, not sacrifice.' For I have
come to call not the righteous but sinners."

Matthew 2.1–13 [ca. 85 CE][26]

Social consequences of Empire

The following passage, regardless of its historicity, provides a fine illustration of the impact of Roman imperial success on traditional Roman ways of life. The passage purports to relay the plight of a Roman general; the situation of the rank-and-file soldier on long-term service with a small farmstead in Italy would have been much more dire.

Atilius Regulus (consul in 250 BCE) . . . learned that his [African] command had been extended for another year. He wrote to the consuls that the overseer on his seven-iugera* farm in Pupinia had died and that a worker had left after having taken the farm equipment. He therefore requested that his successor be sent out, so that his land not be deserted and his wife and children left in poverty.

> Valerius Maximus, *Memorable Deeds and Sayings*, 4.4.6 [ca. 30 CE]

As tribunes the brothers Tiberius (133 BCE) and Gaius Gracchus (123–122 BCE) made the most comprehensive attempt to redress the displacement and impoverishment of the small landholder in Italy. The wars of conquest led to profound socio-economic dislocations in Roman society: the enriched senatorial aristocracy created large private estates by appropriating public land or ager publicus*, which they could afford to work with the mass importation of slave labor; hard-pressed small landholders returned from war to neglected, dilapidated homesteads and gravitated to towns and cities, where they swelled the impover-ished urban sector; and long-term service abroad became unattractive. Military service in Spain was particularly dangerous and unpopular in the second century BCE. In 151 and 138 BCE tribunes actually incarcerated the consuls who were attempting to levy legions.[27] Since many males in the towns and cities now fell below the requisite property qualification for military service, military recruitment crises arose. The Gracchi attempted to redress the problem by limiting the amount of public land which could be held by individuals, thereby freeing up land for redistribution to those who were landless.[28]

Tiberius' brother Gaius states in a certain writing that when Tiberius was journeying through Tuscany on his way to Numantia and observed the depopulation of the countryside, and that those who worked its soil or tended its flocks were imported barbarian slaves, he then first came upon the public policy which was to be the cause of great evils for the two brothers.

> Plutarch, *Life of Tiberius Gracchus*, 8.7 [ca. 115 CE]

At the same time the rich increased their wealth through their slaves' offspring, who increased because they were exempt from military service. In this way certain powerful men became exceedingly rich and the slave class multiplied throughout Italy, while the free Italians dwindled in numbers and in strength, as they were oppressed by poverty, taxes, and military service. And if they had any relief from these evils, they passed their time idly, since the rich held the land, and employed slaves instead of free men as workers. . . . Tiberius Sempronius Gracchus, of illustrious birth and eager to make a name for himself, delivered an eloquent oration in the office of tribune in which he bemoaned the plight of the Italians, a people valiant in war and related to the Romans, who were falling into abject poverty and decimation without any hope for improvement.... After speaking in this way he again brought forward the law which provided that no one should hold more than 500 iugera of the public land. But he added a provision that the sons of the occupants might each hold half that amount, and that the rest should be divided among the poor by three annually elected commissioners.

Appian, Civil Wars, 1.7–8 [ca. 160 CE]

The Romans sold off part of the neighboring land they had conquered, but part of it they made into common land (*ager publicus*), and this they assigned to the poor for a nominal rent into the state treasury. After the rich started offering larger rents and in this way drove out the poor, a law was passed which forbade the holding by one person of more than 500 iugera. For a time this law placed a check on the rapaciousness of the wealthy, and it was an aid to the poor, who stayed in their places on rented land and occupied the lots they had been initially assigned. But in time the neighboring rich men, by the contrivance of fictitious people, transferred these rentals to themselves, and finally they held the land themselves openly in their own names. At that point the poor, thrown off their land, no longer displayed any zeal for military service, and they failed to rear their children, so that before long all of Italy was conscious of the paucity of the free-born, and was glutted with hordes of foreign-born slaves, through whom the rich worked their great estates, from which they had driven off the free citizens.... Tiberius Gracchus, once elected tribune of the plebeians, attempted to rectify these problems.

Plutarch, Life of Tiberius Gracchus, 8.1–3 [ca. 115 CE]

Not long after Gaius Gracchus' death [121 BCE] legislation was enacted allowing landholders to sell off the land which had caused so much strife. This Tiberius Gracchus' law forbade. Immediately the wealthy began buying up the plots of the poor, or they found reasons for seizing them forcibly. As a consequence the plight of the poor became worse than before, until the tribune Spurius Thorius brought forth legislation which discontinued the land redistributions, stating that the land should belong to the current possessors who would pay rent to the state for it, and that these revenues should be distributed. This distribution was a sop to the poor, but it did not help to increase population. In these ways the Gracchan laws – most excellent and beneficial had they been carried out – were once and for all frustrated. Shortly thereafter the rental itself was abolished by the action of another tribune.[29] The plebeians in this way lost everything, and a further diminution in population resulted, both of citizens and of soldiers, and there was also a decline in revenue from the land and land distributions, and the allotments themselves.

Appian, Civil Wars, 1.27 [ca. 160 CE]

The large estates (*latifundia*) have ruined Italy and are now ruining the provinces – six magnates were holding half Africa when the emperor Nero had them put to death.[30]

Pliny the Elder, Natural History, 18.35 [ca. 75 CE]

Attempt to retard immigration and the increase of the citizen-body in Rome (177 BCE)

Then Gaius Claudius proposed a law regarding the allies with the Senate's authorization, and he issued an edict that all allies of the Latin confederation, if they or their ancestors had been registered among the Latin allies of the confederation during the censorship of Marcus Claudius and Titus Quinctius [189 BCE] or thereafter, should all return to their own states before the beginning of November. Lucius Mummius the praetor* was given the task of investigating those who should not comply with the law. The Senate added a decree that a dictator*, consul*, interrex*, censor*, or praetor*, who was then in office and those who should come later, before whom a slave had been brought for manumission, should require an oath that the manumitter was not freeing him for the purpose of changing his citizenship. If the oath was not taken, the manumission was to be disallowed. These were precautions for the future, and orders were issued under the edict of the consul Gaius Claudius [for the return of the allies to their homes].

Livy, *History of Rome*, 41.9.9–12 [ca. 25 BCE]

State subsidizes grain shipments to Rome[31]

Grain was extremely inexpensive in this year (200 BCE). A great quantity was shipped in from Africa. The curule aediles* Marcus Claudius Marcellus and Sextus Aelius Paetus distributed the grain to the Roman people at the price of two asses per modius.

Livy, *History of Rome*, 31.50.1 [ca. 25 BCE]

Slave labor: war captives, mass enslavement, slave breeding[32]

After a siege of six months [262/1 BCE] the Romans became masters of Agrigentum in the manner described and carried off all the slaves, to the number of more than 25,000.

Diodorus of Sicily, *Universal History*, 23.9.1 [ca. 30 BCE]

[M. Popillius Laenas] disarmed them all [10,000 Ligurian Statelliates], destroyed their town, and sold them off into slavery with all their property.... The Senate considered this an outrage, because these people alone had not made war against the Romans, and even now had been attacked even though they were not at war, after having given themselves over to the good faith of the Romans [173 BCE].

Livy, *History of Rome*, 42.8.4–5 [ca. 25 BCE]

Just as [the people of Chalcis] considered that, rather than depart from their loyalty, they should suffer everything, even more grievous injuries than those they were now suffering, so also, as far as Lucretius and Hortensius were concerned, they were aware that it would have been safer to bar their gates than to receive those Romans into their city [171/0 BCE]. Those cities which had shut them out – Emathia, Amphipolis, Maronea, Aenus – were unharmed. In Chalcis, temples had been stripped of all their adornments, and the loot of these profanations Gaius Lucretius had transported in his ships to Antium; free persons had been rushed away into slavery; the possessions of allies of the Roman people had been plundered and daily were being plundered.

Livy, *History of Rome*, 43.7.9–11 [ca. 25 BCE]

Aemilius Paullus in Epirus (167 BCE)

All the gold and silver was gathered together early in the day, and then the rank-and-file were unleashed to plunder the towns at the fourth hour of the day. The haul was so great that each cavalryman received 400 denarii; each infantryman received 200. One hundred and fifty thousand people were taken away into slavery. The plundered communities numbered about 70; their walls were destroyed. All the war booty was sold off, and this was the source of the amounts given to the soldiers which I have recorded above.

Livy, *History of Rome*, 45.34.4–6 [ca. 25 BCE]

During Marius' Cimbric campaign [104 BCE] the Senate gave him permission to seek military assistance from overseas peoples friendly to Rome. Marius sent a request to King Nicomedes of Bithynia. The king answered the request by stating that most of the Bithynians were now in slavery in a Roman province, having been seized by the tax farmers.

Diodorus of Sicily, *Universal History*, 36.3.1 [ca. 30 BCE]

Let me continue discussing the mines. The slaves who are put to work in them produce an unbelievable amount of wealth for their masters, but they themselves wear out their bodies digging in the earth day and night, dying in droves because of the exceptional hardships they endure. No break or rest is given to them in their work, but driven on by blows of their overseers to endure the severity of their lot, they throw away their lives in a wretched way, although some of them who can endure it, because of their bodily strength and their strong spirit, manage to live a long time. Indeed they desire death more than life, because of the magnitude of their hardships.

Diodorus of Sicily, *Universal History*, 5.38. 1–2 [ca. 30 BCE]

Although he did not campaign in Gaul for a full ten years, during his time there [Caesar] took by force 800 cities, subjected 300 nations, and fought set-piece battles at various times with 3,000,000 men, of whom he killed 1,000,000 in actual fighting; the rest he took off into slavery.

Plutarch, *Life of Caesar*, 15.5 [ca. 115 CE]

In view of the [Frisians'] narrow resources, Drusus had imposed on them a moderate tribute, consisting in a payment of ox-hides for military purposes. No one had given attention to their firmness or size, until Olennius, a leading centurion appointed to the Frisian governorship selected the hide of the aurochs [an extinct European ox] as the standard [28 CE]. The demand was burdensome enough to any people, but it was less endurable in Germany, where the forests teem with huge animals, but the domesticated herds are of moderate size. First their cattle only, next their lands, finally the persons of their wives and children, were handed over into slavery.

Tacitus, *Annals*, 4.72 [ca. 115 CE]

Vernae, or home-bred slaves

In fact, I now and then avenge those who have just cause for grievance, as well as punish those who incite the slaves to revolt, or who slander their taskmasters; and, on the other hand, I reward those who conduct themselves with energy and diligence. To women, too, who are unusually prolific, and who ought to be rewarded for the bearing of a certain number of offspring, I have granted exemption from work and sometimes even freedom after they had reared many children. For to a mother of three sons exemption from work was granted; to a mother of more her freedom as well.

Columella, *On Farming*, 1.8.18–19 [ca. 50 CE]

Slave rebellions

In the consulship of Quintus Fabius and Aemilius[33] they made an expedition to Volsinii to secure the freedom of its citizens; for they were under a treaty of obligation to them. The Volsinii were the most ancient of the Etruscan people. They had acquired power and constructed a well-fortified citadel, and they lived by a just constitution. As a result, when they were once involved with war against Rome, they held out for a long time. After they had been conquered, however, they fell into slothful inertia, they left the management of the city to their domestic slaves, and they used these slaves to carry out their military campaigns. Finally they encouraged them to such an extent that the slaves grew in power and ambition, and they felt that they had a right to their freedom. Indeed, they eventually obtained this through their own efforts. After that they became accustomed to wed their mistresses, to succeed their masters, to be enrolled in the senate, to hold offices, to hold all authority. Furthermore, they were not hesitant to repay their masters for any insults they had received. Consequently the old citizens, not being able to endure them, and yet having no power of their own to punish them, secretly despatched envoys to Rome.

John Zonaras, *Epitome*, 8.7 [twelfth century CE]

A slave insurrection made Etruria into what looked like a battlefield [196 BCE]. The praetor Manius Acilius Glabrio ... was sent out with two of the city legions to look into the matter and restore order. He destroyed some of the insurrectionists who formed a body of opposition. Many of these he killed; many he took prisoner. Some of the instigators of the revolt he crucified; others he handed back to their masters.

Livy, *History of Rome*, 33.36.1–3 [ca. 25 BCE]

The great slave rebellions [34]

There were three major slave rebellions in the history of the Roman Republic. Two occurred in Sicily in the second century BCE (135–132, 104–100 BCE). These were risings of agricultural slaves, slave pastoralists and herders, led by charismatic figures. The Sicilian rebellions gained massive followings, and Roman authorities had difficulty in restoring order. The most famous slave revolt against Rome was the uprising led by the fugitive gladiator Spartacus (73–71 BCE). Spartacus' band defeated several Roman armies before being crushed by Marcus Crassus, with the assistance of Pompey.

The First Sicilian Slave War (135–132 BCE)

The praetor L. Hypsaeus was in command of the Roman forces. He arrived from Rome with 8,000 troops recruited in Sicily under his command. When the two sides confronted each other in battle, however, the rebels were victorious. Their numbers by this time had reached 20,000. But not long afterward their numbers swelled to 200,000. As a result they were victorious in many battles against the Roman forces; only occasionally did they come out the loser. When the news from Sicily spread, a slave revolt involving 150 broke out in Rome. There was another one involving about 1,000 insurgents in Attica; another took place at Delos; and yet more broke out in many other places. In these instances relief was swift and the punishment severe, so that the men in charge in the localities quickly put down these risings. But in Sicily the evils grew in scale. The rebellious slaves besieged and captured whole cities along with their inhabitants. The rebels completely destroyed many armies.

Diodorus of Sicily, *Universal History*, 34/5.2.18–19 [ca. 30 BCE]

The Second Sicilian Slave War (104–100 BCE)

[Manius] Aquillius [was consul] for the first time [101 BCE]. He was sent to Sicily to put down the rebels, and he destroyed them in a brilliantly fought battle, largely because of his personal bravery. He fought single-handedly with the king of the slave rebels, Athenion, and killed him in heroic combat. In the fight he sustained a serious head wound. Doctors treated him and he later recovered, and then he continued his campaign against what were left of the rebels, who now numbered 10,000. After they failed to withstand his assault and retreated to rugged defensive positions, Aquillius tried every avenue until he finally defeated the besieged. There were about 1,000 still left after this, ranged around their leader Satyros. Aquillius' first thought was to defeat them by main force, but he then gained their surrender through the use of negotiators. He spared the slave prisoners from capital punishment and instead took them to Rome, where he intended to have them fight in the arena as gladiators against wild beasts. Some report that these men ended their lives gloriously when they killed each other in front of the public altars, refusing to do battle with the wild beasts. The leader Satyros himself slew the last man, then took his own life in heroic fashion. The Sicilian slave war, having lasted for nearly four years, reached its tragic conclusion in this way.

Diodorus of Sicily, Universal History, 36.10.1–3 [ca. 30 BCE]

The Spartacid rebellion (73–71 BCE)

The gladiators' uprising and their devastation in Italy, what is generally known as the war of Spartacus, began in this way. A man named Lentulus Batiatus had a training school for gladiators at Capua. Most of these men were Gauls and Thracians. They hadn't done any mischief, but simply because of the cruelty of their master they were being kept in confinement until they were needed for gladiatorial combat. Two hundred of them planned their escape, but they were betrayed (some of them realized this in advance); and only 78 managed to take action and to get away in time ... On the way out of the school, the slaves happened upon some wagon loaded with weapons on its way to gladiators in another city. They took these arms for themselves. Then, after they had assumed a strong position, they elected three leaders, among whom Spartacus was the first. He was from a nomadic Thracian tribe, and he had not only great spirit and physical strength, but also intelligence and culture (which one would not expect from his condition), being more like a Greek than a Thracian.

Plutarch, Life of Crassus, 8.1–3 [ca. 115 CE]

After [victories over the Roman praetors Gaius Claudius Glaber and Publius Varinius in 73 BCE] even greater numbers flocked to Spartacus until his slave army swelled to 70,000. He manufactured weapons and gathered equipment for these men, whereas the Romans now sent out the consuls with two legions.

Appian, Civil Wars, 1.116 [ca. 160 CE]

The [final] battle was protracted and bloody, as you would expect from so many thousands of desperate men. Spartacus was wounded in the thigh and sank down on a knee, holding out a shield to protect his front and meeting his attackers in this way, until finally he and a large number of his men were surrounded and cut down. The rest of his army was thrown into disorder and confusion; they were slaughtered in droves. It was impossible to count the numbers of the dead. The Romans suffered about 1,000 casualties. Spartacus' body was never found. A large number of his men fled to the hills, and Crassus pursued them. They split up into four segments and continued resisting until they were destroyed, except for 6,000. They were taken and crucified along the highway [Appian Way] running from Capua to Rome.

Appian, Civil Wars, 1.120 [ca. 160 CE]

Piracy and the slave trade[35]

In the aftermath of the Third Macedonian War (172–167 BCE), Rome was displeased with the island republic of Rhodes, which had attempted to pose as a third-party mediator in the war's latter stages. The senators debated going to war against Rhodes for the insult, but later determined to name the island of Delos as a free port. This act served to cripple Rhode's maritime economy, and ultimately to destroy its ability to police the seas against pirates, a problem which would return to haunt the Romans in the following century. In the following excerpt the Rhodian stateman Astymedes instructs the Roman Senate on the effects of this action.

"You see that you have imposed a heavier tribute on the Rhodians for a single mistake than on the Macedonians who had always been your enemies. But the greatest calamity inflicted on our state is this. The revenue we drew from our harbor has ceased owing to your having made Delos a free port, and deprived our people of that freedom by which our rights regarding our harbor and all the other rights of our city were justly guarded. It is not difficult to convince you of the truth of this. For while the harbor dues were formerly farmed out for 1,000,000 drachmae, now they fetch only 150,000; so that your displeasure, Roman gentlemen, has only too heavily visited the vital resources of the state."

Polybius, *Histories*, 30.31.9–13 [ca. 150 BCE]

The Roman destruction of Corinth [146 BCE] increased the fame of Delos even more, because the businessmen now used Delos, attracted as they were both by the immunity enjoyed by the temple and by the well-situated harbor. Delos is fortunately placed for those sailing from Italy and Greece to Asia. The festival is a commercial affair, and the Romans attended it more than any other people, even while Corinth was still in existence.

Strabo, *Geography*, 10.5.4 (C 486) [ca. 15 BCE]

Tryphon, along with the worthless line of kings who came to rule over Syria and then Cilicia, caused the Cilicians to form their bands of pirates [early 130s BCE]. The upheavals of others made these men attempt the same sort of thing, and so the disputes of brothers made the country vulnerable to attack. But what induced them to their evil practices most of all was slave export, which was tremendously lucrative. Slaves were not only easily obtained, but the market, large and rich in property, was not very far away. I am talking about Delos, which was able to both bring in and send out 10,000 slaves on the same day.... The Romans were the cause of this, since after having become rich with the destruction of Corinth and Carthage, they used many slaves. The pirates' numbers grew, as they saw the easy profit to be gotten, and they went out not only in search for booty but also to traffic in slaves.

Strabo, *Geography*, 14.5.2 (C 669) [ca. 15 BCE]

[Pirates] were emboldened at the time of the Mithridatic wars when they were in the service of the king. And when the Romans were embroiled in their civil wars the seas were unprotected and the pirates moved out farther and farther until they began to ravage the islands and coasts, rather than restrict themselves to actions at sea. Soon men of substance and reputation joined their ranks and shared in their enterprises, as they regarded piracy as an honorable profession.... It is certain that the pirates had more than 1,000 ships and that they captured some 400 cities.

Plutarch, *Life of Pompey the Great*, 24 [ca. 115 CE]

Pompey and the pirates (67 BCE)

[He] divided the waters and the adjacent coasts of the Mediterranean Sea into 13 districts, and assigned to each a certain number of ships with a commander, and with his forces thus scattered in all quarters he encompassed whole fleets of piratical ships that fell in his way, and straightway hunted them down and brought them to port; others succeeded in dispersing and escaping, and sought their hive, as it were, hurrying from all quarters into Cilicia. Against these Pompey intended to proceed in person with his 60 best ships. He did not, however, sail against them until he had entirely cleared of their pirates the Tyrrhenian Sea, the Libyan Sea, and the sea about Sardinia, Corsica, and Sicily, in 40 days all told.

Plutarch, *Life of Pompey the Great*, 26.3–4 [ca. 115 CE]

The popular assembly passed a law ordering Pompey to root out the pirates, who had cut off the trade in grain. He cleared them all from the seas in 40 days; and he brought the war against them in Cilicia to a successful conclusion, received their submission, and gave them land and cities.

Livy, *Summaries*, 99 [ca. 25 BCE]

EDITOR'S NOTES

1 On Roman politics of largesse, see P. Veyne, *Bread and Circuses: Historical Sociology and Political Pluralism*, trans. B. Pierce (New York, 1990).

2 For senatorial attempts to keep numbers down, see Livy, *History*, 39.3.4–6 (187 BCE); 41.8.6–12 (177 BCE); 42.10.3–4 (173 BCE).

3 For further sources on the bribery laws, see T. R. S. Broughton, *The Magistrates of the Roman Republic*, vol. 1 (reprint Atlanta, 1986), pp. 384, 445, with A. W. Lintott, "Electoral Bribery in the Roman Republic," *Journal of Roman Studies*, 80 (1990), pp. 1–16.

4 For a concise and lucid account of the Gracchan revolution and its background, see H. H. Scullard, *From the Gracchi to Nero: A History of Rome 133 BC to AD 68*, 5th edn. (London and New York, 1982), pp. 1–41.

5 For the sources, which do not provide exact terms of the Calpurnian law, see Broughton, *Magistrates of the Roman Republic*, p. 459.

6 For Roman power in Spain, see J. S. Richardson, *Hispaniae: Spain and the Development of Roman Imperialism, 218–82 BC* (Cambridge, 1986).

7 For the political dimensions of the courts in the Middle and Late Republic, see E. S. Gruen, *Roman Politics and the Criminal Courts, 149–78 BC* (Cambridge, Mass., 1968).

8 Caesar thus altered legislation of the praetor L. Aurelius Cotta, who in 70 BCE had reversed the dictator Sulla's settlement by dividing the criminal juries between senators, equestrians, and this class, the tribunes of the treasury (*tribuni aerarii*).

9 See further the classic study of E. Badian, *Roman Imperialism in the Late Republic* (Oxford, 1968); and M. Beard and M. Crawford, *Rome in the Late Republic* (Ithaca, NY, 1985).

10 For Marius' military reforms and the armies of the warlords of the Late Republic, see E. Gabba, *Republican Rome, the Army, and the Allies*, trans. P. J. Cuff (Berkeley and Los Angeles, 1976). Gabba (pp. 1–52) argues that Marius' reform represents the culmination

of a long process of professionalization of the Roman army that began at least as early as the third century BCE.

11 The best study of Pompey's political career remains R. Seager, *Pompey: A Political Biography* (Berkeley and Los Angeles, 1979), now available again as *Pompey the Great* (Oxford, 2002). For Pompey's eastern campaign, see collected sources in Broughton, *Magistrates of the Roman Republic*, pp. 155, 159–60, 163–4, 169–70, 176.

12 On Caesar see the classic study of M. Gelzer, *Caesar: Politician and Statesman*, trans. P. Needham (Cambridge, Mass., 1968); and for a concise account, see my biographical essay in *The Dictionary of Literary Biography*, vol. 211 (Detroit, San Francisco, London, Boston, and Woodbridge, Conn.), pp. 109–17.

13 See the detailed study of A. N. Sherwin-White, *The Roman Citizenship*, 2nd edn. (Oxford, 1973).

14 The *lex Plautia Papiria* of 89 BCE completed the enfranchisement of the Italians; on which see Gabba, *Republican Rome*, pp. 89–96.

15 See now R. MacMullen, *Romanization in the Time of Augustus* (New Haven and London, 2000).

16 The tribute was imposed on Queen Teuta in the aftermath of the First Illyrian War in 228 BCE; see Polybius, *Histories*, 2.12.3–4.

17 Valerius Antias and Claudius Quadrigarius were earlier annalistic historians whom Livy used as sources; their works are now lost. See E. Badian, "The Early Historians," in *Latin Historians*, ed. T. A. Dorey (New York, 1966), pp. 1–38. On the indemnity imposed on Philip V in 196 BCE, see also Polybius, *Histories*, 18.44.7.

18 On the Roman commander T. Quinctius Flamininus' activities in Greece, see E. Badian, *Titus Quinctius Flamininus: Philhellenism and Realpolitik* (Cincinnati, 1970).

19 Cf. Livy, *History of Rome*, 38.38.13–14.

20 The times of composition of Strabo's *Geography* are mysterious. He apparently worked on his massive work from the mid-20s down to about 2 BCE and then stopped abruptly, only to resume in the reign of Tiberius (14–36 CE). See *The Cambridge History of Classical Literature*, vol. 1 (Cambridge, 1985), pp. 642–3.

21 See T. Frank, *An Economic Survey of Ancient Rome*, vol. 1 (Baltimore, 1933), p. 138, who estimates that public booty surrendered to the state treasury down to the year 167 BCE amounted to 70,000,000 denarii from the East, with another 40,000,000 from other areas, for a grand total of 110,000,000 denarii (see Glossary for the currency unit of the denarius).

22 See E. Badian, *Publicans and Sinners: Private Enterprise in the Service of the Roman Republic* (Ithaca, NY, 1972).

23 See Badian, *Roman Imperialism*, pp. 84–6.

24 Ibid.

25 Cf. Livy, 45.29.11 [ca. 25 BCE].

26 Cf. Luke 5.30–2.

27 For the events of 151 and 138 BCE see Broughton, *Magistrates of the Roman Republic*, pp. 455, 483, with the excellent study of L. R. Taylor, "Forerunners of the Gracchi," *Journal of Roman Studies*, 52 (1962), pp. 19–27.

28 See P. A. Brunt's classic study, "The Army and the Land in the Roman Revolution," *Journal of Roman Studies*, 52 (1962), pp. 69–86. For recent criticism, see J. Rich, "The Supposed Manpower Shortage of the Later Second Century BC," *Historia*, 32 (1983), pp. 287–331; N. Rosenstein, "Marriage and Manpower in the Hannibalic War: *Assidui, Proletarii* and Livy 24.18.7–8," *Historia*, 51 (2002), pp. 163–91; and briefly N. Rosenstein, "Republican Rome," in *War and Society in the Ancient and Medieval Worlds*, eds. K. Raaflaub and N. Rosenstein (Cambridge, Mass., and London, 1999), pp. 206–8.

29   This is probably a reference to an extant Latin inscription recording legislation of 111 BCE: *Corpus Inscriptionum Latinarum*, vol. 1, 2nd edn., no. 585; for a translation see N. Lewis and M. Reinhold, eds., *Roman Civilization: The Republic and the Augustan Age*, vol. 1, 3rd edn. (New York, 1990), pp. 276–83.

30   Pliny probably refers to a development unknown in the Gracchan age: the creation of vast estates run largely by tenants, as opposed to the slave-staffed villas of earlier times.

31   See further Livy, *History of Rome*, 30.26.6 (203 BCE), 31.4.6 (201 BCE), 33.42.8 (196 BCE).

32   For a table of mass enslavements in Roman history, see A. J. Toynbee, *Hannibal's Legacy*, vol. 2 (London and New York, 1965), pp. 171–3.

33   265 BCE. Zonaras is in error; the consuls were Q. Fabius Maximus Gurges and L. Mamilius Vitulus. See Broughton, *Magistrates of the Roman Republic*, vol. 1, p. 201.

34   For excellent introduction, collection of documents, and bibliography on the slave rebellions, see B. D. Shaw, ed., *Spartacus and the Slave War: A Brief History with Documents* (Boston and New York, 2001). See also K. R. Bradley, *Slavery and Rebellion in the Roman World, 140 BC–70 BC* (Bloomington and Indianapolis, 1998).

35   On piracy in classical antiquity, see now Philip de Souza, *Piracy in the Graeco-Roman World* (Cambridge, 1999), and pp. 149–78 on Pompey's subjugation of the Cilician pirates.

3

Ideology and Government of Empire

Introduction

The two selections in this chapter raise problems of the ideologies, presuppositions, justifications, and rationalizations which the Romans constructed in order to legitimate their imperial dominion. Brunt discusses several Roman ideologies of empire: the glory of imperial expansion, the predestination of the Roman Empire, the idea of a Roman empire that encompasses the world, the Roman theory of the "just war" (*bellum iustum*), and notions of Roman clemency and justice. Like all ideologies, these ideas served largely to obfuscate ugly realities, and Brunt grimly concludes that "provincial revenues were spent lavishly on feeding and amusing the inhabitants of Rome and beautifying the city, to say nothing of court expenditure. These privileges were not challenged by provincials in the senate or on the throne. Equality as between Italians and provincials was not attained, until all were sunk in equal misery."

Mattern studies the constant Roman quest to assert dominance and to avert submission in relation to outside powers. In these desires the Romans did not follow the dictates of any rational international security concerns. "This study suggests that international relations, for the Romans, were not so much a complex geopolitical chess game as a competition for status, with much violent demonstration of superior prowess, aggressive posturing, and terrorization of the opponent. The Romans behaved on an international level like Homeric heroes, Mafia gangsters, or participants in any society where status and security depend on one's perceived ability to inflict violence. Image or national 'honor' emerges as the most important policy goal."[1] Consequently, according to Mattern, Roman emperors were preoccupied with martial glory and Roman military superiority. Roman virtues were set up against the alleged moral failings of non-Roman barbarians, and Roman emperors sought to legitimate their rule by claiming stunning victories over barbarian forces, erecting victory monuments and celebrating spectacular triumphal ceremonies to that end. Individual glory and material rewards were of course part of Roman imperial motivations, but Mattern focuses upon the moral imperatives for the exercise or pretended exercise of Roman military might, which Roman emperors advertised for public consumption. "Greed and glory were plausible, though not necessarily respectable, causes for war. Still more plausible and respectable was the motivation of revenge, and of asserting or enhancing the honor and majesty of the Roman empire – provided, of course, that this could be done without causing invasion, revolt, civil war, or crippling expense."

NOTE

1   Susan Mattern, *Rome and the Enemy: Imperial Strategy in the Principate* (Berkeley, Los Angeles, and London, 1999), preface, p. xii.

Laus Imperii

P. A. Brunt

THE GLORY OF IMPERIAL EXPANSION

In the political programme Cicero sketched in his defence of Sestius ([*pro Sest.*] 96ff) he maintained that all good men should seek *otium cum dignitate*. *Otium* must have included security from external attack (*de orat.* 1.14), and *dignitas* suggests, among other things, the glory of the whole state (*pro Sest.* 104); *provinciae, socii, imperii laus, res militaris* are expressly named among the *fundamenta otiosae dignitatis*. ["provinces, allies, the praise of imperial power, military affairs...the foundations for a dignified leisure"]. Much of Cicero's programme can have had no appeal to the poor either in Rome or in the country, but the urban plebs at least could apparently be moved by the glamour of imperial glory; in his speech for the Manilian law Cicero enlarges on the dishonour Rome had suffered from the pirates and from Mithridates, and on the necessity of entrusting the eastern command to Pompey, in order to restore 'the prestige of the Roman people which has been transmitted to you by our ancestors and whose greatness appears in every way and above all in the military domain' ([*pro Manil.*] 6; cf. 7–11, 53ff). No other people, he says there, had ever had such an appetite for glory, and we know that in his own judgement this had been a dominant motive for the old Romans (*de rep.* 5.9). He can argue for the propriety or wisdom of any practices which have in the past served to aggrandize the empire (*pro Rosc. Am.* 50, *Phil.* 5.47), or which its long existence in itself justifies. Both Pompey and Caesar are lauded for making its boundaries coterminous with the *orbis terrarum*,[1] a boast that Pompey made for himself on a monument recording his deeds in Asia (Diod. 40.4). The speech *de provinciis consularibus* is particularly significant in this connexion. As an encomiast of Caesar in 56, Cicero was in a delicate position. Both he and the majority of the senate had recently been in opposition to Caesar. However, he finds it plausible to assert that Caesar's achievements in Gaul had changed their attitude, and rightly changed it, hence the extraordinary honours the senate had already voted to the conqueror ([*de Prov. cons.*] 25; cf. *in Pis.* 81). In the long letter he wrote to Lentulus in 54, which was obviously intended as an apologia for a wider public, Cicero exculpates his own change of course in much the same way: it is now, he claims, the triumvirs who are doing most to secure *otium cum dignitate*, and Caesar's conquests are part of his case (*ad fam.* 1.9.12–18 and 21). It seems to me highly improbable that these sentiments, however insincere on the lips of Cicero, whose correspondence in the 50s, even with his brother Quintus in Gaul, betrays little interest and no pride in the conquests, were not genuinely felt by Romans, who had less than Cicero to lose from the dominance of the triumvirs, or that Caesar himself was untruthful in recording that in 49 the councillors of Auximum, from Pompey's homeland of Picenum, declined to exclude from their town *C. Caesarem imperatorem, bene de republica meritum, tantis rebus gestis* ["the general Gaius Caesar, well deserving of the Republic, with such great deeds performed"] (*BC* 1.13).

There is abundant evidence for the value individual Romans set on *gloria*,[2] but, as Cicero says in his defence of Archias, they could win no greater renown than by victories in war, renown in which the whole people shared (21ff; cf. 30). In *de officiis* Cicero admits that most men rank success in war above achievements in peace (1.74), and that it had been the most natural and traditional objective for a young aristocrat (2.45); in public he declared that military talent had brought eternal glory to Rome and compelled the world to obey her commands and that it was to be more highly valued than the orator's eloquence (*pro Mur.* 21ff). He scoffed at the Epicurean Piso's professed disdain for a triumph as preposterous and incredible (*in Pis.* 56ff), and for all his own rational expectation to be immortalized as the Roman Demosthenes and perhaps as the Roman Plato, he magnified his own petty exploits in Mount Amanus in hope of the honour.[3] The triumph, properly granted only to the general who had slain 5,000 of the enemy in a single battle (Val. Max. 2.8.1), was itself the institutional expression of Rome's military ideal. According to Cicero (*de rep.* 3.24) the words *finis imperii propagavit* ["he extended the boundaries of empire"] appeared on the monuments of her great generals; in his speeches he takes it for granted that victory and the extension of empire are the objectives of any provincial governor (*de prov. cons.* 29, *Phil.* 13.14), and at his most theoretical he prescribes that wise statesmen should do their utmost in peace and war *ut rem publicam augeant imperio agris vectigalibus* ["that through their imperial power they augment the state with tax-paying territory"] (*de offic.* 2.85), thus accepting in 44 B.C. a principle of statecraft that no contemporary had done more to fulfil than Caesar, whom at this very time he was concerned to vilify (1.26, 2.23–8, 3.83 etc.). In *de oratore* 1.196 he roundly asserted that no fatherland deserved so much love as Rome, *quae una in omnibus terris domus est virtutis, imperii, dignitatis* ["which is throughout all lands the one home of virtue, imperial majesty, dignity"].

VIRTUS, FORTUNA AND THE WILL OF THE GODS

Thus Cicero could not free himself from the militarism of the traditions he revered, which appeared in the old prayer of the censors for the aggrandizement of Rome (Val. Max. 4.1.10), in the rule that the *pomerium* might be extended only by those *qui protulere imperium* (Tac. *Ann.* 12.23) – among them was Sulla – and perhaps in the alleged predictions of *haruspices* that the wars with Philip V, Antiochus and Perseus would advance *terminos populi Romani*. If these predictions recorded by Livy (21.5.7, 36.1.3, 42.30.9) are not annalistic fabrications, they cast doubt on the view that any of these wars were merely defensive in motivation, but even if they were invented by Valerius Antias or Claudius Quadrigarius (if not earlier), they still illustrate the imperialistic conceptions dominant in the time of their invention, and accepted by Livy, in whose work *belli gloria* is naturally a pervasive theme. In particular, the legend of Marcus Curtius, for which our earliest source is a contemporary of Cicero, Procilius, enshrined the truth that it was *arma virtusque* that guaranteed Rome's perpetuity (7.6.3). In Livy's view it was the number and valour of Rome's soldiers and the talents of her generals – elsewhere he also stresses military discipline, to which Cicero only once alludes (*Tusc. disp.* 1.2) – which with the help of fortune had made Rome unconquerable.[4]

It was, however, not only military qualities that were thought to have made Rome great. Wise policy was another factor (*de rep.* 2.30). Like Polybius, Cicero clearly laid great weight on Rome's balanced constitution.[5] Most Romans were not political theorists, but traditions counted heavily with them; as Cicero's innumerable allusions in speeches to ancestral wisdom[6] indicate; in his defence of Murena (75) he casually refers to *instituta maiorum quae diuturnitas imperi comprobat* ["the institutions of our ancestors confirm the permanence of our empire"], and we may conjecture that a widely shared conviction that these institutions had contributed to the acquisition of empire was one reason why Augustus felt it necessary to veil the extent to which he had subverted them.[7] In one speech Cicero suggested that Rome's readiness to share political rights with other peoples, even with defeated enemies, had been of the highest importance in her aggrandizement (*pro Balb.* 31); more was to be made of this theme by Livy, and by Dionysius who doubtless drew the idea from Romans he met or from the annals he read.[8] Posidonius too was obviously following Roman mentors when he extolled the frugality, simplicity, good faith and piety of the old Romans in a passage in which he is accounting for Rome's rise to power:[9] *moribus antiquis res stat Romana virisque* ["the Roman state stands upon ancient virtues and men"]. Sallust and others apprehended danger to Rome from the degeneration from those pristine standards which they detected in their own day.[10]

Romans themselves acknowledged that fortune as well as virtue had assisted them; for instance the situation of the city, and the centrality of Italy within the Mediterranean world, had favoured expansion, and Italy's natural resources were actually exaggerated.[11] But the Roman conception of fortune tended to be that of which Cicero speaks: *divinitus adiuncta fortuna* ["Fortune divinely adjoined"] (*de imp. Cn. Pomp.* 47). The gods were the guardians of city and empire.[12] It was Roman piety that had earned their goodwill. In Propertius' words (3.22.21), *quantum ferro tantum pietate potentes stamus* ["we stand powerful as much by piety as by force of arms"]. Virgil's Aeneas, *pietate insignis et armis* ["outstanding in piety and in arms"], was the prototype of the people aided and destined by the gods to conquer. In public Cicero gave the most eloquent expression to the notion, which we can trace from a praetor's letter of 193 B.C. to the time of Augustine, that 'it was by our scrupulous attention to religion and by our wise grasp of a single truth, that all things are ruled and directed by the will of the gods, that we have overcome all peoples and nations'.[13]

It may be doubted if Cicero himself had firm religious convictions. There is no hint of personal devotion in his intimate letters; above all, he never expresses hope of assistance from the gods in moments of the deepest distress or anxiety.[14] But he held that it was expedient to imbue the citizens with religious faith, in order that they might be deterred by the fear of divine retribution from infringing oaths and treaties, and from crimes in general. If men ceased to think that the gods took no care for mankind and to pay them due honour, good faith, social cooperation and justice would surely be extinguished. Polybius had already traced the high moral standards of old Rome to the prevalence of a scrupulous fear of the gods.[15] The ideal system of sacred law Cicero sketches in the second book of *de legibus* is expressly modelled on the Roman (2.23). He lays great emphasis on the powers of the aristocratic priest-hoods, 'for it helps to hold the state together that the people should always need the advice and authority of the *optimates*' (2.30). Cicero unhesitatingly approved the abuse of priestly authority for obstructing 'seditious' proposals.[16] The truth of beliefs implicit in the ancestral rituals was irrelevant to their utility. In the same way Varro adopted the view of Q. Mucius Scaevola that philosophic views on religion were unsuited to the masses and that traditional rites should be kept up for their benefit. Varro indeed held that there was a basis of truth in the old religion, which he reconciled with Stoic pantheism.[17] In *de legibus* Cicero adopted a similar standpoint.

In this work he accepted the Stoic justification of divination; it was at least credible in principle, though Cicero already denied that the augurs of his own day (he was one himself) any longer enjoyed knowledge of the future,[18] and insisted above all on their political importance. By the end of his life he had come to reject every kind of divination. Yet in the very treatise, *de divinatione*, in which he discredits belief in the supernatural power of *haruspices* and augurs as mere superstition, he reiterates that for political reasons the old practices should be maintained.[19] This work is a sequel to his *de natura deorum*, in which his mouthpiece, Cotta, refutes all Stoic teaching on divine providence in a way which could be said *deos funditos tollere* ["to destroy the gods to the root"] (*de div.* 1.9). Cotta is actually made to say that experience throws doubt on the very existence of gods, though as a pontiff, bound to maintain the cults, he would never avow this *in contione* (*de nat. deor.* 1.61).[i] It is true that at the end Cicero makes Cotta indicate that he would like to be convinced that the Stoics were in the right (3.95), and declare that no philosophic reasoning could induce him to question the truth of ancestral beliefs on the worship of the gods, and that Rome could never have achieved such greatness but for her supreme care in placating them (3.5ff; cf. 14). Strictly this means that Cotta accepts on authority all the traditional *beliefs* including those which Cicero was to ridicule in *de divinatione*. I suspect that Cicero has gone further than he really intended here, and that he should have made Cotta say merely that all the ancient *practices* were to be preserved, irrespective of their truth.

Whatever Cicero's personal convictions may have been, they are primarily of biographical interest; we cannot properly generalize from a single individual. But the cynical manipulation of the official religion for political ends is itself one piece of evidence for the decay of belief in it among the controlling aristocracy. Of course it does not stand alone: at this time many cults were neglected, the calendar was often in disarray, priesthoods were unfilled, temples were falling into disrepair, the pontifical law was no longer studied, and in public and private life auspices were not duly observed.[20] Can we then suppose that the conception that the empire depended on divine favour really had much influence on men's minds?

The answer is surely that Cicero and other highly educated aristocrats were not representative figures. It is significant that Cicero in his speech *de haruspicum responsis* (18) finds it necessary to deny that his philosophical studies have alienated him from the old religion. The frequency of his public appeals to religion is surely proof that belief was still widespread.[21] There can be no doubt that superstition was rife among the ignorant masses.[22] But Cicero was just as apt to play on religious sentiment when addressing members of the higher orders. To take only one example, *religiones* and *auspicia* come first in the *fundamenta otiosae dignitatis* as a part of the programme that was to enlist the support of all *boni et locupletes* throughout Italy (*pro Sest.* 98). I do not suppose that they were meant to think only of the opportunities for political obstruction which the old religion furnished. The so-called religious revival that Augustus was to attempt may well have appealed to the old-fashioned municipal gentry, who were already playing a larger part in the political life of Cicero's time and whose support he sought, like Augustus after him.[23] It may be noted that the incest of Clodius in 62 aroused indignation first among the lower ranks in the senate, a body of which probably under thirty per cent belonged to noble houses.[24] Most Romans may well have retained the conviction that it was to the gods that they owed their empire, an empire that was said to be coterminous with the *orbis terrarum*.

THE CONCEPTION OF WORLD EMPIRE

Virgil's Jupiter was to bestow on Rome a dominion without limits in space or time (*Aen.* 1.277ff). Cicero and his contemporaries, and perhaps Virgil's, were somewhat less confident. More than once Cicero avers that Rome had no external enemies to fear, but that her eternity could only be assured if she remained faithful to the institutions and customs that had made her great.[25] On the other hand he constantly speaks, and sometimes in quite casual ways with no rhetorical inflation (e.g. *de orat.* 1.14), as if Rome already ruled all peoples or the whole *orbis terrarum*.[26] This conception also appears in an admittedly rather grandiloquent preamble to a consular law of 58: *imperio amplificato pace per orbem terrarum* ["with the empire having been enhanced by peace throughout the world"]. A century earlier, Polybius had held that by 167 B.C. the whole, or virtually the whole *oikoumene* ["inhabited world"] or its known parts, had come under Roman dominion. His true meaning is better conveyed in other texts in which he ascribes to Rome mastery over land and sea *kath'hemas*,[ii] or of those which had fallen under inquiry (*historian*); evidently these did not embrace all the parts of the world that geographers had described but only those which formed Polybius' political universe.[27] *Orbis terrarum* was often used in the same restricted sense (cf. n. 26).

Even so, it is obvious that in the time both of Polybius and of Cicero Rome did not herself administer the whole of this political universe. Both must then have conceived that her dominion extended beyond the provinces to the kings, tribes and cities who were bound to Rome by alliances, even if the terms of the treaty, as with little Astypalaea,[28] affected a formal equality between the High Contracting Parties which harsh reality rendered meaningless, or who were linked by the looser tie of *amicitia*, which within Rome's own society was often a courteous synonym for clientage.[29] In form the status of such allies and friends of Rome beyond provincial frontiers was no different from that of others like Massilia whose territories constituted enclaves within a province. In reality the degree of their dependence was determined by the advantages or disadvantages that might induce Rome to punish or overlook disobedience to her will.

Augustus was to regard all *reges socios* ["allied kings"] as *membra partisque imperii* ["members and parts of empire"] (Suet. *Aug.* 48). Owing their thrones to recognition, if not to appointment, by Rome, they were not necessarily scions of an established royal house nor even drawn from the people they ruled; normally they now enjoyed Roman citizenship, a symbol of their function as creatures and agents of the suzerain. Augustus naturally included his dealings with them in his record of the deeds *quibus orbem terrarum imperio populi Romani subiecit* ["by means of which he subjected the world to the imperial majesty of Rome"]. In his view Armenia was in revolt when it rejected the princes he named. He justified by ancestral practice his decision not to annex that country; Lucullus and Pompey had in fact already reduced it to vassalage.[30]

Under his more efficient regime 'client' states were perhaps more closely controlled than in the republic, but Cicero had already included all kingdoms and *liberae civitates* ["free states"] in the *orbis terrarum* ["the world"] where every Roman in virtue of his citizenship should be safe from arbitrary punishment (II *Verr.* 5.168), and in 47 B.C. an attack on king Deiotarus could be construed as a violation of *populi Romani ius maiestatemque* ["the justice and majesty of the Roman people"] (*B. Alex.* 34). In Cicero's phrase Rome was *dominus regum* ["the house of kings"] (*de dom.* 90), and when Tacitus declared it to be an ancient and long-approved practice of the republic to make kings *instrumenta servitutis* ["instruments of servitude"] (*Agr.* 14), he was echoing Sallust, who represents Mithridates as telling how Eumenes of Pergamum had been reduced by Rome to the most wretched slavery (*ep. Mith.* 8; cf. *BJ* 31.9). Sallust too makes Adherbal recall to the senate that his father, Micipsa, had enjoined on him *uti regni Numidiae tantummodo procurationem existumarem meam, ceterum ius et imperium eius penes vos esse* ["that I am merely a custodian of the Numidian kingdom, but that the right and authority are in your [Roman] hands"].[31] From the second century such rulers had had to look to Rome for recognition, and like free cities and friendly tribes, they were expected to conform their policy to Rome's will, to furnish military aid and money or supplies, when occasion demanded; some were actually tributary. In return they had a moral claim to Rome's protection (e.g. *BJ* 14, *B. Alex.* 34). In 51 B.C. king Ariobarzanes of Cappadocia plainly depended wholly on Rome to defend him against Parthian attack or internal discontent, fostered no doubt by the exactions required to meet the usurious demands of Pompey and Brutus. Modern descriptions of such client kingdoms or peoples as 'buffer states' is never adequate and often quite misleading. Analogies with the princedoms of British India or the system of 'indirect rule' in British Nigeria would be more to the point.[32] A recent writer has drawn a distinction between the Roman empire *stricto* and *lato sensu*, the former comprising only territory under Rome's own administration and the latter the subordinate states as well. This is clearly a useful tool of analysis, but it does not correspond to Roman usage.[33]

Unlimited expansion

The duty acknowledged by the Romans (but not invariably performed) of protecting their friends and allies could involve them in wars with peoples who had hitherto lain beyond their orbit. Victory made these peoples in turn Rome's subjects. Thus the limits of the *orbis terrarum* within which she claimed dominion were continually advancing. There was no point at which such expansion could halt, so long as any independent people remained. Indeed, as P. Veyne has recently argued, the very existence of a truly independent power was viewed at Rome as a potential threat to her own security.[34]

The early treaties with Carthage, and perhaps one with Tarentum, had bound Rome to keep out of certain lands or seas.[35] There is no certain evidence that she ever accepted such a restriction after the war with Pyrrhus. Livy indeed says that under the pact with Hasdrubal the Ebro became *finis utriusque imperii* ["boundaries of either empire"] (21.2.7), but Polybius that it simply forbade the Carthaginians to cross that river, and there is no hint that Hannibal argued that Rome had infringed its terms by intervening on behalf of Saguntum.[36] At one time Flamininus offered Antiochus III a line of demarcation between his sphere of authority and Rome's, but the treaty of Apamea certainly set bounds for Antiochus, without debarring Rome from interfering beyond them.[37] Caesar would not accept either Rhine or Channel as limits to Roman power. Whatever the practice of earlier ages, his attitude was characteristic for his own time.

It is true that according to Orosius (6.13.2) the Parthian king complained that Crassus' crossing of the Euphrates was an infringement of 'treaties' made by Lucullus and Pompey; Florus (3.11.4) refers instead to 'treaties' made with Sulla and Pompey. Many scholars suppose that one or more of these generals had in fact recognized the Euphrates as a boundary delimiting the Roman and Parthian spheres of influence or at least as one which neither party was to cross in arms. Yet, since Crassus was patently launching an offensive against Parthia, the Parthian king was perhaps merely reminding him of previous pacts of friendship, which need have comprised no such precise stipulation. Certainly none is recorded in the other texts, admittedly meagre, which relate to the negotiations between these generals and the Parthians.[38] Lucullus was actually quartered far east of the Euphrates at the time, having overrun much of Armenia. Pompey too invaded Armenia, reduced king Tigranes to vassalage, and sent troops into Gordyene. According to Plutarch (*Pomp.* 33.6) Phraates then proposed the Euphrates as a frontier, but Pompey merely replied that he would adopt the just boundary. That was manifestly an evasion. In his monument he claimed to have 'given protection to' not only Armenia but Mesopotamia, Sophene and Gordyene (Diod. 40.4), and if he was unwilling to fight the Parthians, who did indeed forbid him to cross the Euphrates again (Dio 37.6), for Tigranes' right to Gordyene, he successfully offered Roman arbitration between the rival claims there of Tigranes and Phraates (Dio 37.6f). It is significant that he denied Phraates the title of 'king of kings' (Dio 37.5; Plut. *Pomp.* 38), which might have suggested that his state was on a parity with Rome. He entered into friendly relations with the rulers of Osrhoene, Media Atropatene and even Elymaitis,[39] as well as Armenia; when and if it suited Rome, she could intervene to defend her friends beyond the Euphrates against Parthia.

When Crassus did cross the river, he was received as a liberator from Parthian oppression at least by many Greek cities (Dio 40.13, Plut. *Cr.* 17), and he had the support of the vassal king of Armenia (Dio 40.19), while the ruler of Osrhoene pretended to be friendly (ibid. 20).

Although Cicero denied that Crassus had any justification for war (*de fin.* 3.75), and our authorities all represent him as the aggressor, perhaps condemning him, as Plutarch suggested (*comp. Nic. et Cr.* 4), only because he failed, we can easily surmise that he had excuses for intervention, on behalf of peoples with whom Rome had already entered into friendly relations, as plausible as Caesar for his Gallic offensives. It is, moreover, significant that even though Romans could see the disaster at Carrhae as divine retribution for an unjust and undeclared war, just as Cicero ascribes the destruction of Piso's army by pestilence to the judgement of heaven on Piso's alleged aggressions (*in Pis.* 85), they continued to assume down to 20 B.C. that it was right for them to punish the Parthians and even to conquer them, in order to vindicate Rome's honour and secure her eastern dominions.

Whatever the provocation they had received, foreign peoples which attacked Rome could at best be said to wage a *bellum prope iustum* (*de prov. cons.* 4). It would be hard to say how far the conviction that the gods had destined them to rule the world predisposed Romans to treat as legitimate *casus belli* which the uncommitted observer would have thought nugatory.

Reluctance to annex territory

It is then quite mistaken to deny that Roman policy was imperialistic whenever it did not result in outright annexation. Until the first century B.C. Rome was notoriously slow to annex territory.

Gelzer explained this on the ground that the Roman state absolutely lacked an organ for carrying through far-reaching plans of expansion, with annual magistrates whose choice rested on the caprice of the electorate, who were often incapable, and who in any event could not assure continuity in policy, and a senate which met only when summoned by a magistrate to consider such matters as he referred to it.[40] It seems to me that he unduly depreciated the real power of the senate to make decisions, and that the fluctuations in its policy did not differ significantly from those we find in the policy of imperial states governed either by absolute rulers or by parliamentary democracies; for instance, no change in senatorial foreign policy was more marked than that which occurred when Hadrian succeeded Trajan.

Badian, while rightly insisting that at any rate after 200 Rome was determined 'to dominate whatever was within reach and to build up strength to extend that reach' and practised what he calls 'hegemonial imperialism', argues that the Roman governing class was reluctant to resort to annexation, because it early became conscious 'that large increases of territory could not easily be administered within the existing city-state constitution'. I know of no evidence for such consciousness, and I doubt if it be true that 'under the Roman Republic no real system of administering overseas territories was ever evolved'.[41]

As Gelzer observed, we must not think in terms of a modern bureaucracy when we speak of Roman government. But this applies almost as much to government in the

Principate as in the republic. Pliny actually had not so many high officials to assist him in governing Bithynia and Pontus under Trajan as Cicero in Cilicia.[42] The activities of government were far fewer than they are today, and they were largely left to local authorities; at most these were gradually subjected by the emperors to somewhat closer supervision. It was only rarely under the Principate that even barbarous tribes were directly governed by Roman military officers; the centralized administration of Roman Egypt was always exceptional.

Nor was there anything unusual by ancient standards in Roman practice. In the Persian empire Greek and Phoenician cities had been left to manage their own affairs; so had the Jews, and doubtless most other unurbanized peoples of whom we know nothing; it is immaterial that the Persian kings, like Rome, sometimes installed local rulers on whose loyalty they could count. Athens and the Hellenistic kings (except again in Egypt) had followed the same practice. The Romans had no reason to think that they were less able than other ruling powers to administer subjects in this loose way. The only puzzle is that they did not always choose to demand tribute (as distinct from heavy war indemnities, which could ultimately be paid off), outside the frontiers of a province; the first known cases are those of Macedon and Illyria in 167 (Livy 45.18.7f).

In the republic the tasks of provincial government may be classified under four heads.

(a) *Taxation.* Collection of taxes was left to publicans or to local authorities; a host of officials employed by the central government was not needed. This long remained true under the Principate.[43]

(b) *Jurisdiction.* The governor was omnicompetent, outside privileged communities, but we need not assume that he as yet possessed that monopoly of jurisdiction over serious crimes which may be inferred from evidence of later centuries, and in civil cases he may generally have limited himself to suits in which Romans were concerned. A *lex provinciae* might actually reserve many types of case to local courts. In Cilicia such rules evidently did not exist, and Cicero makes out that it was his innovation to let the Greeks settle their own disputes in local courts under local laws, but I suggest that he did no more than *guarantee* this 'autonomy' to them, whereas his predecessors had been ready to assume jurisdiction if ever they saw fit, perhaps to the advantage of influential magnates and to their own pecuniary gain.[44]

(c) *Supervision of local government.* Cicero praised his brother for ensuring that the Asian cities were administered by the *optimates*. This was no doubt normal policy, though in Asia, for instance, popular assemblies were allowed to retain some power,[45] and Caesar on occasion installed kings in Gallic *civitates*.[46] In general local rulers, whether or not Rome had placed them in control, were left to administer their own communities with little interference. Cicero indeed must have spent much time in checking municipal accounts and unveiling corruption, but the mere fact that he examined accounts for the past ten years indicates that within that period no proconsul had thought this a task necessary to perform.[47]

(d) *Internal order and defence.* Here lay the governor's inescapable obligation. Spain, Gaul, Macedon and some parts of the east nearly always required legionary garrisons. As Badian saw,[48] this was costly to the treasury and burdensome to the Italian peasantry.[49] Generations of war in Spain might well have made the senate apprehensive of assuming military responsibilities that could be shifted on to reliable vassals. Even with the threat of a Parthian invasion in 51, the worthy consul, Servius Sulpicius, vetoed a *supplementum* for the weak forces in Syria and Cilicia.[50] The elder Cato is said to have opposed annexation of Macedon in 168 because Rome could not afford protection (*HA Hadr.* 5.3).

It may be thought that this aversion to assuming the task of military defence ill fits the Roman passion for military glory. But we have to reckon, as Badian argued (cf. n. 48), with the prevalence of mutual jealousy among the Roman aristocracy. Provincial commands gave particular individuals better than average chances of augmenting their personal glory and wealth, and their influence at home. This jealousy is manifest in the *leges annales*, in the normal restriction of provincial commands to a single year, and in the strength of the objection in the late republic to extraordinary commands. In 57–56 no agreement could be reached on the restoration of Ptolemy Auletes to the Egyptian throne, whether by Pompey or any one else; success would bring too much honour even to such a respectable figure of the second order as Lentulus Spinther. Moreover, once a commander was in the field, it was hard for the senate to exercise any control over him. For over two years (57–55) the proconsul L. Piso did not so much as send a single despatch to Rome, though Cicero claims that this was abnormal. The provisions that appeared in Sulla's law on *maiestas* and in Caesar's on *repetundae*, and in many older enactments, forbidding governors *exire de provincia, educere exercitum, bellum sua sponte gerere, in regnum iniussu populi Romani ac senatus accedere* ["to leave the province, to lead out an army, to wage war on their own initiative, to enter a kingdom without the command of the Roman People and Senate"] (*in Pis.* 50) were clearly unenforceable.[51] Both in order to restrict the opportunities for individuals to attain preeminence and to preserve its own authority, the senate had good reason to frown on annexations. And that was not all. Just because annual commands were preferred, there was always the danger that incompetent nonentities would sustain ignominious defeats, and it became hard for generals to carry through a systematic course of expansion or pacification; hence it was not until Augustus' time that order could be established throughout Spain, though it is hard to believe that the complete conquest of that country can ever have seemed undesirable.

THE THEORY OF THE JUST WAR

Following Panaetius, Cicero implied that states as well as individuals should respect the just principle of *suum cuique*. Men should not only abstain from doing wrong themselves but so far as possible prevent wrong-doing by others (*de offic.* 1.20–4). Wars should therefore be fought only *ut sine iniuria in pace vivatur* ["in order to live in peace without injustice"] and as a last resort, if diplomacy failed; they were, however, justified not only in self-defence but also for the protection of friends and allies against injury.

Cicero claimed that Numa had implanted in the Romans a 'love of peace and tranquillity, which enable justice and good faith most easily to flourish', and in rebutting an argument, which had been advanced by Carneades on his visit to Rome in 155, that all men necessarily followed their own interests without regard to justice, and that Rome had naturally pursued a policy of aggrandizing her own wealth and power, he maintained that her wars had been just: in particular, it was by defending her allies that Rome had secured world dominion. (Sallust propounds a similar view.) According to Cicero, by strict observance of the old fetial procedure, or of a procedure modelled on it, under which war had to be formally declared, and was to be declared only when reparation had been sought and refused, with the gods invoked to punish unjust demands, Rome had demonstrated her respect for the rights of others. Cicero's insistence that every war must have a *iusta causa* was certainly not peculiar to himself, but corresponded to Roman practice or propaganda since at least the third century.[52] Nor, despite lamentations on the supposed decay of moral standards, had it been abandoned in Cicero's own time. Caesar followed it with as much, or rather as little, scrupulosity as the senate had done in the second century. Augustus was later to boast that he had pacified the Alps *nulli genti bello per iniuriam inlato* ["with war having been waged unjustly against no people"] (*RG* 26).

In fact the primitive fetial procedure was certainly formalistic and permitted the enforcement in arms of demands that had no equitable basis. Livy, to whom we owe the preservation of what he took to be the ancient ritual (1.32), put into the mouth of the Alban dictator the cynical observation that though both Romans and Albans were putting forward claims for reparation *ex foedere*, 'if we are to say what is true rather than what is plausible, it is lust for empire that rouses two kindred and neighbouring peoples to arms' (1.23.7). For Livy himself the two cities were contending for *imperium servitiumque* (1.25.3); as Drexler observed, we are in a world where there can only be rulers and subjects, not equal independent powers. It was particularly hard for others to concede that Rome was merely fighting in defence of her friends and allies if (as was sometimes the case) she admitted states to her friendship and offered them protection at a time when they were already threatened or under attack; it was all too obvious that she was then acting for her own interest,[53] and of course victory would give her control of the conquered *iure belli*, and justify mass-enslavements, heavy indemnities or annexation, at her own discretion. Moreover, even Cicero adopted a wide formulation of the rights of a state to defend itself and its friends: 'we may ward off any disadvantage that may be brought to us' (*si quid importetur nobis incommodi propulsemus, de offic.* 2.18).

To an enemy like Perseus (Livy 42.52.16), and even to so sympathetic an interpreter of Roman policy as Polybius (1.10.6), it could appear that Rome took the mere existence of a powerful and potentially dangerous neighbour as such a disadvantage, and Cicero's principles were quite compatible with Cato's argument for finishing Carthage off: 'the Carthaginians are our enemies already; for whoever is directing all his preparations against me, so that he may make war on me at the time of his own choice, is already my enemy, even if he is not yet taking armed action' (*ORF*[2] fr. 195). In all cases the Romans were in Hobbes' words 'judges of the justness of their own fears'. In retrospect Lactantius could aver that 'it was by using fetials to declare war, inflicting injuries under cover of law and unceasingly coveting and carrying off what belonged to others that Rome obtained possession of the world' (*de div. inst.* 6.9.4). Roman reactions to the possibility of a threat resembled those of a nervous tiger, disturbed when feeding. It is hardly surprising that Polybius, although in his analysis of the origins of many particular wars Rome's policy appears to be defensive, concluded that Rome had persistently and deliberately aimed at extending her dominion.[54]

Cicero himself casually refers to Roman wars like those waged with Italian peoples, Pyrrhus and Carthage, the purpose of which was empire or glory. Such a purpose was hardly consistent with Panaetius' general account of justice, and I take it that it was Cicero who inserted the reference to them, half-conscious that Panaetius' doctrine did not after all permit the justification of all Rome's wars. He does indeed hasten to add that just causes must be found even in such cases.[55] But a just cause is now nothing but the 'decent pretext' that Polybius (36.2) thought the Romans were right to look for, after deciding on war for reasons of self-interest; it might be as legalistic and inequitable as those adduced for the Third Punic War.

Polybius thought that Rome needed them to impress the world, i.e. the Greek world, and it may be that as late as c. 150 the senate still had some regard for Greek public opinion, such as it had shown in the previous generation. This sort of consideration is certainly ascribed to the Romans on other occasions,[56] and their propagandist assumption of the role of protector of Greek liberty finds an analogy in Caesar's attempt to parade himself in 58 as the champion of the freedom of Gallic peoples against German invaders (*BG* 1.33 and 45); indeed his relations with the Gauls in a single decade offer a sort of telescoped parallel to those of Rome with the Greek cities between 200 and 146.

But Polybius may have been both too cynical and too inclined to overrate the importance in Roman eyes of his own fellow-Greeks. We must not forget that for Romans a just war was one in which the gods were on their side. The very formalism of Roman religion made it possible for them to believe that this divine favour could be secured, provided only that all the necessary ceremonies and procedures had been duly followed. Drexler (p. 110) suggested that the Romans fought better because they were convinced in this way of the rightness of the cause, even in cases when it does not seem morally defensible to us.[57] However Machiavellian the *principes* may have been in directing policy, they had perhaps to think of the morale of the common soldiers. Dio at least supposed that the near-mutiny at Vesontio in 58 was inspired not only by fear of Ariovistus but also by the suspicion that Caesar was entering on a campaign out of personal ambition without a just cause (38.35).

. . .

Roman 'clemency'

Wherever necessary, the most brutal methods of repression were therefore in order. Death or enslavement was the common penalty for freedom-fighters. Caesar was alleged to have made a million slaves in Gaul;[58] he himself casually refers to a load of captives he shipped back from Britain in 55 (*BG* 5.23.2), the only kind of booty, Cicero had heard (*ad Att.* 4.16.7), that could be expected from this poor island; he was delighted at Quintus' promise to send him some of them (*ad QF* 3.7.4). Caesar did all he could to extirpate the Eburones (*BG* 6.34 and 43). On one occasion, like Scipio Aemilianus, that paragon of Roman *humanitas* (App. *Iber.* 94), he had the right hands of all his prisoners cut off (8.44). Yet he speaks, as does Hirtius, of his clemency.[59]

It was characteristic of Romans as early as Cato (Gell. 6.3.52) to boast of what Livy calls their *vetustissimum morem victis parcendi* ["ancient custom of sparing the defeated"] (33.12.7). Once again Cicero held that Roman practice conformed to Panaetian laws of war; especially when wars were fought for glory, the conquered were to be treated with mercy. Only the destruction of Corinth had perhaps marred Rome's record. Not indeed that Cicero considered that mercy was always proper; it was not due to enemies who were themselves cruel or who were guilty of violating treaties, Rome naturally being the judge, nor when Rome's own survival was at stake. He does not make it clear how he would have justified the destruction of Numantia, which he approves.[60] But Numantia had rebelled; to Romans rebellion was in itself proof of perfidy. Polybius reports Flamininus as saying in 197 that the Romans were 'moderate, placable and humane', since they did not utterly destroy a people the first time they fought them (18.37). By implication repeated resistance might call for severity, which was also regarded as a virtue. When Virgil defined Rome's mission as *parcere subiectis et debellare superbos* ["to be lenient to the subjected and to war down the arrogant"], he was in effect dividing mankind into two categories, those too insolent to accept her god-given dominion, and those who submitted to it. The latter were to be spared: what of the former? Germanicus was to set up a monument boasting that he had 'warred down' the Germans, after exterminating one community with no distinction of age or sex (Tac. *Ann.* 2.21f).

Naturally this was not the practice Romans preferred. We may readily believe Augustus' claim that it was his policy to preserve foreign peoples who could safely be spared rather than extirpate them (*RG* 3). After all, the dead paid no taxes. Moreover it was usually more expedient to accept the surrender of an enemy, offered in the hope or expectation of mercy, rather than to incur the expense of time, money and blood in further military operations, and then to fulfil that expectation, if only to encourage others not to prolong their own resistance. Hampl found a precedent for Rome's normal conduct in Hittite inscriptions. It was not motivated primarily by humanity, but by rational consideration of self-interest.[61]

It is true that Cicero connected with Rome's supposed clemency to the vanquished her liberality with the franchise. In degree, if not in kind, this was undoubtedly a practice for which we can find no parallel in the policy of other city states. But for Cicero himself it was not altruistic generosity, but a device by which Rome had extended her empire (see p. 165). In early days it must have been prompted by self-interest, however enlightened, and it was not always welcome to beneficiaries such as the Capuans, if they did not attain to full equality of rights in the Roman state. By the time that Roman citizenship had come to be an object of the subjects' aspirations, it was a privilege granted reluctantly and sparingly. In Cicero's youth the Italians had had to wrest it from Rome by force of arms. Few now wished to go further and add to the numbers of *Romanos rerum dominos gentemque togatam* ["Romans, masters of affairs, and the people of the toga"]. All efforts to enfranchise the Transpadani failed until Caesar could carry the measure by military power in 49.[62] It was Caesar too who began to extend citizenship to provincial communities. More often he was content to bestow the Latin right, as to the Sicilians. They were Cicero's old clients, whose loyalty to Rome he had extolled in fulsome terms in 70; none the less, he regarded this grant as 'insufferable'.[63]

JUSTICE FOR THE SUBJECTS

In general Cicero speaks with contempt of provincials. Thus the most eminent of Gauls is not to be compared with the meanest of Romans; they were an arrogant and faithless people, bound by no religious scruples, the true descendants of those who had burned down the Capitol (*pro Font.* 27–36). Conceivably there might be Sardinians whose testimony a Roman court might believe, but most of them were mere barbarian half-breeds, more mendacious than their Punic forebears, and not one community in the island had earned the privileges of friendship with Rome and liberty (*pro Scaur.* 38–45). Even the Greeks, to whom Rome owed her culture, as Cicero often allowed,[64] were now for the most part degenerate,[65] yet they stood at a far higher level than such peoples as Mysians and Phrygians (*ad QF* 1.1.19), who constituted most of the population of the province of Asia. Jews and Syrians were 'nations born for servitude' (*de prov. cons.* 10). Admittedly in most of the passages cited Cicero was trying to discredit witnesses hostile to his clients, and he could speak, when it suited him, honorifically of provincial magnates and communities, but none the less such statements are eloquent of the prejudice he could easily arouse, and some of his private remarks even on Greeks are disdainful (e.g. *ad QF* 1.2.4).

The '*ideal* of inclusiveness' which Last treats as an 'outstanding feature of the political technique devised by the Roman Republic' had not in fact emerged.[66] The third book of Cicero's *de republica* preserves traces of an argument in which imperial dominion seems to have been defended as just in much the same way as the rule of soul over body or masters over slaves; men who were incapable of governing themselves were actually better off as the slaves or subjects of others.[67] The theory naturally did not imply that any actual slaves or subjects belonged to this category, but a Roman could easily persuade himself that experience showed the subjects to be unfitted for independence.

Under Roman private law the master was entitled to exploit his slaves as he pleased, and the *iura belli*, accepted throughout antiquity, allowed similar rights to the victor in war. Beyond doubt Romans took it for granted that Rome was justified in profiting from her empire. Yet in Panaetius' theory, which Cicero adopted, just as masters were bound to give slaves just treatment (*de offic.* 1.41), so an imperial power had a duty to care for the ruled, which Rome had faithfully discharged in the 'good, old days' before Sulla (2.27). Good government was due even to Africans, Spaniards and Gauls, 'savage and barbarous nations' (*ad QF* 1.1.27).

Many or most of Rome's subjects had come under her sway, not always after defeat, by *deditio*, which involved the surrender of *divina humanaque omnia* ["all things human and divine"] (Livy 1.38) and the extinction of the community concerned, but Rome regularly restored to the *dediti* their cities, lands and laws, often recognized them as her friends and sometimes concluded treaties with them; they thus acquired rights that *fides* or *religio* bound Rome to respect. In practice Rome left them all to manage their own internal affairs, at most ensuring that they were administered by persons loyal to the sovereign.[68]

Indemnities or taxes might be demanded from defeated enemies as *quasi victoriae praemium ac poena belli* ["as if the reward for victory and the penalties of war"] (II

Verr. 3.12), and provinces could be described as virtual estates of the Roman people (ibid. 2.7), yet Cicero at least felt it necessary to argue that taxation was in the interest of the provincials themselves: armies were required for their protection, and revenue was indispensable to pay them (*ad QF* 1.1.34). Thus taxation of the subjects was justified by the benefits conferred on them. Precisely the same argument was to be advanced by Tacitus.[69] There was not even anything new in Tiberius' celebrated dictum that he would have his subjects sheared, not shaved (Suet. *Tib.* 32): Cicero rebutted Verres' claim that he had acted in the public interest by selling the Sicilian tithes at unprecedentedly high amounts, by observing that neither senate nor people had intended him to act in such a way as to ruin the farmers and jeopardize future returns (II *Verr.* 3.48). This, however, is only a question of rational exploitation of the subjects, not of justice towards them.

We may indeed ask how far Cicero spoke for many more than himself in advocating justice to the subjects. Here I attach some significance to his denunciations of the misgovernment prevalent in his time, in the Verrines written for an upper-class audience, in his speech before the people on the Manilian law, and even in a despatch from Cilicia to the senate.[70] He assumes that his own sentiments are generally shared. He actually tells the senate that because of the oppressive and unjust character of Roman government the *socii* are too weak or too disloyal to contribute much to defence against Parthia. About the same time he wrote to Cato that it was his principal object, given the lack of adequate military resources, to provide for the protection of his province by his own mild and upright conduct that would ensure the fidelity of the *socii*, and he later claims that he had reconciled the provincials to Roman rule by the excellence of his own administration.[71] It was indeed a commonplace of ancient political thinking, doubtless based on oft-repeated experience, that in Livy's words *certe id firmissimum longe imperium est quo oboedientes gaudent* ["clearly an empire is by far most sound in which the obedient subjects are happy"];[72] it recurs, for instance, in discussions of absolute monarchy, which teach the king to show justice not only for its own sake but in order to secure the affection of his subjects and make his rule more secure.[73]

However, Cicero's letters from Cilicia and his advice to his brother in Asia (*ad QF* 1.1) do not suggest that good government was to be practised purely for this prudential reason. Cicero tells Atticus, for instance, that his integrity as a governor afforded him the greatest intrinsic satisfaction of his life. It mattered to him, he says, more than the fame it brought (*ad Att.* 5.20.6). But the allusion to fame should also be marked. 'Fame' he says in the first *Philippic* (29) 'is demonstrated by the testimony not only of all the best men but by that of the multitude.' It was in this sense that he expected his reputation to be enhanced by his virtues as a governor. So too he surely supposed that denunciations of misrule would evoke indignation – Pompey in 71, he tells us (I *Verr.* 45), had actually roused the people in this way – and equally that there would be a popular response to his laudation of Pompey, not only as a great general but as one whose upright behaviour won the hearts of the subjects (*de imp. Cn. Pomp.* 36–42); he does not add in this encomium that his behaviour would strengthen Roman rule. In the same way Caesar in his *Civil War* digresses to excoriate the cruelty and rapacity of Metellus Scipio and his officers in the east (*BC* 3.31–3); this was in part a propagandist work, and Caesar evidently hoped that his readers would condemn his enemies for their ill-treatment of provincials. The author of the

Bellum Africum also contrasts Caesar's care for African provincials (3.1, 7.2) with the depredations, and worse, of his adversaries (26).

Perhaps the constant use of the term *socii* to describe provincials in itself indicates something about Roman attitudes to them; it could hardly have been totally divested of the nuance imparted by its other senses. Much more striking, however, is the history of *repetundae* legislation. At least from the late third century the senate had been ready to hear complaints from the *socii* against Roman officials and to provide for reparation or punishment.[74] The statutes on this subject passed between 149 and 59 were the work of politicians of varying complexion, but according to Cicero (*de offic.* 2.75) each enactment made the law stricter. It is notable that the clause authorizing recovery of money from third parties who had benefited from the governor's extortions, a clause that could affect *equites* and was apparently often invoked, was introduced by Glaucia, who sought their political backing, and was simply adopted in later statutes (*Rab. post.* 8–10). Cicero briefly characterizes Sulla's law as *lex socialis* (*div. in Caec.* 18). Caesar's statute, comprising no less than 101 clauses (*ad fam.* 8.8.3), and approved by Cicero (*pro Sest.* 135; *in Pis.* 37), remained in force until Justinian's time and formed the basis of the law throughout the imperial period.[75] Our accounts of the eventful year in which it was passed are fairly full, yet they do not allude to its enactment. It was probably uncontroversial. Like earlier *repetundae* laws, it was concerned only with the wrong-doing of senatorial officials. The governor himself was supposed to protect subjects in his courts against publicans and usurers. On paper even Verres promised heavy damages against the former, if they were guilty of illicit exactions (II *Verr.* 3.26), and some governors gave the provincials real protection.[76]

No proof is needed that provincials found insufficient aid in the *repetundae* laws, *quae vi, ambitu, postremo pecunia turbabantur* ["which are agitated by force, by canvassing, finally by money"] (Tac. *Ann.* 1.2), or that many governors, for prudence or profit, connived at or participated in the rapacity of tax-gatherers and moneylenders. Personal or political connexions could also distort the conduct of senators who, like Cicero, had no wish for their own part to pillage the subjects.[77] In practice the provincials were usually at the mercy of the proconsul, who was virtually absolute in his province, *ubi nullum auxilium est, nulla conquestio, nullus senatus, nulla contio* ["where there is no appeal, no protest, no Senate, no public addresses"] (Cic. *ad QF.* 1.1.22). Their best hope lay in his probity and courage. In general he was restrained from indulging in or permitting extortion only by his conscience, or regard for his own reputation. Cicero enjoins upon Quintus and claims for himself, and for Pompey, such virtues as justice, mercy, accessibility and diligence. No quality is more often commended than that elementary honesty for which the most revealing Latin term is *abstinentia*.[78] The very frequency with which it is ascribed, whether truly or falsely, to individuals shows how little it could be assumed as a common characteristic of officials (cf. n. 81). Still, we must not too lightly treat a Verres or an Appius as typical of republican governors. Others are known to have been men of personal integrity, or, like Scaevola, Lucullus and perhaps Gabinius (n. 76), to have protected the subjects against usurers and publicans. Scaevola remained an exemplar; Cicero took his edict as the model for his own (cf. n. 76). In 50 Cicero tells Atticus that he had heard only good reports of all but one of the eastern governors; they were behaving in conformity with the high principles of Cato, *a quo uno omnium sociorum querelae audiuntur* ["by whom alone the complaints of all the allies are heard"], [79] and, incidentally, with those which Atticus had himself repeatedly recommended to Cicero.[80] The standards of good government were already recognized and approved in the republic, and the only change that came about in the Principate in this regard was that they were somewhat better observed, an improvement that it is easy to exaggerate.[81]

When Cicero included *provinciae, socii* among the *fundamenta otiosae dignitatis*, I feel sure that he meant among other things care for their welfare (cf. *de leg.* 3.9). But *aerarium* is another of the *fundamenta*, and in his day it was the provinces which supplied most of the revenue. It was probably not until the nineteenth century that any imperial power scrupled to tax subjects for its own benefit; the Romans were not ashamed to do so, and I imagine that most of them would have thought Cicero's justification of the practice, which I cited earlier, as superfluous. In one way or another senators and equites, soldiers and grain recipients at Rome all profited from the empire. In addressing the people Cicero can refer to 'your taxes' and 'your lands'.[82] He did not forget in advocating the Manilian law to argue that it served the interests of the treasury and of Romans with business in the east (*de imp. Cn. Pomp.* 14–19). Pompey boasted of the enormous accretion of revenue his conquests had brought (Plut. *Pomp.* 45). Nor must we overlook what Romans seldom mentioned, that victorious wars stocked Italian estates with cheap slaves.

I will add only one further point. Under the Principate the worst features of republican misrule were obliterated; above all peace and order were better preserved. But exploitation did not end. Italy benefited as much as the provinces from the Roman peace, yet until Diocletian the land there was immune from tax.[83] While contributing less than the provinces to the common needs for expenditure, Italians continued, as late as the third century, to enjoy a share of the higher posts disproportionate to that of provincials, if we simply equate Italy with an area in the provinces of like size and population.[84] Moreover provincial revenues were spent lavishly on feeding and amusing the inhabitants of Rome and beautifying the city, to say nothing of court expenditure. These privileges were not challenged by provincials in the senate or on the throne. Equality as between Italians and provincials was not attained, until all were sunk in equal misery.

NOTES

1   e.g. *in Cat.* 3.26; *pro Sest.* 67; *de prov. cons.* 30, 33; *pro Balb.* 64.

2   *pro Arch.* 12–32 is the *locus classicus.* Much evidence in U. Knoche's paper, reprinted in H. Oppermann, [ed., *Römische Wertbegriffe* (Darmstadt)], (1967), 420–46. On the old Roman *virtus*, manifest in services to the state, see [D.C.] Earl, [*The Political Thought of Sallust* (Cambridge)], (1961), ch. II.

3   See esp. *ad fam.* 15.4–6. Cicero retained the title of *imperator* at least till May 49 (ibid. 2.16).

4   Cf. Livy 1.16.7, 8.7.16: *disciplinam militarem, qua stetit ad hunc diem* ["military discipline, upon which the Roman state has stood to this day"] (340 B.C.) *Romana res;* 9.17.3: *plurimum in bello pollere videntur militum copia et virtus, ingenia imperatorum, fortuna per omnia humana, maxima in res bellicas potens; ea et singula intuenti et universa sicut ab*

aliis regibus gentibusque, ita ab hoc quoque (Alexander) *facile praestant invictum Romanum imperium* ["The most important factors in war seem to be the numbers and bravery of soldiers, the commanders' skills, and fortune, which, powerful in all human affairs, is especially so in war. These things, whether taken together or singly, make it clear that just as against other princes and nations, so against this one [Alexander the Great] Rome would have proved invincible"]; 9.17.10 (discipline); *praef.* 7: *ea belli gloria est populo Romano ut cum suum conditorisque sui parentem Martem potissimum ferat, tam et hoc gentes humanae patiantur aequo animo quam imperium patiuntur* ["So great is the martial glory of the Romans that when they claim that their father and the father of their founder was Mars himself, the peoples of the earth may well submit to this with as good grace as they submit to Rome's empire"]. (The idea that subjects accept an imperial power as 'deserving' to rule because of military prowess is in Thuc. 2.41.3.) [H.] Drexler, ["Iustum Bellum," *Rheinisches Museum*, 102] (1959), [19–140], cites many other texts from Livy on the concept of military glory.

5   *de rep.* 2 *passim*; cf. Polyb. 6.50.

6   See [H.] Roloff, [*Maiores bei Cicero* (Göttingen)], (1938).

7   F. Millar, *JRS* LXIII (1973), 50ff, and E. A. Judge in J. A. S. Evans, ed., *Polis and Imperium: Studies in honour of E. T. Salmon* (Toronto, 1974), 279ff, may be right in denying that Augustus officially claimed to have 'restored the Republic' in so many words, but Vell. 2.89 (and much else) shows that such a claim would well have summarized the official view of his settlement; it is significant that Velleius, a new man himself, is so concerned to stress that *prisca illa et antiqua rei publicae forma revocata (est)* ["that pristine and ancient form of state has been recalled"].

8   Livy 4.3ff (whence Claudius' speech in *ILS* 212 and Tac. *Ann.* 11.24); 8.13 (*voltis exemplo maiorum augere rem Romanam victos in civitatem accipiendo? materia crescendi per summam gloriam suppeditat* ["Would you follow the example of your ancestors, and increase the Roman state by receiving your conquered enemies as citizens?"]); Dionys. *Ant.* 2.16ff; 14.6; cf. [P.A.] Brunt, [*Italian Manpower, 225* BC –AD *14* (Oxford)], (1971), 538f. Cf. Cic. *de offic.* 1.35.

9   Jacoby, *FGH* 87 F 59. 111b (military discipline) and 112. I would ascribe Diod. 37.2–6 to Posidonius, who also deplored the decay of the old standards; cf. n. 10.

10 e.g. Sall. *Cat.* 6–13; Cic. *pro Marc.* 23; *Tusc. disp.* 1.2; Hor. *Odes* 3.6 and 24, etc. [F.] Hampl, ["Römische Politik in republikanischer Zeit, und das Problem des Sittenverfalls," *Historische Zeitung*, 188] (1959), [497–525], cites further texts and argues that such complaints (cf. also n. 9), which are just as common in classical Greece, have no basis in history and may actually betoken a heightened moral consciousness in the ages when they are made; I agree.

11 Cic. *de rep.* 2.5–11; Livy 5.54 (site of Rome); Vitruv. 6.1.10ff; Strabo 6.4.1 (strategic centrality of Italy). *Laudes Italiae* ["praises of Italy"], a theme dear to Varro: Brunt, [*Italian Manpower*], 128ff.

12 e.g. *in Cat.* 2.29, 3.18–22 (a remarkable testimony to popular superstition); *de dom.* 143; *pro Sest.* 53; *in Vat.* 14; *pro Scaur.* 48; *pro Mil.* 83; Sall. *BJ* 14.19.

13 *de har. resp.* 18ff, with particular reference to the skill of the *haruspices* in advising on the placation of the gods. Cicero was bound, if he was to persuade senators who credited this nonsense, not to let his own scepticism appear. Cf. *de nat. deor.* 2.8 ('Stoic'); *SIG*³ 601; Hor. *Odes* 3.6.1ff; *Mos. et Rom. Leg. Coll.* 6.4.8 (Diocletian); Aug. *Civ. Dei*, books 4 and 5 *passim*.

14 K. Latte, [*Römische Religionsgeschichte* (Munich)], (1960), 285f. [R.J.] Goar, [*Cicero and the State Religion* (Amsterdam)], (1972) ascribes a more sincere religious belief to Cicero, but his candid analysis of the letters yields a similar result.

15 *de leg.* 2.15ff; *de nat. deor.* 1.3ff, 77; Polyb. 6.56; cf. Posidonius (n. 9). Cicero also suggests that Athenians and Romans were civilized respectively by the Eleusinian Mysteries and by Numa's rituals (*de leg.* 2.36; *de rep.* 2.26ff). It is hard to see how Roman religion was ever thought to deter men from wrong-doing. Goar, [*Cicero*], notes that Cicero only twice threatens his enemies with punishment after death (*in Cat.* 1.33; *Phil.* 14.32); see Latte, [*Römische Religionsgeschichte*], 286ff, for lack of belief in an after-world, cf. esp. *pro Cluent.* 171. *de leg.* 2.25 suggests that religion makes men fear immediate punishment by the gods, but *de har. resp.* 39, *de leg.* 1.40 that they merely afflict the wrongdoer with *furor*, to which *de leg.* 2.43ff adds posthumous infamy.

16 *de leg.* 2.30–4, 3.27; *post red. sen.* 11, etc.; cf. Goar, [*Cicero*], 48ff. Yet, as Latte, [*Römische Religionsgeschichte*], 299, justly remarks, Bibulus' *obnuntiatio* had no effect even on the masses.

17 Varro, who himself accepted Stoic theology (Tert. *ad Nat.* 2.2), regarded it as superstition to fear the gods, disapproved of images and thought sacrifices futile (Arnob. 7.1), none the less followed Q. Mucius Scaevola in distinguishing three kinds of theology, philosophic and political, and approved of the last for the people, whom it was expedient to deceive; though he would not have instituted the old Roman religion in a new city, it was the duty of the priests to keep up the cults *ut potius (deos) magis colere quam despicere vulgus velit* ["so that the people would be more likely to cherish the gods than to despise them" (Aug. *Civ. Dei* 4.31; cf. 4.11.13 and 27; 6.5f). Cf. Latte, *Römische Religionsgeschichte*], 291ff.

18 *de leg.* 2.32ff; cf. *de div.* 2.75. On Appius Claudius see Latte, [*Römische Religionsgeschichte*], 291.

19 *de div.* 2.28.70 and 148.

20 Latte, [*Römische Religionsgeschichte*], ch. X; F. Schulz, *Roman Legal Science* (Oxford, 1946), 80ff.

21 They are collected by Ursula Heibges, *Latomus* XXVIII (1969), 833–49. I do not accept her assumption that Cicero shared, as well as adapted himself to, the vacillating beliefs of his contemporaries.

22 See W. Kroll, *Kultur der ciceronischen Zeit* (Leipzig, 1933), I, ch. 1, who in my view overestimates the continuing strength of the traditional religion even in educated circles.

23 Tac. *Ann.* 3.55, 16.4; Pliny, *Ep.* 1.1.4, apply *a fortiori* to this period; cf. Cic. *pro Rosc. Am.* 43–8; it is reasonable to believe that piety was as much valued as other ancient virtues.

24 This is based on analysis of the list of senators in 55 in P. Willems, *Le Sénate de la République rom.* (Paris, 1878), ch. XV, which, though antiquated, will serve for a rough estimate; I assume that *novi* preponderated among the *ignoti*. Clodius' *incestum*: *ad Att.* 1.13.3; cf. 12.3, 14.1–5, 16.1–9. I can see no evidence that Cicero or the other *principes* acted from outraged religious feeling.

25 *in Cat.* 2.11; *pro Rab. perd.* 33; *pro Sest.* 50; *de rep.* 3.41. Cf. Hor. *Epodes* 16; Livy 9.19.17.

26 [J.] Vogt, [*Orbis* (Freiburg im Breisgau, 1960)] assembles texts and interprets the meaning of the phrase. *ad Her.* 4.13 is the earliest extant instance in Latin. Alternatively, Cicero speaks of Rome's power over all peoples, II *Verr.* 4.81; *de leg. agr.* 2.22; *de dom.* 90; *pro Planc.* 11; *Phil.* 6.19.

27 *SEG* 1.335, cf. Cic. *ad Att.* 4.1.7 (consular law of 57 *de annona*); Polyb. 1.1.5, 1.3.10, 3.1.4, 6.50.6; for his true meaning 1.3.9, 15.9.5 with 2.14.7 and 4.2.2. A gloss in Vell. 1.6.6 shows that Aemilius Sura dated Rome's world dominion to the defeat of Antiochus III; some hold that he wrote before 171, see [J. W.] Swain, ["The Theory of the Four Monarchies: Opposition History under the Roman Empire," *Classical Philology*, 35] (1940), [1–21]. Polybius' conception was then perhaps shared by Romans in his own lifetime.

28   [R. K.] Sherk, [*Roman Documents from the Greek East* (Baltimore)], (1969), no. 16.

29   [E.] Badian, [*Foreign Clientelae* (Oxford)], (1958), part I *passim*.

30   [M. R.] Cimma, [*Reges Socii et Amici Populi Romani* (Milan)], (1976) gives the fullest recent treatment of 'client' kings. Citizenship: PIR^2 A 900; H 153; I 65, 131f, 149, 175ff, 274ff, 276ff, 472, 512–17, 541, 637, 644. Armenia: *RG* 27. Lucullus had overrun Armenia; Pompey received the humble submission of Tigranes and recognized him as king, friend and ally of Rome (Cic. *Sest.* 58ff; Plut. *Pomp.* 53, etc.). When Corbulo proposed *parta olim a Lucullo Pompeioque recipere* ["to recover places once [taken] by Pompey and Lucullus"] (Tac. *Ann.* 13.34), he designed (as the context shows) to force the Parthian nominee on the throne to recognize, like Tigranes, the suzerainty of Rome: there was no thought of annexation.

31   *BJ* 14.1; cf. Livy 42.6.8 (Antiochus IV); 45.44.19 (Prusias I); also the Rhodian speech in 37.54.

32   In 47 Caesar required the kings and dynasts near Syria to protect that province as friends of Rome (*B. Alex.* 65.4). But most of them had territories that did not lie *between* Syria and Parthia. Ariobarzanes: Cic. *ad fam.* 15.1–4 *passim*; *ad Att.* 6.3.5. Tribute: Livy 45.18.7f; [E.] Badian, [*Roman Imperialism in the Late Republic*, 2nd edn. (Oxford, 1968)], ch. VI.

33   [T.] Liebmann-Frankfort, [*La Frontière orientale dans la politique exterieure de la République romaine* (Brussels, 1969)], 7ff and *passim*.

34   [P.] Veyne, ["Y-a-t-il eu un imperialisme romain?," *MEFR*, 87] (1975), [793–855], is no doubt right that in the third and early second centuries, with which he is concerned, 'Rome ne songe pas encore à dominer le monde, mais plûtot à être seule au monde' ["Rome does not yet dream of dominating the world, but rather to be independent to the world"], but 'defensive' wars fought for this purpose were bound to appear aggressive to others and to be interpreted in the light of the dominance Rome attained, which in turn created the ideal of world rule.

35   Polyb. 3.22–5 (the last renewal was in 279) for Carthage; App. *Bell. Samm.* 7.1 (Tarentum); the clause was perhaps ambiguous.

36   2.13.7 (cf. [F. W.] Walbank, [*A Historical Commentary on Polybius*, vol.1 (Oxford, 1957), 168–72], for varying views); 3.15, 3.20ff and 28–30.

37   Livy 34.58; see Badian, [*Foreign Clientelae*], 76ff, Livy 38.38.

38   [K. H.] Ziegler, [*Die Beziehungen zwischen Rom und den Parthenreich* (Wiesbaden, 1964)], 20ff; Liebmann-Frankfort, [*La Frontière*], 171ff, 237ff, 263ff, 276ff, 296ff, 308ff for evidence and discussion. Of course there was never any formal treaty ratified at Rome, and perhaps no more than a vague understanding; cf. Dio 37.5.

39   Plut. *Pomp.* 36; Dio 37.5–7; 40.20.1.

40   [M.] Gelzer, ["Die Anfange des römischen Weltreichs," in *Kleine Schriften*, vol. 2 (Wiesbaden)], (1963), 15ff (first published in 1940).

41   [E.] Badian, [*Roman Imperialism*] (1968), 9ff.

42   Cicero had a quaestor, four legates, a *praefectus fabrum* (*ad fam.* 3.7.4) and other equestrian prefects, of whom he sent one to do justice in Cyprus (*ad Att.* 5.21.6). Pliny had only one legate (*Ep.* 10.25); there were also an equestrian procurator with one or two freedmen assistants – Epimachus perhaps succeeded Maximus – and the prefect of the *ora Pontica* (21ff, 27ff, 83–6a). Both could call on a *cohors amicorum*, and on military officers, of whom there were far more in Cicero's province. No doubt the procurator had more clerical staff than Cicero and his quaestor.

43   A. H. M. Jones, [*The Roman Economy* (Oxford)], (1974), ch. VIII for a brief survey.

44   Cic. II *Verr.* 2.32; *ad Att.* 6.1.15, 6.2.4. I am not convinced by D. Kienast's rejection in [*ZSS*] LXXXV (1968), 330ff, of the orthodox view that grants of *libertas* did not give cities exemption from the governor's jurisdiction.

45 *ad QF* 1.1.25; cf. A. H. M. Jones, [*The Greek City from Alexander to Justinian* (Oxford)], (1940), 170ff.

46 *BG* 4.21, 5.25 and 54; but Commius (4.21) ultimately turned against the Romans, and the native leaders most dangerous to Rome were sometimes kings or aspirants to kingship backed by popular support (1.3ff, 7.4; cf. the case of Ambiorix, 5.27, 6.31).

47 *ad Att.* 6.2.5.

48 Badian, [*Roman Imperialism*], ch. I.

49 Brunt, [*Italian Manpower*], 432ff, 449. Conscription: ch. XXII.

50 Cic. *ad fam.* 3.3.1. Cicero's army: Brunt, [*Italian Manpower*], 689.

51 See also the Cnidus inscription published in *JRS* LXIV (1974), col. III 5ff. Despite Cicero's *plurimae leges veteres* ["many old laws"], the prohibition might have been introduced first in Saturninus' *maiestas* ["treason"] law, as a result of recent disasters incurred by aggressive proconsuls. But were all provincial frontiers clearly defined? And was a proconsul debarred either from striking first at an enemy force mustering outside the province, or from pursuing it after repelling an incursion? In Cicero's Cilicia the land route from the Phrygian *conventus* to Cilicia Pedias actually passed through the Cappadocian kingdom; he went outside his province three times in a year. Caesar felt no inhibition in attacking Ariovistus, etc., and there is no indication that his apparent violation of his own rule was censured even by his enemies except in one instance.

52 *Iustae causae* ["just causes"] and fetial law: Cic. *de offic.* 1.34–6 and 80: *de rep.* 2.31 (cf. 26 on Numa), 3.34ff, part of the answer to Furius Philus' speech, 8ff, which derives from a discourse of Carneades (Lactant., *div. inst.* 5.14ff), delivered at Rome in 155; cf. [C.] Capelle, ["Griechische Ethik und römischer Imperialismus," *Klio*, 25] (1932), [86–113], and [F. W.] Walbank ["Political Morality and the Friends of Scipio," *JRS*, 55] (1965), 13; it is immaterial here whether Panaetius supplied the answer (*contra* [H.] Strasburger, ["Posidonius on Problems of the Roman Empire," *JRS*, 55] (1965), 45). See also Sall. *Cat.* 6.5; *or. Lepidi* 4; Drexler, ["Iustum Bellum"] collects much material from Livy. For adaptation of fetial procedure in the middle republic, see [W.] Dahlheim, [*Struktur und Entwicklung des römischen Völkerrechts* (Munich, 1968)], 171ff; but see now J. W. Rich, *Declaring War in the Roman Republic in the Period of Transmarine Expansion* (Collection Latomus CXLIX) (1976), ch. III. Neither its origins, cf. [F.] Hampl ["Stoische Staatsethik und frühes Rom," *Historische Zeitung*, 184] (1957), [249–71], nor Roman practice, when documented, can warrant Cicero's claims that it embodied a distinctively high moral standard.

53 Witness the cases of Saguntum and of the Greek cities in Asia, whose freedom Rome professed to protect against Antiochus III, while perfectly willing to abandon it in her own interests, Badian, [*Foreign Clientelae*], 75ff.

54 1.3.6ff, 1.6, 1.10 with 20; 1.63.9, 2.31 with 21; 3.2.6, 3.3.8ff, 6.50.6, 9.10.11, 15.10.2. For Greek views of Roman imperialism, see also 5.104, 9.37.6, 11.5; Livy (P) 31.29.6. Polybius' general judgements deserve attention although they conflict with the details of his narrative perhaps derived from Roman informants, which fit a defensive interpretation of Roman policy ([F. W.] Walbank, ["Polybius and Rome's Eastern Policy," *JRS*, 53] (1963), [1–13], with a different explanation of the apparent inconsistency). See also Walbank, ["Political Morality,"] on his cynicism in analysing many Roman actions after 168. Perhaps his experience of contemporary Roman conduct and knowledge of the actual consequences of earlier wars made it hard for Polybius to credit that Rome's policy had ever been so defensive as the information he accepted in his narrative naturally suggested.

55 *de offic.* 1.38, 3.87. On the Hannibalic war see Lucret. 3.836ff; Livy 22.58.3, 27.39.9, 28.19.6ff, 29.17.6, 30.32.2. Unlike some Stoics (Cic. *de fin.* 3.57), Panaetius probably allowed some value to glory, but could hardly have regarded its pursuit as condoning injustice.

56 Polyb. 36.2 and 9, on which see [W.] Hoffmann, ["Das römische Politik des 2. Jahrhunderts und das Ende Karthagos," *Historia* 9] (1960), [309–44]; for a parallel, 32.9 and 13. There is nothing peculiarly Roman in insistence on a *iusta causa* for a war prompted by very different motives, cf. Thuc. 6.93 and 105; 7.18 (Sparta); 6.6 and 8 (Athens); Polyb. 3.6 and Arr. *Anab.* 2.14 (Macedon). For public opinion, Drexler, ["Iustum Bellum,"] cited Livy 3.72.2ff, 30.16.8ff, 45.18.1.

57 Drexler, ["Iustum Bellum,"] cited Livy 5.51ff, 31.9.5, 45.39.10 and many other texts. Cf. Thuc. 7.18 (Sparta).

58 Plut. *Caes.* 15; App. *Celt.* 2, misinterpreted by [W. L.] Westermann, [*The Slave Systems of Greek and Roman Antiquity* (Philadelphia)], (1955), 63, though naturally unreliable. Note *BG* 7.89.5.

59 *BG* 2.14.28 and 31ff, 8.3.5, 21.2. In 8.44.1 and 3.16 note apologies for special severity; but cf. Cic. *de offic.* 3.46.

60 Cic. II *Verr.* 5.115; *de offic.* 1.33–5, 1.82, 2.18, 3.46. Numantia: see [A. E.] Astin [*Scipio Aemilianus* (Oxford)], (1967), 153–5 on App. *Iber.* 98.

61 ...*Deditio*: Dahlheim, *Struktur*, ch. 1. Especially significant on Roman motives for clemency: Livy 42.8.5ff, 44.7.5 and 31.1; Jos. *BJ* 5.372ff. Cf. generally Livy 30.42.17: *plus paene parcendo victis quam vincendo imperium auxisse* ["to have increased the empire almost more by sparing the conquered than by conquest"].

62 Cicero sought to arouse prejudice against L. Piso, *cos.* 58, because his mother was Insubrian, *in Pis.* fr. 9–12 (OCT); *post red. sen.* 15.

63 *ad Att.* 14.12.1. Contrast II *Verr.* 2.2–8.

64 *pro Flacc.* 62; *ad QF* 1.1.27ff; *de rep.* 2.34; *Tusc. disp.* 1.1–7 (but stressing Roman moral superiority).

65 *pro Flacc.* 9, 16, 57, 61; *ad QF* 1.1.16, 1.2.4; *pro Sest.* 141; *pro Lig.* 11. He found it necessary to differentiate the Sicilians (who were almost like old Romans!) from other Greeks, II *Verr.* 2.7.

66 *CAH* XI 437.

67 *de rep.* 3.37–41, whence Aug. *Civ. Dei* 19.21, cf. Capelle, ["Griechische Ethik"], 93.

68 Dahlheim, [*Struktur*], chs. I and II.

69 *Hist.* 4.74. Dio makes Maecenas add that taxation should be levied on all alike (52.28ff). That was still not the case when he wrote.

70 See esp. II *Verr.* 3.207 (in 2.2–8, 5.8 he implausibly claims that the Sicilians loved their master, but treats them as exceptional); *de imp. Cn. Pomp.* 65; *ad fam.* 15.1.5.

71 *ad fam.* 15.3.2 and 4.14; *ad Att.* 5.18.2.

72 Cf. Polyb. 5.11, 10.36; Sall. *BJ* 102.6; Cic. II *Verr.* 3.14; Livy 8.13.16.

73 e.g. Sen. *Clem.* 1.3, 8.6ff, 11.4, etc., as in Polyb. 5.11.

74 [A.] Toynbee, [*Hannibal's Legacy*, 2 vols. (London)], (1965), vol. 2, 608ff. Particularly significant are the activities of the elder Cato in seeking to redress or punish wrongs done to subjects (*ORF*[2] frs. 58ff, 154, 173, 196–9); note also the indignation that Gaius Gracchus tried to arouse at ill-treatment of the Italians (Gell. 10.3). Even if personal or political feuds explain why some or most charges were brought, it would remain true that injustice to subjects was a suitable pretext for assailing personal adversaries.

75 [P. A.] Brunt, ["Charges of Provincial Maladministration under the Early Principate," *Historia*, 10] (1961), part I.

76 On the duty of governors and its delicacy, Cic. *ad QF* 1.1.32–6; *ad Att.* 5.13.1. Posidonius held (with some anachronism) that equestrian control of the courts made governors too fearful to restrain equites in the provinces (Jacoby, *FGH* 87 F 108d and 111b). There were certainly exceptions like Q. Mucius Scaevola and L. Sempronius Asellio (Diod. 37.5 and 8 from Posid.), Lucullus (Plut. *Luc.* 20) and perhaps Gabinius in Syria (Cic. *de prov.*

cons. 10; *ad QF* 3.2.2); Cicero adopted Scaevola's edict on the publicans, while that of Bibulus in Syria was overtly still stricter (*ad Att.* 6.1.15, but see *ad fam.* 3.8.4).

77 From Cilicia Cicero pressed administrators of other provinces to comply with Roman moneylenders' demands (e.g. *ad fam.* 13.56 and 61) in terms perhaps not very different from the pleas on Scaptius' behalf that he resented. Despite his condemnation of Appius Claudius' conduct as governor (e.g. *ad Att.* 5.15ff and 6.1.2), he did what he could to hinder his conviction at Rome (*ad fam.* 3.10.1; *ad Att.* 6.2.10), and showed his displeasure with hostile witnesses from Cilicia (*ad fam.* 3.11.3). Similarly in 70 L. Metellus had reversed Verres' *acta* in Sicily (II *Verr.* 2.62ff, 138–40, 3.43–6, 5.55) but obstructed his prosecution (2.64ff, 160–4, 3.122, 152ff, 4.146–9).

78 *ad QF* 1.1 (a letter presumably intended for publication) commends *aequitas, clementia, comitas, constantia, continentia, facilitas* (for the meaning of which see *de imp.* Cn. *Pomp.* 41; *ad Att.* 6.2.5), *gravitas, humanitas, integritas, lenitas, mansuetudo, moderatio, severitas, temperantia,* ["equitability, clemency, courtesy, steadiness, restraint, facility, seriousness, humanity, integrity, gentleness, civility, moderation, severity, temperance"]. Several of these virtues (also *fides, innocentia* ["trustworthiness, innocence"]) recur in Cicero's eulogy of Pompey (*de imp.* Cn. *Pomp.* 13.36–42) and in the claims he makes on his own behalf in 51–50 B.C. (*ad Att.* 5.9.1, 15.2, 17.2, 18.2, 20.6, etc.; *ad fam.* 15.4.1 and 14), along with *abstinentia* (for whose meaning see also *ad Att.* 5.10.2, 16.3, 21.5; *continentia, innocentia, integritas, temperantia* ["trustworthiness, innocence, integrity, temperance, justice and modesty"] are more or less synonymous), *iustitia* and *modestia*. See R. Combès, *Imperator* (Paris, 1966), ch. VIII.

79 *ad Att.* 6.1.13; *ad fam.* 15.4.15.

80 *ad Att.* 5.9.1, 10.2, 13.1, 15.2, 21.5 and 7. Conceivably in pressing Scaptius' case, Atticus did not know all the facts.

81 Brunt, ["Charges"], part II.

82 *de imp.* Cn. *Pomp.* 4ff, 7; *de leg. agr.* 2.80ff.

83 Aurelius Victor, *Caes.* 39.31.

84 G. Barbieri, *L'Albo senatorio da Severo a Carino* (Rome, 1952), 441, found that forty-three per cent of senators whose origins were known or probable were Italian. H.-G. Pflaum, *Les Procurateurs équestres* (Paris, 1950), 193, assigned an Italian origin to twenty-six out of ninety-one third-century procurators.

EDITOR'S NOTES

i Cotta would not express his own convictions on the gods in a public speech before the Roman people.

ii *kath'hemas* may be roughly translated as "with which we are familiar."

Rome and the Enemy: Imperial Strategy in the Principate

Susan Mattern

THE PRESTIGE OF THE EMPEROR

Just as Rome depended on repeated and vigorous proof of its military prowess to maintain its superior international status and, as the Romans saw it, the integrity and security of their empire, so the defeat and humiliation of barbarians was highly valued within Roman society and conferred immense *personal* prestige on anyone who could accomplish it.[i] This is easily inferred from the extensive publicity that such success always received. The theme of the humiliated and submissive enemy – always easily recognizable by his long hair, beard, and characteristic ethnic clothing or, alternatively, nudity or partial nudity – is extraordinarily popular in the iconography of the Principate; the kneeling barbarian and especially the bound barbarian prisoner were favorite themes on coins and monuments.[1] Colossal statues of bound Dacian prisoners decorated Trajan's forum; his gigantic *tropaeum* at Adamklissi was surmounted by a trophy with four prisoners at its foot.[2] Barbarians trampled under the foot of a victorious emperor, or under his horse in an equestrian representation, or being speared by the emperor on a horse, were also very popular; an extant statue of Hadrian shows the emperor in military uniform stepping on a barbarian; and the famous equestrian statue of Marcus Aurelius on the Capitoline hill may have originally crushed a barbarian[3] (the equestrian trampling theme was also popular on the tombstones of cavalrymen throughout the western empire).[4] The lower register of the Gemma Augustea, a large cameo, shows a bound barbarian prisoner, a kneeling, suppliant barbarian, and a woman being dragged by the hair, while Roman soldiers erect a trophy; the upper register shows Augustus, naked to the waist and enthroned like Jupiter, being crowned by a personification of *oikoumene* – the inhabited world – amid symbols of world rule.[5]

Emperors advertised their military successes on triumphal arches and other victory monuments and in spectacular triumphal ceremonies, as well as on coins announcing territories "captured," "conquered," and "subjugated"; proclaiming victories *de Britannis, de Germanis, de Sarmatis*, or reading simply *Victoria Britannica, Parthica*, or *Germanica*, with a representation of the goddess; this last type becomes especially popular beginning with Commodus.[6] Poets and panegyrists praised the emperors' military victories at every opportunity, and their victories were accumulated and celebrated in the imperial titulature itself. The martial element in this titulature was quite prominent. Augustus took the title *imperator* – traditionally voted to a victorious general by acclamation of the army – as his first name, and after Nero this became standard. It would appear again toward the end of the title, with a numeral to indicate the total number of acclamations.[7] All the Julio-Claudians were *Germanicus*, and Domitian took this title after his war with the Chatti; Trajan was the first to hold multiple victory titles (*Dacicus, Germanicus, Parthicus*), and after that, inflation seems to have set in. Marcus and Verus were *Parthici Maximi*, and after Severus, *Maximus* – greatest – became a standard part of any victory title.[8] Beginning with Marcus and Verus, too, miscellaneous titles like "Extender of the Empire," "Invincible," or "Pacifier of the World" become popular.[9] An inscription from a milestone dedicated to Caracalla gives an idea of the cumulative effect; the title in the inscription reads: "To the Emperor Caesar Marcus Aurelius Severus Antoninus, Pious, Blessed, Augustus, victor of Arabia, victor of Adiabene, greatest victor of Parthia, greatest victor of Britain, chief priest, in the fifteenth year of his tribunician power, *imperator* twice, consul three times, father of his country."[10] It was usual for the emperor's full titulature to appear on milestones, and thus it was rather conspicuous; it would also appear on public monuments, on military *diplomata* (discharge documents granting citizenship) and other official documents, and parts of it (though obviously not all) would fit on coins. This raises the question of whom the emperor was trying to reach by publicizing his victories. For some publicity – including triumphal parades, the lavish ceremony of Tiridates' coronation, and perhaps monuments at Rome such as the imperial fora – the urban plebs may have been the chief audience. But another obvious candidate is the army, since not only *diplomata* but coins and milestones would all have been effective here, especially since their inscriptions were in Latin and not in Greek.[11] It is significant that ancient sources perceive a relationship between a martial, victorious image and the loyalty of the army.[12] We might well believe that such an image also had a great deal of appeal for the emperor's own class – the senatorial aristocracy – as well, and that the emperors themselves must have shared these values, and been genuinely eager to defeat barbarians and genuinely proud of their successes. Certainly emperors with unwarlike images attracted sharp criticism from the literary sources, and a military background was considered a good qualification for the office.[13] And, while it is possible that Domitian could announce *Germania capta* on his coins to provincials and perhaps even to the army with impunity, the senatorial aristocracy could distinguish between honors and triumphs that reflected a "real" defeat of barbarians . . . and undeserved honors voted in flattery.[14]

It is therefore not surprising that many emperors are supposed to have undertaken aggressive campaigns purely or mainly in order to enhance their own prestige. Understandably, the desire to acquire personal glory (i.e., *ambitio*, or φιλοτιμία), or a concern for *fama*, or δόξα, was considered an insufficiently "just" cause for waging unprovoked wars of conquest;[15] nevertheless, to the ancient sources the desire for a title, a triumph, or a glorious reputation seemed a perfectly plausible explanation for war, including such a monumental effort as Trajan's Parthian war, or one with such important cultural consequences as the conquest of Britain.[16]

It is possible that the provincial aristocracy of the Greek east was less impressed with the emperor's military exploits than were his senatorial colleagues. It is possible to see something of a "language gap" on the foreign-relations issue: writers of Greek are more likely to describe the empire as surrounded by barriers and troops, thus emphasizing the defensive function of the army; they are more likely to protest the expense of new conquests and to deride the barbarians outside the empire as "useless" and "unprofitable."[17] Thus a martial emperor like Trajan might find himself listening to an extended parable by a Greek sophist on the follies of excessive militarism.[18] As ambassadors, doctors, secretaries *ab epistulis*, and hangers-on, Greek intellectuals were very prominent presences in the emperor's entourage.[19] It may have been this group that most influenced the philhellene Hadrian, whose foreign policy contrasts sharply with that of other emperors: he used no victory titles, he took the controversial step of abandoning conquered territory, and Cassius Dio associates him with a policy of intensified military exercises, nonaggression, and money payments to barbarians – all of which the historian himself approves.[20]

It is an indication of the immense prestige that military victory could bring to an individual that by the middle of the first century A.D. all of its honors – triumphs, victory titles, monuments, acclamations of *imperator* – became the sole privilege of the emperor or his designated successor. Already early in the reign of Augustus, Cornelius Gallus was exiled for the publicity he gave his accomplishments in Egypt, and Licinius Crassus celebrated a triumph for his conquests in Moesia and Thrace but was denied the *spolia opima*[iii] for the defeat of an enemy commander in single combat.[21] The only military honors regularly offered to imperial legates were the *triumphalia*, or triumphal ornaments, which were often granted for nonmilitary reasons, and the ancient sources sometimes perceive them as hopelessly trivialized.[22] But other evidence indicates that senators were proud of this distinction nevertheless: Suetonius writes that Claudius granted them so frequently that "a joint letter in the name of the legions arose, asking that *triumphalia* should be given to consular legates at the same time as their commands, so that they would not seek every excuse for war";[23] and Plautius Silvanus boasts of receiving the *triumphalia* in his epitaph (*ILS* 986). Thus legates like Suetonius Paulinus might still be motivated to win glory through victory; he is supposed to have invaded Mona "desiring to equal the honor (*decus*) of the recapture of Armenia by conquering enemies" (*Ann.* 14.29).

But it was not in the emperor's interest to allow too much of this. It was dangerous to permit others of high rank to achieve military success.[24] Emperors are often supposed to be suspicious or jealous of victorious subordinates; and successful commanders are described as threats. On several occasions legates are supposedly recalled from potentially glorious conquests for this reason.[25] Verus entrusted the war against Parthia to Avidius Cassius, who revolted with the army of Syria; in Marcus' speech to the troops, it is apparently Cassius' fame "for his deeds against the Parthians" that is his main attraction.[26] More and more, emperors tended to assume command of campaigns themselves, if the provincial army was insufficient.

All of this meant that, paradoxically, the very great prestige attached to military victory partially explains the slow pace of conquest under the Principate. Governors may have been relatively indifferent to new conquests for which they would receive minimal glory, or they may have feared the fate that too much success might bring – with good reason; emperors, also with good reason, would be suspicious of anyone who won glorious victories, and might well discourage this. Thus the ferocious competition for glory that fueled the conquests of the late Republic did not exist in the Principate. In addition, it was probably the need to prevent large armies from falling into the hands of rivals that accounts for the division of provinces like Moesia, Pannonia, and Germany; this was of strategic significance to the empire, because attacks that could not be handled by a provincial army required special commands and long delays. Thus the emperor's need to control the prestige associated with victory contributed significantly to the general shape of foreign relations in the Principate. Finally, we should note that the goals of Roman foreign policy – domination and humiliation of the enemy, which did not necessarily, for example, involve the occupation of new territory – made it easier to substitute propaganda for more substantial achievement; and an emperor motivated mainly by prestige concerns, rather than more familiar, geopolitical strategic preoccupations, might well find it easier and cheaper to propagandize.[27] Nero's baroque ceremonial humiliation of Tiridates substituted for the more costly and difficult military effort that would have been necessary to achieve the reinstatement of Rome's nominee in Armenia – though as we have seen, emperors who chose this path risked criticism from their own class.

DISCIPLINE

So far this study has described a culture that placed immense value on the subjection of foreign peoples. This value system had, for example, a geographical element, as place-names figure prominently in the rhetoric of imperialism; and an economic element, as part of the glory of conquest lay in the acquisition of the material wealth of the conquered. It also had a social element, the prestige that accrued to successful military commanders; and a moral and psychological element, more difficult to define, where foreign policy was perceived as a system of national honor, insult, and retribution that justified conquest and maintained security. The value attached to warfare also emerges in the very important Roman concept of discipline, which requires a brief separate treatment. If one were to ask the Romans to explain their success in building and maintaining their empire, it is unquestionable that a large part of the answer would be the discipline of the army. By this, Romans seem to have meant a certain sophistication of tactics and organization; but *disciplina*, or ἄσκησις, also had an important moral dimension; it is the opposite of decadence and luxury, and it is easily corrupted by money and peace.

At the beginning of a long digression on the training, organization, tactics, and equipment of the Roman army, Josephus writes that his discussion will show "that they hold such a great empire as a prize of valor (ἀρετῆς κτῆμα), not as a gift of fortune."[28] Aelius Aristides includes an encomium of the Roman army's self-control and organization in his panegyric to Rome (86–88). Centuries later, Vegetius begins his treatise *On Military Matters* with the statement "It is evident that the Roman people have subjected the world by no other means than the exercise of arms, the discipline of the camps, and warlike practices." He adds, "What indeed could the small number of Romans have accomplished against the multitude of the Gauls? What could their shortness have dared against the tallness of the Germans?" (1.1).

As this passage suggests, the Romans often contrast their own superior discipline with the indiscipline of their barbarian enemies. Barbarians are often associated with a fighting style that is frenzied, sporadic, and disorganized. The stereotype can be found in Seneca's treatise *On Anger*: "What indeed is it that shatters the barbarians, so much more robust in body and so much more enduring of labors, if not anger, the quality most inimical to themselves?" If one were to give the Germans reason (*ratio*) and discipline, "it will certainly be necessary for us to return to Roman ways" (1.11.1–4). Barbarians, who tend to "rush into war," "disorganized, unafraid, reckless," are easily cut down by the Roman legions (3.2.6). Similar ideas can be found in Strabo, Tacitus, and elsewhere. Parthians, like other barbarians, cannot endure long campaigns;[29] Germans, Gauls, and other northern barbarians are quick to attack and strong initially but lack perseverance and organization.[30] ... this stereotype antedates the Principate and can be found, for example, in Polybius. Also in Polybius we discover a type of battle narrative that pervades the literature of the imperial period: the story of the triumph of Roman military virtues over barbarian vices. Again and again we read of the defeat of undisciplined barbarians by the superior hard work, organization, and self-control of the legions, sometimes against overwhelming odds.[31]

The topos of Roman military virtue contrasted with barbarian vice is especially prominent in Tacitus: Caecina escapes from near disaster when the Germans, ignoring Arminius' advice to wait until the Romans march out of their camp, instead follow the advice of Inguiomerus, "fiercer and pleasing to barbarians (*atrociora... et laeta barbaris*)," impatiently storming the camp (*Ann.* 1.68). Similarly, the defeat of Tacfarinas is accomplished in a night battle where "the Romans had drawn together the infantry, posted the cavalry in position, and prepared everything for battle; the enemy, on the other hand, ignorant of everything, had no arms, no order, no plan, but like beasts they were dragged, killed, and captured" (*Ann.* 4.25). Similar themes arise in the extended narrative sculpture on Trajan's column, which portrays the Roman army as constantly at work building forts, roads, and bridges; barbarians are notoriously lazy.[32]

Sometimes the barbarians' drunkenness – another typical trait – or greed for plunder plays a role, as in Germanicus' slaughter of the Marsi, who are lying in a stupor with no guards posted, thus displaying laziness as well (*Ann.* 1.50–1). Tacitus' Sarmatian marauders in the invasion of A.D. 69 are dispersed and weighted down in their greed for booty; but "on the Roman side all was ready for battle," and the raid is easily repelled.[33] In Cassius Dio's account of the defeat of the Nasamones, the barbarians have plundered the legionary camp and especially the wine (67.4.6).[34] On the other hand, Suetonius Paulinus carefully chooses a position and deploys his small force of ten thousand against Boudicca's enormous army, which leaps about excitedly in all directions (*Ann.* 14.34); urging his soldiers to remain in formation and forget plunder, he succeeds in killing eighty thousand of the enemy with only four hundred Roman losses (14.36–7).

It was therefore important to the Romans that their army should be kept constantly in training either by warfare or by military drills and exercises. Josephus emphasizes that the Romans train even in peacetime (*BJ* 3.72–5). In the speech composed for Maecenas by Cassius Dio, he advises Augustus that the troops "should always be under arms and should perform military exercises continually" (52.27.2). The Romans sometimes, still in the Principate, show a deep suspicion of long peace as a source of corruption and frequently express the idea that foreign war is a positive thing from this point of view.[35] Horace looks forward to war with the Parthians, which will restore Rome to its ancient military virtues (*Carm.* 3.2.1–6). Augustus is supposed to have undertaken campaigns in Illyricum and Dalmatia "lest that thing most inimical to discipline, leisure, should corrupt the army" (Vell. Pat. 2.78.2); similarly, Cassius Dio writes that Severus "made a campaign against Britain, seeing that his sons were going astray and that the army was dissipated from idleness" (76[77].11.1; see Herodian 3.14.2). In Tacitus, the dangers of peace and lack of discipline can lead to mutiny.[36] During the suspension of duties at the death of

Augustus, the soldiers "desired luxury and leisure, and scorned discipline and work" – thus the Pannonian mutiny (*Ann.* 1.16); it spreads to the Rhine army (1.31), where the cure is, naturally, foreign war – specifically, the campaigns of Germanicus.[37]

The ancient sources frequently criticize the perceived luxury and degeneration of the soldiers, and praise emperors and commanders who restore old-fashioned discipline. Corbulo stands out in this respect: in Tacitus' tangled account of his eastern campaigns, one image that emerges clearly is that of Corbulo walking around bareheaded in the Armenian winter, encouraging his frostbitten troops; he had found them "sluggish from long peace," but quickly rectified this situation.[38] Paetus, in contrast, fails properly to plan and organize his campaign (15.8), and grants leave to his troops liberally (15.9); thus his disastrous loss to the Parthians. Later, Hadrian compensates for a policy of nonaggression with increased discipline, constant visits to the troops, and the unusual legend *Disciplina Augusta* on the coinage.[39]

Emperors were themselves supposed to set an example of discipline for the soldiers, by sharing their hardships and their training,[40] and also to enforce it.[41] To Fronto, this means returning to a warlike policy after years of peace; he considers Hadrian's substitution of exercises and training maneuvers for real war a disaster.[42] Fronto tells us that the typical soldier whom Lucius Verus found when he arrived in the east was, once again, "reduced to idleness from long discontinuance of warfare" (*Principia historiae* 11 [Loeb 2:209]); it is Verus who, he writes, restored discipline in preparation for his Parthian war.[43]

But the most striking passage concerning the importance of military discipline in Rome's success comes at the very end of our period of discussion – almost at the very end, in fact, of the history of Cassius Dio. He has recently retired from his post as legate of the prestigious military province of Upper Pannonia; a man of wide experience, *amicus* of three emperors, he offers his own assessment of a new menace on the eastern horizon:

> He [Ardashir, king of Persia] has become fearful to us, ... not because he himself seems worthy of any note, but because our army is in such a condition that some are even going over to him, and others do not want to fight him off. For they enjoy such luxury, license, and irresponsibility that those in Mesopotamia have dared to kill their own commander, Flavius Heracleo, and the praetorian guard even accused me before Ulpianus because I governed the soldiers in Pannonia strictly. ... (80.4.2–3)

The value the Romans ascribed to their superior tactics, engineering, and organization was inseparable from a broader moral background of discipline and degeneracy against which the Romans tend to project their ideas about the army and its maintenance, even as they tend to describe their foreign-relations goals in terms of honor or dignity, disgrace, and revenge.

CONCLUSION

> Pillagers of the world, when the earth is insufficient for their plundering, they search the sea; if the enemy is rich, they are greedy; if he is poor, they are ambitious. Neither the east nor the west has satisfied them: they alone lust after wealth and poverty with equal

passion. They call theft and slaughter and pillage by the false name of "empire," and when they have made a wasteland, they call it peace. (Tac. *Agr.* 30)

The famous speech composed by Tacitus for the rebel Calgacus is of course a rhetorical exercise. It is easy to imagine the opposite argument: the Romans conquer not out of desire for money, land, or fame, but to retaliate for a wrong; they practice clemency when it is safe to do so, extermination in the face of stubborn arrogance and intransigence. In either case, this rare statement about Roman aims in the conduct of foreign relations reflects a reality. Greed and glory were plausible, though not necessarily respectable, causes for war. Still more plausible and respectable was the motivation of revenge, and of asserting or enhancing the honor and majesty of the Roman empire – provided, of course, that this could be done without causing invasion, revolt, civil war, or crippling expense. And if a tribe caused too much trouble, the Romans saw no moral or ethical argument against wiping it off the face of the earth. The relatively slow pace of conquest under the Principate should not be explained as the result of substituting a "defensive" strategy for the ideology of glory and conquest that prevailed in the Republic. The Romans at all times valued victory and conquest, as part of a system in which aggression, especially in retaliation for a perceived wrong, was crucial for maintaining honor and security. However, there were certain factors, mainly fiscal ones, that limited the size of the army; the Romans recognized manpower constraints as a limit on the growth of empire. And conquests that did not promise the immense profits of, for example, the acquisition of Egypt perhaps did not look as attractive as the lucrative ventures of an earlier era.

An extraordinary passage from Pliny's *Panegyric* praises the emperor Trajan for attacking the Dacians at the worst possible time: "at that time that is most favorable to them and most difficult for us, when the banks of the Danube are bridged with ice, and, frozen solid, it carries vast wars across on its back, when ferocious tribes are armed no less with their weather and their climate than with arrows" (12.3). As with the speech of Calgacus, one is at first tempted to dismiss this statement as mere rhetoric. Surely, we might argue, the terms the Romans used to frame their decisions about war and peace must have been quite different from those employed by Pliny here: the unscientific ethnic stereotype (ferocious tribes, grim climate); the idea that to demonstrate one's superior military prowess by attacking an enemy in midwinter was far more important than more practical considerations – in this case, of tactics.[44] But as this study has demonstrated, it is not necessary to make this assumption at all. Pliny the Younger came from precisely that small group of individuals that was entrusted with making Rome's most important decisions; and it was in rhetorical terms that this group was trained to think.

Pliny did not imagine Dacia as a territory of certain shape and extent, bounded by certain geographical features; such information, and such a picture, would be formed only after conquest, if at all. Dacia was a land beyond the Danube, a mighty river, which divided the Romans from the barbarians the way it had divided the king of Persia from the ferocious Scythians, in a half-mythical tale of conquest centuries ago. It was inhabited by a fierce, savage, warlike, barbarous people. In its icy and inhospitable climate it approached the earth's farthest, uninhabitable regions; it bordered on the frigid, sluggish ocean of the north. It was one of the remote corners of the earth – like Arabia, or India – still not subject to Roman domination. Such was the image that was most likely in Trajan's mind when he invaded it, proudly subjecting this wild and remote territory to land surveys, taxes, roads, a Roman colony. Trajan, like Darius, bridged the Danube.[45] No conquest in the imperial period brought any emperor greater glory; none was depicted on monuments so vast; none was commemorated in language so reverent.

To achieve this success, Trajan required approximately half of the Roman army and a vast amount of money. He was rewarded not only with fame and reputation but with immense sums in booty and ultimately from gold mines. But we must consider the likelihood that the Dacian wars, for all the immense effort that they required, would have happened even in the absence of greed. There were other considerations as well. Its king had humiliated Rome by inflicting defeats on the Roman army, and by wresting from Rome a treaty in which one clause especially – the financial subsidies paid to Decebalus – clearly conceded this defeat. Imagine, for example, some insignificant nation in Central America or the Middle East daring to behave in the same way toward, say, the United States!

The comparison is not totally inappropriate. Considering the disparity in size between Rome and the Dacian kingdom, one might well question whether the latter could ever have posed a "real" strategic threat to the empire. But for the Romans, their hegemony and their very security depended on universal recognition of their empire's *maiestas*, its "greaterness." Their policy depended on perceived and acknowledged military superiority, on the terror and awe of the enemy; and if this image was challenged by invasion, defeat, or revolt, the Romans reasserted it with the maximum possible brutality and ferocity. Both of Trajan's Dacian wars were wars of punishment and revenge. Mainly for this, and for no other reason, the emperor was willing to commit military and financial resources of immense proportions.[iv] Modern superpowers occasionally behave in ways that are just as difficult to explain without invoking motivations similar to those that drove the Romans. Perhaps we can learn, from our study of the Roman mind, not only something about the forces that shaped the boundaries of one of the world's great empires, but something about ourselves as well.

NOTES

1 For kneeling Parthian and Armenian kings on Augustus' coins of 18 B.C., see Levi 1952, 7–9; Brilliant 1963, 72; *RIC*^{2} Augustus 287, 290. The theme appears also on famous silver cups from Boscoreale (Brilliant 1963, 73–4); see Zanker 1988, 187, for more kneeling barbarians under Augustus. On the coins of Domitian, who advertised his German victory in an extensive program, see Strobel 1987, 435–6; Parthians kneel on coins of Trajan (Brilliant 1963, 109–10; see *RIC* Trajan 667–8); Dacians kneel (ibid., 214, 447, 448, 485–8, 499; nos. 510–12 show the goddess Pax with a kneeling Dacian). Prisoners are especially common – e.g., in Vespasian's famous *Judaea capta* series (*RIC* Vespasian 424–6; Hannestad 1988; 121; Levi 1952, 10–11). These coins were struck and distributed in Palestine, too, with Greek legends (Goodman 1987, 235–6). On the importance of costume in Strabo's ethnography, see van der Vliet 1984, 63–4; nude or seminude depictions of barbarians include, e.g., the metopes of the Adamklissi monument, the Gemma Augustea, and the "Ammendola" battle sarcophagus. Barbarians being crushed

by horses on the tombstones of cavalrymen (see n. 4 below) are typically naked or partially clothed.

2   On Trajan's forum, see Levi 1952, 14–15; on the Adamklissi monument, Rossi 1971, 55–65; Florescu 1965; Strobel 1984, 34–40.

3   Coins show Trajan with his foot on a Dacian (*RIC* Trajan 210); on the statue of Hadrian, see Levi 1952, 16–18 with plate VI.1. Equestrian representations: Domitian's equestrian statue, described by Stat. *Silv.* 1.1, trampled the hair of the Rhine underfoot (vv. 50–1); that the barbarian is in this case the personification of a river hardly changes the gist of the message. For equestrian assaults depicted on Trajan's coins, see *RIC* Trajan 257, 284, 344, 361; and barbarians are trampled by the horse in ibid., 208, 534–45. For the theme in general, see Brilliant 1963, 96; see Hannestad 1988, 221, for a discussion of the original appearance of Marcus' statue. A twelfth-century guidebook indicates that the barbarian survived at least until then. Cf. also Suet. *Ner.* 41.2, where the emperor, on his way back to Rome during the revolt of Vindex, happens to notice "a Gallic soldier sculpted on a monument, being crushed by a Roman *eques* and dragged by the hair." Only a small number of examples have been gathered here; a full-length study of the portrayal of the barbarian on Roman coins and monuments is needed.

4   See Koepp 1924–30, 3:9, with plates 6–10; Will 1955, 93–103; Collingwood and Wright 1965, nos. 108, 109, 121, 201.

5   On the Gemma Augustea, see Zanker 1988, 230–2.

6   A search of the index of legends in *Roman Imperial Coinage* yields the following incomplete list: *Aegypt[o] capta* with crocodile (Augustus 275); *Armenia capta* (ibid., 513–15); the famous *Judaea capta* series (Vespasian 393, 424–7, 489–91, etc.); *Parthia capta* (Trajan 324–5); *Dacia capta* (ibid., 96, 585); *Germania capta* (Domitian 278a); *Judaea devicta* (Vespasian 148b, 289, 373); *Germania subacta* (Marcus Aurelius 1021, 1049, 1094); *De Britannis* (Claudius 30, 33, 44); *De Germanis* (ibid., 3, 35; Marcus Aurelius 629 [Commodus], 1179, etc.); *De Sarmatis* (ibid., 630, 632, 1185, etc.); *Victoria Britannica* (Commodus 440, 451–2, 459; Severus 247, 808; Caracalla 169, 172, 230, 483, 487; Geta 172, 178, etc.); *Victoria Germanica* (Marcus Aurelius 240, 256, 257, 1000, 1029, 1722; Caracalla 316; Maximinus 23, and on medallions, Maximinus 115, 121); *Victoria Parthica* (Marcus Aurelius 160; Verus 562, 571, 929, 1455; Severus 295–7; Caracalla 78, 144–5, 168a, 297, 299, etc.). Cf. Kneissl 1969, 25.

7   On *Imperator* as praenomen, see Hammond 1957, 21–41; on Augustus, Syme 1958; acclamations, Campbell 1984, 122–8; statistics, ibid., 124. The record holder was Claudius with twenty-seven.

8   On victory titles, see Kneissl 1969, with convenient appendices citing the inscriptions on which the titles can be found (pp. 186–241) and a list of the titles of each emperor (pp. 242–4); see also Rosenberger 1992, 168–70.

9   Marcus and Verus were *Propagatores imperii* (Birley 1987, 253–4), as was Septimius Severus (id. 1974). *Invictus* occurs first under Commodus as part of the formula *Pius Felix Invictus* but also occurs alone beginning with Severus (Storch 1968, 200–2). For *Pacator Orbis*, see Commodus' letters to the senate in Cass. Dio 72[73].15.5.

10 Imp. Caes. M. Aurelio Severo Antonino Pio Felici Aug. Arabico Adiabenico Parthico Max. Brit. Max. Pontif. Max. trib. pot. XV imp. II cos. III P. P. On milestones, see Chevallier 1976, 39–47; this inscription appears among the samples given on p. 42; it is *CIL* XIII.9129.

11 The point about milestones is made by Isaac (1992, 304–9). It is interesting that the literacy rate among legionaries was strikingly high, and even auxiliaries may have been more literate than the general population (Harris 1989, 253–5). There is some debate about the intelligibility of Roman coin types and the involvement of the emperor in choosing them; in favor of intelligibility, see mainly Sutherland 1959 and more recently

id. 1983; against intelligibility, see mainly Crawford 1983, with bibliography in n. 2, arguing from the silence of ancient sources about *reverse* coin types, though substantial testimony on the obverse portrait of the emperor, which lent authority to the coin and was a mark of sovereignty, survives. Cf. also the argument of Levick (1982) that coin types were chosen not by the emperor but by sycophantic mint officials with a view to flattery; in either case the value attached to victory is obvious.

12   Campbell (1984, 383–7) argues that there is no clear-cut relationship between "martial" emperors and the loyalty of the army, which depended mainly on money; on the other hand, Germanicus tries to win over mutinous troops by reminding them of the victories and triumphs of Tiberius (Tac. *Ann.* 1.34); Tacitus writes that Suetonius Paulinus might have been nominated by the soldiers because of his military reputation (*Hist.* 2.37); and Marcus' speech to the troops in Cassius Dio also portrays the revolutionary Cassius' military reputation as his main attraction for them (71[72].25.3). Herodian also believes that a military reputation and image are important here; see, e.g., 2.2.8 (Pertinax), and see Campbell, op. cit., 385.

13   Criticism and contempt for unwarlike emperors: Suetonius records a couplet levied at Nero: "while our man plucks the cithara, the Parthian draws his bow; ours will be Paean, the other Hecabeletes" (*Ner.* 39.2);[ii] and the sentiment is expressed at greater length and with even greater scorn by Cassius Dio (63[62].8). Dio also criticizes Domitian for living luxuriously and decadently while sending others to conduct the war in Dacia (67.6.3). See Herodian 1.15.7, where Commodus should be proving himself fighting barbarians instead of in gladiatorial combat. Qualifications: on Vespasian, see Suet. *Vesp.* 4.1–2, Cass. Dio 65[64].8.3; on Titus, Suet. *Titus* 4.1; on Pertinax, Herodian 2.1.4.

14   Especially in the case of Domitian – e.g., Cass. Dio 67.7.3–4; in his case the celebration of triumphs was especially offensive (in Tac. *Germ.* 37.6, the Germans are "triumphed over rather than defeated"; Pliny *Pan.* 16.3–5 contrasts Trajan, as often, with Domitian); cf. Campbell 1984, 398. See also the case of Gaius, who is acclaimed *imperator* several times, "having won no battle nor killed any enemy" (Cass. Dio 59.22.2; cf. Suet. *Gaius* 47). That the aristocracy was sensitive to the fine points of these issues is suggested by Dio's criticism of Claudius for accepting multiple salutations of *imperator* for the same war; strictly speaking, this should not happen (60.21.4–5). Cassius Dio also distinguishes between salutations that Claudius received deservedly, when his legates inflicted defeats on the Germans and retrieved the last of the standards lost with Varus, and triumphal ornaments for a campaign that preceded his accession, which he did not deserve (60.8.6–7). Macrinus misrepresents his achievements in the east but is ashamed to take a victory title after being defeated by the Parthians (ibid., 78[79].27.3).

15   "Ambition" is often coupled with greed as an unjust cause – e.g., in the case of Crassus (Plut. *Crass.* 14.4; App. *B Civ.* 2.18; Vell. Pat. 2.46.3) and of Caesar (Suet. *Jul.* 22.1, where Gaul is rich and will furnish triumphs; see Mantovani 1990, 35–6, for further references). Domitian wages an unnecessary war for wealth and *dignitatio* in Suet. *Dom.* 2.1; and cf. Calgacus' famous speech in Tac. *Agr.* 30: "if the enemy is rich, they [the Romans] are greedy; if he is poor, they are ambitious (*ambitiosi*)." See also Florus 2.20.2 on Antony's *cupiditas titulorum* – desire for the titles of conquered peoples – engraved in the *elogium* under his statue; he attacks the Parthians "without cause or plan and without even the pretense of a declaration of war."

16   Claudius attacked Britain mainly to get a triumph (though a convenient provocation presented itself; Suet. *Claud.* 17.1); Severus' British wars are said to be motivated by his desire for a victory title (Herodian 3.14.2, 5); Caracalla desires the title "Parthicus," hence his eastern war (Herodian 4.10.1; indicating an "unjust" war). Trajan's Parthian war (Cass. Dio 68.17.1) and Severus' conquest of Mesopotamia (ibid., 75.1.1; Herodian 3.9.1) are motivated by a desire for δόξα (good reputation). In other cases where literary

evidence fails, the desire of a new emperor for an enhanced military reputation seems probable – e.g., Domitian's first war with the Chatti (Strobel 1987, 427–8) and the advance beyond Hadrian's wall under Pius (Breeze 1988, 18). Cf. Cass. Dio 53.6.3, where Augustus says in a speech that many make war on account of τὸ εὐκλεές (renown).

17 On defenses, see [Mattern, *Rome and the Enemy,*] ch. 3, pp. 110–11; for "unprofitable," ch. 4, n. 156.

18 Dio Chrysostomus *Or.* 4, with Moles 1983. It is interesting that the imperialist boast at the head of the *RGDA* is missing from the Greek version (Gagé 1977, 72–3). See Nutton 1978, 210–11; and cf. Whittaker 1994, 36–7. On Greek attitudes to Rome generally, see recently Swain 1996.

19 See Bowersock 1969, chap. 4, for Greek intellectuals in the emperor's court. Ambassadors, e.g., Aelius Aristides (Bowersock, op. cit., 44–6); hangers-on, e.g., Dio Chrysostomus (ibid., 47–8). On sophists as secretaries *ab epistulis*, a prestigious post, see ibid., 50–8; on doctors, ibid., chap. 5 (on Galen); Trajan's doctor accompanied him on campaign in Dacia and wrote a commentary (ibid., 65).

20 69.9; note that, according to Cassius Dio, Hadrian succeeded in terrifying the barbarians with his ostentatious military exercises, so that they "used him as an arbitrator of their differences with each other," thus maintaining Roman dignity. On victory titles, see Kneissl 1969, 91–6; Hadrian initially used Trajan's titles on his coins, perhaps in connection with his questionable adoption, but took none of his own; also see Hannestad 1988, 190–2.

21 See Kneissl 1969, 24–5, and Campbell 1984, 348–62, on the control of victory honors. Suetonius notes that triumphs were still celebrated by nonemperors under Augustus (*Aug.* 38.1; cf. Cass. Dio 54.12.1); but the last such triumph was that of Cornelius Balbus in 19 B.C. (Campbell, op. cit., 358–9). Agrippa set the example in the same year by refusing a triumph for his exploits in Spain (Cass. Dio 54.11.6). Tiberius made a special exception and allowed Blaesus to be acclaimed *imperator* after his defeat of Tacfarinas (Tac. *Ann.* 3.7; Kneissl, op. cit., 24; Campbell, op. cit., 351). The last nonemperor to dedicate a trophy was L. Apronius Caesianus, for a defeat of Tacfarinas in A.D. 20 (Picard 1957, 247–8; cf. Tac. *Ann.* 3.21); and the last nonemperor to take a victory title (that of Chaucius) was P. Gabinius Secundus in A.D. 41 (Kneissl 1969, 24–5). On Gallus' boasting, exile, and suicide, see Cass. Dio 53.23.5–7; cf. Suet. *Aug.* 66.1–2; and see *PIR* II, C1369, and above, sec. 1. Crassus would have received *spolia opima* (Cass. Dio 51.24.4); on his triumph, see ibid., 51.25.2; for the argument that Augustus denied the *spolia opima* on the pretext that Crassus was not a consul, see Syme 1939, 308 n. 2; on Crassus and Gallus, ibid., 308–10.

22 On *triumphalia*, see Campbell 1984, 359–61. Tacitus ascribes a lull in activity on the Rhine to "the temperament of the generals, who, because the triumphal ornaments had become so debased, hoped for honor (*decus*) rather by having continued the peace" (*Ann.* 13.53). Nero is supposed to have granted *triumphalia* even to quaestors and *equites*, "and not always for military reasons" (Suet. *Ner.* 15.2); Tiberius is supposed to have granted them for informing (Cass. Dio 58.4.8).

23 *ne causam belli quoquo modo quaererent* (Suet. *Claud.* 24.3); in Tac. *Ann.* 11.20 the petition circulates after soldiers are forced by their ambitious commander to dig gold and silver mines.

24 Agrippa points out how dangerous it is, under a monarchy, to entrust military commands to men of high rank (Cass. Dio 52.8.4); Maecenas gives similar advice (ibid., 52.20.4); Pliny complains that when he served in the army under Domitian, "virtue was suspected, inertia was prized…no authority for the generals, no respect in the soldiers" (*Ep.* 8.14.7). See Campbell 1984, 337.

25 On imperial jealousy generally, see ibid., 334–7. Famous examples include Tiberius and Germanicus (Tac. *Ann.* 2.26); Claudius recalls Corbulo from exploits across the Rhine; "learning of his ἀρετή (valor) and ἄσκησις (discipline), he would not allow him to become too great (ἐπὶ πλέον αὐξηθῆναι)" (Cass. Dio 60[61].30.4–5; and see Tac. *Ann.* 11.2 for the same story); Corbulo exclaims, "How fortunate the generals of yesteryear!" Later, Domitian hears of Agricola's success in Scotland "with a happy face but an anxious heart . . . for within he was aware that his recent false triumph over the Germans had been a source of scorn for him" (Tac. *Agr.* 39); for Agricola's recall, see ibid., 40, and see Cass. Dio 66.20. The latter's contention that Domitian murdered Agricola out of jealousy is reflected in Tacitus' report of the rumor that Agricola was poisoned (*Agr.* 43). Threats: Corbulo could have become emperor because he had "a great force and no small reputation" (Cass. Dio 62.23.5); Suetonius Paulinus could have been nominated during the civil wars because of his British campaigns (Tac. *Hist.* 2.37). Commodus entrusts Ulpius Marcellus with the British war and then nearly executes him because of "his personal ἀρετή" (Cass. Dio 72[73].8.2–6).

26 On Cassius being entrusted with the war, see Cass. Dio 71.2.3; on his revolt, 71[72].17, 22; Marcus' speech, 71[72].25.3.

27 Gruen (1990 and 1996) argues that this was the policy of Augustus.

28 *BJ* 3.71; the question of whether Romans owed their success to valor or fortune seems to have been a popular one; cf. Plut. *Mor.* 316–26 (*De fortuna Romanorum*), making the opposite case. On the subject of military discipline generally, see Davies 1968, especially for training and military exercises; Isaac 1992, 23–6; and Wheeler 1996.

29 Trogus (Justin) 41.2; Tac. *Ann.* 11.10 ("the Parthians, though victors, rejected a distant campaign"); Cass. Dio 40.15.6. Also see Lucan 8.368–90: Parthians are invincible on their own territory because they have room for flight, but cannot endure hardship, have no military machines, and flee quickly.

30 Strabo, describing the Rhoxolani, comments of all barbarians: "against an organized and well-armed phalanx, all of the barbarian race is weak" (7.3.17). Tacitus presents the Chatti as especially organized and disciplined, for Germans (*Germ.* 30; "others go to battle, the Chatti go to war"); the traditional stereotype appears in 4.3: "large bodies strong only in assault; they have not the same tolerance of labor and work." Germanicus encourages his troops by reminding them of the weaknesses of the enemy's weapons; the Germans might look impressive and be "strong in a brief assault" but will turn and run after a setback (Tac. *Ann.* 2.14). Ariovistus' Germans are "not enduring of hardship in battles, nor do they employ reason or knowledge or anything except passion (θυμός), like beasts" (App. *Gall.* 3). On Gauls, see Strab. 4.4.2, Cass. Dio 38.45.4–5. Severus Alexander, encouraging his troops for the Persian war, tells them that in general barbarians are "daring in the face of withdrawal and hesitation, but against one who resists they [the barbarians] by no means stand their ground in the same way, since for them the fight at close quarters with rivals does not promise success, but they consider that it is by raiding and flight that they gain what they seize by plunder. To us belongs organization and good order (τὸ εὔτακτον ἅμα τῷ κοσμίῳ), and we have learned to defeat them always" (Herodian 6.3.7).

31 On Polybius, see Eckstein 1995, ch. 6.

32 The emphasis on the hard work of the Roman army is noticed by Rossi (1971, 99), Richmond (1982, 2–3), and Hannestad (1988, 158–9). For plates, see the recent edition of Settis et al. (1988). On laziness, see, e.g., Tac. *Germ.* 4.3 and 15.1.

33 *Hist.* 1.79. Cf. Dauge 1981, 752–3.

34 See also Tac. *Hist.* 4.29–30, contrasting Civilis' drunken, frenzied Germans with the well-ordered, better-equipped legions. Very similar is Livy's account of Camillus' defeat of the sleeping, drunken, lazy Gauls (5.44–5). On the drunkenness of Germans, see Tac. *Germ.*

22–3, *Ann.* 11.16; of Parthians, Pliny *HN* 14.144, 148; of Gauls, Polyb. 2.19.4, Diod. Sic. 5.26.3; cf. Cass. Dio 51.24.2, where Crassus takes advantage of the notorious drunkenness of the Scythians.

35 Most obvious in the still-popular idea that the destruction of Carthage marked the beginning of Rome's decline. See Vell. Pat. 2.1.1; Pliny *HN* 33.150; Florus 1.47.2 ("the overhanging fear of the Punic enemy preserved the old discipline"); Earl 1967, 18–19. On the subject of discipline in the Republic, cf. Rosenstein 1990, ch. 3.

36 On corruption and indolence due to peace, see *Hist.* 1.88, this time of the Roman aristocracy; cf. 2.17. Of the army in Britain under Trebellius Maximus (A.D. 69), Tacitus writes that "soldiers accustomed to campaigns became licentious in leisure" (*Agr.* 16.3; but cf. *Hist.* 1.60, where he blames Trebellius' greed and stinginess for the mutiny). See also *Hist.* 1.40–3 on the atrocious behavior of the army in the civil war.

37 *Ann.* 1.49: "The desire then entered their still-fierce minds to march against the enemy, in expiation of their frenzy; nor could the ghosts of their fellow soldiers be placated until they had received honorable wounds on their impious breasts."

38 *Ann.* 13.35; Corbulo had also brought harsh discipline to the Rhine (ibid., 11.18) and was famous for this quality (Walser 1951, 42–3).

39 On Hadrian's program, see Cass. Dio 69.9; and see Davies 1968 for detailed discussion. On virtues and personifications on Hadrian's coins, see Wallace-Hadrill 1981, 311–14; see also Hannestad 1988, 191.

40 A very common topos – e.g., Tac. *Hist.* 2.5 (Vespasian); Pliny *Pan.* 13 (Trajan); Fronto *Principia historiae* 13 (Loeb 2:209–11; Verus); Herodian 2.11.2, 3.6.10 (Severus); cf. Tac. *Ann.* 13.35 on Corbulo, above, and *Agr.* 20 on Agricola; also MacMullen 1976, 26, with n. 11; and Campbell 1984, 32–59.

41 Pliny *Pan.* 18; cf. Dio Chrys. *Or.* 1.29.

42 *Principia historiae* 10 (Loeb 2:207), with the article of Davies (1968, 75–84). On the idea of military discipline in the east, see recently Wheeler 1996, emphasizing that the literary topos arises from the Roman perception of the effete easterner and does not necessarily reflect a reality.

43 See Fronto's letter to Verus (Loeb 2:149–51) and *Principia historiae* 13 (Loeb 2:209–11). These passages are discussed extensively in Davies 1968 and Wheeler 1996.

44 Very similar is Caesar's decision to construct a bridge over the Rhine, which he subsequently destroys, rather than cross by the usual method of lashing boats together; this would have been beneath Roman dignity (*B Gall.* 4.17–19).

45 Cf. Hdt. 4.89, with Hartog 1988, 58–60. His footnote 107 is also appropriate for the Roman period: "Note that, nearly always, any engineering is Greek."

EDITOR'S NOTES

i The most exhaustive study of Roman conceptions of the barbarian is (in French), Dauge, 1981.

ii These are epithets of the god Apollo; Nero exemplifies the god's softer side.

iii The *spolia opima* were the spoils that a Roman general would offer, taken from an enemy in single combat. Before Augustus there were only three recorded instances (under Romulus, 437 BCE, 222 BCE).

iv Cf. the Roman siege of Masada (besieged by Flavius Silva with eight Roman encampments and circumvallation for some six months in 73 or 74 CE).

REFERENCES

Birley, A. R. 1974. Septimus Severus, *propagator imperii*. In *Actes du IX congrès internationale d'études sur les frontières romaines*, ed. D. M. Pippidi (Bucharest: Editura Academie), 297–9.

——. 1987. *Marcus Aurelius: A Biography*, 2nd edn. New Haven: Yale University Press.

Bowersock, G. W. 1969. *Greek Sophists in the Roman Empire*. Oxford: Clarendon Press.

Breeze, D. J. 1988. Why did the Romans fail to conquer Scotland? *Proceedings of the Antiquaries of Scotland* 118: 3–22.

Brilliant, R. 1963. *Gesture and Rank in Roman Art*. Memoirs of the Connecticut Academy of Arts and Sciences, no. 14. New Haven: The Academy.

Campbell, J. B. 1984. *The Emperor and the Roman Army, 31* BC–AD *235*. Oxford: Clarendon Press.

Chevallier, R. 1976. *Roman Roads*, trans. N. H. Field. Berkeley: University of California Press.

Collingwood, R. G., and R. P. Wright. 1965. *The Roman Inscriptions of Britain*, vol. 1: *Inscriptions on Stone*. Oxford: Clarendon Press.

Crawford, M. 1983. Roman imperial coin types and the formation of public opinion. In *Studies in Numismatic Method Presented to Philip Grierson*, ed. C. N. L. Brooke, 47–64. Cambridge: Cambridge University Press.

Dauge, Y.-A. 1981. *Le Barbare: recherches de la barbarie et de la civilisation*. Collection Latomus, vol. 176. Brussels: Latomus.

Davies, R. W. 1968. Fronto, Hadrian, and the Roman Army. *Latomus* 27: 75–95.

Earl, D. 1967. *The Moral and Political Tradition of Rome*. Ithaca, NY: Cornell University Press; London: Thames and Hudson.

Eckstein, A. M. 1995. *Moral Vision in the Histories of Polybius*. Berkeley: University of California Press.

Florescu, F. B. 1965. *Das Siegesdenkmal von Adamklissi: Tropaeum Traiani*. Bucharest: Verlag der Akademie der rümanischen Volksrepublik; Bonn: Habelt.

Gagé, J. 1977. *Res gestae divi Augusti*, 3rd edn. Paris: Les Belles Lettres.

Goodman, M. 1987. *The Ruling Class of Judaea: The Origins of the Jewish Revolt against Rome*, AD *66–70*. Cambridge: Cambridge University Press.

Gruen, E. S. 1990. The imperial policy of Augustus. In *Between Republic and Empire: Interpretations of Augustus and His Principate*, ed. K. A. Raaflaub and M. Toher, 385–416. Berkeley: University of California Press.

——. 1996. The expansion of the empire under Augustus. In *Cambridge Ancient History*, 2nd edn., vol. 10: *The Augustan Empire, 43* BC–AD *69*, 188–94. Cambridge: Cambridge University Press.

Hammond, M. 1957. Imperial elements in the formula of the Roman emperors during the first two and a half centuries of the Empire. *Memoirs of the American Academy in Rome* 25: 17–64.

Hannestad, N. 1988. *Roman Art and Imperial Policy*. Aarhus: Aarhus University Press.

Harris, W. V. 1989. *Ancient Literacy*. Cambridge, Mass.: Harvard University Press.

Hartog, F. 1988. *The Mirror of Herodotus: The Representation of the Other in the Writing of History*, trans. J. Lloyd. Berkeley: University of California Press.

Isaac, B. 1992 [1990]. *The Limits of Empire: The Imperial Roman Army in the East*, 2nd edn. Oxford: Clarendon Press.

Kneissl, P. 1969. *Die Siegestitulatur der römischen Kaiser*. Göttingen: Vandenhoeck and Ruprecht.

Koepp, F. 1924–30. *Germania romana: Ein Bilder-Atlas*, 2nd edn., 5 vols. (in 2). Bamberg: C. C. Buchner.

Levi, A. C. 1952. *Barbarians on Roman Imperial Coinage*. Numismatic Notes and Monographs, no. 123. New York: American Numismatic Society.

Levick, B. 1982. Propaganda and the imperial coinage. *Antichthon* 16: 104–16.

MacMullen, R. 1976. *The Roman Government's Response to Crisis*, AD *235–337*. New Haven: Yale University Press.

Mantovani, M. 1990. *Bellum Iustum: Die Idee des gerechten Krieges in der römischen Kaiserzeit*. Bern: P. Lang.

Moles, J. J. 1983. The date and purpose of the fourth kingship oration of Dio Chrysostom. *Classical Antiquity* 2: 251–78.

Nutton, V. 1978. The beneficial ideology. In *Imperialism in the Ancient World*, ed. P. D. A. Garnsey and C. R. Whittaker, 209–21. Cambridge: Cambridge University Press.

Picard, G. C. 1957. *Les Trophées romains: contribution à l'histoire de la religion et de l'art triomphal de Rome*. Paris: de Boccard.

Richmond, I. 1982. *Trajan's Army on Trajan's Column*. London: British School at Rome.

Rosenberger, V. 1992. *Bella et expeditiones: die antike Terminologie der Kriege Roms*. Stuttgart: F. Steiner.

Rosenstein, N. 1990. *Imperatores Victi: Military Defeat and Aristocratic Competition in the Middle and Late Republic*. Berkeley: University of California Press.

Rossi, L. 1971. *Trajan's Column and the Dacian Wars*. London: Thames and Hudson; Ithaca, NY: Cornell University Press.

Settis, S. et al. 1988. *La colonna Traiana*. Turin: G. Einaudi.

Storch, R. H. 1968. The "absolutist" theology of victory: its place in the late Empire. *Classica et Medievalia* 29: 197–206.

Strobel, K. 1984. *Untersuchungen zu den Dakerkriegen Trajans*. Bonn: Habelt.

——. 1987. Der Chattenkrieg Domitians: historische und politische Aspekte. *Germania* 65: 423–52.

Sutherland, C. H. V. 1959. The intelligibility of Roman imperial coin types. *Journal of Roman Studies* 49: 46–55.

——. 1983. The purpose of Roman imperial coin types. *Revue numismatique* 6.25: 73–82.

Swain, S. 1996. *Hellenism and Empire: Language, Classicism, and Power in the Greek World*, AD *50–250*. Oxford: Clarendon Press.

Syme, R. 1939. *The Roman Revolution*. Oxford: Clarendon Press.

——. 1958. Imperator Caesar: a study in nomenclature. *Historia* 7: 172–88.

van der Vliet, E. C. L. 1984. L'Ethnographie de Strabon: idéologie ou tradition? In *Strabone: Contributi allo studio della personalità e dell'opera*, ed. F. Prontera, 1: 27–86. Perugia: Università degli Studi.

Wallace-Hadrill, A. 1981. The Emperor and his virtues. *Historia* 30: 298–323.

Walser, G. 1951. *Rom, das Reich, und die fremden Völker in der Geschichtsschreibung der frühen Kaiserzeit*. Baden-Baden: Verlag für Kunst und Wissenschaft.

Wheeler, E. L. 1996. The laxity of the Syrian legions. In *The Roman Army in the East*, ed. D. L. Kennedy, 229–76. Ann Arbor: Journal of Roman Archaeology.

Whittaker, C. R. 1994. *Frontiers of the Roman Empire: A Social and Economic Study*. Baltimore: Johns Hopkins University Press.

Will, E. 1955. *Le Relief culturel gréco-romain: contribution à l'histoire de l'art de l'empire romain*. Paris: de Boccard.

Zanker, P. 1988. *The Power of Images in the Age of Augustus*, trans. A. Shapiro. Ann Arbor: University of Michigan Press.

Sources

Empire of force

Certain Roman generals were seeking the right of celebrating triumphs* for insignificant skirmishes. As a result a law was promulgated stating that no one should celebrate a triumph unless he had killed 5,000 of the enemy forces in a single engagement.

> Valerius Maximus, *Memorable Deeds and Sayings*, 2.8.1 [ca. 30 CE]

According to an ancient Roman legend, in the reign of King Tullus Hostilius (traditional dates, 672–640 BCE), conflict between Romans and Albans was resolved by a mortal contest of three champions from either side; the Horatii, according to Livy, fought for Rome, while the Curiatii represented Alba.

When they had come to terms, the brothers armed themselves, according to their mutual understanding. The soldiers on both sides exhorted their champions, reminding them that their fathers' gods, their native land, their parents, and all their countrymen, whether at home or with the army, were watching only their swords and their right hands. Zealous for combat, which was only increased by their native spirit as well as by the shouts of encouragement, the brothers advanced into the space between the two lines of battle. The two armies were drawn up, each in front of its own camp, no longer in any immediate danger, but their concern unabated; and no wonder, since empire was staked on those few men's valor and good fortune.... With a downward thrust Horatius buried his sword in the Alban's throat, and stripped his corpse. The Romans welcomed their hero with cheers and blessings, and their joy was all the greater that they had come near to utter hopelessness. The two armies then buried their dead – with widely different feelings, since one nation was elevated to imperial power, while the other was made subject to foreign domination.

> Livy, *History of Rome*, 1.25.1–2, 12–13 [ca. 25 BCE]

The council and the people [of Ilium] honored Titus Valerius Proculus, procurator* of Drusus Caesar, who destroyed the pirate ships in the Hellespont and kept the city free of burdens in every way.

> *Inscriptiones Graecae ad res Romanae pertinentes*, 4.219 [ca. 20 CE]

It is appropriate for a good governor who is serious about his duties to make sure that the province he administers is kept quiet and peaceful. He will easily do this if he takes conscientious measures that ensure that the province is free from malefactors and that he hunts them down. Besides hunting down temple robbers, kidnappers, and thieves, he should inflict on them the penalties they deserve and punish anyone who gives them refuge; without such people a robber cannot last long.

> Ulpian, *Digest*, 1.18.13, Introduction [ca. 160 CE]

The "spoils of honor" (spolia opima)

But while [the Sabines] were dispersed and engaged in pillage, Romulus appeared with his troops and showed, by an easy victory, how useless anger is without strength. He broke and routed their army, and pursued it as it fled; their king he killed in battle and despoiled; their city, once their leader was slain, he captured at the first assault. He then led his victorious army back, and being not more splendid in his deeds than willing to display them, he arranged the spoils of the enemy's dead commander upon a frame, suitably fashioned for the purpose, and, carrying it himself, mounted the Capitol.

Livy, *History of Rome*, 1.10.4–5 [ca. 25 BCE]

Even if [rebellious allies] were embroiled in a war with neighbors concerning local boundaries, and even if they thought that one battle could determine the issue, they still would be better equipped and prepared than they now are. It is even more unbelievable that with such ill-prepared forces they would try to gain the world sovereignty that all civilized peoples, kings, and barbarians have accepted, partly compelled by force, partly of their own volition, when crushed either by Roman arms or saved by Roman generosity.

[Cicero] *Rhetorical Precepts for Herennius*, 4.13 [ca. 85 BCE]

Evocation of Juno from conquered Etruscan Veii (396 BCE)

When the inhabitants' wealth had now been carried out of Veii, they began to remove the possessions of the gods and the gods themselves. . . . For out of all the army youths were chosen, and made to cleanse their bodies and to put on white garments, and to them the duty was assigned of conveying Queen Juno to Rome. Reverently entering her temple, they first hesitated to approach her with their hands, because according to Etruscan practice none but a priest of a certain family was accustomed to touch the image; when one of them, whether divinely inspired or jokingly, asked, "Will you go, Juno, to Rome?" – and then the others cried out that the goddess had agreed. The embellishment was later added to the story that she had also been heard to say that she was willing. At all events we are told that she was moved from her place with ease, as though she accompanied them voluntarily, and was lightly and easily transferred and carried safely to the Aventine hill, the eternal home to which the prayers of the Roman dictator* had called her; and there Camillus afterwards dedicated to her the temple which he himself had vowed.

Livy, *History of Rome*, 5.22.3–7 [ca. 25 BCE]

Empire of destiny

For these [Romans] I place neither physical bounds nor temporal limits; I have given empire without end.

Vergil, *Aeneid*, 1.278–9 (Jupiter's blessing) [ca. 20 CE]

When [Scipio Aemilianus] as censor* was concluding the census and in the sacrifice of suovetaurilia*, the scribe recited before him from public tables the formula of prayer in which the immortal gods were asked to make the Roman state better and greater.

Valerius Maximus, *Memorable Deeds and Sayings*, 4.1.10a [ca. 30 CE]

It has now finally come about that the limits of our empire and of the earth are one and the same.

Cicero, *On the Consular Provinces*, 33 (June/July, 56 BCE)

But you will realize my point more easily if you watch our republic as it progresses, and, by a path which we might call Nature's road, finally reaches the perfect condition. What is more, you will judge our forefather's wisdom praiseworthy since, as you will learn, we have improved those institutions which we have borrowed from abroad so that they are much better than they were in those places from which we received them and where they had their origins. And you will learn that the Roman people has grown great, not accidentally, but by planning and discipline, though most certainly Fortune has smiled upon us.

Cicero, *On the Republic*, 2.30 [54 BCE]

It was by piety and religious scruples and our sagacious understanding of a single truth, that all things are directed and ruled by the gods' will, that we have conquered all peoples and nations.

Cicero, *On the Responses of the Priests*, 19 [56 BCE]

It is not permitted for the Roman people to be in servitude, whom the immortal gods wanted to rule over all peoples.

Cicero, *Philippics*, 6.19 [43 BCE]

In the Augustan age the designation of Rome as an *urbs aeterna*, or Rome as "eternal city" and seat of a world empire, appears for the first time. The earliest attestation is from the Augustan poet Tibullus.

Romulus had not yet formed the walls of the eternal city, which could not accommodate his brother Remus, but then cattle grazed on the grassy Palatine, and humble homes stood on Jupiter's heights.

Tibullus, *Elegies*, 2.5.23–6 [ca. 20 BCE]

Climatic and geographical determinism for Roman rule

The inhabitants of Italy are perfectly disposed in either direction, both in terms of bodily structure and of mental strength for endurance and courage. Like the planet Jupiter which is tempered by running the middle course between torrid Mars and frigid Venus, in the same way Italy exhibits good qualities tempered by the mixing of the extremes of north and south. As a result Italy's qualities are unsurpassed. It therefore checks the courage of the northern barbarians by its policy, and the imaginative southerners by its strength. In this way the divine will has given Italy a most excellent and temperate climatic condition in order that it may rule the world.

Vitruvius, *On Architecture*, 6.1.11 [Age of Augustus][1]

After the apotheosis of Rome's first king, Romulus (traditional dates, 753–716 BCE), Proculus Julius reported the epiphany and advice of Romulus to the distraught Roman populace.

"Quirites[*], Romulus, father of our country, suddenly descended from the sky at dawn this morning and appeared to me. Confused, I stood reverently before him, praying that it might be granted to me to look upon his face without sin. 'Go,' said he, 'and tell the Romans Heaven's will that my Rome shall be the capital of the world; so let them love the art of war, and let them know and teach their children that no human strength can resist Roman arms.'"

Livy, *History of Rome*, 1.16.6–8 [ca. 25 BCE]

The historian Livy reports the following divine signs of the stability, longevity, and growth of the Roman Empire in the reign of the mytho-historical king Tarquinius Superbus (traditional dates, 534–510 BCE).

While the birds of augury allowed that consecrations of all other shrines should be rescinded, they refused for the shrine of Terminus. This omen and augury was understood as follows: the fact that Terminus was not moved, and that of all the gods he alone was not called away from the place consecrated to him, meant that the whole kingdom would be firm and steadfast. After this divine sign of permanence, there followed another prodigy foretelling their empire's greatness. A human head, its features intact, was found, so it is said, by men who were digging for the foundations of the temple. This appearance plainly foretold that here was to be the citadel of the empire and the head of the world.

Livy, *History of Rome*, 1.55.3–6 [ca. 25 BCE]

Empire of virtue

[The Romans] began asking what constituted Roman strength; for the priests had said that whatever this was, they must offer it up in sacrifice on that spot, if they wished for their empire to endure.... And then Marcus Curtius, a young soldier of great abilities, admonished them, so the legend goes, for questioning that any blessing could be more Roman than arms and virtue [362 BCE].

Livy, *History of Rome*, 7.6.3–4 [ca. 25 BCE]

And if our fatherland is a pure delight, as it well ought to be.... with what great love must we certainly be stirred for a country like ours, as it stands alone among all others as the home of virtue, imperial power, and dignity! It is our country's spirit, customs, discipline that we first must learn, both because she is the mother of us all, and

because we must realize that that wisdom was perfect which went into the establishment of our laws, as well as the acquisition of the immense power of our empire.

Cicero, On the Orator, 1.196 [55 BCE]

And now it is not with exhortation and precept but with prayers that I ask that you, as
a brother, bring all your thoughts and concerns to gathering universal praise from all
quarters. If the public talk and recognition of our achievements were not outstanding, nothing exceptional, nothing beyond what other Roman governors have done,
would be demanded of you. . . . As it has happened, my public career has been made in
Rome, and yours in the province. If my achievement stands second to none, see to it
that yours surpasses the rest. Consider also that we aren't now working for some
glory hoped for in a future time but rather fighting for what we have won, and we are
obligated to maintain this rather than to seek it out.

Cicero, Letters to Brother Quintus, 1.1.41 [60/59 BCE]

Virtue and empire building

Most of all men praise [Aemilius Paullus'] liberality and great-heartedness; for he
refused even to look at the masses of silver and gold gathered together from the royal
treasuries [of Macedonia], but he relinquished these to the quaestors for the public
treasury.

Plutarch, Life of Aemilius Paullus, 38.6 [ca. 115 CE]

When Aemilius Paullus obtained Macedonia's wealth [167 BCE] – and it was enormous – he deposited so much money that the spoils of a single general did away with
the need for tax on property in Rome for all time to come. But he brought nothing
save the glory of an immortal name to his own estate. Africanus [P. Cornelius Scipio
Aemilianus] emulated his father's example and was none the richer for his destruction
of Carthage [146 BCE]. And what shall we say of Lucius Mummius, his colleague in
the censorship? Was he one bit richer when he had destroyed to its roots the richest of
cities [Corinth]? He preferred to adorn Italy rather than his own house. And yet by the
adornment of Italy his own house was, as it seems to me, still more splendidly adorned.

Cicero, On Duties, 2.22.76 [mid-40s BCE]

An upright Roman governor: Cicero in Cilicia (51/0 BCE)

He received Cilicia as his province by lot, with an army of 12,000 infantrymen and
1,200 cavalrymen, and he sailed with instructions to keep Cappadocia friendly and
obedient to King Ariobarzanes. He accomplished this and arranged affairs satisfactor-
ily without resorting to arms, and estimating that the Cilicians were in an agitated
state because of the Parthian disaster to the Romans and the rising in Syria, he
pacified them with mild government. He refused to accept gifts, not even when
kings offered them, and he relieved the provincials of the expenses of entertainments;
but he himself daily received refined gentlemen at banquets which were generous but
not expensive. . . . He never ordered any man to be beaten with rods or to have his

clothes torn from him, and he never made angry or insolent allegations. He discovered that much of the public property had been embezzled, and by restoring it he improved the cities' economic condition, and men who made restitution he maintained in their civil rights with no further penalties.

Plutarch, Life of Cicero, 36.1–4 [ca. 115 CE]

Caesar gave a lengthy speech in order to demonstrate why he could not now give up the task he had set for himself. He said that it was his own practice and the practice of the Roman people not to allow the abandonment of deserving allies ... If the standard was to be priority of time, then Roman sovereignty in Gaul was completely justified. And if the Senate's decision was to be observed, Gaul should be a free state, for after the country's conquest the Senate had decided that it should continue to observe its own laws.

Caesar, Gallic War, 1.45 [ca. 50 BCE]

For I do not approve of the same nation being the ruler of the world and also its tax-gatherer; on the other hand, I consider frugality the best revenue both for private families and for states.

Cicero, On the Republic, 4.7 [54 BCE]

Devotio, the supreme self-sacrifice to the Commonwealth

The Latin War (340 BCE)

Amid confusion Decius the consul[*] [340 BCE] called out to Marcius Valerius: "We need the gods' help, Marcus Valerius. Come therefore, state pontiff of the Roman people, dictate the words, that I may devote myself to save the legions." The pontiff told him to put on the purple-bordered toga and, with veiled head and one hand thrust out from the toga and touching his chin, to stand upon a spear laid under his feet, and say as follows: "Janus, Jupiter, Father Mars, Quirinus, Bellona, Lares, divine Novensiles, divine Indigites, you gods who have power over both us and our enemies, and you, divine spirits of the dead – I invoke you and worship you, I beseech and crave your favor, that you make prosper the might and the victory of the Roman People of the Quirites[*], and cast the enemies of the Roman People of the Quirites into fear, shuddering, and death. As I have pronounced the words, even so in behalf of the republic of the Roman People of the Quirites, and of the army, the legions, the auxiliaries of the Roman People of the Quirites, do I devote the legions and auxiliaries of the enemy, together with myself, to the divine spirits of the dead and to the Earth." Having uttered this prayer he ordered the lictors go to Titus Manlius and lose no time in announcing to his colleague that he had devoted himself for the good of the army.

Livy, History of Rome, 8.9.4–9 [ca. 25 BCE]

The battle at Sentinum (295 BCE)

Decius ... cried aloud on the name of his father Publius Decius: "Why," he asked, "do I seek any longer to postpone the doom of our house? It is the privilege of our family that we should be sacrificed to avert the nation's perils. Now I shall offer up the legions of the enemy, to be slain with me as victims to Earth and the Manes*." On going down into the field of battle he had ordered Marcus Livius the pontifex not to leave his side. He now commanded this man to recite before him the words with which he proposed to devote himself and the enemy's legions on behalf of the army of the Roman People, the Quirites. He was then devoted with the same form of prayer and in the same habit his father, Publius Decius, had commanded to be used, when he was devoted at the Veseris, in the Latin War; and having added to the usual prayers that he was driving before him fear and panic, blood and carnage, and the wrath of the gods celestial and gods infernal, and should blight with a curse the standards, weapons, and armor of the enemy, and that one and the same place should witness his own destruction and that of the Gauls and Samnites – having uttered these imprecations upon himself and the enemy, he spurred his charger against the Gallic lines, where he saw that they were thickest, and hurling himself against the weapons of the enemy he met his death.

Livy, History of Rome, 10.28.13–18 [ca. 25 BCE]

The bellum iustum or "just war"[2]

By now the Helvetians, having brought their forces through the defiles and the Sequanians' borders, had come to the lands of the Aeduians, and they were ravaging their territory. Being unable to protect themselves and their property from the invaders, the Aeduians sent legates to Caesar asking for assistance. They pleaded that the Aeduians had always served the Romans too well to be deserving of the ruin of their lands, the loss of their children to enslavement, and the seizure of their towns, almost within the sight of the Roman army.... In light of all these events Caesar determined that he must not wait until the Helvetians should penetrate into the Santonians' land, having destroyed the fortunes of Rome's allies.

Caesar, Gallic Wars, 1.11 [ca. 50 BCE]

But the Romans, investing all of their energies at home and abroad, did not lose time, got themselves ready, exhorted each other, went out to meet their enemies, and protected their freedom, their country, and their parents by arms. Later, when their virtue had warded off danger, they came to the aid of allies and friends, and established cordial relations by granting rather than by receiving favors.

Sallust, The Conspiracy of Catiline, 6.5 [ca. 40 BCE]

I brought about the restoration of peace in the Alps, from the region nearest to the Adriatic Sea as far as the Tuscan Sea, without undeservedly making war against any people.... The Cimbrians, the Charydes, the Semnones, and other German peoples of the same region through envoys sought my friendship and that of the Roman people.

Augustus, Accomplishments (Res Gestae Divi Augusti), 26 [14 CE]

The Romans make it a point to embark only upon wars that are just, and to make no casual or precipitate decisions about such matters.

Diodorus of Sicily, Universal History, 32.5 [ca. 30 BCE]

The fetiales[*] *(fetial priesthood)*

Equity in war has been most sacredly transmitted by the fetial code of the Roman people; and we may understand from this that no war is just, unless a formal demand for satisfaction has been given and a formal war declaration issued.

Cicero, *On Duties*, 1.36 [44 BCE]

It is [the fetials'] duty to take care that the Romans do not enter upon an unjust war against any city in alliance with them; and if others begin the violation of treaties against them, to go as ambassadors and first make formal demand for justice, and then, if the others refuse to comply with their demands, to sanction war. In like manner, if any people in alliance with the Romans complain of having been injured by them and demand justice, these men are to determine whether they have suffered anything in violation of their alliance; and if they find their complaints well grounded, they are to seize the accused and deliver them up to the injured parties. They are also to take cognizance of the crimes committed against ambassadors, to take care that treaties are religiously observed, to make peace, and if they find that peace has been made otherwise than is prescribed by the holy laws, to set it aside; and to inquire into and expiate the transgressions of the generals insofar as they relate to oaths and treaties.

Dionysius of Halicarnassus, *Roman Antiquities*, 2.72 [ca. 10 BCE]

When the envoy has arrived at the frontiers of the people from whom satisfaction is sought, he covers his head – the cover is of wool – and says: "Hear Jupiter; hear, ye boundaries of" – naming whatever nation they belong to – "let righteousness hear! I am the public herald of the Roman People; I come duly and religiously commissioned; let my words be credited." Then he recites his demands, after which he takes Jupiter to witness: "If I demand unduly and against religion that these men and these things be surrendered to me, then let me never enjoy my native land." ... It was customary for the fetial to carry to the bounds of the other nation a cornet-wood spear, iron-pointed or hardened in the fire, and in the presence of not less than three grown men to say: "Whereas the tribes of the Ancient Latins have been guilty of acts and offences against the Roman People of the Quirites; and whereas the Roman People of the Quirites has commanded that war be made on the Ancient Latins, and the Senate of the Roman People has approved, agreed, and voted a war with the Ancient Latins; I therefore and the Roman People declare and make war on the tribes of the Ancient Latins and the men of the Ancient Latins." Having said this, he would hurl his spear into their territory. This is the manner in which at that time redress was sought from the Latins and war was declared, and the custom has been received by later generations."

Livy, *History of Rome*, 1.32.6–8, 12–14 [ca. 25 BCE]

Empire of inclusion

That legal system which our ancestors devised with divine guidance from the very beginnings of the Roman name is so admirable! Their legal precepts ruled that nobody can be the member of more than one state ... that no one can be removed from the citizen register against his will, nor forced to remain a part of it against his will! This is the solid foundation of our freedom: each one of us has absolute power of keeping or giving up his citizenship. But what is most responsible for the establishment of the Roman Empire and the fame of the Roman people is that Romulus, the founder of the city, instructed us by the treaty with the Sabines that this state should be increased even by the admission of enemies to the [Roman] citizenship. Our ancestors through his authority and example never ceased to grant and bestow the citizenship.

Cicero, *In Defense of Balbus*, 31 [56 BCE]

Romulus, Rome's founder, was said to have made his new city a safe haven for refugees and vagabonds. In order to increase the population of the fledgling city, the Romans abducted the neighboring Sabine women. On the verge of war over this incident, the pleas of the Sabine women averted war and led to the incorporation of Sabines into the Roman state. According to ancient Roman legend, King Tullus Hostilius (traditional dates, 672–640 BCE) punished the treachery of his Alban allies only with the execution of Mettius Fufetius, their commander, while incorporating the Alban people into the Roman state. Ancus Marcius (traditional dates, 640–616 BCE) also adopted this policy of inclusion.

Meanwhile Rome was growing. More and more ground was coming within the circuit of its walls. Indeed, the rapid expansion of the enclosed area was out of proportion to the actual population, and evidently indicated an eye to the future. In antiquity, the founder of a new settlement, in order to increase its population, would as a matter of course shark up a lot of homeless and destitute folk and pretend that they were "born of earth" to be his progeny. Romulus now followed a similar course. To help fill his big new town, he threw open, in the ground – now enclosed – between the two copses as you go up the Capitoline hill, a place of asylum for fugitives. All the lowliest elements from neighboring peoples fled here for refuge: some free, some slaves, and all of them wanting a fresh start. That mob was the first real addition to the city's strength, the first step to its future greatness.[3]

Livy, *History of Rome*, 1.8.4–7 [ca. 25 BCE]

The city of Rome, as far as I can make out, was founded and first inhabited by Trojan exiles who, led by Aeneas, were wandering without a settled home, and by rustic natives who lived in a state of anarchy uncontrolled by laws or government. When once they had come to live together in a walled town, despite different origins, languages, and habits of life, they coalesced with amazing ease, and before long what had been a heterogeneous mob of migrants was welded into a united nation.

Sallust, *The Conspiracy of Catiline*, 6.1–3 [ca. 40 BCE]

"If you regret," [the Sabine women] continued, "the relationship that unites you, if you regret the marriage tie, turn your anger against us; we are the cause of the war, the cause of the wounds, and even death to both our husbands and our parents. It will be better for us to perish than to live, lacking either of you, as widows or as orphans." It was a touching plea, not only to the rank-and-file, but to their leaders as well. A stillness fell on them, and a sudden hush. Then the leaders came forward to make a truce, and not only did they agree on peace, but they made one people out of the two. They shared the sovereignty, but all authority was transferred to Rome.

Livy, *History of Rome*, 1.13.3–5 [ca. 25 BCE]

Thereupon the centurions*, sword in hand, surrounded Mettius, while the king proceeded: "May prosperity, favor, and fortune be with the Roman people and myself, and with you, men of Alba! I purpose to bring all the Alban people over to Rome, to grant citizenship to their commons, to enroll the nobles into the Senate, to make one city and one state. As formerly from one nation the Alban nation was divided into two, so now let it be reunited into one.... Rome... was increased by Alba's downfall. The number of citizens was doubled, the Caelian hill was added to the city, and, that it might be more thickly settled, Tullus chose it for the site of the king's house and from that time onwards resided there. The chief men of the Albans he made senators, that this branch of the nation might grow too. Such were the Julii, the Servilii, the Quinctii, the Geganii, the Curiatii, and the Cloelii. He also built, as a consecrated place for the order he had enlarged, a Senate house.

Livy, *History of Rome*, 1.28.7–8, 30.1–2 [ca. 25 BCE]

Ancus dedicated the care of the sacrifices to the flamines* and other priests, and having enlisted a new army proceeded to Politorium, one of the Latin cities. He took this place by storm, and adopting the plan of former kings, who had enlarged the state by making enemies into citizens, transferred the whole population to Rome. The Palatine was the quarter of the original Romans; on the one hand were the Sabines, who had the Capitol and the citadel; on the other lay the Caelian, occupied by the Albans. The Aventine was therefore assigned to the newcomers, and here too were sent shortly afterwards the citizens recruited from the captured towns of Tellenae and Ficana.

Livy, *History of Rome*, 1.33.1–3 [ca. 25 BCE]

A schism which occurred between the advocates of war and those of peace amongst the Sabines resulted in the transfer of some part of their strength to the Romans. For Attius Clausus, afterwards known at Rome as Appius Claudius, himself a champion of peace, was hard pressed by the turbulent war-party, and finding himself no match for them, left Inregillus, with a large band of clients, and fled to Rome. These people were made citizens and given land across the Anio River. The "Old Claudian Tribe" was the name used later, when new tribesmen had been added to designate those who came from this territory. Appius, having been enrolled in the Senate, came in a short time to be regarded as one of its leading members.

Livy, *History of Rome*, 2.16.3–6 [ca. 25 BCE]

Unroll the family tree of any nobleman you like; you will arrive at low birth if you go back far enough. Why should I list individuals? I could use the whole city as my example. Once these hills stood bare and within the extensive confines of our walls there is nothing more distinguished than a lowly hut.... Can you reproach the Romans? They could conceal their humble beginnings but instead they make a display of them and do not regard all this as great unless it is made obvious that it rose from a small beginning.

Seneca, *Controversies*, 1.6.4 [ca. 35 CE]

Empire of terror

Those whose object is to gain dominion over others use courage and intelligence to get it, moderation and consideration for others to extend it widely, and paralysing terror to secure it against attack. The proofs of these propositions are to be found in attentive consideration of the history of such empires as were created in ancient times as well as of the Roman domination that succeeded them. . . . In more recent times the Romans, when they went in pursuit of world empire, brought it into being by the valor of their arms, then extended its influence far and wide by the kindest possible treatment of the vanquished. So far, indeed, did they abstain from cruelty and revenge on those subjected to them that they appeared to treat them not as enemies, but as if they were benefactors and friends. Whereas the conquered, as former foes, expected to be visited with fearful reprisals, the conquerors left no room for anyone to surpass them in clemency. Some they enrolled as fellow citizens, to some they granted rights of intermarriage, to others they restored their independence, and in no case did they nurse a resentment that was unduly severe. Because of their surpassing humanity, therefore, kings, cities, and whole nations went over to the Roman standard. But once they held sway over virtually the whole inhabited world, they confirmed their power by terrorism and by the destruction of the most eminent cities. Corinth they razed to the ground, the Macedonians (Perseus, for example) they rooted out, they razed Carthage and the Celtiberian city of Numantia, and there were many whom they cowed with terror.

Diodorus of Sicily, *Universal History*, 32.2, 4.4–5 [ca. 30 BCE]

The sack of Pometia (502 BCE)[4]

When a short time had elapsed, long enough for healing wounds and recruiting the army, [the Romans] returned, with heightened resentment and also with augmented forces, to the attack of Pometia. They had repaired their mantlets and the rest of their equipment, and they were already upon the point of sending their men against the walls when the town capitulated. But the fate of the Aurunci was no less awful from their having surrendered their city than if it had been stormed. Their chief men were beheaded and the rest of the colonists were sold as slaves. The town was razed; its land was sold.

Livy, *History of Rome*, 2.17.4–6 [ca. 25 BCE]

Savagery against the Tarquinienses (353 BCE)

Two wars were successfully prosecuted this year, and the Tarquinienses and the Tiburtes were forced to make submission. The city of Sassula was taken from Tibur, and the rest of their towns would have met with the same fortune, had the whole nation not laid down their arms and cast themselves upon the mercy of the consul. A triumph was celebrated over them, but in all other respects the victory was used with clemency. There was no mercy for the Tarquinienses. Many were slain on the battlefield, and out of the vast number taken prisoners 358 were selected – the noblest of them all – to be sent to Rome, and the rest of the populace were put to the sword. Neither were the Roman people less stern towards those who had been sent to Rome, but scourged them all with rods in the middle of the Forum and struck off their heads.

Livy, *History of Rome*, 7.9.1–3 [ca. 25 BCE]

Roman retribution against rebellious Sora (314 BCE)

Sora was already taken when the consuls arrived at dawn and accepted the surrender of those whom fortune had allowed to survive the rout and carnage of the night. From these, 225, who were designated on all hands as the authors of the revolt and the hideous massacre of the colonists, they sent to Rome in chains. . . . All those who were taken to Rome were scourged and beheaded in the Forum, to the great delight of the commoners, whom it most nearly concerned that the people who were sent out here and there to colonies should in every case be protected.

Livy, *History of Rome*, 9.24.13–15 [ca. 25 BCE]

Scipio Africanus and the sack of New Carthage (209 BCE)

Finally, when the walls had been taken . . . those who entered through the gate occupied the hill on the east after dislodging its defenders. When Scipio thought that a sufficient number of troops had entered he sent most of them, as is the Roman custom, against the inhabitants of the city with orders to kill all they encountered, sparing none, and not to start pillaging until the signal was given. They do this, I think, to inspire terror, so that when towns are taken by the Romans one may often see not only the corpses of human beings, but dogs cut in half, and the dismembered limbs of other animals, and on this occasion such scenes were very many owing to the numbers of those in the place.

Polybius, *Histories*, 10.15.3–7 [ca. 150 BCE]

Surrounding [the city of Lutia in Spain] at dawn, [Scipio Aemilianus] ordered the inhabitants to deliver up their leaders. After the citizens claimed that they had already fled from the town, Scipio sent a herald to tell the citizens that he would sack their city if the men were not handed over to him. Terrified, they handed over about 400 men. Scipio cut off their hands, withdrew his troops, and rode off, arriving in his own camp at about daybreak the next day.

Appian, *Spanish Wars*, 94 [ca. 160 CE]

Sulla's siege and sack of Athens (87–86 BCE)

But when he learned of the famine in Athens, that they had eaten all their cattle, boiled the hides and skins, and licked what they could get from them, and that some had even tasted human flesh, Sulla ordered his soldiers to surround the city with a ditch so that the besieged might not escape secretly, even one by one. Then he brought up his ladders and simultaneously began to break through the wall. The enervated defenders soon fled, and the Romans rushed into the city. A massive and pitiless slaughter in Athens followed. The starving inhabitants were too weak to flee, and Sulla ordered an indiscriminate massacre, not sparing women or children. He was angry that they had so suddenly joined the barbarians [Mithridates] without cause, and had displayed such violent hatred toward himself. Most of the Athenians when they heard the order given rushed upon the swords of the slayers willingly. A few had taken their feeble course to the Acropolis, among them Aristion [leader of the rebellion], who had burned the Odeum, so that Sulla might not have the timber in it at hand for storming the Acropolis. Sulla prohibited the burning of the city, but allowed his soldiers to plunder it. In many houses they found human flesh prepared for food. The next day Sulla sold the slaves.

Appian, *Mithridatic Wars*, 38 [ca. 160 CE]

Julius Caesar and the rebellion at Uxellodunum (51 BCE)

Caesar knew that his clemency was renowned, and he did not fear that harsher action might seem due to an innate cruelty; he also could not see success for his plans if more of the enemy in different districts engaged in this sort of behavior. He therefore determined that the rest must be deterred by an exemplary punishment; and so, while granting them their lives, he cut off everyone's hands who had borne arms, to proclaim the more openly the penalty of evildoers.

Caesar, *Gallic Wars*, 8.44 [ca. 50 BCE]

EDITOR'S NOTES

1   For classic statements on climatic and geographical determinism, see the Hippocratic treatise, *Airs, Waters, Places*, conveniently translated in the Loeb Classical Library, *Hippocrates*, vol. 1 (Cambridge, Mass., repr. 1984), pp. 65–137; Aristotle, *Politics*, 1327a23–33; also 1285a19–22. See further K. Clarke, *Between Geography and Empire: Hellenistic Constructions of the Roman World* (Oxford, 1999).

2   For a spirited argument that Romans subscribed to the idea of the just war, see (in German) M. Kostial, *Kriegerisches Rom? Zur Frage von Unvermeidbarkeit und Normalität militärischer Konflikte in der römischen Politik* (Stuttgart, 1995); for criticism, see my review in *Bryn Mawr Classical Review*, 97.2.8 (1998), on-line journal <http://ccat.sas.upenn.edu/bmcr/>. See generally M. Walzer, *Just and Unjust Wars: A Moral Argument with Historical Illustrations*, 3rd edn. (New York, 2000).

3   See also the lengthy speech of the tribune C. Canuleius in 445 BCE at Livy, *History of Rome*, 4.3.1–5.6.

4   See W. V. Harris, *War and Imperialism in Republican Rome, 327–70 BC* (Oxford, 1979), pp. 263–4 ("Roman killing in captured cities"); A. Ziolkowski, "*Urbs direpta*, or how the Romans sacked cities," in *War and Society in the Roman World*, ed. J. Rich and G. Shipley (London and New York, 1993), pp. 69–91.

4

"Romanization": Cultural Assimilation, Hybridization, and Resistance

Introduction

The selections in this chapter open up questions of the politico-cultural dimensions of Roman imperialism. They all address the difficult concept of "Romanization." What was it? Were there conscious motivations on the part of Romans, provincials, or both in the diffusion and acceptance, rejection, or modification of Roman cultural forms? Or was all this largely an unconscious process?

MacMullen takes up the question of replication of Roman culture in Italy outside the capital and in the provinces. For a pre-industrial society, the rapid spread of Roman culture in the East, in Africa, in Spain, and in Gaul during Augustus' reign is remarkable. How do we account for it? MacMullen argues against any "push or pressure" from Rome as metropole upon susceptible, peripheral provincials. There was no Roman cultural program, and, as MacMullen observes, "the alien civilization was embraced: its speech, its dress, its leisure customs, its rituals of burial and commemoration, most particularly the value it placed on euergetism [public benefactions bestowed by wealthy elites], and so on through a catalogue of borrowings. Sometimes what was borrowed seemed in itself better, sometimes a means rather of gaining some further good: favor among the powerful, community esteem."

Woolf, focusing on the culture of Roman Gaul, argues for a somewhat more complex picture. It is not the persistence of regional cultural forms and cultural diversity, "the default condition of the perpetual creativity of human societies," that needs explanation, but rather "the brief convergence of Roman provincial cultures" in the age of Augustus. Local elites above all embraced Roman culture as a means to power and privilege, but this process was "more complex than simple emulation." Becoming Roman created social and cultural hierarchies and stratification that served to distance Gaul from Gaul, and we may see this as a function of Roman power. This was "a cultural system structured by systematic differences." To be sure, in the cultural sphere in Gaul there was convulsion and disruption in the formative period of Gallo-Roman society in the second half of the first century BCE and the first half of the following century, but Woolf stresses that this tension was short-lived: "The contrast between the uses made of Roman-style culture in the formative period, and those characteristic of the succeeding two centuries strongly suggests that Roman values *were* internalized by the Gallo-Roman elite."

Wells looks at cultural interactions between Romans and the conquered peoples of temperate Europe, with a special focus on Roman perceptions of indigenous peoples. Roman constructions of those who did not speak Latin or Greek, the *barbari*, were highly stereotypical: they were either represented as uncouth savages or idealized as unspoilt, noble, and simple folk. And these constructions persisted for a long time. But the historical reality was much more complex and nuanced. Linguistic evidence, for example, indicates that the idea of peoples in temperate Europe speaking either Celtic or Germanic is grossly reductionist; and archaeological evidence has led some scholars even to deny that there were recognizable groups of people, the "Celts" and the "Germans." Moreover, we must not only be wary of the Classical texts' representations of these peoples, but we must also recognize that these tribal societies had *already* been profoundly transformed by contact with Roman civilization before the conquests and the arrival of those Romans (and Greeks) who wrote about them. Yet native responses to Roman cultural forms were highly selective, complex, and heterogeneous.

Romanization in the Time of Augustus[i]

R. MacMullen

REPLICATION

The means

Some generations before Augustus, a very great Roman achievement took its place not in the usual history books (it is barely recorded by Livy) but in the capital. It was, or is, the public storage barn called the Porticus Aemilia. Parts survive. Designed to receive comestibles on a capital scale, it measured two hundred feet by sixteen hundred and fifty, with two stories, divided into some two hundred chambers.[1] Nothing like it had ever been seen for sheer size, and practicality. As the second century went on, the limitless powers of construction here demonstrated were demonstrated in other Roman storage barns as well, though none so big as the Aemilian; they were demonstrated elsewhere in Italy again and yet again, most spectacularly in the footings of gigantic structures like the terracing of Palestrina or of temples at Tivoli or Tarracina.

There was a trick to such building: foundations and vaults and other parts not meant to show could all be done in plain poured concrete. You needed carpenters to build the forms that would contain and shape the pouring till it cured; then you took away the forms and their supports and moved them down the line, or up the wall, to repeat the process. There was nothing terribly complicated about it. Under proper direction, a little-trained work-force would do.[2]

The trick lay in the forms – but of course not only there. Concrete itself was essential. This was the material that set Roman architecture apart from Greek, liberating it for its most characteristic achievements. Combining mortar with stones, as big as two fists or just chips that needed little or no shaping, *opus caementicium* proved infinitely adaptable to any project at hand. And cheap. For at least the gross elements of major projects, "observing how soon the quarrymen would cut half a ton of *Spawls* [that is, chips] from an unformed block," who would go to the trouble of ashlar?[3] And the bare concrete could always be made more pleasing to the eye, and better protected against moisture, too, if it was faced with small stones unshaped ("petit appareil") or shaped only on the side that showed, or with segments of brick, in a random over-all arrangement or in a net pattern, *opus reticulatum*. For *opus reticulatum*, stones in the desired arrangement toward the outer sides of a wall, to a height of several layers, would be set in mortar as the wall rose, so as to make small forms themselves, between which the core-space was then filled in more roughly, and smoothed off, and the process repeated. This had become the technique of choice in Augustus' time, used even on his mausoleum, the Theater of Marcellus, and so on.[4]

Such simple economical methods were soon learnt. With or without admixture of traditional building techniques, they appear in a great deal of public construction already noticed in eastern and western provinces alike. They explain the terracing on vaults that transfigured the center of so many cities. In the late 40s B.C., Narbo got a cryptoportico tucked into sloping ground near the forum with 126 chambers along three hundred feet of vaulted aisles; and not long after Augustus' death, in Vienna, a storage barn almost double the size of the Aemilian was constructed – double, that is, assuming it had no second story (but it probably did).[5]

Terms used by scholars to describe the techniques of construction outlined here make plain their particular character: "industrialization," "mass production," capable of endless mechanical repetition because in their essence they consisted of quite simple forms – *Roman* forms.

In an extended sense, lines and holes on pavement could serve as a form, by the rules of which the hands and calculations of game-players were governed. Wherever such a thing was drawn and put to use, bystanders learned how to become Roman. The ball-court constructed for the people of Nemausus by prince Gaius served the same purpose, inviting them to a set activity and thus shaping their behavior.[6] Baths-buildings with their tripartite plan afforded a form into which life itself was poured, and cured; theaters in which everyone knew who was who and where he was supposed to sit inculcated distinct ideas about social place, quite aside from ideas of entertainment. And so forth – not excluding the form of bronze tablets conspicuously displayed "at eye level and in a much-frequented part of the city" (as the standard phrasing so often insisted).

Texts like those defining a constitution for Spanish cities were certainly prominent by the hundreds, even if they don't survive, spread across the provinces in Augustus' time. They were first at home in Italy, shaped there in their teachings and requirements, carefully considered by due authority as to necessary content and wording, publicized from the 40s B.C. if not earlier, and repeated without any very significant modification thereafter for the benefit of one urban center after another, again and again. It is a safe guess that [urban centers] had such a text on the wall of their finest temple, perhaps rather in the basilica, but in any case where no one could miss it.

Once its essential content had been more or less decided on, early in Augustus' time, the imposing of it on a fresh population was as easy as putting up work-forms for a wall; pouring the population into it was as quickly done; and the hardening of their habits of at least partial conformity could be expected to yield an equally durable set of institutions: prescribing nomenclature, guardianships, social ranks, religious ceremonies, and so on and so forth, all, thoroughly Roman. There was no need to re-invent them each time.

We in our modern world might expect some force to be applied to produce conformity. The masters of the provinces could call up their legions ad lib. and compel obedience to a charter, could they not? But there is never a hint that this was even thought of.

Still, the legions did play some part. They built major highways serving as arma-tures on which might depend a dozen, indirectly a hundred, urban centers needing access to each other for commerce and growth. Spain, Gaul, and the most habitable parts of the province of Africa, equipped with such gigantic structures laid down across their whole expanse, took on the look of Italy. In Augustus' time, Italy's network was long familiar, a characteristic of its civilization. The width of the roadway, depth of stone, and delimitation in Roman miles were all so well known, they could be laid down in the provinces with perfect confidence and ease. Once in place, the indigenous populations took advantage of them to develop their economy.

The legions proved useful in other tasks of civil engineering. Many clear instances have turned up in the previous chapters,[7] along with others less clear, where an army role must be inferred from surviving construction. Does the crossing of *kardo* and *decumanus* at some provincial city's center, and the arrangement of the open space and surrounding municipal offices, replicate the headquarters-area at the center of a camp? There are differences; but the plan of Barcino or Forum Segusiavorum must surely recall Italian Republican colonies like Ostia or the later Augusta Bagiennorum, laid out by army surveyors.[8] For the imperial authorities set over a province, legionary legate or governor, the only experts at hand to help in preparing some center for its share of responsibility were attached to the Commanders of Engineers, *praefecti fabrum*. So Vitruvius had served outside of Italy. Others like him have appeared in construction roles, above. The forum-form they imposed serves my purpose equally well whether derived from camps or ordinary Italian town centers, so long as it is clear that it was ready and waiting for implementation – that it shows Romans' capacity to transfer designs ready-made from their homeland to the lands they conquered. There was certainly a call for their help in the Augustan "building-boom."

No need, perhaps, to rehearse the role they played in surveying the lands set aside for the use of veteran settlers. It does need to be said again, however, that the form of squares of twenty *actus* pressed down on the land by centuriation marked it forever as Roman, and redistributed the farming population in a manner to change their farming practices. Land reclamation and sedentarization followed.[9] At the same time everyone came under the authority of the town in their midst, according to a pattern of responsibility at home in Italy; or rather, they or at least the richest persons among them took their place in the town's *curia* to exercise that responsibility, presided over by magistrates just like those to be found in Italian municipalities and just as the town's charter prescribed. The *curia* was a form, the basilica where magistrates held court was one other; so was the forum for public assemblies, perhaps equipped with a replica of Rome's rostra, even of the Roman forum's Marsyas statue, and dignified by a great podium temple at one end. Assemblies would be held according to form, that is, with preliminary Roman rites in the temple or at an altar in front of it. Indeed, the more fully Roman centers, *coloniae*, were marked out from their very inception by a priest's plowing of a sacred furrow, depicted on the coins of Emerita or Philippi, for example, according to the same rites that had initiated Rome itself; and from that moment forward, if there was any doubt just how a cult should be conducted, questions could be directed to the capital, to find out what was the custom, the form, at the shrine of Diana or of some other appropriate deity. Provision that this be done was written up on bronze in the charter "at eye level and in a much-frequented part of the city."

Toward the end of a remarkable book, Lopez Paz takes into one single vision the Roman city surrounded by its centuriated lands: "The entirety of this huge structure, the territory of the Roman community, realized itself in something changeless over time, destined to endure, stable, eliminating all conflict that might destroy it." It was "the ideal community but not utopian," Roman not Greek; and, everywhere, its exact specifications, their permanence, and their advertisement for future reference were of particular concern to Augustus. It was he who proclaimed by edict just what should be the width of border-roads around *centuriae* and how corner-termini should be set up and inscribed; he who arranged that site-plans and allotments should be registered and preserved. Much of the map of one area of assignment in the provinces is still before us, once posted in public to remind people exactly who owned what, near what inscribed boundary-stone – this, the well-known marble plan of Arausio.[10]

Even in quite remote areas in Augustan times the application of the Romans' Standard Operating Procedure is described: "their soldiers were wintering there [near the Rhine] and towns were being formed: the barbarians were adapting themselves to orderly Roman ways and were becoming accustomed to holding markets and peaceful assemblies" (Dio 56.18.2f). Evident in the passage is the need as yet unsatisfied for a built assembly place, a forum with a *comitium*, and a built market-hall, a *macellum*; but the future would supply these; for it was a particular characteristic of a Romanized urban center, even in Corinth or Antioch, that it should have accommodations in stone for the activities thought to define a city.[ii]

The design of them needn't depend on the moment's inspiration. There were forms easily followed from handbooks. Vitruvius' is only the most pretentious and complete. Something much simpler could have dictated the plans of private houses and fora, *capitolia* or theaters, aqueducts or *tropaia*.[11] All of these structures could be laid out according to modules in prescribed ratios; all accustomed the eye to the Roman aesthetic, for all had in sight the corresponding structures of Italy, often, of the center of Rome itself. The decorative elements of the temples of Apollo and of Mars-the-Avenger were particularly favored for imitation. One had only to ask for a drawing or plaster cast to copy, as local architects and stone-cutters can be shown to have done in many provinces.

Nothing, however, taught the Italian aesthetic more ubiquitously than Italian pottery. In one variety or another it could be found everywhere, within the reach of people of almost every level of wealth. It is too much to say that its characteristic shapes, suited to the Italian diet, served as a form to impose that diet. No, lessons under that heading worked through other means; but the new appetites would certainly be accommodated by Italian shapes. As to the decoration, from Arretium = Arezzo in Tuscany (still today a center of ceramic production) flowed a stream of the most striking wares marked, from early Augustan times on (about 30 B.C.), by reliefs, many of them of the highest quality. *Terra sigillata* relied on a simple trick: a hollow form, a baked clay matrix, in the inner walls of which had been impressed reliefs by stamps; and the matrix was then cooked to be hard; and a soft clay vessel could be placed inside the matrix and its sides pressed out into the matrix-walls so as to take on the reliefs; whereupon, as it dried and lost bulk, it could be removed from the matrix to be fired without damage to either, and the matrix re-used indefinitely. Many matrices and stamps have been found both at Arretium and in the western provinces. The stamps could be applied in any arrangement ad lib.[12] In the preceding chapter an indication was given of the extraordinary flow of finished vessels from only one, though by far the most active, cluster of little workshops in the Province in Augustus' time. "Mass production" thanks to mechanical replication of designs is the obvious term by which to describe this whole business. Its principles could be applied wherever the rewards of efficiency of manufacture were evident: for example, in meeting the great demand for an entirely different kind of vessel, crude large amphorae required for oil-export from Spain. The Spanish kilns turned out "large numbers of surprisingly uniform bulbous containers."[13] Another example is the mass production of terracotta figurines by mould to sell to pilgrims at a Gallic shrine, or the identical bronze figurines of Aphrodite and Asclepius from scattered western sites.[14] Moulds, again, or forms.

No one would expect that stone sculptures of some undeniable artistry might be standardized and mass-produced. Explanation of the process may best begin with the mass-produced: portraits of the imperial family in quite remarkable numbers. They are found in army camps, carried around with the troops; in places of imperial cult, most naturally, after the mid-20s B.C.; in or near theaters, sometimes in special galleries; and on fora. Those more than life-size are of the emperor.[15] Beginning in the east in the 40s B.C., the wish of the greatest Romans to present themselves in portraits to the people had taken hold, producing rare Antony's (but many were destroyed), a thin scattering of Caesar's (some thirty survive), but a very great number of Augustus's. Though a majority of the more than 250 of the latter that survive do so without context, some seventy can be traced to Italy (the most) and the rest, to all regions. On the assumption that every least city in the empire that might think itself worthy of the name would have wanted some public advertisement of its proper loyalty to be set up in more than one choice location, Augustus-portraits must have numbered above twenty thousand by the end of his reign. With others in proportion for the various princes, the total spread over a generation or so is a match for the output of La Graufesenque. It is undeniably mass production.

From this effort, Romanization resulted intangibly, as the identity of supreme power took on a specific human shape in poses and costumes that were specific to the civilization of the masters of the world. That is, provincial populations were taught a political lesson of the most obvious importance, and, along with it, lessons in art and image. The rapid approximation of portraits of private individuals in Spain, and of a native king in Africa, to the face and expression of the emperor, has been noticed.[16] Provincials were taught the habit of advertisement itself through statues

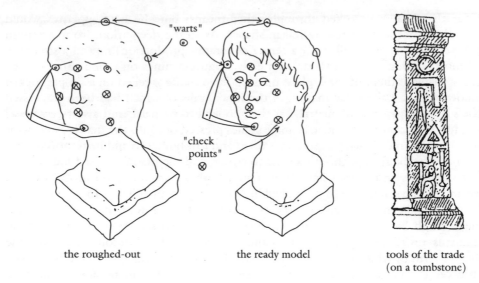

| the roughed-out | the ready model | tools of the trade (on a tombstone) |

Figure 6   *Copying-methods for statuary.*

set up in public, along with lessons in the epigraphic habit. In these various respects, then, the output of carved stone and its ubiquitous display deserves a place in these pages.

But by what trick could mass production be achieved in this marble art? Michael Pfanner has drawn attention to what he calls "warts" or, in the modern craftsman's language, "puntelli," to be noticed on a number of not quite finished pieces of Roman sculpture – notably, on a full-length barbarian destined for a monument in Rome a century after Augustus, but found unused on the Field of Mars.[17] On this work there are two dozen little protuberances left after the surrounding stone had all been cut away to the proper figure. They must correspond to their like, of plaster, temporarily and identically situated and attached to a now-lost model of which the barbarian was a copy. The sculptor decided what would be the most convenient points on his model by which to measure with calipers a matching distance, in three dimensions, on the roughed-out block of stone he had before him. Preliminary roughing-out he could do by eye, but more accuracy was attainable through his calipers, and the greater the number of "warts," the more perfect the outcome. Modern methods explain "warts" left on dozens of pieces of ancient statuary. Slight variations in technique and instruments can be added to the picture of the stone-cutters at work; and the extraordinary accuracy they could attain can be demonstrated by comparing the profiles of Augustus-heads of the several most famous, frequently copied styles, of Prima Porta and so forth.[18] These latter derived from models, or in my metaphor, from "forms," most often made available in plaster casts for reproduction, the process beginning in the Carrara quarries that the emperor controlled and being completed on site in Emerita or Caesarea-in-Pisidia. The patterns of distribution of the result indicate the surprising speed with which the work could be done. "Roman imperial culture," Pfanner concludes, "had become a mass culture."

He is not the first to have been struck by the sculptural evidence that rather abruptly appears in the 20s B.C., transforming the character of public areas in cities everywhere. The trick of replication, not unknown in Hellenistic times and therefore no Roman invention, was nevertheless applied on an altogether new and Roman scale, exactly like the trick of concrete wall-building. In architecture, too, so far as it was official and public, a special degree of standardization [existed]. At Tarraco, standardization was applied even to private individuals' votive portraiture set up in the city's principal shrine – a place semi-public. The replication of bronze statuary to meet private demand, having nothing to do with political correctness and everything to do with being Roman, established itself at the same time. It too used "warts" and favored reproductions of the best-known classics in the art.[19] That such classics were also Greek made them no less Roman.

The opportunity

It was of course essential that replication should be physically possible on a scale to respond to demand, whether in art or pottery or typical comestibles, chiefly olive oil and wine. Otherwise, no historically significant acculturation could take place. Yes, but every reader of the more classical detective stories knows from their last chapter, when the dark mystery is explained under three headings, there must be not only *means* but *opportunity* as well (with *motive* first and last of all).

In the earlier decades of Augustus' time, while war was threatened or actively waged, the antagonists must seek everywhere for support. For example, in Massilia. Wooed by both Pompey and Caesar with rich favors, its people were in no hurry to end their courtship: they declared it absolutely beyond their intellectual powers to tell who was in the right. Or in Baetica, Pompey lavished his *beneficia* on the chief cities, and Caesar mentally added up those favors and estimated their danger to his cause, and topped them.[20] What was promised in pressing circumstances had to be delivered afterwards, for years. A usual award was some reassignment of taxes or direct gift of plunder taken from other parties. To all such, there must be some limit. Better by far were generous gifts of charters and citizenship. These cost no one anything and could be indulged in so long as they did not too much offend public opinion in Italy. A shower of gifts to provincial communities set in in the 50s B.C. and continued into the 40s and beyond. As a result, long before the end of Augustus' reign, in the Province there was no one left outside the boundaries of some chartered city – all of southern Gaul could fairly be called "Latinized" – while southern Spain was treated almost equally well.[21] Similarly, in large areas of north Africa and parts of north western Greece. It was owing to the opportunity of civil strife that the process of partial or complete incorporation into the Roman state should have been offered to those who wanted it, on a scale unmatched in any previous time.

Then, too, it was only by the opportunity or accident of war that several dozen legions came together at Philippi and, at Actium, dozens again with huge naval forces to support them, while still other troops were serving at the same time in other theaters; and something had to be done with them all when the fighting was over. Victorious commanders could maintain their position only by post-war demobilization, which had to be seen as generous, or at least acceptable, and not too long delayed by further campaigning against external enemies. The salience of the problem is clear in Augustus' *Achievements*, where he gives an early paragraph (3) and some monumental sestertius-totals to his handling of it. Resettlement in Italy was what the men wanted. Much along this line was achieved. But seizing land there involved a political cost and buying it at a fair price, a prohibitive cost in money. There was a third possibility: to settle the men overseas. Even then, their farms had often to be purchased, not confiscated. As against the 600 million sesterces Augustus had to spend in Italy, he paid out 260 in compensation to provincials. Italian land was certainly more expensive per acre. To bring up the total cost of provincial land to 260 millions, we must suppose that a very substantial proportion of the 300,000 veterans whom he re-settled were sent overseas. That would fit with the total of perhaps sixty colonies attributed to him, if each received 1,500–2,000 men. As many again must be added, from Caesar's and the Triumvirs' colonies, earlier, at some forty sites, counting, too, a huge number of civilians from Rome dispatched by the dictator to Carthage and elsewhere.[22]

Both the beneficiaries of these policies and the form in which they were settled proved effective instruments of acculturation, though by no means sufficient in themselves to explain the process that interests me. Among movements of people in ancient history, nothing compares with these more than 200,000 veterans and scores of thousands of civilians set down in successive waves at well over a hundred points of colonization, with close to a hundred other, mostly pre-existing centers newly chartered in a Roman fashion. Mighty changes! and over the course only of a generation.

Had there been no such changes. . . . To imagine the provinces instead untouched makes us confront the import of what was actually done. Plain statistics – or call them approximations – indicate its scale. At the same time, it is well to remember that areas in southern Gaul and southern Spain, where Roman culture was already familiar at Augustus' birth, at his death still retained much of their non-Roman character, while in the east, in most of its aspects, imported Roman culture faded out after two or three generations.

So far as Romanization resulted, sheer numbers played a very important part; but the particular quality of the settlers made a difference, too. It was a matter of opportunity, here again. The vast majority of them were legionaries, used to hanging together, to acting for a common end, and they had special skills applicable to community projects.[23] Even where, as in "Old" Africa, some were scattered among villages in little clusters, they were assured of a dominant position by reason both of their civic status and the relatively generous acreage of land they were assigned; and where, in the great western areas of the empire, there was the most changing to be done toward those city-centered Roman-Hellenistic customs and institutions, Roman warriors even at rest counted for something.

This last point surely should be given a good deal of weight. Positions of leadership among the Celtiberi or Helvetii, the respect accorded to an opinion or a choice, had been generally won through war. Contemporary sources make that plain.[24] Now by the verdict of war the victors, whether Roman or peregrine collaborators, had been declared; in terms of native values they had won the right to lead and to be heard. This right remained to them even in peace, or especially so, since warriors of the old style were now forbidden to flaunt their swords and spears and soon ceased even to be buried with them. In their place were "ACO" cups and Arretine.

To afford such civilian collectibles cost money. It was opportune that much became available for free expenditure in the course of civil strife. The losers are not heard of, only the winners. These latter, however, if they enjoyed some local prominence to begin with, found themselves competed for by Roman leaders just like their communities, with the opportunity similarly to offer their *officia* for *beneficia*. In the confusion of the times, by means and methods they could excuse as no different from their leaders', they might hope for sudden wealth, and can be seen applying it to the purchase of prestige through conspicuous consumption and largesses, little different in Roman terms than in indigenous. They built aqueducts and theaters, they put on gladiatorial games. A fair number of individuals of the sort have been instanced in earlier chapters.[25] Had they been in any doubt that lavish public giving would serve their ambitions, Caesar and Augustus set an example – the latter over a very long period and with very obvious help from Agrippa. To add up the amounts spent by Augustus and Agrippa in the west, by some extrapolation from their attested acts of patronage, is surely to understand a great deal about the "building-boom" of the period; and it was crucial to their means, and at the center of their opportunity, that the wealth of Egypt had fallen to the victor at Actium. Civil war paid for much of that construction.

The motive

Comparison of the degree of acculturation achieved in these western regions, with that achieved in the east, suggests, however, how important was the intrinsic attractiveness of the Roman way of life seen through the eyes of the indigenous population. The point was made in the preceding chapter (at nn. 65ff.), with illustrations that could have been drawn from any province at all. Baths and wine and so forth recommended themselves to the senses without need of an introduction. They felt or they looked good.

It is thus possible to speak of a higher civilization, in conventional terms, in contact with a lower. Romans of Augustus' time had no hesitation in doing so, untroubled by cultural relativism and post-colonial guilt. They could use the term "barbarian" in a value-neutral sense of "native," true, but usually in a sense of more or less horrified denigration.[26] There are instances of the latter before a company of the natives themselves. To make quite tactless comments was one of the pleasures of *maiestas*.[iii] The natives would be taught, if it was not plain enough on its face, that they could better rise into the ranks of the master race by reforming themselves – by talking, dressing, looking, and in every way resembling Romans. They would and did respond as ambition directed. They *pulled* Roman civilization to them – to their homes, their families, their world.

It used to be supposed that acculturation was more a matter of push. Long after Augustus a pair of comments, one from Tacitus and the other from Pliny the Elder, articulated the Romans' *maiestas* in cultural terms: their heaven-sent mission was "to soften people's ways, *ritus molliret*, to bring the clashing wild speech of infinite different peoples to a common conversation through a common tongue, and to supply civilization, *humanitas*, to men, that all races might, in a word, belong to one single *patria*." So Pliny; and Tacitus described his father-in-law's "intention" as a governor in Britain "that people who lived in widely dispersed and primitive settlements and hence were naturally inclined to war should become accustomed to peace and quiet by the provision of amenities. Hence he gave encouragement to individuals and assistance to communities to build temples, fora, and Roman-style houses. He praised those that responded and censured the dilatory. Ambition for promotion, *honoris aemulatio*, took the place of compulsion. Further, he educated the sons of the leading men in the liberal arts. . . . Thus even our style of dress came into favour and the toga was everywhere to be seen. Gradually, too, they went astray into the allurements of evil ways, colonnades and warm baths and elegant banquets. The Britons, who had no experience of this, called it 'civilization,' *humanitas*, although it was a part of their enslavement."[27]

The general tendency to minimize these two passages seems to me correct.[28] Pliny is simply noting the fact that Latin is spreading. The pride he felt in the ascendancy of his own tongue makes him treat the phenomenon in grand terms, as something the very gods wanted (else, perhaps, they would have awarded the western half of the "known world," too, to the Greeks and their tongue). As for Tacitus' account, it might have more weight except for its singularity. There is no match for it elsewhere, in words, nor any indication of it indirectly in the actions of governors. They betray an interest only in making their jobs easier. That need not involve more than bringing down the native populations from elevated strong-places to the plains, facilitating communication, clarifying approved forms of local oligarchy, and making clear through routine publication of laws and imperial orders that a knowledge of Latin would be taken for granted. All these steps have indeed been readily discerned in all the provinces, especially in the west. They looked, quite rationally, to the end the Romans always had in mind, the realities of power. More than that was not on governors' minds, gratifying as that "more" might be, if it were imitation of their way of life, and generally to be smiled on as it was by Agricola.

For the period with which I am properly concerned, something not said may count for more. Strabo, describing the whole empire from his knowledge of it in the middle years of Augustus' principate, says nothing about acculturation. He saw the Romans' power exerted in administration and the spread of colonies in the east while, in the west, it was exerted in pacification by force of arms, and, here too, in colonizing and diffusing Latin and law. For him, the barbarism to be overcome was violent, savage behavior, not boorish ignorance or bad manners. It stood in the way of peace and prosperity, without such peace also requiring atrium houses, worship of the lares, or gladiatorial games in every town on every weekend, a vision at which Strabo would have shuddered.[29] His testimony thus fits well with the distinction made in the preceding chapter between the public and the private spheres. In the public sphere, the spread of citizenship, charters, law, and imperial cult was obviously initiated or at least encouraged by imperial authority. In that sense, they represented push, with cultural consequences already sufficiently emphasized – but yet, consequences not foreseen or cared about by the Romans.

It may qualify as push or pressure from the center of the empire, that the bellicosity of "barbarians" was seen as something in need of chastening. Barbarians weren't fit to govern themselves nor even able to draw due benefit from peace. It was for Romans to preside not only over law-courts but commerce as well. For the chastening needed, there was Caesar with illustrative passages in his works; for the handling of business and respect for law, Cicero; but Cicero's bland claims extend over the Greeks of the east as much as over the Gauls.[30] His testimony proves too much: he had in sight only materialistic exploitation. Add to the picture a little note: that in an inscription of Ephesus we see the Triumvirs in 43 B.C. providing large tax-exemptions for physicians and professors, not out of any reverence for the civilization they represented, surely, but because the Roman ruling class had personal need of such skills and extended their favor to the purveyors as to clients.[31]

The notion of an abstract "Rome" with a cultural mission has been often enough dismissed.[32] Of any individual, specific champion there is no sign. A claim is sometimes entered for Augustus – a claim implied in the detection of an "Augustan ideology" of undefined content, but somehow "moral." The message was read in the art. Risk here of Procrustean subjectivity, so as to force the past "to make sense," is obvious. To discount it, evidence was offered in the preceding chapter, showing the adoption of new styles across all genres without confusion of esthetics and ethics or any flowing of the one into the other (where, too, the quality or impact of the style has been variously interpreted).

It makes no sense, in the face of some centralized culture-push, that Augustan style should have been quite unobserved in the homeland, around the corner from Augustus, so to speak, but in quite déclassé localities, then and now – localities outside the capital, then, and today to be found in local Italian museums rarely visited by art historians.[33] What determined choice were local tastes, not imperial "ideology." They retained their independence because that independence was never challenged.

It was different in the provinces. The populations there knew their land was not Italy, nor their ways Roman regardless of their being "provincial." Above and beyond their taking on of Roman traits in the public sphere, then, they must do so to some significant degree in the private sphere as well. It was the eagerness particularly of the urban well-to-do, the pull of that rich class, that so greatly accelerated the process. For all the reasons often noted, the alien civilization was embraced: its speech, its dress, its leisure customs, its rituals of burial and commemoration, most particularly the value it placed on euergetism, and so on through a catalogue of borrowings. Sometimes what was borrowed seemed in itself better, sometimes a means rather of gaining some further good: favor among the powerful, community esteem. "It was a process that went on through imitation, by osmosis – assimilation of oneself in the knowledge that one could live better and more easily if one played the game by Roman rules."[34]

NOTES

1 Lugli (1957) 371, 375, 450; Carettoni et al. (1960) 1.81, 95; Sear (1982) 74; MacMullen (1993) 61f.

2 Explained by Lugli (1957) 387f (use of *cassoni lignei*), 416; by Goudineau (1979) 190f, 195, "*opus caementicium* required both less time and less specialization," to which, add as a variant or development *opus reticulatum*, representing, "one may say, industrialization . . . , techniques of mass production, and use of shuttering, coffrages de bois recuperables

à l'infini"; also MacDonald (1982) 147, who offers further information in conversation (my cordial thanks to my omniscient friend). Grenier (1958–60) 3, 1.24 was right to emphasize the call for very large numbers of unskilled or semi-skilled labor that must explain the "building-boom" in Gaul under Augustus. Cf. the ca. 11,000,000 quite uniform blocks required for a single project, Autun's walls, Varène (1987) 45.

3   Roman production of "spawls" for concrete, of any size, cannot have been different from the method (quoted) in eighteenth-century Weymouth, England, Smeaton (1793) 65.

4   On *opus incertum* and *reticulatum*, Lugli (1957) 372, 422, 446, esp. 488; Goudineau (1979) 196, "petit appareil constitutes the equivalent of *reticulatum*. It represents a regional adaptation of the Italian technique and its attribution to Roman influence can give rise to no disagreement."

5   Above, on exported Roman wall techniques, chap. 1 nn. 78, 81; 3 n. 55; 4 n. 85; in the Province, Goudineau (1979) 191f.; and cryptoporticoes, chap. 4 n. 78 (to say nothing of those in Spain, e.g. Conimbriga).

6   Grenier (1958–60) 3, 1.15, a *sphaeristerium* in A.D. 4.

7   Chaps. 1 at n. 67; 2 at n. 7; 3 at nn. 3, 10, 22f.; and 4 at n. 65.

8   Barcelona, cf. Pfanner (1990) 70f, 87 (date in 30s B.C.?), compared with Ostia or other Italian colony plans; Balty (1991) 361 versus Euzennat and Hallier (1986) 90, 96f, nn. 110, 112, both citing MacMullen (1959) 221f and nn; and above, chap. 1 n. 67 and 3 n. 3. Cf. Kienast (1982) 364, supposing "that the greater part of Augustan construction ... was carried through by soldiers."

9   Above, chap. 2 n. 8, 3 n. 18, and 4 nn. 52, 84.

10   Lopez Paz (1994) 333; Blume et al. (1967) 1.172 lines 2f and 194 lines 9f; on the surveyor Balbus, 239 lines 15ff, with controversy in Dilke (1971) 38, Moatti (1993) 93, and Perez (1995) 45, from all which, I see the man in question as, at the least, handling sources of Augustus' time, and perhaps himself of that time. On the fragment of the Arausio plan, first extensively studied by A. Piganiol, see e.g. Hinrichs (1989) 123 n. 28, 125, Assénat (1994–5) 53f, and Moatti (1993) chaps. 2, 3, 5, and *passim*, to show that durability on which Lopaz Paz insists (and to refute the suggestion of N. Purcell in a review, *JRS* 80 (1990) 180, that the map amounted only to "the rhetoric of display of wealth" without relevance to "the ability to retrieve meaningful information from the record").

11   Chap. 3 at nn. 51ff., 4 at nn. 59, 81ff.

12   The best explanation of technique that I know is Paturzo (1996) 128f, 132ff, 141; or see A. Stenico, s. v. "Aretini, vasi" in the *Enciclopedia delle arte antica classica e orientale* 1 (1958) cols 609f; in English, Baur (1941) 245f (with thanks for reff. to my friend C. Lucas).

13   Whittaker (1985) 50.

14   Grenier (1958–60) 4, 2.796; Menzel (1985) 160, where the identical nature is clear in the photographs, Pl. 13; compare the identical (or virtually identical) Jupiter bronzes in discussions of Sucellus-figurines, above, chap. 4 n. 24.

15   Antony's portrait, e.g. Braemer (1948–9) 112f or Holtzman and Salviat (1984) 265f, 271f, Thasos, Narbo, etc.; Caesar's portrait, above, chap. 1 n. 18, Lämmer (1975) 102, and Keay (1995) 310; colossal statues for Augustus, in the east, above, chap. 1 n. 18; in Africa, chap. 2 n. 42, Gsell (1972) 8.225, Smajda (1978) 180 (with smallest size for princes, p. 181), Bejor (1987) 104f, Leveau (1984) 16, and Fittschen (1979a) 232; and in Spain, chap. 3 n. 95 and Garcia y Bellido (1949) 1.22f. For group displays, cf. above, chap. 1 nn. 18, 72; 2 nn. 42, 62f; and 3 nn. 94f. Totals in Walker and Burnett (1981) 25 with map, 48, and Pfanner (1989) 178, proposing a total of 25–50,000.

16   Trillmich (1993) 57; Fittschen (1979) 218.

17 Pfanner (1989) 188 or Boschung and Pfanner (1990) 138 Fig. 12a-b-c; but I prefer to cite the 1989 article, which the 1990 severely abbreviates.

18 Pfanner (1989) 194, the method sketched; its accuracy, 205–12 with Abb. 22–30; a half-dozen examples of Augustan times of "puntelli," 237f, 240, 245, 247, 250; further thorough, excellent discussion, *passim*; and the quotation, 226, with emphasis on the accompanying "Gleichförmigkeit und ihre normative Monotonie," or standardization. Cf. G.-C. Picard (1982) 180 on "the uniformity of imperial Roman art . . . , the chief types of official sculpture turn out almost identical in the different parts of the empire" (as is self-evident in any large selection of photographs). On plaster casts, presumed as vehicles of copying, see Fittschen (1979) 212 or Zanker (1983) 8 or (1991) 215.

19 Chap. 4 at nn. 115ff.; Pfanner (1989), 226, "überall sehr ähnliche Bauten mit ähnlichem Bauschmuck . . . mit Recht als Ausdruck einer 'Reichskunst' an[zu]sehen"; Alföldy (1979) 189 on "the remarkable strictness of unity in the character of monumental statue bases"; and Landwehr (1990) 148, remarking on "une véritable industrie. L'art de la copie connut un premier sommet sous le règne d'Auguste." For a good illustration of the supply of the market, cf. Gsell (1972) 8. 248ff.

20 Caes., *BC* 1.35, *neque sui iudicii neque suarum esse virium discernere, utra pars iustiorem habeat causam* [it is not within our discretion or our power to decide which side has the more just cause]; Pompey's *beneficia*, 2.18, matched by Caesar, 2.21, with Dio 41.24.1 and Galsterer (1988) 63f, regarding Gades, cf. chap. 3 at n. 59, on [Caes.], *Bell. Hisp.* 42, *beneficia* to Hispalis.

21 On the "Latinization" of Provincia attributed to Caesar, see Sherwin-White (1973) 232 or C. Goudineau in *CAH* 10, ed. 2 (1996) 473, without the process being really explained or the attribution well defended. There is a tendency to see Caesar as more generous with citizenship than Augustus, but cf. Vittinghoff (1951) 97f and Sherwin-White (1973) 233. The latter (225) finds generosity during wartime, where I emphasize its role in post-war settlements. Of urban centers, several dozen were made *municipia* by Caesar or Augustus in the east, Africa, and Spain, and perhaps 14 Latin colonies in Gaul.

22 Mattern (1999) 84, 38 legions at Philippi; at Actium, 16 (Octavian's) and 23 (Antony's, undersized); more complicated calculations in Brunt (1971) 480–501; the land costs, ibid. 337 (*Res Gestae* 16.1). . . . for the civilians, [see] Suet., *Iul.* 42.1, "80,000 citizens distributed among [Caesar's] overseas colonies, to relieve the crowding of the over-strained city."

23 MacMullen (1990) 226; above, n. 5 with reff.

24 MacMullen (1990) 64.

25 The foremost is the elder Balbus, chap. 3 and n. 70; for other examples, sure or likely, of non-Roman individuals taking an active part in the civil wars and being rewarded afterwards, see above, chap. 1 nn. 18, 29, 31, 72, 89; chap. 3 nn. 7.63f.; and chap. 4 nn. 11, 13, 46, 48, 87, 89.

26 Apparently not in a hostile sense, in [Caes.], *Bell. Hisp.* 35; clearly hostile, against an artifactually or institutionally or morally backward society, ibid. 35; Caes., *B. G.* 2.15, 5.34, 36; Cic., *Pro Balbo* 19.43; *Ad. Q. frat.* 1.1.27, quoted in the first chapter, above; Strabo 4.1.12, 4.4.4ff; Pomp. Mela, *Chorography* 3.2.18f, from Poseidonios, in Brunaux (1996) 196.

27 Virg., *Aen.* 1.263, on Aeneas' destiny to give laws, etc., is aimed only at Italy and is either irrelevant or significant in what it does not say. Plin., N. H. 3.39, quoted, on *Italia* and *Roma, numine deum electa quae caelum ipsum clarus faceret, sparsa congregaret*, etc.; and Tac., *Agr.* 21, where I borrow parts of the translation of Birley (1999) 17, with (p. 80) an alternative English for *domus* which I adopt, and the comment, "This chapter is unique in the literary sources for Roman history as a record of officially sponsored 'Romanization.'"

But I prefer my own ((1990) 64) translation of the two Latin words that Birley gives as "they began to compete with one another for his approval."

28   Ibid., and Fear (1996) 17ff and Haley (1997) 496, and "the new orthodoxy" in between, noted by Hanson (1997) 67, which "sees the process [of Romanization] as an incidental, even accidental one." To this, Hanson doesn't subscribe, nor Ramage (1997) 150, "Romanization was surely one of the long-term goals...," nor Whittaker (1997) 144, e.g., "It was cultural regeneration that was the intention of Augustus" (!), to be sought empire-wide through "the ideology of cities coupled to the moral order of society as a whole."

29   Lassèrre (1983) 889–93.

30   Frézouls (1991a) 100–11.

31   Engelmann and Knibbe (1989) 102 – and add in explanation Suet., *Caes.* 42.

32   Vittinghoff (1951) 9 describes the Roman "imperial conception" in a long emphatic statement, too long to quote; similarly, Syme in 1983, quoted with agreement by Koch (1993) 24, on Rome's "kulturpolitischer Indifferenz," with all of which I agree; Beaujeu and Brunaux to the same effect, above, chap. 4 n. 17; also Thébert (1978) 72, leaving more room for the *Agricola*-passage and (77), with Frézouls (1991) 112f, seeing the Roman elite in friendly, tolerant yoke with provincial elites, regardless of way of life.

33   Fuhrmann (1949) 65; *per contra*, the most effective advocate for an ideological content in Augustan art, Zanker (1988), with equal thoroughness, includes in his presentation generally rare objects, many post-Augustan for lack of contemporary works, and selected out of a mass that generally ignores the motifs he emphasizes, esp. pottery – in sum, an evidentiary base less sure than it seems. See further the arguments in chap. 4 at nn. 97ff., above.

34   Pflaum (1973) 67, going on to say, quite rightly, "Still, this behavior was a function of Rome's power"; and still, "the Romans never wanted to Romanize."

EDITOR'S NOTES

i   References to previous chapters and chapter notes are to the book from which this extract is taken: R. MacMullen, *Romanization in the Time of Augustus* (New Haven and London, 2000).

ii   On Roman building, see K. D. White, *Greek and Roman Technology* (Ithaca, NY, 1984), pp. 73–112.

iii *maiestas*: a difficult Roman concept to translate. "Dignity," "sovereignty," and "majesty" are approximations.

REFERENCES

Alföldy, G. (1979) "Bildprogram in den römischen Städten des Conventus Tarraconensis – Das Zeugnis der Statuenportamente," *Revista de la Universitad Complutense*, ser. 2, 28, iv, pp. 177–275.

Assénat, M. (1994–5) "Le Cadastre colonial d'Orange," *Rev. archéologique de Narbonnaise*, 27–8, pp. 43–55.

Balty, J. C. (1991) *Curia ordinis: recherches d'architecture et d'urbanisme antiques sur les curies provinciales du monde romain* (Brussels).

Baur, P. V. C. (1941) "Megarian Bowls in the Rebecca Darlington Stoddard Collection of Greek and Italian Vases in Yale University," *American Journal of Archaeology*, 45, pp. 229–48.

Beaujeu, J. (1976) "Cultes locaux et cultes d'empire dans les provinces d'Occident aux trois premiers siecles de notre ère," in *Assimilation et résistance à la culture gréco-romaine dans le monde ancien*, Travaux du VI Congres international d'Études Classiques, 1974, ed. D. M. Pippidi (Paris), pp. 433–43.

Bejor, G. (1987) "Documentazione epigrafica di complessi statuari nell'Africa romana: alcuni esempi," in *Africa Romana: Atti del IV Convegno, 1986* (Sassari), pp. 101–16.

Birley, A. R. (1999) *Tacitus, Agricola and Germany* (Oxford).

Blume, F. et al. (eds.) (1967) *Die Schriflen der römischen Feldmesser*, 2nd edn. (Hildesheim).

Boschung, D. and M. Pfanner (1990), "Les Méthodes de travail des sculpteurs antiques et leur signification dans l'histoire de la culture," in *Pierre éternelle du Nil au Rhin: carrieres et préfabrication*, ed. M. Waelkins (Brussels), pp. 127–42.

Braemer, F. (1948–9) "Un Buste présumé de Jules César," *Bull. Soc. Nationale des Antiquaries de France*, pp. 112–16.

Brunaux, J.-L. (1986) *Les Gaulois: sanctuaires et rites* (Paris).

Brunaux, J.-L. (1996) *Les Religions gauloises: rituels celtiques de la Gaule* (Paris).

Brunt, P. A. (1971) *Italian Manpower, 225 BC–AD 14* (Oxford).

Carretoni, G. et al. (1960) *La pianta marmorea di Rome antica: forma urbis Romae*, 2 vols. (Rome).

Dilke, O. A. W. (1971) *The Roman Land Surveyors: An Introduction to the Agrimensores* (Newton Abbot).

Engelmann, H. and D. Knibbe (1989) "Das Zollgesetz der Provinz Asia," *Epigraphica Anatolica*, 14, pp. 1–209.

Euzennat, M. and G. Hallier (1986) "Les Forums de Tingitane: observations sur l'influence de l'architecture militaire sur les constructions civiles de l'Occident romain," *Ant. afr.*, 22, pp. 73–103.

Fear, A. T. (1996) *Rome and Baetica: Urbanization in Southern Spain c. 50 BC–AD 150* (Oxford).

Fittschen, K. (1979) "Bildnisse numidischer Könige," in *Die Numider: Reiter und Könige nördlich der Sahara*, ed. H. G. Horn and C. B. Rüger (Cologne), pp. 209–25.

Fittschen, K. (1979a) "Juba II. und seine Residenz Jol/Caesarea (Cherchel)," in *Die Numider: Reiter und Könige nördlich der Sahara*, ed. H. G. Horn and C. B. Rüger (Cologne), pp. 227–42.

Frézouls, E. (1991) "Villes augustéennes de l'est et du nord-est de la France," in *Les Villes augustéennes de Gaule: Actes du colloque 1985* (Autun), pp. 107–15.

Frézouls, E. (1991a) "La Perception des rapports gouvernants/gouvernés à la fin de la République," *Cahiers des études anciennes*, 26a, pp. 95–113.

Fuhrmann, H. (1949) "Zwei Reliefbilder aus der Geschichte Roms," *Mitt. des deutschen arch. Inst.*, 2, pp. 23–68.

Galsterer, H. (1988) "The Tabula Siarensis and Augustan Municipalization in Baetica," in *Estudios sobre la Tabula Siarensis*, ed. J. Gonzales and J. Arce (Madrid), pp. 61–74.

Garcia y Bellido, A. (1949) *Esculturas Romanas de España y Portugal*, 2 vols. (Madrid).

Goudineau, C. (1979) *Les Fouilles de la maison au Dauphin: recherches sur la romanisation de Vaison-la-Romaine* (Rome).

Grenier, A. (1958–60) *Manuel d'archéologie gallo-romaine*, vols. 3–4 (Paris).

Gsell, S. (1972) *Histoire de l'Afrique du Nord*, 8 vols. (reprinted Osnabrück).

Haley, E. (1997) "Town and Country: The Acculturation of Southern Spain," *American Journal of Archaeology*, 10, pp. 495–503.

Hanson, W. S. (1997) "Forces of Change and Methods of Control," in *Dialogues in Roman Imperialism: Power, Discourse, and Discrepant Experience in the Roman Empire*, ed. D. J. Mattingly (Portsmouth), pp. 67–80.

Hinrichs, F. T. (1989) *Histoire des institutions gromatique: recherches sur la répartition des terres, l'arpentage agraire, l'administration et le droit foncier dans l'Empire Romain*, trans. D. Minary (Paris).

Holtzmann, B. and F. Salviat (1984) "Les Portraits sculptés de Marc-Antoine," *Bull. de Correspondance Hellénique*, 105, pp. 265–88.

Keay, S. (1995) "Innovation and Adaptation: The Contribution of Rome to Urbanism in Iberia," in *Social Complexity and the Development of Towns in Iberia: From the Copper Age to the Second Century AD*, ed. B. Cunliffe and S. Keay (Oxford), pp. 291–338.

Kienast, D. (1982) *Augustus, Princeps und Monarch* (Darmstadt).

Koch, M. (1993) "Animus Meus Praesagit, Nostram Hispaniam Esse," in *Hispania Antiqua: Denkmäler der Römerzeit*, ed. W. Trillmich et al. (Mainz), pp. 1–40.

Lämmer, M. (1975) "Die Kaiserspiele von Cesarea im Dienste der Politik des Königs Herodes," *Kölner Beitr. zur Sportswiss.*, 3, pp. 95–164.

Landwehr, C. (1990) "Bronze grec original, moulage en plâtre et copie romaine en marbre," in *Pierre éternelle du Nil au Rhin: carrières et préfabrication*, ed. M. Waelkins (Brussels), pp. 143–61.

Lassèrre, F. (1983) "Strabon devant l'Empire romain," *ANRW* II, 30 (Berlin), pp. 867–96.

Leveau, P. (1984) *Caesarea de Maurétanie, une ville romaine d'Afrique et ses campagnes* (Paris).

Lopez Paz, P. (1994) *La ciudad romana ideal, I: El territorio* (Santiago de Compostela).

Lugli, G. (1957) *La tecnica edilizia romana con particolare riguardo a Roma e Lazio*, 2 vols. (Rome).

MacDonald, W. L. (1982) *The Architecture of the Roman Empire*, vol. 1: *An Introductory Study*, 2nd edn. (New Haven).

MacMullen, R. (1959) "Roman Imperial Building in the Provinces," *HSCP*, 64, pp. 207–35.

MacMullen, R. (1990) *Changes in the Roman Empire: Essays in the Ordinary* (Princeton).

MacMullen, R. (1993) "The Unromanized in Rome," in *Diasporas in Antiquity*, ed. S. J. D. Cohen and E. S. Frerichs (Atlanta), pp. 47–64.

Mattern, S. (1999) *Rome and the Enemy: Roman Imperial Strategy in the Principate* (Berkeley).

Menzel, H. (1985) "Römische Bronzestatuetten und verwandte Geräte: ein Beitrag zum Stand der Forschung," *ANRW* II, 12.3 (Berlin), pp. 127–69.

Moatti, C. (1993) *Archives et partage de la terre dans le monde romain (IIe siècle avant J.-C.–Ier siècle après J.-C.)* (Rome).

Paturzo, F. (1996) *Arretina vasa: la ceramica aretina da mensa in età romana: Arte, storia e tecnologia* (Cortona).

Perez, A. (1995) *Les Cadastres antiques en Narbonnaise occidentale: essai sur la politique coloniale romaine en Gaule du Sud (IIe s. av. J.-C.–IIe ap. J.-C.)* (Paris).

Pfanner, M. (1989) "Über das Herstellen von Porträts: Ein Beitrag zu Rationalisierungsmassnahmen und Produktionsmechanimen von Massenware im späten Hellenismus und in der römischen Kaiserzeit," *Jahrbuch deut. arch. Inst.*, 104, pp. 157–257.

Pfanner, M. (1990) "Modelle römischer Stadtentwicklung am Beispiel Hispaniens und der westichen Provinzen," in *Stadtbild und Ideologie: Die Monumentalisierung hispanischer Städte zwischen Republik und Kaiserzeit*, ed. W. Trillmich and P. Zanker (Munich), pp. 59–115.

Pflaum, H.-G. (1973) "La Romanisation de l'Afrique," in *Akten des VI. internationalen Kongresses für griechische und lateinische Epigraphik, 1972* (Munich), pp. 55–68.

Picard, G.-C. (1982) "La Sculpture dans l'Afrique romaine," in *150-Jahr Feier deutsches archäologisches Institut Rom* (Mainz), pp. 180–95.

Ramage, E. S. (1997) "Augustus' Propaganda in Gaul," *Klio*, 79, pp. 117–60.

Sear, F. (1982) *Roman Architecture* (Ithaca, NY).

Sherwin-White, A. N. (1973) *The Roman Citizenship*, 2nd edn. (Oxford).

Smajda, E. (1978) "L'inscription du culte impérial dans la cité: l'exemple de Lepcis Magna au début de l'Empire," *Dialogues d'histoire ancienne*, 4, pp. 171–86.

Smeaton, J. (1793) *A Narrative of the Building and a Description of the Construction of the Edystone Lighthouse with Stone*, 2nd edn. (London).

Thébert, Y. (1978) "Romanisation et déromanisation: histoire décolonisée ou histoire inversée?," *Annales*, 33, pp. 64–82.

Trillmich, W. (1993) "Hispanien und Rom aus der Sicht Roms und Hispaniens," in *Hispania Antiqua: Die Denkmäler der Römerzeit*, ed. W. Trillmich et al. (Mainz), pp. 41–7.

Varène, P. (1987) "L'Enceinte augustéenne de Nîmes," in *Les Enceintes augustéennes dans l'Occident romain*, ed. M.-G. Colin (Nîmes), pp. 17–23.

Vittinghoff, F. (1951) *Römische Kolonisation und Bürgerrechtspolitik unter Caesar und Augustus* (Mainz).

Walker, S. and A. Burnett (1981) *The Image of Augustus* (London).

Whittaker, C. R. (1985) "Trade and Aristocracy in the Roman Empire," *Opus*, 4, pp. 49–75.

Whittaker, C. R. (1997) "Imperialism and Culture: The Roman Initiative," in *Dialogues in Roman Imperialism: Power, Discourse, and Discrepant Experience in the Roman Empire*, ed. D. J. Mattingly (Portsmouth), pp. 143–63.

Zanker, P. (1983) *Provinzielle Kaiserporträts: Zur Rezeption der Selbstdarstellung des Princeps* (Munich).

Zanker, P. (1988) *The Power of Images in the Age of Augustus*, trans. A. Shapiro (Ann Arbor).

Becoming Roman: The Origins of Provincial Civilization in Gaul

G. Woolf

BEING ROMAN IN GAUL

Becoming Roman

The culture of Roman Gaul had its origin in a single historical moment, a formative period shared with other provincial cultures in the East and the West, itself one aspect of a much broader reconfiguration of Roman power and culture.[1] That formative period lasted a short century that spanned the turn of the millennia and centred around the principate of Augustus, although the shift to autocracy was only one component of these transformations. The life and manners of the south of Gaul, conquered at the end of the second century BC, were thus transformed at much the same time as those of the interior which Caesar added to the Roman empire almost seventy years later. Naturally it took the Gauls some time to satisfy the new cultural aspirations learnt in that period. The technology gap was formidable, and the cost of building a new civilization ruinous. But little by little imported wine and marble were replaced by local products, and stop-gap solutions like wooden *fora* and imitation *sigillata* were replaced with the real thing. Eventually, distinctively Gallo-Roman cultural forms appeared, some, like *villae* and *fana*, the results of Mediterranean technology applied to traditional structures, others simply local creations, like Gallo-Roman theatre-amphitheatres and the Jupiter columns of the north-east, that developed within the increasingly loose complex that formed Roman imperial culture.[i] That increasing looseness is also evident in the appearance of regional traditions in everything from burial rites to ceramic tablewares. The regional diversity of Gallo-Roman culture in the second and third centuries AD recalls that of the very different cultures of the late La Tène period. Cultural diversity is unsurprising, the default condition of the perpetual creativity of human societies, especially when unrestrained by modern communications and industrial production, and uncoerced by the cultures of the nation-state. Regional diversity has in any case long been characteristic of France, a product in part of an environment that, without insulating populations, has permitted their circumscription into local communities and traditions.[2] It is the brief convergence of Roman provincial cultures during the formative period that demands explanation.

Various factors have been invoked to account for that moment of convergence. The initial stimulus was the extraordinary disruption of Gallic societies by the extension of Roman power into Gaul. Trade, and even military conquest, were relatively minor and early components of this process. The formative period coincides more closely with a structural transformation manifested in the imposition of much more intense structures of exploitation and control, institutions that bound Gallic communities and individuals more and more tightly within the empire of cities and the empire of friends. The census, the levy, new taxes, new constitutions, the spread of a cash economy, of Roman education, of citizenship and of law, and the *pax Romana* itself were just the most prominent features of this penetration of Gallic societies by Roman power. But imperialism, even understood in these terms, provides only a partial explanation for cultural change. Also important were the attitudes that accompanied it, the notion of a civilizing process, that divinely sanctioned ideology of the Roman empire, or the idea that Roman identity was intimately connected with *mores*, and the significance that those attitudes gave to culture as a basis for patronage and privilege. Roman imperialism and the attitudes that accompanied it provided the opportunity for some groups in Gallic society – notably the emergent aristocracies of the new Gallo-Roman communities, but also auxiliary soldiers, the neighbours of veteran colonists and others in close contact with Romans – to make strategic use of Roman culture to acquire privileged places for themselves in the new order of things. Those uses were more complex than simple emulation, even if they were seen as such by Romans confident of their own civilization. Roman civilization also offered more sensual attractions, and a consolation for conquest. Nevertheless, the public contexts of the earliest manifestations of this process – civic centres and monuments, equipment for dining and burial and so forth – suggest that, to begin with, Roman culture satisfied public needs more than private desires. Other enabling factors can be inferred by comparing the Gallic experience to that of other provincial populations. There is no sign, for example, that Rome had to make concessions to the defining symbols of Gallic identities as they did to the customs of the Jews or the language of the Greeks. Even the gods of the Gauls might be accommodated within Roman religion, if they were prepared to give up their traditional priests and a part of their ancestral rites.

Romans, too, played a part in the creation of Gallo-Roman culture that was not limited to tolerant approbation of those who civilized themselves. Emperors, governors, landowners, teachers, architects, sculptors, craftsmen, traders, colonists, soldiers, and many others, played active roles in the creation of Gallo-Roman civilization. That process confirmed the imperial conceits of some Romans, and made some rich, especially during that initial period when the demand for Roman goods seems to have been insatiable. The pace and profits of the civilizing process inevitably slowed, as the capacity of Gaul to produce Roman goods of its own increased, and as the need to prove oneself Roman declined with the Gauls' progressive integration into the empire. By stages now difficult to measure, the styles and goods that had once symbolized Roman and not Gaulish, civilized and not barbarian came to mean rich not poor, and educated not boorish. But by the late first century, an elite who regarded themselves as both Gallic and Roman were advertising their social status with a culture of exclusion that was thoroughly Roman in form. Naturally, areas existed which were in some senses 'backward' and 'peripheral', but that status reflected their location in an imperial geography of civilization, and they were far from cultural Galapagos Islands, inhabited by remnant La Tène societies. Nothing could have been more Roman (in the sense of characteristic of living in the Roman empire) than to be culturally peripheralized.

It is meaningless to ask, then, how Roman (let alone how Romanized) were the Gauls. Those Roman aristocrats who had taken on themselves the burden of regulating civilization had defined Roman culture in such a way that it might function as a marker of status, not of political or ethnic identity. That situation has not been uncommon in the past,[3] but its rarity in more recent times may have led us to misunderstand Roman culture in the provinces. Modern national cultures are organized around a distinction between metropolitan sophistication and uncultivated provincialism.[4] That situation existed to a much more limited extent in the Roman empire, and by the middle of the first century claims based on relative civilization were over-riding those based on Roman or Italian identity, not just in Claudius' speech on behalf of the leading citizens of Gaul, but much more widely, as leading provincials from all over the empire were recruited successively into each level of the imperial ruling hierarchy.[5] By the middle of the second century AD, cultural distinctions between powerful men from different parts of the empire were much less marked than those maintained between them and their social subordinates everywhere.[6] A symbolic centre did exist in the Roman cultural system, but it was located not in any one place or region but rather in the set of manners, tastes, sensibilities and ideals that were the common property of an aristocracy that was increasingly dispersed across the empire. Naturally there were geographical expressions of this system. The city of Rome occupied one central position in the empire of the imagination, the emperor's court (wherever it happened to be at the time) another, and conversely, distant provinces like Germania and northern Britain might stand (in literary contexts) for the limits of civilization. But from the Roman aristocrat's perspective, civilization was to be found anywhere that he was, and he was surrounded everywhere by the primitive or degenerate beliefs and manners of peasants, artisans, slaves and the like. Modern analysts might prefer a more inclusive notion of imperial culture, one perhaps that embraced the experience of the excluded majority. Yet even from that viewpoint the uncivilized Gauls have their counterparts in the uncivilized masses of every province, and also of Italy. The Gallic provinces, in this respect, were as Roman – but also as un-Roman – as any part of the empire.[ii]

Becoming Roman, becoming different

An immense cultural gap separated the Gallo-Romans from their ancestors. The building and adornment of cities; the red tile roofs that replaced thatch on farms, temples and town houses; statues of men and gods; and meals cooked in olive oil, flavoured with fish sauces, and accompanied by wine (now mixed with water) sipped from shiny red pottery goblets were among the external manifestations of this distance. Where older ways persisted they were marginalized, revalued as signs of a lack of sophistication, of *urbanitas*, rather than as signs of un-Roman behaviour or cultural resistance. Nor were these changes simply a convenient façade, concealing a core of Gallic sensibility. Material culture is not, in any case, so easily separable from mentality, habit and moral culture. The novelty of Gallo-Roman society was also expressed in new tastes, new senses of style, of cleanliness and of propriety. The Gauls had also gained a new conception of the divine and lost any sense of a past distinct from that of the Romans, and in the process they had become a different people. It is possible in any case that the category of 'Gauls' had no agreed meaning before the conquest,[7] and that it was classical ethnographers and Roman administrators who had invented the identity on which the *imperium Galliarum* of AD 69–70 was based and floundered.[8]

But the creation of Gallo-Roman culture made the Gauls different in other ways. The new order was itself much more highly differentiated than iron age societies had ever been. Becoming Roman did not involve becoming more like the other inhabitants of the empire, so much as participating in a cultural system structured by systematic differences, differences that both sustained and were a product of Roman power. This aspect of cultural change can be explored in several ways. At one level it comprised the differentiation of roles and spaces within Gallo-Roman society. Gauls thus became more different from each other, as they became more Roman. The emergence in the first century AD of divides between rich and poor, artisans and peasants and slaves and freedmen marks the appearance of a more complex society, within which some individuals had new opportunities to change their roles, homes and identities. Economic growth and participation in much larger systems created a differentiation of its own.[9] Naturally it is the most dramatic examples – the rise of senators like Valerius Asiaticus, for example – that attract the most attention, but most mobility was far more localized within the Gallic provinces.[10] Countrymen moved into the new towns, and craftsmen and traders and some landowners moved between them, settling as *incolae* in neighbouring or distant communities. The capacity to escape the local community in this way was a direct result of the Roman peace in Gaul, and it was the common cultural framework of Gallo-Roman culture that made it possible. Finally, greater differentiation was reflected in the specialized place occupied by the Gallic provinces within the empire as a whole.

These themes are neatly brought together and illustrated by consideration of the development, over the first century AD, of an increasingly distinct militarized zone in the north-east.[11] Even if the traditional picture of unbroken tranquillity needs to be nuanced a little, the Gallic provinces were nevertheless probably as typical as any area was of the peaceful, productive core of the empire, protected by and sustaining the military, and supplying the emperors and imperial aristocracies with the wealth on which *pax, luxuria* and *indulgentia* depended. Yet for many Gauls, becoming Roman took place in a rather different environment, in the course of military service of one kind or another. That experience evolved over time. During the Caesarian and triumviral wars, Gallic aristocrats had led irregular levies in support of Roman armies, and although the organization of both the *auxilia* and the imperial command structure underwent gradual transformations, there were always Gauls serving in the Roman military as commanders, volunteers and conscripts. The epigraphic evidence is not as abundant for Gaul as it is for other regions, but it seems clear that the Rhine legions were increasingly recruited from Narbonensis, their accompanying auxiliaries were largely drawn from northern and eastern Gaul, and conversely, most Gauls who joined the army were stationed on the northern frontier, in Germany or Britain.[12] The Roman culture of the German frontier zone bore a superficial resemblance to that of the cities and landscapes of the Gallic provinces, but on closer inspection there are marked differences. Patterns of epigraphic commemoration illustrate graphically the bonds that held together one of the few ancient societies not based on kinship. Rank, unit affiliation and comradeship supplanted social status, community of origin and familial relationships on the mortuary epigraphy of the north-east, just as they did in the social life of the camps.[13] Analysis of faunal remains and transport *amphorae* reveals distinctions between the diet of military populations and that of surrounding populations;[14] graffiti reveal the local forms of Latin that provided recruits with a *lingua franca*;[15] and military calendars and private dedications alike list distinctive festivals and cults.[16] The culture of the frontier zones may usefully be considered as civilization without cities. While in the eastern provinces soldiers were often billetted in cities,[17] in the north-west permanent stone-built legionary bases began to be constructed from the late first century AD, equipped with main roads and side streets, 'public' juridical and religious areas around the *praetorium*, and, scattered around the edge of the camp, bathhouses and amphitheatres, cemeteries and shrines.[iii] The army provided education, too, and offered mobility – social, economic and geographical – but the Romans it produced were rather different to those that emerged from the civil societies of the Gallic provinces.

Likewise those populations among whom Roman soldiers lived had their own peculiar experiences of becoming Roman. For those who inhabited the *canabae*, the informal settlements that grew up around the forts, there was a variety of close relationships with soldiers, which may have been commercial, filial, sexual, or amicable. Their experience was the underside of the civilization of the troops, a chaotic mixture of those aspects of civic and familial life that had been carefully edited out of the design of the 'military cities'. Others in the vicinity lived lives closer to those of the farmers and artisans of the Gallic provinces, but were exposed to a rather different series of models of Roman life than those presented by the Narbonensian *coloniae*, or in the Gallic interior, where few Romans from other provinces or from Italy ever penetrated. The nature of each different 'contact culture' inevitably left its trace on the new provincial cultures that emerged in each region.[18] Other communities in the frontier zones were transformed into almost wholly militarized societies. The Batavians of the Low Countries provide a good example. Encouraged to maintain their military customs, they were recruited in great numbers into the Roman *auxilia* and were used both on the Rhine and in Britain. Their cults, and especially their burials, show how their position in the new order had entailed a distinctive selection from both iron age and Roman culture.[19] Often these different worlds were physically juxtaposed, as in the complex of forts, *canabae* and civilian native settlements around Nijmegen.[20] The culture of the militarized zones of the empire is an enormous subject. The object of introducing it here is simply to indicate some of the variety in the Gallic experience of becoming Roman. There were so many kinds of Romans to become that becoming Roman did not mean assimilating to an ideal type, but rather acquiring a position in the complex of structured differences in which Roman power resided.

Cultural distinctions in the West traced, for the most part, the contours of Roman power.[21] While the complexity, wealth and antiquity of pre-Roman cultures might be expected to have made major differences to the speed or completeness with which indigenous forms were replaced by Roman ones, it is striking how similar the sequence seems to have been in the huge tribal communities of inland Gaul to that in the tiny hilltop villages of southern Iberia or the ancient Punic cities of Tripolitania. The same seems true for Rome's temperate empire as far east as the Black Sea. To be sure, local traditions left a trace in the forms of houses, in regional distributions of cults and rural settlement patterns, in the languages spoken by most of the inhabitants of the empire. But in most respects western cultures were artefacts of Roman imperialism. It is difficult to see any explanation other than the equal contempt in which all these cultures were held by Rome. Elsewhere, the picture is more complex. The place occupied by the Greeks in Roman conceptions of civilization seems to have resulted in a distinctly different handling of provincial communities. Nevertheless, the formative period is evident here, too, although it took different forms, limited in those areas of Greek culture which were central to Greek self-definition in this period, such as language and cult, although more noticeable in fields like civic constitutions, architecture and technology.[22] Roman attitudes to Jews, Syrians and Egyptians were less clear cut, a result of a mixture of respect for antiquity and contempt for the present day, but without the history of interchange that mediated a similar relationship with Greeks.[23] The compromises differed according to Roman assessments of each group's claims to antiquity and civilization, and according to the different ways in which each group constructed its identity. Discussion of these regions is beyond the scope of this study, but some of the factors adduced in it – the idea of a formative period, the importance of Roman notions of civilization and of the specific ways in which culture participated in the construction of identity – may be applicable in the East as well as in the West.[iv]

Roman culture and the Roman empire

Rome was not the most seductive of ancient civilizations. Hellenism, in different ways, fascinated Lydians and Carians, Macedonians and Italians, Parthians, Jews and

Romans among many others, even when there were few obvious material or political benefits, while Judaism and Christianity exercised even more powerful attractions, enticing some individuals to jeopardize relatively privileged positions in their own communities and in the empire in exchange for membership of minorities who were at best tolerated and occasionally persecuted. Yet if the Greek world seems at times to have been surrounded by a penumbra of would-be Greeks, with others keen to imitate specific aspects of Greek culture from architecture to athletics, the limits of early imperial Roman culture were much more precise. A few items were imported into late La Tène Gaul as they were later into Free Germany or Ireland, but the phenomenon of becoming Roman, in the sense in which it has been discussed here, was firmly limited by the boundaries of the empire.

One possible explanation for the limits of Roman culture would be that no one had ever really wished, in their heart of hearts, to become Roman as an end in itself. Togas and baths, inscriptions and mosaics would then be no more than the props for an elaborate ruse played on the Roman elite, and Tacitus' comment in the *Agricola* would need to be turned on its head, since it was the Romans who mistook servility for civilization.[24] That view is superficially attractive for a number of reasons: it stresses the active role played by the subjects of the empire in the creation of an imperial culture, it offers to expose the conquerors' perceptions of the civilizing process as an ideology that deceived themselves more than anyone else, and it entails a view of culture as a means of adaptation employed strategically by individuals and communities to achieve material goals. This explanation will naturally appeal to those committed to any of those positions on general grounds – among them most New Archaeologists, many Marxists, a few post-colonial historians, and those prehistorians and Romanists most concerned to emancipate themselves from historical and classical paradigms at any price. [My argument] however, does not support such an explanation. The contrast between the uses made of Roman-style culture in the formative period, and those characteristic of the succeeding two centuries strongly suggests that Roman values *were* internalized by the Gallo-Roman elite. Otherwise it is difficult to understand the continuing use of Roman culture after the crisis in which its use had been adopted. A deception that lasted generations is unimaginable. No means existed for reproducing such a tradition in secret alongside publicly owned values rehearsed in education, in political rhetoric and action, in acts of euergetism and so forth.

The implausibility of the 'thin veneer' view of Gallo-Roman culture has been a leitmotif of this study. Certainly Roman culture did not remain frozen in the shape it had taken in the formative period, and its evolution encompassed both a growth of regional diversity and a shift in the terms in which Roman identity was defined. The re-appearance from the third century of some stylistic forms of pre-Roman origin has been taken as evidence for a 'Celtic renaissance',[25] but there is nothing to suggest that La Tène motifs on common ceramics – if indeed that description of Argonne ware is accepted – had any political connotations, and the phenomenon is best seen as a feature of that loosening of Roman culture that has already been remarked on. Cultural conformity was less of an issue precisely because anxieties about Gallic membership of the empire were less acute. The same attitude is expressed in the opinion of a jurist writing just after Caracalla's extension of citizenship to most of the inhabitants of the empire, that the trusts known as *fideicommissa* were valid even if made in the Celtic language.[26] This relaxation of the definition of Roman culture can be exemplified from all over the empire in this period, along with other changes such as the de-centring of urbanism within notions of civilization, and the increasing importance attached to education. Yet when the military crisis of the third century finally spread to the Gallic provinces, the local elites and the military commanders of the region set up their own emperors not as a rejection of Rome but in order to protect Roman life in Gaul from the barbarians.[27] Roman culture can hardly have been adopted simply as a gesture of loyalty to the empire if Gauls would resort to rebellion in order to remain Roman.

The problem, then, is to understand why Roman identity remained so attractive to those within the empire, yet failed to enchant those beyond it. One starting point is provided by the comparison already drawn with Hellenism, Judaism and Christianity. The seductiveness of those cultural movements did not derive from any material rewards open to those who adopted Greek, Jewish or Christian identities, but rather from the content and organization of those cultural systems. Roman culture equally demands to be treated in terms of its content and structure as well as of any pragmatic advantages Roman identity offered to adherents. This is an area where cultural analysis is underdeveloped, but it is helpful to return to the notion of culture as organized around symbolic centres, points in an interconnected symbol system which are less open to negotiation and change than others, values which operate as points of reference in relation to which other values may be calculated, concepts which articulate the symbol system, spaghetti junctions in a semantic field through which all travellers pass frequently and where chains of significance meet, intersect and depart again. Symbolic centres do not all occur in the same area of culture. For Greeks of the Roman period, for instance, language, cults and a mythology through which religion was linked to descent, often via the Homeric poems, were central to cultural definition, while for Jews, religion was central but language less so.[28] The stress Romans placed on customs (*mores*) and the central articulating function acquired by the notion of civilization (*humanitas*) have already been discussed. One explanation for the limits of Roman culture would be to posit a similar centrality for the relationship conceived between Roman civilization and the Roman empire, between being Roman in a cultural sense and being a member of the Roman political community. Such a notion might be contrasted with the weaker association of cultural and political identity in the case of the Greeks, for whom panhellenism rarely provided the basis for common political action. Roman identity, on the other hand, had not been formulated in conditions of political pluralism, and at least since the late Republic, political dissidents had been represented as culturally deviant, whether barbarizing like Sertorius or hellenizing like [Antony], or flirting with both as in the case of Catiline. *Humanitas* may have been formulated as a universalizing concept, but Roman identity was perhaps more jealously guarded and closely defined, to the extent that it was simply not available beyond the limits of the empire. That intimate relationship between Roman civilization and Roman empire is also a reminder of the centrality of imperialism in the Roman culture of the principate.

Any temptation to elevate these defining features of early imperial culture into enduring constants should, however, be resisted. Just as Hellenism came in the East to mean paganism, and Greek-speaking Christians in Byzantium came to define themselves as Romans, so, too, in the West the content and structure of Roman culture underwent changes. At some point in the fifth century AD Roman cultural identity became finally dissociated from any particular political membership,[29] and the ethnic 'Roman' came to refer to a people scattered throughout a series of barbarian kingdoms, rarely in positions of power but maintaining, for a time, separate legal and educational systems, and distinguished by their own language, religion (now Catholic Christianity) and literature. Perhaps the political division of the empire had made it thinkable that the Romans might live in several different polities even before the fragmentation of the West, and perhaps the introduction of barbarians into the empire had already raised Roman awareness of themselves as a group distinguished by culture above all, an impression that Christianity will have reinforced in areas that came under the control of pagans or heretics. At some moments in this process of redefinition, a Sidonius might identify himself with the attitudes and lifestyle of a Pliny, but the conceit was purely literary. Being Roman no longer meant the same thing in a changing Gaul.

NOTES

1 See Ward-Perkins (1970), Woolf (1995) for this perspective and (1994) for a study of its distinctive manifestation in the Greek East. On this transformation of imperial culture, see most recently Zanker (1988) with Wallace-Hadrill (1989) and Nicolet (1988).

2 See Fox (1971) on this enduring feature of inland France. For a historical perspective, see Weber (1979) and Braudel (1988).

3 Gellner (1983), although his schematic representations of the cultural anatomy of modern and pre-industrial states are best treated as ideal types. Cultures of exclusion (promoted by dominant social groups) and cultures of inclusion (unifying political communities) have co-existed in most societies, although Gellner is right to note the dramatic shift in their relative importance. The Roman solution was not the only one possible, however, as the experience of Hellenistic kingdoms demonstrates.

4 A claim implicitly accepted by those in some modern regions who reject the nation-state on the basis of the antiquity (real or imagined) of their own culture, for which see Trevor Roper (1983). For the spread of the notion that national communities were or should be co-terminous with cultural ones, see Anderson (1983).

5 A full discussion of the issue would require consideration of the shifting valency of Roman and Italian identities in this period. The *locus classicus* is Statius *Silvae* 4.5.45–8. For some preliminary discussion, see Woolf (1990, 223–7).

6 The existence of two high cultures, Greek and Latin, slightly complicates the picture, as do the close cultural links between former slaves and their ex-masters. The prominence of cultures of exclusion also reflects to some extent the threat posed to elite exclusiveness by upwardly mobile individuals, especially in the cities of the empire where large numbers of individuals are difficult to classify as either rich or poor.

7 Goudineau (1983). For modern analogies, see Ardener (1972).

8 As in the case of the Italian identity at the time of the Social War. If provincial boundaries and cults promoted the Roman view of the Gauls as a single people, with a collective identity which provided the basis for the anti-Roman coalition, they also asserted differences between Gauls and Germans which operated as a powerful argument for Gallic loyalty to Rome; see Tacitus *Histories* 4.54–79. Julius Sabinus' claim to be descended from Julius Caesar and his adoption of the title 'Caesar' illustrates the Roman form in which the *imperium Galliarum* was conceived.

9   For a similar approach to the complexification of Anglo-Saxon society and ensuing social mobility, cf. Runciman (1984), and, applied to Rome, Woolf (1996).

10 Krier (1981), Wierschowski (1995).

11 On the significance of these developments, see Drinkwater (1983, 64–9), stressing the establishment of separate German provinces. Those arrangements were simply one stage in a longer process whereby frontier arrangements became institutionalized and the Gauls and Germanies more differentiated.

12 On the development of the *auxilia*, see Holder (1980) and Saddington (1982). Mann (1983, 25–8) shows that the German legions were largely recruited from Italy and Narbonensis, with the balance shifting in favour of the latter in the course of the first century. Holder (1980, 110–19) discusses the prominence of Belgic Gauls in the *auxilia*, throughout the first century, and argues that the majority were stationed on the Rhine.

13 Saller and Shaw (1984) on commemoration patterns. MacMullen (1984) on the social organization of military life; see also MacMullen (1963).

14 King (1984), Desbat and Martin-Kilcher (1989).

15 Adams (1994).

16 See Rüpke (1990, 165–98) on the official cult of the army, Derks (1991), (1995) and Zoll (1994), (1995) on private cults patronized by soldiers.

17 Isaac (1990, 269–82).

18 See Foster (1960) for the notion of contact culture. The distinctive development of frontier societies is the main theme of Whittaker (1994).

19 Roymans (1993).

20 See Bloemers (1990) for a clear discussion, suggesting in addition that Xanten and Tongres might be comparable.

21 Woolf (1997).

22 Woolf (1994), perhaps understressing the religious dimension of interaction.

23 The nature of pre-Roman identities is not always clear in these regions, and in many areas the issue was further complicated by the prior encounter with Hellenism, which often provided a bridge to Roman culture, for which see Millar (1993) and, for a later period, Bowersock (1990).

24 See Reece (n.d.) for a similar perspective on Roman Britain.

25 MacMullen (1965), but cf. King (1990, 172–9).

26 Digest 32.1.11. [*The Digest of Justinian*, ed. A. Watson (Philadelphia, 1985).]

27 Drinkwater (1987), with a good discussion of the implication of the iconography of the coins of Postumus and his successors.

28 Schwartz (1995).

29 For the most recent attempts to trace this process, see Drinkwater and Elton (1992) and Harries (1994).

EDITOR'S NOTES

i   Definitions: *fora* = public meeting places; public squares sometimes surrounded by monumental buildings; (*terra*) *sigillata* = popular, mass-produced ceramic ware, characterized by a red gloss-coat, often copied metal-work; *villae* = rural estates associated with agriculture; *villae* of the rich were sumptuous countryside retreats in the Augustan age; *fana* = consecrated ground; usually places for shrines or temples.

ii The highlanders of the Italian Apennine mountains provide an analogous case of the complexities of the Roman acculturation process; see E. Dench, *From Barbarians to New*

Men: Greek, Roman, and Modern Perceptions of Peoples from the Central Apennines (Oxford, 1995).

iii *praetorium* = the Roman general's tent; by extension, the residence of a Roman provincial governor.

iv See J. P. V. D. Balsdon, *Romans and Aliens* (Chapel Hill, NC, 1979).

REFERENCES

Adams, J. N. (1994) "Latin and Punic in Contact? The Case of the Bu Njem Ostraka," *JRS*, 84, pp. 87–112.

Anderson, B. (1983) *Imagined Communities: Reflections on the Origin and Spread of Nationalism* (London; rev. 1991).

Ardener, E. W. (1972) "Language, Ethnicity, and Population," *Journal of the Anthropological Society of Oxford*, 3, pp. 125–32.

Bloemers, J. H. F. (1990) "Lower Germany: Plura Consilio Quam Vi: Proto-Urban Settlement Developments and the Integration of Native Society," in *The Early Roman Empire in the West*, ed. T. F. C. Blagg and M. Millett (Oxford), pp. 72–86.

Bowersock, G. W. (1990) *Hellenism in Late Antiquity* (Cambridge).

Braudel, F. (1988) *The Identity of France, I: History and Environment* (London).

Derks, T. (1991) "The Perception of the Roman Pantheon by a Native Elite: The Example of Votive Inscriptions from Lower Germany," in *Images of the Past: Studies on Ancient Societies in Northwestern Europe*, ed. N. Roymans and F. Theuws (Amsterdam), pp. 235–65.

Derks, T. (1995) "The Ritual of the Vow in Gallo-Roman Religion," in *Integration in the Early Roman West: The Role of Culture and Ideology*, ed. J. Metzler et al. (Luxembourg), pp. 111–27.

Desbat, A. and S. Martin-Kilcher (1989) "Les Amphores sur l'axe Rhône-Rhine à l'époque d'Auguste," in *Amphores romaines et histoire économique: dix ans de recherche*, ed. M. Lenoir et al. (Rome), pp. 339–65.

Drinkwater, J. F. (1983) *Roman Gaul: The Three Provinces, 58 BC–AD 260* (London).

Drinkwater, J. F. (1987) *The Gallic Empire: Separatism and Continuity in the North-Western Provinces of the Roman Empire* (Stuttgart).

Drinkwater, J. F. and H. Elton (eds.) (1992) *Fifth-Century Gaul: A Crisis of Identity?* (Cambridge).

Foster, G. M. (1960) *Culture and Conquest: America's Spanish Heritage* (Chicago).

Fox, G. W. (1971) *History in Geographic Perspective: The Other France* (New York).

Gellner, E. (1983) *Nations and Nationalism* (Oxford).

Goudineau, C. (1983) "La Notion de Patrie Gauloise durant le Haut-Empire," in *La Patrie Gauloise* (Lyon), pp. 149–60.

Harries, J. (1994) *Sidonius Apollinaris and the Fall of Rome, AD 407–85* (Oxford).

Holder, P. A. (1980) *Studies in the Auxilia of the Roman Army from Augustus to Trajan* (Oxford).

Isaac, B. (1990) *The Limits of Empire: The Roman Army in the East* (Oxford).

King, A. C. (1984) "Animal Bones and the Dietary Identity of Military and Civilian Groups in Roman Britain, Germany, and Gaul," in *Military and Civilian in Roman Britain: Cultural Relationships in a Frontier Province*, ed. T. F. C. Blagg and A. C. King (Oxford), pp. 187–218.

King, A. C. (1990) *Roman Gaul and Germany* (London).

Krier, J. (1981) *Die Treverer ausserhalb ihrer Civitas* (Trier).

MacMullen, R. (1963) *Soldier and Civilian in the Later Roman Empire* (Cambridge, Mass.).

MacMullen, R. (1965) "The Celtic Renaissance," *Historia*, 14, pp. 93–104.

MacMullen, R. (1984) "The Legion as a Society," *Historia*, 33, pp. 225–35.

Mann, J. C. (1983) *Legionary Recruitment and Veteran Settlement during the Principate* (London).

Millar, F. G. B. (1993) *The Roman Near East, 31 BC–AD 337* (Cambridge, Mass.).

Nicolet, C. (1988) *L'Inventaire du Monde: géographie et politique aux origines de l'Empire Romain* (Paris); English trans.: *Geography, Space and Politics in the Early Roman Empire* (Ann Arbor, 1991).

Reece, R. (n.d.) *My Roman Britain* (Cirencester).

Roymans, N. (1993) "Romanisation and the Transformation of a Martial Elite – Ideology in a Frontier Province," in *Frontières d'Empire: Nature et Signification des Frontières Romaines*, ed. P. Brun, S. van der Leeuw and C. R. Whittaker (Nemours), pp. 33–50.

Runciman, W. G. (1984) "Accelerating Social Mobility: The Case of Anglo-Saxon England," *Past and Present*, 104, pp. 3–30.

Rüpke, J. (1990) *Domi militiae: Die religiöse Konstruktion des Krieges in Rom* (Stuttgart).

Saddington, D. B. (1982) *The Development of the Roman Auxiliary Forces from Caesar to Vespasian, 49 BC–AD 79* (Harare).

Saller, R. P. and B. D. Shaw (1984) "Tombstones and Roman Family Relations in the Principate: Civilians, Soldiers and Slaves," *JRS*, 74, pp. 124–56.

Schwartz, S. (1995) "Language, Power and Identity in Ancient Palestine," *Past and Present*, 148, pp. 3–47.

Trevor-Roper, H. (1983) "The Invention of Tradition: The Highland Tradition of Scotland," in *The Invention of Tradition*, ed. E. Hobsbawm and T. Ranger (Cambridge), pp. 14–41.

Wallace-Hadrill, A. (1989) "Rome's Cultural Revolution," *JRS*, 79, pp. 157–64.

Ward-Perkins, J. B. (1970) "From Republic to Empire: Reflections on the Early Imperial Provincial Architecture of the Roman West," *JRS*, 60, pp. 1–19.

Weber, E. (1979) *Peasants into Frenchmen: The Modernisation of Rural France, 1870–1914* (London).

Whittaker, C. R. (1994) *Frontiers of the Roman Empire: A Social and Economic Study* (Baltimore and London).

Wierschowski, L. (1995) *Die regionale Mobilität in Gallien nach den Inschriften des 1. bis 3. Jahrhunderts n. Chr.* (Stuttgart).

Woolf, G. D. (1990) "Food, Poverty, and Patronage: The Significance of the Epigraphy of the Roman Alimentary Schemes in Early Imperial Italy," *PBSR*, 58, pp. 197–228.

Woolf, G. D. (1994) "Becoming Roman, Staying Greek: Culture, Identity and the Civilising Process in the Roman East," *PCPhS* n.s. 40, pp. 116–43.

Woolf, G. D. (1995) "The Formation of Roman Provincial Cultures," in *Integration in the Early Roman West: The Role of Culture and Ideology*, ed. J. Metzler et al. (Luxembourg), pp. 9–18.

Woolf, G. D. (1996) "Monumental Writing and the Expansion of Roman Society in the Early Empire," *JRS*, 86, pp. 22–39.

Woolf, G. D. (1997) "Beyond Romans and Natives," *World Archaeology*, 28, pp. 339–50.

Zanker, P. (1988) *The Power of Images in the Age of Augustus*, trans. A. Shapiro (Ann Arbor).

Zoll, A. L. (1994) "Patterns of Worship in Roman Britain: Double-Named Deities in Context," in *Proceedings of the Fourth Annual Theoretical Roman Archaeology Conference, Durham 1994*, ed. S. Cottam et al. (Oxford), pp. 32–44.

Zoll, A. L. (1995) "A View Through Inscriptions: The Epigraphic Evidence for Religion at Hadrian's Wall," in *Integration in the Early Roman West: The Role of Culture and Ideology*, ed. J. Metzler et al. (Luxembourg), pp. 129–37.

The Barbarians Speak: How the Conquered Peoples Shaped Roman Europe

P. S. Wells

IDENTITIES AND PERCEPTIONS

[There is] evidence – textual, epigraphic, and archaeological – that informs us about the Roman conquests in temperate Europe and about some of the effects of those conquests on the native peoples. We need next to turn to a different set of aspects of the interactions, those of identity and perception. The ways in which the authorities in an imperial society view indigenous groups plays a determinative role in the character of interactions and of the societies that develop in the colonial context. What did the Roman conquerors think about the indigenous peoples they encountered? What did the indigenous peoples think about the Romans? How did these perceptions affect the interactions, and how did the perceptions change through the process of interaction? What role did perceptions about the others play in the creation of new societies in the Roman provinces? To address these questions, I turn to four main categories of evidence – textual, pictorial, linguistic, and archaeological.

Roman perceptions of indigenous Europeans

Texts

The Roman–native interactions in temperate Europe were classic instances of conquests of smaller-scale, nonliterate peoples by a larger-scale, literate society. The written records left by Roman generals, politicians, administrators, and others have been an immensely powerful force in interpretations of the progress of Romanization. If we are to try to achieve an unbiased view of the changes that took place during and after the Roman conquests, we must escape what Jonathan Friedman calls the dominant discourse of the conqueror.[i] Conquerors' accounts – or indeed any accounts by members of one society about members of a different society – are notoriously biased. But if we can understand, and deconstruct, the biases, then we can make fruitful use of the texts. Texts are cultural constructs, and we need to treat them as such. To make sense of the Roman and Greek accounts, we must determine which of the assertions constitute stereotypes or tropes, then separate those and focus on the significant details left.[ii]

Roman writers represented the peoples of temperate Europe in terms of the characteristics with which they, as outside observers or compilers of information, were familiar. Before and during the Roman conquests in temperate Europe, this familiarity was most often in the form of interactions in military contexts. None of the writers whose works are preserved spent time living in an Iron Age village, nor were any of them merchants who traveled among the late prehistoric peoples north of the

Alps. Hence we learn virtually nothing about everyday life from the textual sources. Some few remarks that the Greek author Polybius makes about apperance and habits of Celts pertain to the groups living in northern Italy, not in temperate Europe beyond the Alps. Instead, we read that the Gauls were brave, fierce, and very aggressive warriors and they used tactics and weapons different from those of the Roman armies. This information derives from a number of encounters, including the invasions of Italy during [the] fourth and third centuries B.C., described by the later historians Polybius and Livy; the well-documented service by Celtic mercenaries in armies of Mediterranean potentates during the fourth, third, and second centuries B.C.; and the direct experience of Caesar and other generals fighting during the final century B.C. and, in the case of the peoples designated Germans, during the first century A.D. Most of the specific information about the native peoples north of the Alps derives from such confrontations. Hence it is highly military in nature, and it reflects the indigenous groups in circumstances of extreme stress, not in the course of daily life nor in circumstances before their conflicts with Mediterranean civilizations.

On a more general level, Roman and Greek writers perceived a fundamental difference between their literate civilizations and the groups they called barbarians – peoples of other regions who did not speak Latin or Greek and who practiced customs they regarded as peculiar. The ancient authors represented this difference in two opposite ways. Sometimes they portrayed barbarians as savage, uncouth, uncivilized peoples who behaved in unpleasant fashion. Other times, the authors idealized them as noble, simple peoples unspoiled by sophisticated lifestyles. But always they represented them as essentially different from the Romans and the Greeks.

Until quite recently, the great majority of modern studies treated the Classical texts as objective representations of the state of affairs in the European landscapes at the time of contact between the Iron Age peoples and the literate Mediterranean civilizations. But especially since the 1960s, a number of scholars have advanced more critical approaches to the texts, in concert with modern thinking and with anthropological models of interaction between more complex and less complex societies. In this section I shall address some of the issues raised in these studies.

In their descriptions of barbarians, the Classical authors almost invariably portrayed them in stereotypical ways, as unusually large, exceptionally strong and fierce, wild in nature, and childlike in many respects. The writers represented their lives as simpler than those of people in the Classical world, and the lands they inhabited were viewed as wilder and less transformed by cultivation than those of the Romans and Greeks. In the case of the peoples of temperate Europe, the further north they resided, the more extreme were these traits that differentiated them from the standard view of the Mediterranean cultures. Like most authors writing about different peoples and foreign lands, the Greek and Roman commentators were especially interested in portraying things they considered strange and outlandish. While Caesar drew a number of parallels between Gallic society and Rome, he also informs us about what he considered bizarre behavior among the Gauls, such as human sacrifice. When he mentioned Germans, he commented on practices that were probably exceptional, not typical. In the *Germania*, Tacitus distinguished groups among the native peoples by their peculiar customs.[iii]

There are two principal kinds of information transmitted by the ancient writers about these indigenous groups of temperate Europe. One concerns geography – where the groups lived. The other concerns their ways of life and character as peoples. The earliest known identification of the Celts is in Greek writers of the sixth and fifth centuries B.C. Hecataeus stated that *Keltoi* inhabited the lands around the Greek colonial city of Massalia (today Marseille on the coast of southern France), and Herodotus writing in the mid-fifth century B.C. indicated that the source of the Danube River was in lands occupied by *Keltoi*. Subsequent Greek writers, including Polybius, Posidonius, Diodorus Siculus, and Strabo, provide additional information about these peoples. But the most detailed account of the indigenous Celts of Europe, to whom the Romans referred with the name Gauls (*Galli*), was that of Julius Caesar, in his commentaries on the peoples of Gaul whom he conquered between 58 and 51 B.C.

In the case of Germans (*Germani*), Caesar is also our principal early source. The Greek geographer Posidonius may have written about the Germans a few decades earlier than Caesar, but his writings have been lost, though some of his observations survive as references in the subsequent works of other authors; it is not always clear which ideas came from Posidonius and which from later writers. The principal information that Caesar provides is that the Germans lived east of the Rhine River, while Gauls (Celts) lived west of it. Caesar went on to indicate that the Germans had a simpler and more rugged lifestyle than did the Gauls. To some extent, his portrayal of the Germans reflected a common attitude among Romans. Groups that inhabited lands near Rome were regarded as like Romans in fundamental ways, while peoples further away were considered more different.

Thus all of our earliest information about peoples named Celts and Germans comes from sources written by outside observers. The Greek and Roman writers defined the categories Celt and German, associated them with particular regions of temperate Europe, and ascribed specific characteristics to the peoples so designated. There is no reason for us to think that all of the groups whom the Classical writers referred to as Celts ever felt that they belonged to a common people, nor that those Caesar and Tacitus called Germans saw themselves as members of a distinct, super-regional population. Outsiders dominated the written discourse, and that domination persists today in the way most researchers approach issues of identity among the indigenous Europeans.

When the ancient texts were rediscovered late in the Renaissance, preserved in copies in European monasteries, the descriptions of the indigenous peoples of temperate Europe by the Greek and Roman writers were accepted as objective accounts of those prehistoric inhabitants. From the development of scholarship during the seventeenth, eighteenth, and nineteenth centuries on, the Classical writers' portrayals of the Celts and Germans have dominated the discourse of historians, archaeologists, and others concerned with the transition from late prehistoric to early historic Europe. In modern Europe, many nations look back for the definitions of their identities to the period in which their inhabitants were first named in written sources. The Gauls, as they were described by Caesar, are an essential part of France's modern national identity. In the minds of modern inhabitants of Great Britain and Ireland, the ancient Celts play a related, but not identical, role. For Germany, the *Germani* described by Caesar and by Tacitus form an important part of the national consciousness. In regard to modern scientific research, much of the archaeology of Iron Age Europe is still driven by the categorization of peoples created by the Classical writers, as a perusal of the many recent books about ancient Celts and Germans reveals.

The information regarding lifestyles of native Europeans is highly stereotypical. Descriptions of the Celts by Greek and Roman writers tell of a heroic, warrior-based society, with chiefs and followers eager for battle and just as enthusiastic about feasting and drinking when they were not fighting. Their courage has been described as reckless, and their politics as volatile. The men are portrayed as large, muscular, and fierce; the women as beautiful and brave.

During the first century B.C. and the first century A.D., when Germans entered the consciousness of Roman and Greek commentators, they were represented in similar terms, but with the frequent observation, especially by Caesar, that they were less civilized than the Celts, lived in smaller communities, and had less highly developed religious practices. Caesar informs us that the Celts had a designated group of religious leaders, the druids. The Germans had no such formal authorities nor did they practice sacrifice. According to him, the Germans were not farmers, but spent most of their time hunting or engaged in warfare. They had no permanent leaders, but elected temporary chiefs for military ventures. Caesar also informed his readers about the unusual creatures of the German forests, among them the unicorn and the elk, an animal without leg joints. Caesar explained that the elk could not raise itself from the ground and hence had to sleep on its feet, leaning against a tree. Locals captured the animals by sawing part way through a tree at its base; when the elk leaned against it, the tree fell over, and the animal fell with it and was easily dispatched. (These bits of fanciful natural history should caution us against relying heavily on details in Caesar's account of the Germans!)

Caesar's statements about the peoples he called Gauls indicate that he became somewhat familiar with their way of life through his experience during the campaigns. However, his portrayals make clear that he judged everything he saw in terms of his own background in Rome. He had none of the objectivity in his observations that we would expect of a modern anthropologist. His remarks about the groups he called Germans indicate that he was very poorly informed concerning peoples east of the Rhine. Even aside from his description of the bizarre forest animals, his statement about the lack of agriculture shows that either he was misinformed or was passing along false information.

The image that Caesar and other Roman writers had of the peoples beyond the Alps derived not only from their direct personal experience, but also from historical traditions of Rome. The migrations of the Cimbri and other groups from northern Europe at the end of the second century B.C. played a major role both in Romans' conceptions of the cultural geography of temperate Europe and in Caesar's attitudes and policies toward the peoples of Gaul and beyond the Rhine. Those incursions were the second major episode of invasions from beyond the Alps, after the sacking of Rome in 387 B.C. by Gauls, a tradition preserved in the writings of Polybius and Livy, and they had rekindled Roman fears of barbarians from the north. As the peoples of Gaul became more familiar to Rome, both through Rome's military and political activity in southern Gaul during the second century B.C. and through the growing trade from southern Gaul northward, Romans developed a model of the European interior. According to this view, the southern, more cultivated zone was inhabited by Celtic peoples; the more distant, northern, more heavily forested region was inhabited by other peoples. The Rhine River formed the boundary between these imagined territories. In his accounts of the Germani living east of the Rhine, Caesar connected the traditions about the Cimbri and the Teutones with the occupants of those landscapes in his time. In Classical geographical thinking, rivers frequently were boundaries between peoples. Thus it may be that lacking a clear understanding of the character of the peoples beyond the Rhine, Caesar followed traditional thinking in making that river the boundary between the Gauls and the Germans.

Pictorial representations

Representations of the indigenous Europeans in the art and iconography of Rome provide another important source of information about perceptions. The earliest portrayals of Celts show battles between Gauls and peoples of Italy and Greece during the fourth and third centuries B.C. The Gauls of northern Italy are represented in heroic fashion as large and muscular warriors, distinguished from their adversaries in being partly or completely naked and sometimes wearing torques around their necks. The great majority of these earliest representations of Gauls in the Mediterranean lands and of later portrayals of Celts and Germans north of the Alps revolve around the theme of war.

Every substantial victory won by Roman commanders against barbarian peoples was accompanied by public representations of the defeated enemies. Some were in the form of monumental architecture on temples and triumphal arches. Others were smaller in scale, such as individual statues and altars. From the time of Caesar onward, coins were much used as means of disseminating propaganda about defeated groups to the wider Roman public. Domitian's victory over the Chatti in A.D. 83 and Trajan's successes were particularly commemorated with the minting of new coins bearing stereotypical images of the barbarians.

The memorial columns erected under the reigns of Trajan (A.D. 98–117) and Marcus Aurelius (A.D. 161–80) are rich sources of information about Roman attitudes toward the barbarians beyond the Alps. Both bear long relief sculptures showing scenes of battles between Roman troops and barbarian peoples east and north of the Rhine and Danube frontiers. Both are idealized representations, showing heroic victorious Romans and defeated, humiliated barbarians. But there are significant differences in the portrayals that signal changes in Roman attitudes during the second century.

Trajan's column is an enormous monument, standing almost 140 ft (43 m) tall and bearing a continuous narrative picture in the form of an upward spiral band. A statue of Trajan crowned the column, and the emperor's tomb was originally built into the base. The pictures portray wars against the Dacians in A.D. 101–2 and 105–6. The column may have served a purpose similar to that of Caesar's commentaries about the Gallic Wars – to present to the people of Rome an account of the military campaigns in which the leaders had invested so much manpower and resources. Just as Caesar told the Roman elites that his campaigns in Gaul were necessary to forestall future barbarian invasions on Rome, so too the Emperor Trajan represented the Dacians as a strong threat to Roman authority on the lower Danube. The barbarian enemies are represented in heroic fashion, as dignified warriors unable to resist the might of Rome. Their clothing, weapons, and the architecture of their settlements appear in realistic portrayals, and these representations match archaeological materials from these groups.

On the column of Marcus Aurelius, erected more than half a century later to commemorate the victories following the long and difficult wars against the Marcomanni and the Sarmatians, there is not the same indication of sympathy and admiration for the enemies. The portrayals do not emphasize as much their dignity and heroism, but rather the glory of the emperor and the invincible power of Rome. Comparison of these two columns, erected for similar purposes and representing similar themes, reveals important changes in Roman public attitudes toward the barbarian peoples on the European frontiers of the empire.

All of these public representations are important indicators for us in that they show how the Roman authorities transmitted information about the indigenous Europeans whom the empire was conquering to the people of Rome. The sculptures were all in prominent places, people saw them regularly in the course of their everyday lives, and the images must have become fixed stereotypes in the minds of the viewers. Coins were an even more immediate source of propaganda that confronted the public constantly. Regularly viewing pictures representing defeated peoples of Europe probably contributed to a widespread and unthinking acceptance on the part of the populace of Rome of the official attitudes toward the barbarians. The dominant content of that notion was that the peoples against whom the Roman armies were warring were different from Romans, and they were unattractive in their personal appearance and habits. These messages were very different from those that Roman soldiers stationed on the frontier received.

Celts and Germans: linguistic evidence

The linguistic patterns in Europe at the time of the Romans constitute an important source of information in the recognition of identities among the indigenous peoples. Language is a critical aspect of cultural and ethnic identity, though language and other aspects of ethnicity rarely overlap completely. The terms "Celtic" and "Germanic" used in designating early languages of temperate Europe are in themselves of complex meaning. These two categories are artificial creations by investigators working in the field of comparative philology in the nineteenth century. The categories "Celtic" and "Germanic" are based on study and comparison of known languages from later times, such as Breton and Irish for Celtic and English, German, and Gothic for Germanic. It is important that we bear in mind this fact that the categories are modern constructions imposed on early languages; the linguistic patterns in Late Iron Age Europe most likely did not correspond to the modern categories. Linguists can nonetheless distinguish between what they consider Celtic and Germanic languages at the beginning of historical times in temperate Europe.

The earliest datable evidence we possess for the languages spoken in temperate Europe is in the form of inscriptions from shortly before and around the time of Christ. Such inscriptions were first written in the context of intensifying contact between the peoples of temperate Europe and those of Greece and Rome, when writing was first introduced by those Mediterranean societies and adopted by some members of the indigenous groups.

For Celtic languages, the earliest datable traces are inscriptions written in Greek characters in southern Gaul, beginning as early as the third century B.C. Personal names that appear in those inscriptions correspond closely to names recorded later by Caesar, in the middle of the first century B.C. But some early inscriptions containing Celtic names occur in other locations. For example, two sherds of characteristic local pottery recovered at Manching bear incised Celtic names, written in Greek letters. At Port in Switzerland was found an iron sword with the name KORISIOS stamped in Greek letters onto the upper part of the blade. The name is believed to be Celtic. We do not know the significance of this stamp, whether it names the swordsmith or the owner. Latin writting was adopted by peoples considered to have been Celts by the first half of the first century B.C. Most common are inscriptions in the Latin alphabet on coins, for example among the Boii in central Europe and among some groups in east-central Gaul. The longest Latin inscription in temperate Europe from before the time of Christ is on the Coligny calendar found in Ain, France, a bronze tablet believed to date to the late second century B.C. and bearing calendrical information in a Celtic language.

The earliest datable evidence for Germanic languages is in the form of inscriptions of runes – short messages written in characters consisting of combinations of straight lines, a system common among Germanic peoples in the early Middle Ages. They include the inscription on the brim of the bronze helmet found at Negau (Ženjak) in Slovenia, probably dating to the second or first century B.C. Another early inscription is on the bow of a fibula from Meldorf in northern Germany, thought to date to the first century A.D., and an inscription from the bog deposit at Vimose in Denmark has been dated at about A.D. 160. By the end of the second century A.D., runic inscriptions were increasingly common. They occur mainly on small, portable objects such as fibulae and weapons found in northern Europe, especially in Denmark, southern Sweden, and northern Germany. Runologists suggest that runes of the late second and early third centuries display a level of skill and confidence indicating that they had been in use for a considerable period of time.

The distributions of early Celtic inscriptions in Gaul and runes mostly in northern continental Europe suggest a general geographical distinction between peoples who spoke Celtic and Germanic languages at the time of the Roman arrival in temperate Europe. Yet the evidence is complex and ambiguous. For example, the incised sherds from Manching with Celtic names written in Greek characters are far east and north of the great majority of early Celtic inscriptions. The Negau helmet is far south of the main distribution of early runic inscriptions. An analysis of early Celtic place-names suggests a distribution similar, but not identical, to that of the Celtic inscriptions. Names ending in -*dunum* attested in the ancient sources are concentrated in southern Gaul, but there are also examples in central and northern Gaul, in the Rhineland, and in the lands south of the upper and middle Danube, as well as in Britain. Names ending in -*magus* concentrate in southern Gaul and on the left bank of the Rhine.

In summary, this complex evidence of language suggests that at the time of intensifying contact with the Roman world during the second and first centuries B.C., peoples in Gaul spoke Celtic languages, and peoples in Denmark and adjoining regions spoke Germanic languages. But we are poorly informed about the languages spoken in other regions. Philologists know virtually nothing about the languages that were spoken in the lands east of the Rhine before the start of the Roman Period. Early Celtic inscriptions are even lacking from the Rhineland, though not, as the sherds from Manching indicate, from the lands east of the Rhine and south of the Danube. In the Roman Period too, names recorded from the province of Germania Superior are of Celtic character, like those of Gaul, not Germanic. In the Rhineland, personal names and names of settlement communities recorded during the Roman Period are mainly Celtic in character. But, curiously, names of deities, such as the mother goddesses that are common in the lower Rhine region, are most often linked with Germanic personal names. This evidence may indicate the survival of Germanic name-elements in populations that otherwise were acculturated to Gallo-Roman society.

Wolfgang Meid interprets the linguistic evidence from the area between Gaul and northern Europe from which we have only sparse epigraphic evidence to indicate the existence of languages that combined elements of what we call Celtic and Germanic.[iv] He thinks that many people in this region probably spoke languages that modern linguists could not readily classify into one or the other of these modern categories. There is even evidence that personal names often included elements of what today would be considered Celtic and Germanic. Before the existence of modern political boundaries and language textbooks, linguistic patterns could vary much more widely.

Archaeological evidence

Celts

We can identify two extreme positions in the question of Celts and archaeology. One is represented by archaeologists who study the European Iron Age and who interpret literally statements by Greek and Roman writers regarding the location and character of the Celts. According to this approach, the people who were living around the upper Danube in the middle fifth century B.C. were, following Herodotus, Celts. The peoples whose fourth and third century B.C. cemeteries have been excavated in northern Italy and whose grave goods are similar to those in eastern France and western Germany during the same period were, following Polybius's and Livy's accounts of the invasions across the Alps, Gauls (or Celts). The people inhabiting the lands west of the Rhine River in Caesar's time were Gauls, as described by Caesar. The statements by ancient authors concerning the society and behavior of the Celts can be linked to the archaeological evidence in the regions described as Celtic homelands. Proponents of this position view the Celts as a clear, unambiguous people whose identity as Celts was recognized both by themselves and by others.

The other extreme position is represented in a recent book by Malcolm Chapman entitled *The Celts: The Construction of a Myth* (1992). Chapman argues that the "Celts" did not exist as a recognizable group of people. The name was used by ancient writers to designate unknown peoples in the northern regions of continental Europe, beyond the shores of the Mediterranean and beyond the Alps. In modern times, the "Celts" were a construction by Romantic writers of the eighteenth and nineteenth centuries, seeking a unity among diverse groups that did not exist in any objective criteria.

How do we develop a reasonable research agenda in light of these two extreme and opposed positions? An important criticism by Chapman is that the ancient authors do not indicate the basis of their ascription of identity. They do not tell what criteria they use in identifying the people of one region as Celts rather than as another named group, such as Scythians. Instead, at least in the earlier texts of the sixth and fifth centuries B.C., "Celts" seems to refer generally to "those people beyond the Alps," barbarians that fit the stereotype. Similarly in Livy's account of the Gauls pouring across the Alps and into northern Italy at the start of the fourth century B.C., there is no reason for us to interpret this designation any more specifically than indicating peoples from beyond the Alps. Only in the final century B.C., when Caesar makes pointed distinctions between Gauls and Germans, can we constructively examine the archaeological evidence in relation to the designations made by the ancient authors. At that stage, it is useful to examine the relevant archaeological evidence first, then turn to the texts and ask what information could Posidonios, Caesar, Strabo, Tacitus, and the others have learned about the people represented in the archaeology that led them to make the assertions they made.

If we accept Herodotus's statement of the mid-fifth century B.C. that *Keltoi* lived around the headwaters of the Danube River, then we can link the name Celts with the material culture known as Early La Tène. This same link can be made another way, through the Champagne region of northeastern France and northern Italy. Greek and Roman texts concerning the fourth and third centuries B.C. refer to Celts living in the Po Plain and eastern central Italy, as the result of the much-discussed migrations across the Alps around 400 B.C. In the latter part of the nineteenth century, archaeologists working in Champagne noted that the style of decoration on objects in burials there, particularly metal ornaments, matched that on similar objects in the cemeteries in Italy. Thus the connection was made of *Galli* with peoples of northeastern France using the La Tène style in the fourth and third centuries B.C. But the problem with this approach is that the written sources of this period do not name any other peoples north of the Alps – any peoples with whom to contrast Celts. Just because groups producing objects ornamented in the La Tène style lived in regions where Herodotus and others say that Celts lived, does not mean that groups on the North European Plain making ornaments in the Jastorf style were not also Celts to the Greeks, if they were aware of them at all. Unfortunately, no other name for peoples in these regions north of the Alps appears in the ancient literature until Caesar's use of Germans. (Herodotus and other ancient writers knew of a group of peoples they called the Scythians, but they were placed far east of our regions, in the lands north of the Black Sea.)

For the early part of the La Tène sequence the connection between this style of ornament and the people known as Celts is problematic, since we know no other names to associate with other styles. In Caesar's time in the mid-first century B.C., the distribution of objects ornamented in the La Tène style does not correspond to the landscapes in which Caesar stated that Gauls lived. The La Tène style is well represented on both sides of the Rhine, both to the west where Caesar said Gauls lived, and to the east where he said Germans lived. This is the earliest clear assertion by an ancient writer concerning the location of Celts and Germans. The same material culture was in use on both sides of the Rhine – similar settlement types, house forms, burial practices, and similar pottery, iron tools, bronze and glass ornaments, and coins. Caesar's repeated assertions that the Rhine was the boundary between Celts and Germans has stimulated a vast literature in archaeology, but the apparent conflict between Caesar and the archaeology has not been resolved using traditional approaches.

Germans

The most important aspects of the Germans as they were described by Caesar and other ancient authors are that they, like the Gauls, inhabited lands beyond the Alps in temperate Europe; they lived east of the Rhine, in contrast to the Gauls; and their society was simpler and smaller-scale than that of the Gauls. But whereas in his account, Caesar emphasized differences between Gauls and Germans, Strabo, writing at about the same time, said that the Germans were very much like the Gauls and were closely related to them. The principal difference, according to Strabo, was that the Germans move more; he referred to substantial migrations that they undertook.

There is no evidence that in Caesar's time the myriad groups east of the Rhine that he lumped together with the term Germans felt any kind of common identity, such as we might recognize in common personal ornaments, designs on pottery, or burial practices. Furthermore, Tacitus, writing around A.D. 100, in the famous passage in the second section of his *Germania*, informs us that the name Germans had only recently come to be applied to the whole group of peoples. The issue is further muddled by the fact that the name Germani originally seems to have designated a much smaller group of peoples in northern Gaul, that is, west of the Rhine, not east of it. Caesar referred to this latter group as *Germani Cisrhenani* and said that they came into Gaul from lands on the other side of the Rhine. Caesar distinguished a small group called the Germani from the larger ethnic group he designated Germani, and that small group he said lived west of the Rhine, where, according to his general model, Gauls lived. Thus the name Germani is fraught with complications.

Caesar's several references to the Germani were all made in the context of his description of the Gauls, among whom he was leading the Roman military campaigns. As noted above, Caesar's account contains two important kinds of information about the Germani – they lived east of the Rhine, and they lived a simpler and less civilized lifestyle than did the Gauls, without towns, permanent governmental institutions, or organized religion. Before Caesar's arrival in Gaul in 58 B.C., the abundant archaeological evidence indicates very similar patterns west and east of the Rhine River. From the archaeology, we would never suppose that the Rhine formed an ethnic boundary or any other kind of major division between peoples. The *oppida* are similar on both sides of the river. Pottery, iron tools, bronze and glass ornaments, coins, and other materials are very much alike in the two regions.

There are two contexts in which the archaeological evidence indicates groups that could be interpreted to correspond to Caesar's characterization of Germans. North of the central regions of temperate Europe, where the *oppida* existed and characteristic Late La Tène material culture was produced, small-scale groups lived. Their settlements were farmsteads and small villages, with no larger centers such as the *oppida*, and they did not produce wheelmade pottery, glass ornaments, or coins. Their ironworking technology was not as highly developed as that of their neighbors to the south, and they were not as much engaged in interaction with the Roman world, to

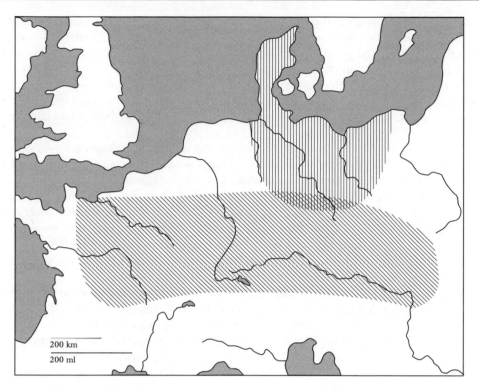

Map 6   *Map showing regions in which the La Tène style* (oblique hatching) *and the Jastorf type* (vertical hatching) *material cultures were common.*

judge by the dearth of Roman imports there compared to those in the *oppidum* zone. The dominant style of material culture in this northerly region is known as Jastorf (map 6). Much of Caesar's characterization of the Germans could fit what we know about groups characterized by Jastorf material culture. If Caesar had said that east of the *lower* Rhine the lands were inhabited by Germans, then this description could correspond to the archaeological situation. But Caesar did not make that stipulation in any of his remarks about the Rhine boundary.

Even more directly relevant to the issues we are considering are changes that took place in lands east of the upper and middle Rhine at about the time that Caesar conducted his campaigns in Gaul. Many of the *oppida* east of the Rhine were abandoned, and considerable changes took place in settlement systems, manufacturing patterns, and burial practices.

Dynamics of identity and the Roman conquests

The complexities of the Roman texts and of the archaeology can be better understood if we examine the evidence in the context of the changes in the archaeological material. Like most descriptions of indigenous peoples written by members of imperial societies, the Roman texts present the indigenous Europeans in static terms.

Caesar, Strabo, Tacitus, and other writers seem to have been largely unaware that the Iron Age peoples of Gaul and Germany were undergoing substantial changes in their social, economic, and political organization well before Caesar's campaigns in Gaul. Nor is there evidence in their writings that they knew that contact with the Roman world was profoundly affecting the structure and organization of those indigenous societies. Surprisingly, a similar lack of attention to the dynamic aspect of the indigenous European cultures characterizes much recent research in the fields of archaeology and ancient history.

Societies in temperate Europe were undergoing significant changes for well over a century before Roman troops marched into Gaul under Caesar's command. Among the changes were the migrations southward and eastward, increased interaction with peoples in the Mediterranean region and in northern Europe, establishment of the *oppida*, and transformation of funerary practices. The arrival of the Roman army, first in Gaul and later east of the Rhine, was another of many factors that stimulated changes. In this section, we need to examine evidence regarding the effects of the Roman conquests and of the establishment of provinces on the identities of the native peoples, both as they saw themselves and as the Romans saw them.

We know from more recent instances of contact between expansionary complex societies and smaller-scale indigenous ones that the latter groups typically change substantially as a result of the contact, frequently well before actual conquest. Studies in different parts of the New World show profound effects of interaction, both among the groups in contact with European explorers and conquerors, and among peoples living beyond the scenes of direct contact. In many of these cases, it is apparent that change brought about through mechanisms of contact took place before Spanish commentators gathered information about the indigenous groups. These well-documented instances in the New World raise the question for Roman Period Europe, how might the indigenous peoples have changed before Caesar and the other Roman writers arrived on the scene? When we pose the question this way, examination of the archaeological evidence in Europe makes clear that interaction with the Roman world had important dynamic effects on indigenous peoples before the Romans who did the recording came into temperate Europe. This observation makes all of the Roman accounts problematic. It is apparent that the writers were unaware of much that was going on around them. But with this question in focus, we can apply both the written and the archaeological sources of information to learn about Rome's early impact on the ways that native Europeans organized and represented themselves.

Tribalization and Rome

Recent analyses of ethnographic and ethnohistorical data show that the phenomenon we know as "tribes" – groups made up of thousands of people with a defined territory and a clearly designated leader – are characteristic of the peripheries of empires and other complex state-level societies. Tribes form in response to interaction between indigenous peoples and larger societies. Research in more recent colonial contexts in the Americas and in Africa reveals the mechanisms involved. When states expand through imperial conquest or colonization, they foster the formation of discrete political and territorial units among complex, multilingual, culturally diverse indigenous peoples. Such "tribal" units are easier for empires to administer than are the typical pre-imperial diverse societies, because they are usually accompanied by a leadership structure that involves a single potentate. This individual can represent the tribe in dealings with the imperial state. Thus a colonizing power establishes static boundaries on groups that had been fluid and not easily understandable or administrable. Indigenous elite individuals play special roles in such tribes as mediators between the colonial power and the newly organized entities.

Jonathan Hill analyzes the process of tribalization in nineteenth-century North America.[v] The conditions he describes are comparable in significant ways to those of indigenous Europeans at the time of the Roman expansion. From an early stage in interactions between colonial enclaves on the east coast of North America and indigenous peoples of the interior, a process began of what he calls the "geopoliticization of indigenous American cultural identities." In his model, the policies pursued by the expanding European state systems – specifically their concept of the nation-state – created tribal entities. The result was fixed tribes with specific territories and leadership structures that enabled interaction with the European American communities. This situation supplanted much more complex indigenous societies with less well defined boundaries and less institutionalized leadership structures. It was not until after 1860 that what we now regard as tribal names such as Cree and Ojibwa became associated with specific individuals and lands. Hill emphasizes what he calls the fluidity of groups before the tribalization process, and also the great extent of interethnic relations before the fixed tribal identities appeared. Both of these patterns could lie behind the archaeological evidence for very active movement and transmission of goods during the final centuries of the prehistoric Iron Age, and they may lie behind some of the phenomena that the Classical writers described as migrations.

The expansion of Roman activity in the south of Gaul during the second century B.C. may have set in motion processes that contributed to the formation of the *oppidum* centers and of the tribal groups that Caesar and other writers describe. Significantly, the distribution of the *oppida* is very similar to that of Roman imports, including amphorae, bronze vessels, fine pottery, and coins. This is not to say that there were no self-recognizing groups in temperate Europe before the Roman activity in southern Gaul in the second century B.C. We know from the accounts by Polybius and Livy of the migrations into Italy that some of these peoples had group names and identified with their kinsmen back in Gaul. But the archaeological evidence shows that they did not have territorial centers comparable to the *oppida* and thus are not likely to have had as strong a territorial identity as tribal groups.

East of the Rhine during the latter half of the final century B.C. we can also identify evidence for a process of tribalization on the edges of the expanding world, but there it did not result in the formation of centers as large and complex as the *oppida*. Before the time of Caesar, the communities of what are now central and northern Germany had broadly similar, but locally varied, kinds of pottery, ornaments, and tools, and they practiced similar burial rituals, all characteristic of the Jastorf culture. At the time of the Roman military and political involvement in Gaul from the 60s B.C. on, the patterns in the lands east of the Rhine changed. Regionally distinctive groups became increasingly apparent, differentiating themselves from their neighbors by burial practice, pottery form, and other such material expressions. Even without the emergence of regional centers on the scale of the *oppida*, these changes appear to represent a process of tribalization across the new frontier of the expanding Roman imperial state. In his remarks about the lands east of the Rhine, Caesar names particular groups of peoples he calls Germans in the same way he describes the tribes of Gaul.

This change in the interregional patterning of material culture is accompanied by the emergence of communities larger and economically more complex than earlier ones. Before the time of Caesar's campaigns in Gaul, settlements in northern regions east of the Rhine were composed of loose agglomerations of farmsteads, typically comprising several buildings. Each farmstead was dominated by a three-aisled structure that combined human residence and livestock stalls. Other buildings included workshops and storage structures. But around the time of the Gallic Wars or shortly thereafter, new, considerably larger settlements were established, of which Feddersen Wierde and Flögeln, both in Lower Saxony, are well-studied examples. These settlements differ from earlier ones in their size and in their degree of economic integration.

The settlement at Flögeln began with four long houses set close together, and several outlying farmsteads. Near the settlement was a complex of fields, defined by walls built of earth and stone. Around A.D. 100, a more substantial village was established at the site, with six farmsteads enclosed within a fenced compound. Each farmstead had up to four house–barn combinations in it, together with other buildings. Altogether some fifteen or twenty dwellings were occupied at any one time during the second and third centuries representing a population of some 150 to 200 persons. The barns accommodated about sixteen cattle each, with a total of some 240 to 320 head at Flögeln. This new arrangement represents both a much greater population than any earlier settlement in the region and a much more highly integrated local economy.

These changes are also apparent in the burial evidence. Cemeteries that had been in use for some time earlier now were distinguished by some graves that were considerably more richly outfitted than others. At Harsefeld, for example, some men's graves during this period are characterized by weapons such as swords and lanceheads, spurs and other accounterments of horseback riding, ornate drinking vessels in the form of horns, and Roman bronze vessels used as urns.

In both of these instances – in Gaul during the second century B.C. and across the Rhine in Germany during the final century B.C. and the first century A.D. – the archaeological evidence suggests processes of change similar to the tribalization processes described by cultural anthropologists among indigenous groups in the New World during the Spanish imperial expansion. If this model is applicable, then in the formation of the *oppida* and of the regional groups across the Rhine we see the expression of new group identities among the indigenous peoples, created in response to Roman activity in the vicinity. There is also evidence that individuals responded to Roman categorization of them in the ways they came to see themselves and their roles in society.

Indigenous responses to Roman categories

During the preconquest decades of interaction, in the course of the conquests, and in the context of relations established after the conquests, there was abundant opportunity for indigenous peoples to become aware of their place in the Roman worldview and of Roman attitudes toward them. The natives surely must have responded to the categories in which the Romans placed them. The clearest archaeological expression of new identities created around Roman categories is in the practice of burying weapons with deceased men, both within the newly conquered lands and in regions beyond the frontiers. The practice of including weapons in graves first became a custom east of the Rhine shortly before the time of Christ. We know from the historical sources that this was shortly after the time when Germanic auxiliaries began serving in the Roman army. Romans established the category of auxiliary soldier, and some indigenous men took on this category and were so designated by the weaponry placed with them in their burials.

There are good examples of this expression by indigenous individuals of their role in the Roman military framework. For example, at Wederath, Grave 1344 contained Roman-style weapons – a *gladius* sword, a *pilum* (spear), and a shield, all the typical equipment of an auxiliary soldier in Roman service. But Roman graves did not contain weapons, hence this burial was most likely that of a Treveri soldier who served in an auxiliary unit and after death was buried with the symbols of that role. Across the Rhine in unconquered territory there are numerous graves that contain Roman weapons and are believed to be those of Germans who served in auxiliary units, returned after their twenty or twenty-five years of service with their weapons, and were subsequently buried with these important signs of their relationship to the Roman world. Many such graves are in the large early Roman Period cemeteries in the lower Elbe region, including Putensen and Ehestorf-Vahrendorf. . . .

Another important example of indigenous people's responding to Roman categorizations is in the practice of burying spurs, an essential piece of equipment for cavalry warfare. Ornate spurs occur in a significant number of men's burials dating to the final half of the last century before Christ, but rarely before this time. Very similar spurs have been recovered in graves within Gaul and beyond the Rhine frontier. In the Moselle River region, a landscape said to be the home of the Treveri, from whom Roman armies hired many cavalry troops, two warriors' graves at Konz, three at Goeblingen-Nospelt, and one at Thür exemplify this practice. Spurs of the type found in these graves also have been recovered in major cemeteries east of the Rhine, for example at Putensen on the lower Elbe and at Grossromstedt and Schkopau in central Germany. The practice of including spurs in warriors' graves just after the time that Caesar reported the employment of auxiliary cavalry troops strongly suggests that the individuals represented in these graves were responding to the Roman use of them as cavalry troops, thus creating for them identities as cavalry in Roman service.

Finally, we know from historical sources that it was Roman policy to establish friendly relations with leaders of peoples along the imperial frontiers, as a means of supporting the defense of the Roman territories. Caesar and other Roman writers mentioned a number of these "friendly kings" by name, but the texts provide little information about their status with respect to Rome or to their own communities. In 1988 a burial was discovered in the course of road construction work at Mušov in Moravia, just north of the Danube frontier, that may provide us with a detailed picture of the complex combination of cultural identities that such an individual encompassed. The excavation report describes a large wooden chamber measuring about 20 by 13 ft (6 × 4 m) and covered with a stone mound, that housed the burial. Although the chamber had been robbed, an extraordinarily rich assemblage of grave goods was found by the archaeologists, including more than 150 objects of metal, glass, and pottery. This grave, situated about 35 miles (60 km) north of the Danube frontier, shows how local rulers displayed their status and wealth through both Roman imports and significant objects of local manufacture. The grave contained eight or more bronze vessels, a set of silver tableware, glass vessels, and ten pieces of provincial Roman pottery. Ornate furnishings also included a Roman bronze folding table and two-part bronze Roman lamp. Iron andirons, several weapons, numerous personal ornaments, sixteen spurs, and handmade pottery represent local craft industries. Some of the objects, such as the lamp and folding table, are characteristic of burial inventories of provincial Roman elites while others, such as weapons and spurs, are characteristic of indigenous, non-Roman traditions. The elaborate sets of Roman ceramic, bronze, and silver dinnerware suggest not just importation of goods or even receipt of diplomatic gifts, but rather a personal familiarity with Roman banqueting customs. This individual was thus represented in his burial as an elite Roman, but also as an elite native of the unconquered territories. His identity, as portrayed in the grave, was thus in part created in response to the Roman category of "friendly king," and in part the re-creation of the traditional position of the elite warrior in European society.

EDITOR'S NOTES

i J. Friedman, "The Past is the Future: History and the Politics of Identity," *American Anthropologist*, 94 (1992), pp. 837–59; and *idem, Cultural Identity and Global Process* (London, 1994).

ii Cf. the classic "constructivist" discussion of ethnicity by F. Barth, Introduction to *Ethnic Groups and Boundaries: The Social Organization of Culture Difference* (London, 1969), pp. 9–38.

iii The most exhaustive study of Roman conceptions of the "barbarian" is (in French) Y.-A. Dauge, *Le Barbare: recherches sur la conception romaine de la barbarie et de la civilisation* (Brussels, 1981).

iv W. Meid, "Hans Kuhns 'Nordwestblock' – Hypothese: Zur Problematik der 'Völker zwischen Germanen und Kelten'," in *Regional Approaches to Mortuary Analysis*, ed. H. Beck (New York, 1986), pp. 183–212.

v J. D. Hill (ed.), *History, Power, and Identity: Ethnogenesis in the Americas, 1492–1992* (Iowa City, 1996), pp. 1–19.

Sources

Honors for a Roman defender of civilization

Year 29 [120/19 BCE], Panemos 20. The politarchai of Lete [executive magistrates of this city in Macedonia], after a preliminary decree was passed by the Boule [council], made the motion: Marcus Annius, son of Publius, a noble and good man, having been sent out as quaestor by the People of the Romans to duty in Macedonia, in the entire earlier period had continued to put above everything else things advantageous in common to all Macedonians and to exhibit the greatest forethought for things of importance for our city in particular, of zeal and ardor omitting nothing, and in the present crisis, when the Gallic nation assembled and made an expedition against the lands towards Argos with a huge army, against which there marched out Sextus Pompeius the praetor* and faced them in battle formation with his own troops, and [when], as it happened, he died in the fighting, and for this reason his troops were disheartened, [against the Gauls] marched Marcus the quaestor with the men attached to him. He routed the opposing forces, recovered the fallen [dead] and killed many of the enemy; he seized many horses and arms, and with concern for the safety of the guards in the forward zones had them sent to the encampment; and after many days even more Gallic horsemen assembled, and with them came Tipas, chief of the Maedi, with a horde even larger, but [Annius] repulsed the oncoming assault of the barbarians; and other soldiers, to fulfill treaty obligations by the Macedonians, he decided not to send for, because he did not wish to inflict the cities with soldiers' pay, preferring the mass [of the population] to remain at their work; he went on the attack with the soldiers he had in the encampment, and, avoiding no danger or suffering, deployed his troops and defeated the enemy in combat, with the providence of the gods, and many of them in hand-to-hand fighting he killed, but he also took some alive, and many of their horses and arms he seized, and in such a way he held events under control in good spirits and has tried to hand over the province to his successors after keeping safe all those in the territory, at peace and in the most splendid settled condition, doing these things in a way worthy of his country and his ancestors and worthy of his own fame and bravery and also of the position of responsibility with which he had been entrusted. Therefore, it is decreed by the Boule and People of Lete to praise Marcus Annius, [son] of Publius, quaestor of the Romans, and to crown him for the sake of his deeds with a crown of [olive] branch, and to establish for him an annual equestrian contest in the month of Daisios, when for other benefactors the contests are held.

Sylloge Inscriptionum Graecarum, 3rd edn., no. 700 [120/119 BCE][1]

A Roman tautology: Rome, urbanization, and civilization

In Italy [Aeneas*] will wage a tremendous war, subdue fierce armies, and then for the people there establish city-walls and a new way of life.

Vergil, *Aeneid*, 1.253–4 [ca. 20 BCE]

You, Roman, remember by your empire to rule the world's peoples (for these will be your arts), to impose the practice of peace, to be sparing to the subjected, and to beat down the defiant.

Vergil, *Aeneid*, 6.851–3 [ca. 20 BCE]

[Rome is called] the nurse and parent of all other lands, elected by the gods' will in order to make heaven itself brighter, to bring scattered peoples into unity, to make manners gentle, to draw together by community of language the jarring and uncouth tongues of nearly countless nations, to give civilization to humankind, and put simply to become throughout all the lands the single fatherland of humanity.

Pliny the Elder, *Natural History*, 3.39 [ca. 75 CE]

Athenaeus talks of Rome as "the populace of the inhabited world," and he says that one would not stray far from the truth in stating that the city of Rome is an epitome of the civilized world.

Athenaeus, *Wise Men at Dinner*, 1.20b [ca. 200 CE]

A relegated person cannot remain in Rome, even if this is not included in his sentence, because it is the common homeland (*patria*), nor in a town or city (*civitas*) in which the emperor is staying or through which he is passing; for only persons who can enter Rome are permitted to look on the emperor, since the emperor is the father of the country (*pater patriae*).

Digest of Justinian, 48.22.18 [from Callistratus,
Judicial Examinations, ca. 200 CE]

But there are still traces of the Massiliots' ancient strengths, especially their aptitude in making instruments and outfitting ships. But on account of the Romans' mastery of the world, the barbarians who dwell beyond the Massiliots became more and more pacified as time went by, and instead of engaging in war they already have turned themselves to civic life and farming. So the Massiliots perhaps also do not pursue their earlier practices so zealously.

Strabo, *Geography*, 4.1.5 (C 180–1) [ca. 15 BCE]

It is indeed difficult to administer a vast empire unless it is turned over to one man, as to a father. In any event, the Romans and their allies have never lived and prospered in such peace and plenitude as Augustus afforded them, from the time that he assumed absolute authority, and now his son and successor Tiberius continues his legacy; Tiberius, who is making Augustus his model for administration and decrees, as are his children, Germanicus and Drusus, who are assisting their father.

Strabo, *Geography*, 6.4.2 (C 288) [ca. 15 BCE]

I believe I am right in thinking that even if Fortune and Virtue are continually at war with each other, at least they suspended their strife in order that dominion and power might be welded together. And these in joining their forces have cooperated in bringing to completion the most beautiful of all human works.... In my opinion Time laid the foundation for the Roman state, and with God's help combined and joined the forces of Fortune and Virtue so that, by taking each's special qualities, he might erect a Hearth for humankind, truly both holy and beneficent, a stout cable, a principle that abides forever... even so, while Fortune was driving about the strongest powers and dominions, and these continued to collide with one another because no one held the supreme power, but everyone wanted to hold it, the continuous motion, fluctuation, and change of all peoples remained with no remedy, until the time came when Rome attained strength and growth, and had attached to itself not only nations and peoples within its own borders, but also kingdoms of foreign peoples beyond the seas, and so this great empire's affairs gained stability and security, since the supreme government, which never experienced a setback, was brought within an ordered and single cycle of peace.

Plutarch, Moralia, 316E–317C [ca. 115 CE]

The province of Asia also must be mindful of the fact that if it were not a part of our empire it would have suffered every sort of misfortune that foreign wars and domestic unrest can bring. And since it is quite impossible to maintain the empire without taxation, let Asia not grudge its part of the revenues in return for permanent peace and tranquility.

Cicero, Letters to Brother Quintus, 1.1.34 [60/59 BCE]

As we have said, you are great and you have set out your city in great dimensions. You have not made it admired in your pride by giving no one else a share in it, but you have sought out a citizen-body worthy of it, and you have brought it about that the word 'Roman' does not just belong to a city, but rather that it is the name of a kind of common race, and this not one out of all the races, but rather a balance to all the remaining ones. You do not now divide the races between Greeks and barbarians, nor have you made your distinction a ridiculous one in the eyes of other men, since one might say that you present a city more populous than the entire Greek race. But you have divided humankind into Romans and non-Romans. So far have you extended the use of the city's name.

Aelius Aristides, Regarding Rome, 63 [ca. 145 CE]

I think it right to say that all men of former times, even those who controlled the largest portions of the earth, ruled over, as it were, only the naked bodies of their people, but you [Romans] have filled your whole empire with cities and adornments. When were there ever so many cities throughout the lands or seas, or when have they ever been so thoroughly adorned? When in former times did anyone ever make such a trip, numbering the cities by the days of his trip, or sometimes even passing through two or three cities on the same day, as it were through avenues? Therefore those men of old were not only greatly inferior in the total extent of their empires, but also where they ruled the same lands as you do now, each people did not enjoy equal and similar conditions under their rule. To the tribe which then existed there then there can be placed the city which now exists among them. One is tempted to say that those men were the rulers of deserts and garrisons, but that you alone are the rulers of cities.

Aelius Aristides, Regarding Rome, 92–3 [ca. 145 CE]

Romanization as forced urbanization[2]

For some reason Augustus, perhaps because he thought that Patrae was a good harbor, took the men from other towns and collected them here, uniting with them the Achaeans from Rhypes, which he destroyed. He gave freedom to the people of Patrae, and to no other Achaeans; and he also granted all the other rights and privileges that the Romans customarily give to their colonists. On the acropolis of Patrae is Artemis Laphria's sanctuary. The name "Laphria" is foreign, and her image too was brought from abroad. For after the emperor Augustus had ravaged Calydon along with the rest of Aetolia so that the Aetolian people might be incorporated into Nicopolis above Actium, the Patraeans secured the image of Laphria.

Pausanias, *Description of Greece*, 7.18.7–8 [ca. 150 CE]

Assimilation

But there is another kind of person, a Chian, or a Galatian, or a Bithynian, who is dissatisfied if he has won glory or power that goes with a certain position among his compatriots; he is in tears because he does not wear the shoes of a patrician senator; if he does wear them, because he is not yet a Roman praetor*; and if he is a praetor, because he is not a consul; and when he is a consul*, because he was not the first to be declared elected, but came in later.

Plutarch, *Moralia*, 470C [ca. 115 CE]

After sailing past Campania and its islands [Augustus] spent the next four days at the villa on Capri, where he rested and entertained himself. As he coasted past the Gulf of Puteoli, the passengers and crew of a ship which had just arrived from Alexandria had put on white robes and garlands, burning incense and wishing him the best of good fortune. They did this, they said, because they owed their lives and the freedom to sail the seas, in short their liberty and prosperity, to him. Augustus was so pleased by this that he gave 40 gold pieces to each of his staff, after making them promise to spend them only on Alexandrian goods. Moreover, he spent the remaining two or three days on Capri distributing other small presents, Roman togas and Greek cloaks to the islanders, insisting that the Romans should speak Greek and dress like Greeks, and that the Greeks should talk Latin and dress in Roman fashion.

Suetonius, *Augustus*, 98.1–3 [early second century CE]

The Lycians revolted and had even gone so far as to kill some Roman citizens [ca. 43 CE]. He [Claudius] stripped them of their freedom and assigned them to the province of Pamphylia. In the course of the investigation [he was conducting in the Senate], he asked a question in Latin of one of the Lycian ambassadors, a man who was originally a Lycian but who had become a Roman citizen. When the man could not understand what Claudius had said he took away his citizenship, remarking that a man who did not understand the language of the Romans had no right to be one.

Cassius Dio, *Roman History*, 60.17.3–4 [ca. 205 CE]

He [Caligula] gave shows in the provinces as well: he gave city games in Sicilian Syracuse, and a mixed program at Lugdunum in Gaul, where he also put on a contest in Greek and Latin oratory, and it is said that in that contest the defeated provided the prizes for the victors, and were made to write eulogies for them, too; but those competitors who had been especially unsuccessful were ordered to erase their compositions with a rubber, or with their tongues – unless they preferred to be caned or plunged into the nearby river.

Suetonius, *Caligula*, 20.1 [early second century CE]

Claudius' speech advocating admission of Gallic nobility into the Roman Senate (48 CE)

I am encouraged by my ancestors, the eldest of whom, Clausus, a Sabine, was at once made a citizen and head of a patrician household, to take up the same policy in my administration, by bringing all true excellence here, from wherever it may be found. I am not ignorant of the fact that the Julii came to us from Alba, the Coruncanii from Camerium, the Porcii from Tusculum; that – not to examine ancient times – senators were brought in from Etruria, Lucania, from all Italy; and that eventually Italy itself was extended to the Alps, so that not only individuals but countries and nationalities should comprise one body under the name of the Romans. Secure peace at home and victory abroad came when regions beyond the Po were admitted to citizenship, and, taking advantage of the fact that our legions were settled all over the world, we added the stoutest provincials to them, and thereby supported a weary empire. Do we regret that the Balbii crossed over from Spain and families of equal distinction from Narbonese Gaul? Their descendants are here; and they do not love this native land of theirs any less than we do. What else was the downfall of Sparta and Athens, than that they held the conquered in contempt as foreigners? But our founder Romulus' wisdom made him on several occasions both fight against and naturalize a people on the same day! We have had strangers as kings; granting high offices on sons of freedmen is not a rarity, as is commonly and mistakenly thought, but rather a commonplace in the old Roman state. . . . And yet, if you examine the whole of our wars, none was finished in a shorter time than that against the Gauls; from then on there has been continuous and loyal peace. Now that customs, culture, and marriage ties have blended them with us, let them also bring their gold and riches instead of holding them apart. All, Conscript Fathers, now thought to be exceedingly old once was new: plebeian magistrates followed patrician; Latin, the plebeian; magistrates from other Italic peoples, the Latin. Our innovation also will become a thing of the past, and what we defend today by precedents will themselves rank as precedents.

Tacitus, *Annals*, 11.24 [ca. 115 CE][3]

How they may obtain citizenship in that municipality

Those who have been or shall be elected magistrates from among the members of the Senate, decurions[*], and enrolled members of the Flavian municipality of Irni in the manner that has been provided for in this law, when they lay down their office are to be Roman citizens along with their parents, wives, and children born in legitimate wedlock who are in the power of their parents, likewise with grandsons and grand-daughters born to a son, each of whom male or female is in the power of their parents; provided no more are Roman citizens than it is appropriate should be magistrates in accordance with this law.

Lex Irnitana, table XXI [late first century CE][4]

Ambivalence regarding the Roman civilizing mission?

Gaul is a whole divided into three parts, one of which is inhabited by the Belgians, another by the Aquitanians, and a third by a people called in their own language Celts, in ours the Gauls. They all differ from one another in language, institutions, and laws. The Gauls are separated from the Aquitanians by the Garonne River, from the Belgians by the Marne and Seine rivers. The Belgians are the most courageous of all these peoples, because they are at the farthest remove from the culture and civilization of the Roman province,[5] and they are least often visited by merchants introducing the commodities that make for unmanliness; and also because they are closest to the Germans who live beyond the Rhine River, with whom they are continually at war. For this reason the Helvetians also excel the rest of the Gauls in valor, because they are struggling in almost daily fights with the Germans, either trying to keep them out of Gallic territory or waging aggressive warfare in German territory.

Caesar, *Gallic Wars*, 1.1 [ca. 50 BCE]

The following winter was spent in carrying out sound measures. [The governor Agricola] would exhort individuals and aid communities in erecting temples, market-places, and houses so that a scattered and uncivilized population, and one proportion-ately ready for war, might grow accustomed by comfort to peace and tranquility. He praised the energetic and scolded the lazy, and rivalry for his approval took the place of coercion. He also began to give the sons of chieftains a liberal education, and to give preference to the native talents of a Briton as opposed to the trained abilities of a Gaul. Consequently, the nation which had rejected the Latin language started aspir-ing to rhetoric. Furthermore, Roman dress became a distinction, and the toga became the fashion, and the Britons gradually drifted into alluring vices: promenades, baths, sumptuous dinners. The naive natives called this part of their servitude "cul-ture."

Tacitus, *Agricola*, 21 [98 CE]

Tacitus on the Fenni: uncouth barbarians or noble savages?

The tribe of the Fenni live in remarkable wildness and foul poverty. They have no arms, no horses, no homes. Their food is wild vegetation, skins provide their clothing; they have the ground as a bed. All their hopes lie in their arrows, but they tip them with bone, since they do not have iron. Hunting is the support of the women as well as the men, for the women willingly accompany the men and lay claim to part of the catch. Their infants have no protection against the elements or wild beasts, except for what a few intertwined branches can provide. These are the places to which young men return; these are the refuge of old age. And yet they think they are happier to live this way than to groan over field work, or to be saddled with building houses, and to be constantly involving the fortunes of both themselves and their neighbors in alternate hopes and fears. They do not care about men; they do not care about heaven. They have achieved something very difficult: they have nothing for which to pray.

Tacitus, Germania, 46 [98 CE]

Roman and native religions, the imperial cult, and Romanization[6]

Hybridization

Roman authors often interpreted foreign deities as their own, as the following passage from Caesar's Gallic Wars attests. The Gallic deities Caesar is most likely referring to are given in brackets. But the inscription following this passage shows that "syncretism," or the amalgamation of Roman and native deities, was practiced.

They [Gauls] especially worship Mercury [Teutates] among the gods. There are many images of him. They claim him as the inventor of all crafts, guide for all roads and journeys; they believe that he has special power over money-making and trade. After him, they worship Apollo [Belen] and Mars [Esus] and Jupiter [Taranis] and Minerva. They have about the same view of these deities as other peoples – that Apollo dispels sickness, that Minerva grants the principles of the arts and crafts, that Jupiter rules heaven, and that Mars controls wars.

Caesar, Gallic Wars, 6.17 [ca. 50 BCE]

To the god Mars Lenus or Ocelo Vellaunus and to the deity of the Emperor, Marcus Nonius Romanus, in return for freedom from the college,[7] gave this gift from his own resources on 23rd August in the consulship of Glabrio and Homulus.

Roman Inscriptions of Britain, 309 [152 CE]

Prototype of the emperor as God: town of Karthaia on Keos

The people of Karthaia dedicate [this statue of] the god and imperator[*] and savior of the inhabited world, Gaius Julius Caesar, son of Gaius Caesar.

Inscriptiones Graecae, XII 5.557 [ca. 48 BCE]

The emperor Augustus (27 BCE–14 CE) established provincial assemblies, beginning in 29 BCE in the East and in 12 BCE in the West. These assemblies centered around the temples put up to Rome and Augustus. Meetings were held annually whose main business was the administration of the imperial cult. These meetings also offered provincials opportunities for appeals to the emperor and review of provincial administration. The office of Augustalis, a priesthood presiding over the cult of the emperor, became a coveted position, and the imperial cult served to solidify Roman imperial rule.

It was decreed by the Greeks in the province of Asia, on motion of the high priest Apollonius son of Menophilus, of Azanium: Whereas the providence which divinely ordered our lives created with zeal and munificence the most perfect good for our lives by producing Augustus and filling him with virtue for the good of humankind, blessing us and those who will come after us with a savior who put an end to war and established peace; and whereas Caesar once he appeared exceeded the hopes of all who had expected good things, not only surpassing the benefactors born before him but not even leaving those to come after him any hope of doing more; and whereas the birthday of the god marked for the world the beginning of good things through his coming, and [the cities of] Asia decreed in Smyrna, when Lucius Volcacius Tullus was high priest and Papas was secretary, that a crown be given to the one suggesting the greatest honors for the god; and whereas Paullus Fabius Maximus, proconsul* of the province sent for its preservation by that god's right hand and intention, bene-fited the province with his own suggestions – the extent of which benefactions no one could succeed in telling adequately – and suggested for the honor of Augustus a thing up until then unknown by the Greeks, namely, beginning the calendar year with the god's birthday. Therefore – may Good Fortune and Safety attend! – the Greeks have decreed in the province of Asia that the New Year shall begin in all the cities on September 23, Augustus' birthday; that, to be certain that the day corresponds in every city, they also use the Greek date along with the Roman date; that the first month – named Caesar, as previously decreed – be reckoned beginning with Septem-ber 23, Caesar's birthday; that the crown decreed for the one suggesting the greatest honors in behalf of Caesar be given to the proconsul Maximus, and that he also be proclaimed in these words at every celebration of the athletic games held at Pergamum in honor of Rome and Augustus: "Asia crowns Paullus Fabius Maximus for most piously inventing the honors for Caesar"; that he be proclaimed in the same way at the city's games in honor of Caesar; that the communication of the proconsul and the decree of Asia be inscribed on a pillar of white marble, which is to be set up in the sacred precinct of Rome and Augustus [in Pergamum]; and that the public advocates for the year shall see to it that in the leading cities of the assize districts Maximus' communication and Asia's decree are inscribed on pillars of white marble, and that these are set up in the temples of Caesar.

> *Orientis Graeci Inscriptiones Selectae*, no. 458 [ca. 10 BCE]

Here is Caesar, and all the descendants of Julus all who one day will come under the vault of the great sky; this is the man, this one, of whom you have heard the promise so often, Caesar Augustus, son of the deified, who will once again bring a golden age to Latium, to the land where Saturn reigned in early times.

> Vergil, *Aeneid*, 789–94 [ca. 20 BCE]

When Augustus died, they declared him to be immortal, assigned priests and sacred rites to him, and they made Livia, who already was called Julia and Augusta, his priestess; they also allowed her to use a lictor* when she performed her sacred office. She herself gave 1,000,000 sesterces* to a man named Numerius Atticus, a senator and former praetor*, because he had sworn that he had seen Augustus ascending to heaven just like the tradition reports of Proculus and Romulus. A shrine was constructed for the dead emperor in Rome, voted by the Senate and built by Livia and Tiberius, and there were others in many different places, some of the communities building them of their own free will and others doing so unwillingly. The house at Nola where he died was also dedicated to him as a precinct. When the shrine at Rome was being erected, they put a golden image of him on a couch in the temple of Mars, and they paid all the honors to this image that they were later to give to his statue.... In addition to all this, Livia held a private festival in his honor for three days in the palace, and this is continued by the incumbent emperor down to the present day.

Cassius Dio, Roman History, 56.46.1–5 [ca. 205 CE]

Further Spain sent an embassy to the Senate at the same time [24 CE], asking permission to follow Asia's example, by putting up a shrine to Tiberius and his mother. Tiberius, who was always steadfastly disdainful of compliments, and was now convinced that an answer was owed to the gossip that he had fallen into vanity, began his speech as follows: "Conscript Fathers, I know that many have deplored my lack of consistency when a short while ago I did not oppose this same request from the cities of Asia. So I must explain my previous silence and the rule I have decided for the future. Seeing that the divine Augustus did not forbid the erection of a temple at Pergamum to himself and the city of Rome, and since I observe his every act and word as law, I followed the precedent which had met with his approval, and I did this more willingly because the worship of myself was combined with veneration of the Senate. But, though it may be pardoned to have accepted this honor once, yet to be consecrated as a divinity throughout all the provinces would be vain and arrogant, and Augustus' honor will soon be a mockery, if it is made common by fawning adulation."

Tacitus, Annals, 4.37 [ca. 115 CE]

Master, a soldier stationed in Nicomedia by the name of Apuleius sent a letter informing me that a certain Callidromus on being detained by Maximus and Dionysius, bakers who employed him, fled to your statue for refuge. When he was brought to a magistrate, he stated that formerly he was a slave of Laberius Maximus, but being taken as prisoner by Susagus in Moesia, he was sent to the king of Parthia, Pacorus, as a gift, and he was in his service for several years; from there he escaped and came to Nicomedia.

Pliny the Younger, Epistles, 10.74 [ca. 110 CE]

[The holder of various public offices], before he announces that he has been elected and appointed, is to administer an oath openly in a public meeting (contio) by Jupiter and the Divine Augustus and the Divine Claudius and the Divine Vespasian Augustus and the Divine Titus Augustus and the genius of the emperor Caesar Domitian Augustus and the Penates[*], that he will do what it is necessary to do under this statute and that he has not done and will not do anything against this law knowingly and with wrongful intent.

Lex Irnitana, table VIIA [late first century CE]⁸

"Romanization" and Greek culture[9]

Greek influences at Rome were nearly coeval with its foundation; in the earliest periods much of this influence was indirect, via Etruria. Romans owed much of their thought, their arts, and their general culture to the Greeks. One of their debts was historiography itself (the first Roman historian, Fabius Pictor, wrote his work in Greek ca. 200 BCE). Yet Rome had conquered this people who had produced such an awesome cultural legacy. Consequently, the Romans exhibited a kind of love/hate relationship, an approach/avoidance conflict, with Hellenism. In the end, however, as Horace's famous lines below suggest, Greece won out culturally; and we may legitimately speak of Graeco-Roman civilization, at least from ca. 150 BCE onwards.

Captive Greece seized its ferocious conqueror and brought the arts into rustic Latium.

Horace, *Epistles*, 2.1.156–7 [ca. 15 BCE]

If it had been your lot to go off to govern wild and barbarous tribes in Africa or Spain or Gaul, you would still be bound as a civilized man to consider their interests and concentrate on their needs and well-being. But we are governing a civilized people, in fact the people from whom civilization is believed to have passed to other peoples, and certainly we must give its benefits most of all to those from whom we have received it. . . . Everything that I have attained I owe to what the literature and teachings of Greece has offered. Consequently, we owe a special duty to the Greeks, beyond our common obligation to mankind; schooled in their teachings, we must want to demonstrate what we have learned before the eyes of our teachers.

Cicero, *Letters to Brother Quintus*, 1.1.27 [60/59 BCE]

Greece is a witness to [what I have said]; Greece, which was kindled with a passion for eloquence, and for long has excelled all other states in this regard. And yet [Greece] had discovered all the other arts, and had even brought them to perfection before this art of effective and eloquent speaking was developed.

Cicero, *Brutus*, 26 [46 BCE]

This is what I have been able to find out about Roman origins from diligent reading of Greek and Roman authors. Let the reader therefore deny any views that make Rome a barbarian retreat, full of castaways and fugitives, and let him confidently assert Rome to be a Greek city. This is easy to see when he demonstrates that it is the most hospitable of all cities, and when he remembers that the Aborigines were Oenotrians, and these in turn Arcadians, and recalls those who settled with them, the Pelasgians who were Argives by descent and came from Thessaly; and when he recalls, moreover, the arrival of Evander and the Arcadians, who settled around the Palatine hill, after the Aborigines had made room for them there; and also the Peloponnesians who came with Heracles, settled on the Saturnian hill; and, last of all, those who left the Troad and intermingled with the earlier settlers.

Dionysius of Halicarnassus, *Roman Antiquities*, 1.89 [ca. 10 BCE][10]

Roman distrust of Greek culture?

Roman senators charged their political opponents in the Senate with an excessive devotion to Greek culture. This charge was brought against P. Cornelius Scipio Africanus, as he was preparing for the African campaign that ultimately would defeat Hannibal (at the Battle of Zama, 202 BCE) and bring the Second Romano-Carthaginian War to an end.

The senators charged that Scipio did not even maintain the appearance of a commander. His appearance, they alleged, was un-soldierly and un-Roman. He wore a Greek cloak and sandals and strolled about in the gymnasium, giving attention to Greek books and physical exercise. And with the same indolence and self-indulgence his army stationed in Sicily was enjoying the charms of Syracuse.

Livy, *History of Rome*, 29.19.11–13 [ca. 25 BCE][11]

Cato did not [desire to get an embassy of eloquent Greek philosophers out of Rome as quickly as possible] because of personal hatred of [the Greek] Carneades, as some people think, but rather because he was opposed to the study of philosophy in principle, and because his patriotic zeal made him contemptuous of Greek culture and Greek education.[12] . . . And in his attempt to turn his son away from Greek culture, he made a statement which I think was ridiculously rash for an old man: he announced with the solemnity of a prophet that if Rome should ever become infected with Greek literature, it would lose its empire. . . . But Cato's aversion to the Greeks was not confined to philosophers: he was also greatly apprehensive of Greek physicians residing in Rome. He knew of Hippocrates' famous reply, when he was summoned to attend the Persian King for an enormous fee, and stated that he would never give his services to barbarians who were enemies of the Greeks. Cato asserted that all Greek physicians had taken an oath along these lines, and exhorted his son to distrust them.

Plutarch, *Life of Cato the Elder*, 23.1–5 [ca. 115 CE]

It was necessary for me to shed light on that branch of wisdom comprised by philosophy in a work in the Latin language; it is true that philosophy can be learned from the Greek writers and teachers, but I have always been certain that our countrymen have demonstrated more wisdom everywhere than the Greeks, either in making their own discoveries or in improving what they have received from Greece – at least in those subjects they have deemed worthy of their efforts.

Cicero, *Tusculan Disputations*, 1.1 [45 BCE]

But in Greece every state is run by irresponsible seated assemblies. Not to consider this later Greece, stirred up and troubled by its own making, let us consider the older Greece, once so renowned for its resources, its power, its glory, but ruined because of this defect alone – the unwarranted freedom and irresponsibility of its assemblies. Untested men, ignorant and inexperienced, participated in the assemblies and then undertook useless wars, then they put turbulent men in charge of the state, and then they banished the most worthy of the citizens. But if such things happened in Athens when that state was preeminent, not only in Greece but in almost the whole world, what chance was there of responsible action in assemblies in Phrygia or in Mysia?

Cicero, *In Defense of Flaccus*, 7.16–17 [59 BCE]

And now I shall speak of a people dear to the hearts of the rich, and one which I avoid like a plague; and I am not reluctant to say it. I cannot tolerate Romans, a Rome of Greeks. And yet what a large part of our dregs comes from Greece! The Syrian Orontes has for a long time now poured into the Tiber, bringing with it its language and its manners; its flutes and its slanted harp strings; bringing also the tambourines of that breed, and the pimps who ply their trade at the Circus.

Juvenal, *Satires*, 3.58–65 [ca. 120 CE]

Provocation and resistance to Roman power

Words cannot express, gentlemen, how bitterly foreign nations hate us because of the wanton and outrageous conduct of the men whom we recently have sent to govern them. For in those countries what temple do you suppose has been held sacred by our officers, what state inviolable, what home sufficiently guarded by its closed doors? Why, they look about for rich and flourishing cities that they may find an occasion of a war against them to satisfy their lust for plunder.

Cicero, *On the Manilian Law*, 22.65–6 [66 BCE]

M'. Acilius Glabrio and the Aetolians (191 BCE)

[Phaineas] interrupted the Roman commander, "We have not handed ourselves over to slavery, but rather we have entrusted ourselves to your good faith, and I am certain that you are acting out of ignorance in giving us these orders which are contrary to Greek custom." The consul answered, "And I do not care very much, by Hercules, what the Aetolians think is the proper custom of the Greeks, since I, in the Roman way, am issuing an order to men who have just now surrendered by their own resolution and who have been conquered by force; therefore, if my command is not immediately obeyed I shall at once order you to be thrown into chains."

Livy, *History of Rome*, 36.28.4–6 [ca. 25 BCE]

C. Popillius Laenas and King Antiochus IV of Syria (168 BCE)

Caius Popillius Laenas, the Roman general, when Antiochus greeted him from a distance and then held out his hand, gave to the king, as he had it with him, the copy of the senatorial decree, and said he should read it first, not thinking it right, I think, to show any conventional signs of friendship before he knew Antiochus' intentions, friendly or hostile. But after the king read it and said he would like to discuss it with his aides, Popillius acted in a way thought to be offensive and exceedingly arrogant.

He had a stick with him cut from a vine, and he drew with it a circle around Antiochus and said he must stay inside this circle until he gave an answer. The king was astonished at this imperious behavior, but after hesitating for a few moments, he said he would carry out Rome's will.

Polybius, Histories, 29.27.1–6 [ca. 150 BCE]

When this report reached Cirta [112 BCE], the Italians, on whose courage the town's defense depended, were certain that in the event of surrender they would be spared because of the prestige of Rome. Therefore they advised Adherbal to give himself and the town over to Jugurtha, demanding only that his life should be spared and the rest left to the Roman Senate. But Adherbal, even though he thought that nothing could be worse than trusting Jugurtha, yet since the Italians were in a position of strength and could compel him if he opposed them, surrendered on the terms they had recommended. Then Jugurtha first tortured Adherbal to death and then made a wholesale slaughter of all the adult Numidians and the [Roman and Italian] traders whom he found bearing arms.

Sallust, Jugurthine War, 26.1–3 [ca. 40 BCE]

Mithridates VI against Rome

Mithridates VI King of Pontus was Rome's most persistent and dangerous enemy in the first century BCE. In the First Mithridatic War (89–85 BCE), Mithridates invaded Asia and massacred some 80,000 Roman and Italian businessmen, with great support in the Greek world (Athens went over to the king). He remained a bitter enemy of Rome until his death in 63 BCE. The following passage describes his treatment of a Roman commander, and reflects the level of hostility against Rome in the ancient Mediterranean world.

Shortly thereafter [Mithridates] captured Manius Aquillius [88 BCE], who was the foremost agitator for this embassy and this war. Mithridates led him around tied to an ass, and proclaimed himself Manius to everyone who saw him. Finally, at Pergamum, Mithridates poured molten gold down his throat as a rebuke against Roman avarice. After setting up governors over the various regions he went on to Magnesia, Ephesus, and Mitylene, all of which received him warmly. The people of Ephesus even went so far as to overthrow Roman statues which had been erected in their city – for which they paid the price not long afterwards.[13]

Appian, Mithridatic Wars, 21 [ca. 160 CE]

Don't you realize that the Romans turned eastward militarily only after the ocean had blocked their westward advance? That since the beginning they have possessed nothing that they have not stolen: home, wives, lands, empire? Once wanderers without a homeland, without parents, the scourge of the entire world, no laws, human or divine, keep them from seizing and destroying their friends and allies, those who are near and those who are far, weak or strong, and from thinking that every government which does not serve them, especially monarchy, is their enemy.... The Romans have weapons against all, the sharpest where victory yields the greatest booty; it is by their audacity, by deceit, and by fighting war after war that they have grown great.

Sallust, *Letter of Mithridates*, 17–21 [ca. 40 BCE]

Gallic opposition to Roman power

Caesar's siege of Alesia in 52 BCE broke Gallic resistance. The speech of the tribal leader Critognatus urges the natives to resist to the bitter end; and the following excerpt warns of Roman motivations.

But the Romans – what else is it that they want or covet than to follow where their envy leads them, to settle down in lands and states whose men they have learned have noble reputations and martial spirit, and to cast these into everlasting slavery? This is the way they have waged their wars. And if you are ignorant of what is going on in distant lands, look now at Gaul which is close by, which has been reduced to a province, with a complete change of rights and laws, and crushed beneath the Roman axes in perpetual servitude.

Caesar, *Gallic War*, 7.77 [ca. 50 BCE]

Rome and the Jewish nation

Judaea was reduced to subjection by Pompey the Great in 63 BCE; and later the governor of the province of Syria, A. Gabinius, reorganized it into five districts. Under Herod the Great (73–4 BCE), the Jewish state was a loyal client kingdom of Rome, and after the banishment in 6 CE of Herod's successor, Arcelaus, it became a Roman province. After 70 CE Vespasian put Judaea under the direction of an imperial legate, with a permanent legion-garrison. The Jewish people enjoyed favored status with Rome; but their culture and traditions were never fully understood by the Roman authorities, and disturbances were common. Particularly provocative were the emperor Gaius' (37–41 CE) mandate that the Jews of Alexandria be forced to eat pork, and the emperor's Hadrian's (117–138 CE) ban on circumcision. Several serious revolts against Roman rule occurred (66–73, 115–18, 131–5 CE). Roman actions regarding the Jews and their attitudes to them were inconsistent, as the following selections attest.[14]

Judas chose Eupolemos son of John son of Accos, and Jason son of Eleazer, and sent them to Rome to establish friendship and alliance, and to free themselves of the yoke, for they saw that the kingdom of the Greeks was enslaving Israel completely. They went to Rome, a very long journey; and they entered the Senate chamber and spoke as follows: "Judas, who is also called Maccabeus, and his brothers and the people of the Jews have sent us to you to establish an alliance and peace with you, so that we may be enrolled as your allies and friends." The proposal pleased them, and this is a copy of the letter that they wrote in reply, on bronze tablets, and sent to Jerusalem to remain with them there as a memorial of peace and alliance: "May all go well with the Romans and with the nation of the Jews on sea and on land forever, and may sword and enemy be far from them. If war comes first to Rome or to any of their allies in all their dominion, the nation of the Jews shall act as their allies wholeheartedly, as the occasion may indicate to them. To the enemy that makes war they shall not give or supply grain, arms, money, or ships, just as Rome has decided; and they shall keep their obligations without receiving any in return. In the same way, if war comes first to the nation of the Jews, the Romans shall act willingly as their allies, as the occasion may indicate to them. . . ."

1 Maccabees 8.17–27 [after mid-second century BCE]

Augustus knew that much of the city of Rome on the Tiber's farther side was inhabited by Jews. Many were freedmen who now had become Roman citizens. They had been brought to Italy as captives and then freed by their owners. They were not forced to violate their national traditions. Augustus knew that they have places for their religious worship and that they meet together in these places, especially on the holy sabbaths, when they come together to learn their ancestral philosophy. He also knew that they take first-fruit collection to raise money for religious uses, and that they send this money to Jerusalem with people who offer the sacrifices. However, he did not banish them from Rome or strip them of their Roman citizenship just because they took pains to preserve their identities as Jews. He did not compel them to abandon their places of worship, or forbid them to gather or receive instruction in the laws, or oppose their first-fruit collections. He respected our interests so piously that with the support of nearly his whole household he adorned our temple through the magnificence of his dedications, and he ordered that forever more whole burnt offerings should be sacrificed every day as a tribute at his own expense to the most high God. And these sacrifices are carried out to the present day and will continue forever more as a reminder of the truly imperial. In regard to the monthly grain doles, when everyone receives his share of money or grain, Augustus never deprived the Jews of this charity. In fact, if the distributions happened to occur on the holy sabbath, when no Jew is allowed to receive or to give anything or to do any regular business at all, particularly financial business, he ordered the officials in charge of the distribution to set aside until the next day the portion of the welfare which belonged to the Jews.

Philo of Alexandria, Embassy to Gaius, 155–8 [ca. 40 CE]

There was also discussion [19 CE] about suppressing the Egyptian and Jewish rites, and a senatorial decree instructed that 4,000 descendants of enfranchised slaves who were infected with that superstition and who were suitable in terms of age, were to be sent to Sardinia and there used to suppress brigandage: "if they were to die because of the pestilential climate, it would be a cheap loss." The rest were ordered to leave Italy, unless they should give up their profane rites by a certain date.

Tacitus, Annals, 2.85 [ca. 115 CE]

Tiberius the emperor suppressed foreign cults, such as the Egyptian and Jewish religions, by compelling those who believed in such superstitions to burn their religious vestments and all their holy objects. Using required military service as an excuse, he assigned young Jews to provinces with harsher climates. Other men of that same race . . . he banished from the city.

Suetonius, Tiberius, 36.1–2 [early second century CE]

Claudius' letter to Alexandria (41 CE)

The Emperor Tiberius Claudius Caesar Augustus Germanicus, pontifex maximus*, holder of the tribunician power, consul* designate, to the city of Alexandria, greeting. . . . As for which party was responsible for the riot and feud (or rather, if the truth must be told, the war) with the Jews, even though your ambassadors, especially Dionysius son of Theo, put your case with great zeal in the face of opposition, nevertheless I was not willing to make a detailed investigation, although I have an undying resentment for those who renewed the strife; and I tell you for the last time that unless you cease from this ruinous and stubborn hatred for each other, I shall be forced to reveal what a benevolent emperor can be when driven to a righteous indignation. And so once again I demand, on the one hand, that the Alexandrians be forebearing and kindly to the Jews, who have lived in the same city for many years, and dishonor none of their religious rites but allow them to keep their customs as in the time of the deified Augustus, which customs I too have affirmed, after hearing both parties. And, on the other hand, I order the Jews in no uncertain terms not to agitate for more privileges than they possessed in the past, and not to send out a separate embassy in the future as if they live in a separate city – unprecedented! – and not to force their way into the gymnastic or cosmetic games,[15] while enjoying their own privileges and the great advantages of a city not their own, and not to bring in or admit Jews from Syria or those who sail from Egypt, a proceeding which will force me to entertain serious suspicions; otherwise I shall proceed against them as agitators of what is a general plague of the whole world.[16]

British Museum papyrus, no. 1912 [41 CE]

Another disturbance occurred at Caesarea [59/60 CE]. The Jews who formed part of the population there were in conflict with Syrians. The Jews claimed that they owned the city, since King Herod, its founder, had been a Jew. The other party recognized that it was a Jew who had sent settlers there, but they maintained that the city belonged to the Greeks all the same, as he would not have put up statues and temples in the city if he had intended it for the Jews. These were the arguments on the two sides; their strife escalated into armed violence, and every day the more reckless of the two sides would rush out to fight, since the Jewish elders were unable to check their own partisans, while the Greeks thought it disgraceful to be overpowered by Jews. Although the Jews had wealth and numerical superiority, the troops supported the Greeks; the greater part of the Roman force there had been recruited in Syria and were prepared to lend aid as kinsmen of the Greeks.

Josephus, Jewish War, 2.266–8 [ca. 75 CE]

At whose house did you have your dinner of vinegar and beans? What shoemaker shared with you his leeks and the lips of a boiled sheep? You won't answer? Speak or I'll kick you. In what Jew's prayer house can I find you?

Juvenal, Satires, 3.292–6 [ca. 120 CE]

Problems in Judaea

Pilate, who had been sent as a procurator to Judaea by Tiberius, brought effigies of Caesar, called standards, under cover during the night into Jerusalem [26 CE]. This action, when daylight came, aroused the Jews to fever pitch; those present were bewildered, thinking that their laws had been trampled underfoot, since their laws disallow any image to be put up in the city; while the townspeople's outrage stirred the countryfolk, who came together in crowds. The Jews rushed after Pilate in Caesarea, begging him to remove the effigies from Jerusalem and to respect the laws of their ancestors. When Pilate refused, they fell prostrate around his home and remained like that motionless for five entire days and nights. On the next day Pilate sat down on his tribunal in the great stadium and summoned the multitude. While he appeared to be ready to answer their request, he gave an arranged signal to his troops to surround the Jews. The Jews now found themselves in a ring of soldiers, three men deep, and they were dumbstruck at the unexpected sight. Pilate threatened to cut them down if they refused to admit Caesar's images, and he signalled the soldiers to draw their swords.

Josephus, *Jewish War*, 2.169–74 [ca. 75 CE]

The Jews saw that war was now fast approaching the capital, and they abandoned the feast and ran to arms. With great confidence in their numerical strength, they ran out in disorder and entered combat with loud cries, not thinking about the seventh day of rest, for it was the sabbath itself which they regarded with a special reverence. But the same zeal which made them ignore their piety also brought them victory in battle [66 CE].

Josephus, *Jewish War*, 2.517–19 [ca. 75 CE]

Most people firmly believed that their ancient holy scriptures contained the prophecy that this was the very time when the East would grow strong and the men starting out from Judaea would take over the world. This mysterious prophecy in reality indicated Vespasian and Titus, but the common people, as is the way of human desire, interpreted these great prophecies in their own interest and could not be dissuaded even in adversity.

Tacitus, *Histories*, 5.13 [ca. 110 CE]

Rabbi Judah and Rabbi Jose and Rabbi Simeon were once sitting in conversation, and Judah, son of proselytes, was with them. Rabbi Judah began, saying: "The accomplishments of this nation [Rome] are so excellent. They have set up market places, they have constructed bridges, they have built baths." Rabbi Jose was silent. Rabbi Simeon ben Yohai said in reply: "All that they have instituted has been done for their own needs. They have instituted market places for their harlots; baths for their own pleasures; bridges to collect tolls."

Babylonian Talmud, *Sabbath* 33b [ca. 135 CE]

A wild lion ate its prey and a bone got stuck in its throat. He declared: "I shall reward the one who pulls the bone out!" An Egyptian heron stuck its beak in, pulled out the bone and demanded its reward. "Go," said the lion, "Boast that you have been in the lion's jaws and survived." So we too should be content that we survived the jaws of Rome.

Joshua ben Hananiah, *Genesis Rabbah* LXIV 10 [late first–early second century CE]

Hatred of Rome

The following excerpt from the speech of the otherwise unknown Briton chieftain Calgacus is placed in Tacitus' account before the climactic battle of the Mons Graupius campaign of 84 CE, which extended Roman power to the Scottish highlands. The speech reflects well-worn themes of the Roman rhetorical schools, and may tell us more about what Romans of the late first century CE were saying about themselves, than it does about the genuine words of Calgacus.

Former battles, which were fought with varying success against Rome, left behind them hopes of help in us, because we, the noblest souls in all Britain, the dwellers in its inner shrine, had never seen any shores of slavery and had preserved our very eyes from the desecration and the contamination of tyranny; here at the world's end, on its last inch of liberty, we have lived unmolested to this day, defended by our remoteness and obscurity. Now the uttermost parts of Britain lie exposed, and the unknown is ever magnified. But there are no other tribes to come; nothing but sea and cliffs and these more deadly Romans, whose arrogance you cannot escape by obedience and self-restraint. Robbers of the world, now that earth fails their all-devastating hands, they probe even the sea: if their enemies have wealth, they have greed; if he be poor, they are ambitious; East nor West has glutted them; alone of mankind they covet with the same passion want as much as wealth. To plunder, butcher, steal, these things they misname empire: they make a desolation and they call it peace.

Tacitus, *Agricola*, 30 [98 CE]

Near at hand is the end of the world, and the last day and judgment of immortal God for such as are both called and chosen. First of all inexorable wrath shall fall on Rome; a time of blood and wretched life shall come. Woe, woe to thee, O land of Italy, great, barbarous nation.

With images of gold and silver and stone be ready, that unto the bitter day ye may come, thy first punishment, O Rome even a gnashing anguish to behold. And no more under slavish yoke to thee will either Greek or Syrian put his neck, barbarian or any other nation, thou shalt be plundered and shalt be destroyed for what thou didst, and wailing aloud in fear thou shalt give until thou shalt repay.

Sibylline Oracles, 8.91–5, 121–9
[end second century CE; trans. M. S. Terry (1890)[17]]

EDITOR'S NOTES

1   Translation from *Rome and the Greek East to the Death of Augustus*, ed. R. K. Sherk (Cambridge, 1984), no. 48, pp. 51–2.

2 On the problematic term "Romanization," see G. Woolf, *Becoming Roman: The Origins of Provincial Administration in Gaul* (Cambridge, 1998), pp. 1–23; J. C. Barrett, "Romanization: A Critical Comment," in *Dialogues in Roman Imperialism: Power, Discourse, and Discrepant Experience in the Roman Empire*, ed. D. J. Mattingly and S. E. Alcock (Portsmouth, 1997), pp. 51–64.

3 For translated text of the famous tablet from Lugdunum, preserving substantial portions of Claudius' speech, see *The Government of the Roman Empire: A Sourcebook*, ed. B. Levick, 2nd edn. (London and New York, 2000), no. 164, pp. 178–82.

4 For full text, translation, and commentary on this municipal law, see J. Gonzales, "The *Lex Irnitana*: A New Copy of the Flavian Municipal Law," *Journal of Roman Studies*, 76 (1986), pp. 147–243.

5 Gallia Narbonensis, founded ca. 121 BCE. For the origins of the province, see C. Ebel, *Transalpine Gaul: The Emergence of a Roman Province* (Leiden, 1976).

6 On the imperial cult of the Roman emperors and Romanization, see the definitive study of S. R. F. Price, *Rituals and Power: The Roman Imperial Cult in Asia Minor* (Cambridge, 1984). For recent discussion and translated sources on Roman religion, see M. Beard, J. North, and S. Price, *Religions of Rome*, 2 vols. (Cambridge, 1998).

7 The college referred to here is probably a priestly college of the god Mars.

8 For full text, translation, and commentary on this municipal law, see Gonzales, "*Lex Irnitana*."

9 See A. Wardman, *Rome's Debt to Greece* (New York, 1976); J. P. V. D. Balsdon, *Romans and Aliens* (Chapel Hill, NC, 1979), pp. 30–58; E. S. Gruen, *Studies in Greek Culture and Roman Diplomacy* (Berkeley, 1990); *idem, Culture and National Identity in Republican Rome* (Ithaca, NY, 1992).

10 For an excellent study of politically motivated ancient Greek constructions of ethnicity, see J. M. Hall, *Ethnic Identity in Greek Antiquity* (Cambridge, 1997); and now *idem, Hellenicity: Between Ethnicity and Culture* (Chicago, 2002).

11 For the political context, see E. S. Gruen, "The 'Fall' of the Scipios," in *Leaders and Masses in the Roman World: Studies in Honor of Zvi Yavetz*, ed. I. Malkin and Z. W. Rubinsohn (Leiden, New York and Cologne, 1995), pp. 59–90.

12 The Roman suppression of the cult of Bacchus-Dionysus in 186 BCE (Livy 39.8–18) is perhaps the most notorious Roman action against a Greek cultural practice; on this see E. S. Gruen, "The Bacchanalian Affair," in *Studies in Greek Culture*, pp. 34–78. For other Roman attempts to suppress Greek writings and expel Greek intellectuals from Rome, see Livy 25.1.6–12 (213 BCE); Livy 40.29.2–14 (181 BCE); Athenaeus 12.547a (173 BCE); Aulus Gellius 15.11.1 (161 BCE).

13 For another case of the Ephesians showing public discontent with Roman rule, see Philostratus, *Life of Apollonius*, 7.5.

14 See P. Schäfer, *Judeophobia: Attitudes towards the Jews in the Ancient World* (Cambridge, Mass., 1997).

15 Compare the gladiatorial games as a force for Romanization; see the provocative study of A. Futtrell, *Blood in the Arena: The Spectacle of Roman Power* (Austin, Tex., 1997).

16 For the Jews' relationship to Hellenistic Greece and Greek culture, see E. J. Bickerman, *The Jews in the Greek Age* (Cambridge, Mass., 1988); E. S. Gruen, *Heritage and Hellenism: The Reinvention of Jewish Tradition* (Berkeley, 1998).

17 This translation is reproduced from N. Lewis and M. Reinhold, eds., *Roman Civilization: The Empire*, vol. 2, 3rd edn. (New York, 1990), p. 336; see also vol. 1: (*The Republic and the Augustan Age*), pp. 403–9.

5

The Frontier: Imperial Strategy and Defense of Empire

Introduction

The study of the Roman frontier has been burgeoning in recent years. E. N. Luttwak's seminal study of the "Grand Strategy" of the Roman Empire (1976), has stimulated much of this scholarly activity. Reprinted here is the introduction to Luttwak's influential book. He argued that there were three distinct periods in Roman imperial defense: (1) the Julio-Claudian system, in which the frontier was more or less stabilized (Claudius' invasion of Britain in 43 CE and Nero's Parthian War of 55–66 CE being exceptions), and client kingdoms (e.g., Galatia, Thrace, Pontus, Armenia, Mauretania) served Rome's interests as buffer states; (2) from the Flavians to the Severans (68 CE to roughly the end of the second century), "scientific" frontiers were developed, and the Empire invested resources in preclusive defense of static borders; (3) the third century witnessed the abandonment of a stable perimeter defense in favor of a system of "defense-in-depth": self-contained strongholds and mobile forces in the field combined to intercept penetration by invading forces, the depth of whose penetration was contained within reasonable limits. At present most Roman historians would argue that Luttwak's book is inaccurate in some details and much too schematic, but all would agree on the tremendous influence it has had – hence its inclusion here. Luttwak wrote: "The firm subordination of tactical priorities, martial ideals, and warlike instincts to political goals was the essential condition of the strategic success of the empire. With rare exceptions, the misuse of force in pursuit of purely tactical goals, or for the psychic rewards of purposeless victories, was avoided by those who controlled the destinies of Rome."

Isaac opposes such notions, and he represents one of the strongest objections to Luttwak's idea of a "Grand Strategy" of the Roman empire. He questions whether the Romans could have had a clear idea of which boundaries would guarantee the security of the Empire, and he contests Luttwak's general thesis that there was any such thing as a "Grand Strategy" of empire. Secure boundaries, according to Isaac, were not a primary concern of the Romans in their frontier policy. Borders, even natural boundaries such as rivers, were to a large degree lines of communication rather than lines of defense. So we should not view veteran colonies in frontier regions as outposts defending the Empire against barbarian onslaughts, but rather as settlements which served to consolidate conquest and subjugation. Safety and security were largely the responsibility of those living in towns and cities near the frontier, rather than that of the Roman imperial army. Roman military activity in the frontier zones was often idiosyncratic, unsystematic, and opportunistic. Just like Roman republican generals before them, the Roman emperors under the Principate were driven by the desire for military glory. Isaac observes: "Decisions were taken by ad-hoc groups: the emperor and his entourage. There was no professional officer class which could persuade or dissuade the emperor to go to war for 'professional' military or economic reasons." Consequently, many of the emperors' military actions defy rational analysis from a strategic perspective, and for Isaac the entire notion of elaborate Roman imperial defensive systems is an anachronistic chimera of modern scholarship. In the excerpt reprinted here, the author considers Roman decisions to go to war, emphasizing their aggressive and haphazard nature, the martial, often irrational, ambitions of Roman emperors, the social and economic advantages to the rank-and-file of belligerence in the frontier zones, and the profitability of annexation to both Roman soldiers and resident Roman citizens.

The Grand Strategy of the Roman Empire

E. N. Luttwak

In our own disordered times, it is natural to look back for comfort and instruction to the experience of Roman imperial statecraft. No analogies are possible in the economic, social, or political spheres of life, but in the realm of strategy there are instructive similarities. The fundamentals of Roman strategy in the imperial age were rooted not in a technology now obsolete, but in a predicament that we share. For the Romans, as for ourselves, the two essential requirements of an evolving civilization were a sound material base and adequate security. For the Romans, as for ourselves, the elusive goal of strategic statecraft was to provide security for the civilization without prejudicing the vitality of its economic base and without compromising the stability of an evolving political order. The historic success of the Roman Empire, manifest in its unique endurance, reflected the high degree to which these conflicting imperatives were reconciled. It was certainly not battlefield achievements alone that ensured for so long the tranquillity of vast territories, lands which have been in turmoil ever since.

Had the strength of the Roman Empire derived from a tactical superiority on the battlefield, from superior generalship, or from a more advanced weapons technology, there would be little to explain, though much to describe. But this was not so. Roman tactics were almost invariably sound but not distinctly superior, and the Roman soldier of the imperial period was not noted for his *élan*. He was not a warrior intent on proving his manhood but a long-service professional pursuing a career; his goal and reward was not a hero's death but a severance grant upon retirement. Roman weapons, far from being universally more advanced, were frequently inferior to those used by the enemies whom the empire defeated with such great regularity. Nor could the secular survival of the empire have been ensured by a fortunate succession of great feats of generalship: the Roman army had a multitude of competent soldiers and some great generals, but its strength derived from method, not from fortuitous talent.[i]

The superiority of the empire, and it was vast, was of an altogether more subtle order: it derived from the whole complex of ideas and traditions that informed the organization of Roman military force and harnessed the armed power of the empire to political purpose. The firm subordination of tactical priorities, martial ideals, and warlike instincts to political goals was the essential condition of the strategic success of the empire. With rare exceptions, the misuse of force in pursuit of purely tactical goals, or for the psychic rewards of purposeless victories, was avoided by those who controlled the destinies of Rome. In the imperial period at least, military force was clearly recognized for what it is, an essentially limited instrument of power, costly and brittle. Much better to *conserve* force and use military power indirectly, as the instrument of political warfare.

Together with money and a manipulative diplomacy, forces visibly ready to fight but held back from battle could serve to contrive disunity among those who might jointly threaten the empire, to deter those who would otherwise attack, and to control lands and peoples by intimidation – ideally to the point where sufficient security or even an effective domination could be achieved without any use of force at all. Having learned in the earlier republican period how to defeat neighbors in battle by sheer tactical strength, having later mastered the strategic complexities of large-scale warfare in fighting the Carthaginians, the Romans finally learned that the most desirable use of military power was not military at all, but political; and indeed they conquered the entire Hellenistic world with few battles and much coercive diplomacy.

The same effort to conserve force was also evident in war, at the tactical level. The ideal Roman general was not a figure in the heroic style, leading his troops in reckless charge to victory or death. He would rather advance in a slow and carefully prepared march, building supply roads behind him and fortified camps each night in order to avoid the unpredictable risks of rapid maneuver. He preferred to let the enemy retreat into fortified positions rather than accept the inevitable losses of open warfare, and would wait to starve out the enemy in a prolonged siege rather than suffer great casualties in taking the fortifications by storm. Overcoming the spirit of a culture still infused with Greek martial ideals (that most reckless of men, Alexander the Great, was actually an object of worship in many Roman households), the great generals of Rome were noted for their extreme caution.[ii]

It is precisely this aspect of Roman tactics (in addition to the heavy reliance on engineering warfare) that explains the relentless quality of Roman armies on the move, as well as their peculiar resilience in adversity: the Romans won their victories slowly, but they were very hard to defeat.

Just as the Romans had apparently no need of a Clausewitz[iii] to subject their military energies to the discipline of political goals, it seems that they had no need of modern analytical techniques either. Innocent of the new science of "systems analysis," the Romans nevertheless designed and built large and complex security systems that successfully integrated troop deployments, fixed defenses, road networks, and signaling links in a coherent whole. In the more abstract spheres of strategy it is evident that, whether by intellect or traditional intuition, the Romans understood all the subtleties of deterrence, and also its limitations. Above all, the Romans clearly realized that the dominant dimension of power was not physical but psychological – the product of others' perceptions of Roman strength rather than the use of this strength. And this realization alone can explain the sophistication of Roman strategy at its best.

The siege of Masada in A.D. 70–3 reveals the exceedingly subtle workings of a long-range security policy based on deterrence. Faced with the resistance of a few hundred Jews on a mountain in the Judean desert, a place of no strategic or economic importance, the Romans could have insulated the rebels by posting a few hundred men to guard them. Based at the nearby springs of Ein Gedi, a contingent of Roman cavalry could have waited patiently for the Jews to exhaust their water supply. Alternatively, the Romans could have stormed the mountain fortress. The Jewish War had essentially been won, and only Masada was still holding out; but this spark of resistance might rekindle at any time the fire of revolt. The slopes of Masada are steep, and the Jews were formidable fighters, but with several thousand men pressing from all sides the defenders could not have held back the attackers for long, though they could have killed many.

The Romans did none of these things. They did not starve out the Jews and they did not storm the mountain. Instead, at a time when the entire Roman army had a total of only twenty-nine legions to garrison the entire empire, one legion was deployed to besiege Masada, there to reduce the fortress by great works of engineering, including a huge ramp reaching the full height of the mountain. This was a vast and seemingly irrational commitment of scarce military manpower – or was it? The entire three-year operation, and the very insignificance of its objective, must have made an ominous impression on all those in the East who might otherwise have been tempted to contemplate revolt: the lesson of Masada was that the Romans would pursue rebellion even to mountain tops in remote deserts to destroy its last vestiges, regardless of cost. And as if to ensure that the message was duly heard, and duly remembered, Josephus was installed in Rome where he wrote a detailed account of the siege, which was published in Greek, the acquired language of Josephus, and that of the Roman East.

The suggestion that the Masada operation was a calculated act of psychological warfare is of course conjecture. But the alternative explanation is incredible, for a mere blind obstinacy in pursuing the siege would be utterly inconsistent with all that we know of the protagonists, especially Vespasian – that most practical of men, the emperor whose chief virtue was a shrewd common sense.

We need not rely upon conjecture to reconstruct in considerable detail the basic features of Roman imperial statecraft from the first century A.D. to the third, the subject of this enquiry. The narrative sources, indispensable to an understanding of the detailed conduct of policy and its motives, are sadly incomplete and sometimes suspect. But the labors of generations of scholars have yielded a mass of detailed evidence on the physical elements of imperial strategy: the force-structure of the army, the design of border defenses, and the layout of individual fortifications. At the same time, enough is known of the salient moments and general nature of Roman diplomacy to form a coherent picture of imperial statecraft as a whole, both the hardware and the software.

Three distinct systems of imperial security can be identified over the period. We may properly speak of *systems*, for they each integrated diplomacy, military forces, road networks, and fortifications to serve a single objective. Moreover, the design of each element reflected the logic of the whole. Each system was intended to satisfy a distinct set of priorities, themselves the reflection of changing conceptions of empire: hegemonic expansionism for the first system; territorial security for the second; and finally, in diminished circumstances, sheer survival for the imperial power itself. Each system was based on a different combination of diplomacy, direct force, and fixed infrastructures, and each entailed different operational methods; but, more fundamentally, each system reflected a different Roman world-view and self-image.

With brutal simplicity, it might be said that with the first system the Romans of the republic conquered much to serve the interests of the few, those living in the city – and in fact still fewer, those best placed to control policy. During the first century A.D. Roman ideas evolved toward a much broader and altogether more benevolent conception of empire. Under the aegis of the second system, men born in lands far from Rome could call themselves Romans and have their claim fully allowed; and the frontiers were efficiently defended to defend the growing prosperity of all, and not merely the privileged. The result was the empire of the second century A.D., which served the interests of millions rather than thousands.

Under the third system, organized in the wake of the great crisis of the third century, the provision of security became an increasingly heavy charge on society, a charge unevenly distributed, which could enrich the wealthy and ruin the poor. The machinery of empire now became increasingly self-serving, with its tax-collectors, administrators, and soldiers of much greater use to one another than to society at large. Even then the empire retained the loyalties of many, for the alternative was chaos. When this ceased to be so, when organized barbarian states capable of providing a measure of security began to emerge in lands that had once been Roman, then the last system of imperial security lost its last support, men's fear of the unknown.

EDITOR'S NOTES

i   There is little evidence that Roman weapons were "frequently inferior to those used by the enemies whom the empire defeated." Indeed, already in the mid-second century BCE the Greek historian Polybius reports that Roman military equipment was superior to that of the Gauls whom Rome faced in the 220s (*Histories*, 2.30.7–8), and he states that both in terms of tactics and equipment the Romans were superior to the Carthaginian forces at the climactic battle at Zama in 202, which ended the Hannibalic War (*Histories*, 15.15.7–16.1).

ii   On Alexander as model for emulation, see A. Stewart, *Faces of Power: Images of Alexander and Hellenistic Politics* (Berkeley: University of California Press, 1993).

iii   Carl von Clausewitz was a Prussian general in the Napoleonic War era whose work *On War* has had a profound impact on modern military strategy. He viewed war as a means of achieving political objectives rather than as an end in itself.

The Limits of Empire: The Roman Army in the East

B. Isaac

Luttwak has described Roman strategy in a systematic manner. He assumes that there was a coherent system built up with an inner logic and that it is possible to describe the coherence and the dynamics of this system. We can admire his lucid analysis of the material, accept many of his insights, and appreciate his systematic approach, but we must still ask whether the system analysed did in fact exist. If we do ask this question, it is thanks to Luttwak's own admirable synthesis. However, his central assumption, that there existed a system whose object was to defend and enhance the security of the empire, is a hypothesis based on analogies with modern army organization. It is not based on an independent analysis of the ancient literary sources or the archaeological material, but derives from a lucid perusal of modern literature, and naturally the result is an approach already implicit in the writings of most specialists on Roman frontiers. The hypothesis suffers from a disadvantage familiar in the study of history: it cannot be proved or disproved by objective means. What we can do, however, is to test the basic assumptions which underly the hypothesis by referring to ancient sources and archaeological material. [Here] it is argued that the results of such a test do not bear out the validity of the hypothesis as it stands.

DECISION-MAKING AND WAR AIMS

It may be asked whether Roman decision-making at the highest level did indeed follow an unconscious inner logic and consistency. The words of an acute observer, speaking of the Second World War, are relevant:

> In fact, it was rare for policy to be clearly thought out, though some romantics or worshippers of 'great men' liked to think so. Usually it built itself from a thousand small arrangements, ideas, compromises, bits of give and take. There was not much which was decisively changed by a human will. Just as a plan for a military campaign does not spring fully-grown from some master general; it arises from a sort of Brownian movement of colonels and majors and captains, and the most the general can do is rationalize it afterwards.[1]

Even today, it is clear, we cannot be certain how often politicians and generals are capable of realizing in practice a well-considered strategy which looks sound in theory. There are now nearly 300 Institutes of Strategic Studies in more than 50 countries, more than 95% of them having been founded within the past two decades. Future students will have to consider what influence these will have had on the course of history.[2] As already noted, the Romans did not even rationalize their actions afterwards.

Even where there is copious information it is hard to determine the aims of even one side, let alone both, in going to war. The stated cause of a war may be merely a convenient excuse. The aims any side professes may not be the real ones. When we are faced with ancient literary sources it is often difficult even to determine whether the aims on record were merely spread by rumour among the upper class, or officially declared. Aims may change in the course of a war, being adapted according to results. Initial modest aims may be replaced by ambitious ones as a result of a successful campaign. Aims may be reinvented in the light of the outcome of a war;[3] this is particularly relevant to our enquiry if it results from a failure of plans for expansion. It would be idle to pretend that we possess sufficient information on many Roman wars to dissect such complicated processes.

In dealing with the principate the following pattern occurs again and again: tribe T. is said to have carried out raids on Roman territory (did they really?). The emperor decides to go to war. He is said to have defeated tribe T. Tribe T. is then incorporated into the empire or not. For information on the initial aims and on the motives for later actions we depend on literary sources, often of doubtful quality. It is very hard to know whether the said raids were more or less serious than we are told, whether the emperor really intended to defend the province or was glad of an excuse to show his mettle, whether he hoped to expand the empire and did so or not, or whether annexation was an afterthought. All this may seem obvious, but these realities are often ignored in discussions of specific wars. It is particularly noticeable that modern historians find it easy to ignore literary sources when these state that a war of conquest was initiated by Rome out of sheer ambition on the part of the emperor. It is then often assumed that it cannot have been as simple as that. However, when the sources state that the emperor marched to the frontier because of the threat posed by tribe T. no such doubts are entertained.[i]

Random factors often decided the objects of Roman wars. Every student of Roman history is familiar with the stories told by Roman historians of wars launched by ambitious generals during the principate, the campaigns of Germanicus in Germany, those of Corbulo in Lower Germany.[4] The location of the war was determined by the area of command of such leaders; and if the war was not pursued further this was because the emperor did not permit it. On the other hand, Pompey and Caesar and many republican generals before them did go on, because there was no one to stop them.[ii] The mere fact that there existed a *lex Iulia* which forbade a governor to start an unauthorized war shows that this was, in fact, common practice. The first encounter with the Teutones resulted from an unprovoked attack by the Romans – and it took place beyond the Alps, another example of Roman disregard for the alleged defensive value of natural obstacles.[5]

This is not a book about Roman imperialism in general, or in the East in particular, but the subject clearly must be touched upon in any discussion of frontier policy. Roman imperialism in Republican Rome is a controversial subject, and so is the imperialism of the principate. For the present discussion it will suffice to indicate a number of elementary differences between the earlier and the later period which affect the issue.

Decisions regarding war and peace were, under the principate, made by the emperor, whose power rested on the support of the standing army, precisely the body which was directly affected when a decision was taken to fight.[6] The civilian population of the empire or of the capital would usually not gain much from such enterprises; but they did not vote for their emperor. Those who hold that wars were often fought to defend the frontier provinces will argue that the population in those areas benefited from enhanced security. Yet it is certain that, at any rate in the first instance, they suffered rather than profited from the passing of armies and the court through their territory. Pliny's correspondence with Trajan shows how much small towns suffered from the passing of travellers even in peacetime. Byzantium, which was a major station for crowds of soldiers on the march, received some support. Smaller frontier towns had to cope by themselves as best they could.[7] Elsewhere Pliny compares the passing of Trajan through the provinces (best case) with that of Domitian (worst):

> Vehicles were requisitioned without chaos, there was no fastidiousness regarding lodgings, food-supplies were the same for all. Your court was strictly organized and obedient . . . How different was the recent journey of another emperor! If it was a journey rather than a devastation, when billeting meant expulsion, and right and left everything was burnt and trampled as if another power or the very barbarians whom he fled had invaded.[8]

Dio's complaint regarding the cost of supplies to the army in the time of Caracalla shows that even senators considered such events a burden.[9]

On the other hand, it is clear that a successful war of expansion was profitable to all participating soldiers.[iii] The acquisition of booty in this period has not, as far as I know, been treated systematically, but there is no lack of sources to indicate that winning a war was lucrative.[10] It was a commonplace that 'in war it is the stronger man who loots'.[11] Following the capture of Jerusalem by Titus 'all troops were so loaded with plunder that in Syria the price of gold was depreciated to half its previous standard'.[12] Titus called up those who had been especially brave and 'placed crowns of gold upon their heads, presented them with golden neck-chains, little golden spears, and standards made of silver, and promoted each man to a higher rank; he further assigned to them out of the spoils silver and gold and raiments and other booty in abundance'.[13] It is no coincidence, of course, that these passages derive from the fullest account available of a military victory under the principate. The well-known career inscription of C. Velius Rufus, who was decorated in the Jewish war, is a clear illustration of the manner in which able men could obtain rapid promotion during and after a war.[14] There is more, however. Tacitus emphasizes the importance of booty in the speeches which he attributes to commanders before a battle. Corbulo 'exhorted his soldiers to secure both glory and spoil'.[15] And indeed, after the battle, the adult men were massacred, 'the civilian population was sold by auction, the rest of the booty fell to the conquerors'.[16] Suetonius, before the decisive battle against Boudicca, similarly spoke of glory and booty.[17] Effortless glory and slaughter (of men, women, and animals) without Roman losses were the happy outcome of the battle. In fact, after a victory licence to kill without inhibition seems to have been part of the prerogatives of Roman soldiers, as of other armies in the ancient and less ancient world.[18] The result is measured in the numbers killed rather than strategic gain.[19] Severus' army was allowed to plunder Ctesiphon and its surroundings at liberty.[20] Dio, critical of this campaign, says Severus did not accomplish anything else, as if plundering the place had been the only purpose of the expedition.[21] It can be argued, of course, that ravaging enemy territory and destroying his economic base is in itself an efficient strategy since he will then not easily be able to carry on the war, but Dio clearly did not think that this was Severus' aim, or if it was, that it was a sensible thing to do.[22] Herodian gives a similar description of Caracalla's Persian campaign.[23] Both Dio and Herodian describe this as an expedition undertaken on a feeble pretext, without provocation.[24] The troops marched through Parthia till they were tired of looting and killing and then returned to the Roman province. Both Dio and Herodian consider it a useless war. Ammianus attributes to Julian the statement that the desire for booty often tempted the Roman soldier.[25] Libanius, Julian's friend, describes how he envisaged Julian's progress in his Persian campaign, assuming all went well: 'ravaging the countryside, pillaging villages, taking forts, crossing rivers, mining walls, occupying cities... the army had exulted in the slaughter of the Persians'.[26]

The suppression of internal unrest too could be profitable. Caracalla allowed his troops to plunder Alexandria in 215 and gave them a donative as well.[27] The army received a donative before as well as after Severus Alexander's Persian campaign.[28] Apart from the booty they took home, valorous soldiers were promoted after a war. This was common practice and is known from literary and epigraphic sources.[29]

A successful war was the best opportunity for soldiers and officers in the imperial army to improve their material and social status without cost to the empire. A letter allegedly written by Aurelian with suggestions how the soldiers are to be kept under control advises: 'let them earn a living from the booty taken from the enemy and not from the tears of the provincials'.[30] Aurelian is praised because he 'commanded the army, restored the frontier districts, gave booty to the soldiers, enriched Thrace with captured cattle, horses, and slaves'.[31] Whether this is the author's fancy or not, it clearly reflects his ideas of a sound ruler. In 360 Constantius gave up the siege of Bezabde very reluctantly because 'he was going back without results while, as it were, the door of a rich house was open before him'.[32] The language of Ammianus is clear enough, and so is his description of the preparations for the next campaign: 'recruits were enrolled throughout the provinces, every order and profession was troubled, furnishing clothes, arms, artillery, even gold and silver, great quantities of provision and various kinds of pack animals'.[33]

Dio levels an interesting accusation against Caracalla: in his desire to spend money on the soldiers he constantly demanded gold crowns from the civilian population on the pretext that he had defeated some enemies.[34] The importance of financial gain or losses was an enduring feature in Roman policy-making and did not diminish in the Byzantine period, as can be seen from the weight attached to the payments made for the garrison in the Darial pass in the fifth and sixth centuries.

The soldiers, on the other hand, did not profit so much from a state of peace: since their length of service was fixed, unlike that of soldiers under the republic, they did not obtain early discharge in peacetime.[35] The troops, it may be concluded, had many practical reasons to welcome a decision to fight. The existence of the standing army as a major factor in Roman politics may well have increased the political will to wage wars of conquest.[36] This tendency was reinforced by the circumstance that military glory would have enhanced the reputation of an emperor and strengthened his ties with the troops.[37]

This is not to suggest that these were simple processes. There was no powerful 'officer class' in Rome, and no centralized army command. If there was a stimulus to initiate wars on the part of the provincial army this would have reached the emperor only through the legionary commanders, provincial governors, and ex-governors. No emperor could rule if there was concerted action to depose him, but the army had no institutionalized means of exerting pressure on political decision-making as in modern military dictatorships. The absence of a class of higher career-officers with permanent commissions, the colonels who, in our times, not only organize military coups but exert constant influence on politics in their countries, made it impossible for the army to interfere in politics in this manner. The centurions, who held permanent appointments, did not have the social status required and those who did, senators and *equites*, did not have permanent appointments. We know a good deal about the mechanism which provided Roman troops with the means to depose and impose emperors of their choice.[38] It cannot be said, however, that the army, as a body, put up emperors. Ambitious military leaders used the troops placed at their disposal to depose rivals and impose their friends or themselves on the empire. Rebellions were organized by commanders, not by the rank and file. There is hardly any evidence of influence being exerted by the army when there was no crisis.[39] It is clear, however, that any emperor was conscious of his dependence on the army. To strengthen his position among the soldiers was indeed imperative if only to avoid a crisis. A ruler enjoyed due respect among soldiers and significant parts of the upper classes only if he was known, among other things, as an experienced and effective warrior. At the same time the army was always a potential threat to the ruling class.

The annexation of new territory was profitable also if it could be achieved without war. It will suffice to refer to the results of the annexations of Cappadocia and of Commagene[40] or to Tacitus' description of the causes of the revolt of Boudicca.[41] While the governor was fighting in Wales the prosperous kingdom of the Iceni was being annexed following the death of its king. 'The kingdom was plundered by centurions, the royal house by (the procurator's) slaves as if they had been captured in war', an expression which merely indicates that this was the usual treatment of peoples conquered in war. The distinguished Iceni were stripped of their ancestral possessions. The Trinobantes, previously incorporated, joined the revolt out of resentment over the veteran colony Camulodunum, founded on expropriated lands. Tacitus, outspoken in these matters, says: 'plunder, slaughter and rapine, the Romans falsely call it empire; they make a desolation and call it peace.'[42]

Annexation remained profitable after the early stages. Aelius Gallus' Arabian expedition was, according to Strabo, undertaken for reasons of long-term profitability.[43] When Trajan reached the Red Sea in his Mesopotamian campaign customs duties were immediately imposed. That was intended to be an enduring source of income. Annexation further afforded a greater possibility of direct interference, as in the giving of support to local Roman citizens. As Strabo heard from a friend who had visited Petra, there lived there 'many Romans and many other foreigners, and he saw that the foreigners were often involved in lawsuits with each other and with the natives, but the natives never prosecuted each other, but they kept absolute peace with each other'.[44] In Caesar's *Bellum Civile* we find as a sort of standard phrase a reference to 'all the people of Antioch and residing Roman merchants'.[45] Antioch had been part of a Roman province for only fifteen years by that time. It is obvious that the imposition of Roman law will have been advantageous to the Roman citizens. Cicero's *Pro Fonteio*, delivered some time after 70 BC, is an obvious case. The province of Gaul was so full of Roman traders that no business could be transacted without the interference of a Roman citizen, no money changed without it being recorded in Roman books.[46] Fonteius was accused of extortion by Gauls, and various groups of Roman citizens resident in the province served as witnesses for the defence. Cicero advised the jury not to accept the testimony of barbarians against that of loyal Roman citizens.

Information on the presence of Roman citizens in such areas is incidental, but the hatred their presence engendered comes out particularly well in the descriptions of the massacres that accompanied rebellions against Roman rule. Best-known are the thousands of Roman citizens who were killed in the province of Asia in 88 BC, evidence both of the numbers involved and the enmity bred by their presence.[47] When the Illyrians revolted in AD 6 'Roman citizens were overwhelmed, traders massacred, and a large number of veterans still serving with the colours in a region far from the commander were exterminated'.[48] The revolt of the Treveri in 21 began with a massacre of Roman business men.[49]

The two groups of Romans, then, that profited from a war of conquest and subsequent annexation were the military and the Romans resident among the subject population. However, that is not to suggest that wars of conquest were primarily undertaken in the interest of these classes or that they had a decisive influence on the process of decision-making at the imperial court in the principate or the later empire. They happened to be the instruments of conquest and annexation and gained by it, but there is no indication at all that they played an active role in politics any more than the subjects in the frontier provinces. Unless we choose to ignore centuries of Roman historiography and literature, the decision to engage in a war of conquest was determined by the imperial will and not by pressures from definable groups with interests at stake.[50] Like generals of all times a Roman emperor could not wage war successfully if the fighting spirit of the troops was broken – as Dio describes that of Severus' army before Hatra.[51] However, the decision to fight was taken by the emperor alone, with the help of advice from those he chose to trust.[52]

These might belong to almost any class: his family, senators, *equites*, freedmen, or worse – in the eyes of noblemen – jugglers and actors. Those advising the emperor were not selected, and did not act, as representatives of specific interest groups.[53] The imperial advisers are sometimes referred to as a group: Dio usually speaks of a collective 'we', and sometimes they are singled out as powerful individuals. Their social class is considered important. A good emperor listens to well-educated senators, a bad one to boorish upstarts. It is not clear, however, that attitudes and ideologies favouring or opposing expansion can be linked to specific social groups. There were, in other words, no permanent 'lobbies' with the ability and the desire to further particular causes at court. Ancient sources frequently describe the emperor as consulting his friends on matters concerning war and peace.[54] Good emperors are described as having good friends.[55] Sometimes it is even stated as rather exceptional that an emperor would consult particular friends because of their expert knowledge regarding the issue involved.[56]

There is never any suggestion that friends were selected as representing a specific ideology. Character, class, and virtue, or the absence of those qualities, are the features described as decisive by ancient authors. Conflict between imperial advisers is invariably about matters of immediate personal interest: influence and wealth, not policy and the affairs of state. The emperor normally did take advice from his friends on important issues, but he was free to ignore it, as Dio tells of Caracalla from personal experience.[57] Dio must have experienced the same under Septimius Severus, for he found the two major campaigns of this emperor useless and even harmful projects. Commodus was criticized for the opposite reason: he decided not to pursue the war in the north, against the counsel of his father's senatorial advisers.[58] Again, Caracalla spent far more money on the army than his mother and advisers found desirable, and Dio complains that his own class no less than wealthy individuals or communities suffered heavy losses. This was a policy which hurt the immediate, personal interests of the emperor's friends.

These are important points in determining the motives which persuaded an emperor to go to war.... Severus merely pretended, according to Dio, that he conquered Mesopotamia for the benefit of the province of Syria. His real motive was the personal desire to obtain military glory.[59] Similarly, Caracalla went to war with Parthia because of his preoccupation with Alexander, again according to Dio who knew him well.[60] Glory, honour, and particularly an identification with generals of the past were a real factor in determining the choice between war and peace. 'Corbulo considered it due to the grandeur of the Roman people to reconquer what once had been captured by Lucullus and Pompey.'[61] 'It is praiseworthy for a private house to retain its own, for a king to fight for another's property.'[62] In Rome there did not exist an established group with political influence and a vested interest in the preservation of peace, the protection of frontier zones, and the avoidance of military adventurism. The only objection to wars of expansion which an emperor was likely to encounter would have been raised by individuals who considered them a waste of money.

NOTES

1   C. P. Snow, *The Light and the Dark*, ch. 34. [J. B.] Campbell, [*The Emperor and the Roman Army* (Oxford, 1984)], ch. 9 and especially p. 393, argues that the emperor in matters of war and peace, foreign policy, the annexation of territory, and the organization and use of the army would in practice consult his advisers and confidants, who were drawn mainly from the upper classes. That may be conceded without admitting that it was a form of decision-making that led to a restrained use of the army.

2   'The Fog of War Studies', *The Economist*, 16–22 April 1988, 72.

3   See B. Lewis, *History, Remembered, Recovered, Invented* (1975).

4   Tacitus, *Ann.* xi 18–20.

5   For the *lex Iulia*, Cicero, *in Pisonem*, 21.50; for the encounter with the Teutones, Appian, *Celt.* 13; both references taken from P. Brunt, *Historia* 10 (1961), 192.

6   The subject of Campbell, *The Emperor and the Roman Army.*

7   *Ep.* x 77f. As Campbell, 250f, points out, Trajan naturally assumes that most of the travellers who caused trouble were soldiers. For the position of Byzantium on the route of armies on the march see also Tacitus, *Ann.* xii 62. On the passing of armies through Asia Minor, S. Mitchell, *AFRBA*, 131–50.

8   *Pan.* 20. 3–4.
9   lxxvii 9. 3; 5–7 (382f). Cf. Rostovtzeff, *Roman Empire*, 358ff, 424ff.
10 For brief remarks, V. A. Maxfield, *The Military Decorations of the Roman Army* (1981), 58f; for Caesar's Gallic war, L. Keppie, *The Making of the Roman Army* (1984), 100f. G. R. Watson, *The Roman Soldier* (1969), 108–14, lists the donatives paid by emperors to the troops on their accession and on special occasions to gain their loyalty. He seems to imply that no payments were made after campaigns. Campbell does not discuss booty.
11 Tacitus, *Agricola* 14.
12 Josephus, *BJ* vi 6.1 (317).
13 *BJ* vii 1.3 (14f), trans. Thackeray, Loeb.
14 *IGLS* vi 2796, cf. D. Kennedy, *Britannia* 14 (1983), 183–96.
15 *Ann.* xiii 39: 'hortatur milites ut . . . gloriaeque pariter et praedae consulerent.'
16 Ibid.: 'et imbelle vulgus sub corona venundatum, reliqua praeda victoribus cessit.'
17 Tacitus, *Ann.* xiv 36.4.
18 Josephus, *passim.*
19 *Ann.* xiv 37: 'clara et antiquis victoriis par ea die laus parta.' It was merely a decisive engagement in a costly and harmful rebellion.
20 Dio lxxvi 9.4 (347); Herodian iii 9.10f; SHA, *Severus* xvi 5.6. Here the permission to plunder and keep the booty is called 'an enormous donative'.
21 See also SHA, *Sev.* 16.5: '. . . donativum militibus largissimum dedit, concessa omni praeda oppidi Parthici, quod milites quaerebant.'
22 On the practice of destroying enemy crops in Greek warfare, G. B. Grundy, *Thucydides and the History of his Age²* (1948), chs. ix and x. Grundy argues that, for social and economic, as well as military reasons, the Greek wars, fought by citizen armies consisting of hoplites, had to be short, sharp, and decisive encounters. The aim was to destroy the other party's crops and to return in time for the harvest. The aims of the Roman imperial army were, of course, dictated by different considerations and needs.
23 iv 11.7f.
24 Dio lxxviii 1; Herodian iv 9.10: Caracalla desired the title 'Parthicus' and an eastern victory.
25 xxiii 5.21.
26 *Or.* i 132. For the same spirit cf. the fanciful description in SHA, *Claudius* 8.6; 9.6.
27 Dio lxxvii 23 (401).
28 Herodian vi 4.1 (before the campaign); 6.4 (after).
29 Maxfield, [*Military Decorations*], 236–40, with numerous examples.
30 SHA, *Aurelian* 7.5: 'de praeda hostis, non de lacrimis provincialium victum habent.'
31 Ibid. 10.2: '. . . exercitum duceret, limites restitueret, praedam militibus daret, Thracias bubus, equis, mancipiis captivis locupletaret . . . '
32 Ammianus xx 11.31: 'quod velut patefacta ianua divitis domus, irritus propositi reverteretur.'
33 xxi 6.6.
34 Dio lxxvii 9.1. Note, by contrast, SHA, *Marcus Antoninus* 17, praising Marcus Aurelius because he financed the Marcomannic war by selling imperial property instead of taxation. After a profitable war he bought everything back.
35 B. Dobson, 'The Roman Army: Wartime or Peacetime Army?', *Heer und Integrationspolitik: Die römischen Militärdiplome als Historische Quelle*, ed. W. Eck and H. Wolff (1986), 10–25.
36 Campbell, ch. 9, rejects this possibility in his treatment of the role played by the army in politics. An example, chosen at random, is the mutiny against Severus Alexander in protest against his policy to trade peace with the Germans in exchange for gold, rather than

marching out to fight them: Herodian vi 78. 9–10, and cf. SHA, *Alexander* 63. 5–6, *Maximini* 7. 5–7.

37 On imperial honours, Campbell, [*Emperor and the Roman Army*], 120–56.

38 Ibid., ch. 9.

39 The regular demands by the troops for salary rises and donatives did not in themselves constitute influence on politics in any other sphere than their own material position.

40 After the annexation of Cappadocia taxes were reduced: Tacitus, *Ann.* ii 42. 6.

41 *Ann.* xiv 31.

42 *Agricola* 30. 6, attributed to a Caledonian chieftain.

43 xvi 4. 22 (780).

44 xvi 4.21 (779).

45 *BC* iii 102: '…omnium Antiochensium civiumque Romanorum, qui illic negotiaren-tur…'

46 *Pro Fonteio* I. I: 'referta Gallia negotiatorum est, plena civium Romanorum. Nemo Gallorum sine cive Romano quidquam negotii gerit; nummus in Gallia nullus sine civium Romanorum tabulis commovetur.'

47 For Roman citizens in the provinces under the republic, [W. V.] Harris, [*War and Imperialism in Republican Rome, 327–70* BC (Oxford, 1979)], 95–102.

48 Velleius ii 110.6.

49 Tacitus, *Ann.* iii 42.1; *Ann.* ii 62.4 describes the presence of such *negotiatores* even among the Marcomanni.

50 See F. Millar, *The Emperor in the Roman World* (1977), ch. 3, 'Entourage, Assistants and Advisers'.

51 lxxv 12.

52 See in general J. Crook, *Consilium Principis* (1955); Millar, ch. 3, 'Entourage, Assistants and Advisers'.

53 Millar, [*Emperor*], 113.

54 e.g. Tacitus, *Ann.* xi 19; xii 20.

55 Suetonius, *Titus* vii 2; and, with the usual reservations: SHA, *Marcus Antoninus* 22.3; *Severus Alexander* 66.

56 Dio lvii 17. 9; SHA, *Severus Alexander* 16.3.

57 lxxviii 11.5; 18.2–4.

58 Dio lxxii 1–2.

59 See also SHA, *Severus* 15: 'Erat sane in sermone vulgari Parthicum bellum adfectare Septimium Severum, gloriae cupiditate non aliqua necessitate deductum.'

60 lxxvii 7–8.

61 Tacitus, *Ann.* xiii 34.4: 'et Corbulo dignum magnitudine populi Romani rebatur parta olim a Lucullo Pompeioque recipere.'

62 *Ann.* xv 1.5: '…et sua retinere privatae domus, de alienis certare regiam laudem esse.'

EDITOR'S NOTES

i   For the Republic, cf. J. Rich, *Declaring War in the Roman Republic in the Period of Transmarine Expansion* (Brussels, 1976).

ii On the autonomy of Roman generals in the Middle Republican period, see A. M. Eckstein, *Senate and General: Individual Decision-Making and Roman Foreign Relations, 264–194* BC (Berkeley and Los Angeles, 1987).

iii For the distribution of war booty under the Republic, see I. Shatzman, "The Roman
     General's Authority over Booty," *Historia*, 21 (1972), pp. 177–205; for Roman sacking of
     cities, see A. Ziolkowski, "*Urbs direpta*, or How the Romans Sacked Cities," in *War
     and Society in the Roman World*, ed. J. Rich and G. Shipley (London and New York,
     1993), pp. 69–91.

Sources

The frontier and expansionist ambitions

[Caesar Augustus] will extend his power beyond the Garamants and Indians, over
far territories north and south of the zodiacal stars, the solar way, where Atlas,
heaven-bearing, on his shoulder turns the night-sphere, studded with burning
stars.

> Vergil, *Aeneid*, 6.794–797 (trans. R. Fitzgerald) [ca. 20 BCE][1]

I extended the boundaries of all the provinces of the Roman people bordered by
nations not subject to our empire. I pacified the provinces of the Gauls, the Spains, as
well as Germany, throughout the region that is bordered by the ocean from Gades to
the mouth of the Elbe River. I pacified the Alps, from that region which is nearest the
Adriatic Sea as far as the Tuscan Sea, without bringing war to any people contrary to
justice. My fleet sailed through the ocean from the mouth of the Rhine eastwards to
the land of the Cimbri, a place to which no Roman had gone before either by land or
by sea, and through their ambassadors the Cimbri, Charydes, and Semnones, and
other Germanic peoples of that region sought my friendship and that of the Roman
people. On my orders and under my auspices two armies were led almost simultaneously into Ethiopia and into Arabia, which is called the "Blessed," and vast forces of
both peoples were slaughtered in battle, and a great many towns captured. Ethiopia
was penetrated as far as Nabata, next to Meroë, in Arabia, the army advanced into the
territory of the Sabaeans to the town of Mariba. I added Egypt to the empire of the
Roman people. I could have made Greater Armenia into a province after its king
Artaxes was killed, but I preferred ... to hand over that kingdom ... to Tigranes ... I
recovered all the provinces extending east beyond the Adriatic, as well as Cyrene,
most of them then ruled by kings, and earlier I recovered Sicily and Sardinia, which
had been seized in the slave war.

> Augustus, *Accomplishments of the Deified Augustus*, 26–7 [ca. 14 CE][2]

The Roman frontier was of diverse geographical features. In some areas these features made the protection of Roman
territory relatively easy: the western extrem-
ity of the Empire was bounded by ocean;
the African frontier was desert, though nomadic raiders sporadically presented security problems. Clearly the most high-level
security concerns, reflected in the concen-
tration of the legions in these areas, lay to
the north, where Germanic tribesmen
posed a constant threat, and to the east,

where Roman power met strong kingdoms, these two troublesome segments of the first Arsacid Parthia, and later Sassanid Roman frontier. Persia. The following selections highlight

The northern frontier

Germanic enemies

If it should happen that the community where they are born is tranquil with long years of peace and quiet, many of the noble youth voluntarily go to those tribes which are engaged in war. This is because peace is unwelcome to these people, and they distinguish themselves more readily among dangers. Besides, a great retinue cannot be maintained except by war and violence.

Tacitus, *Germania*, 14 [98 CE]

The Cimbric/Teutonic invasions (104 BCE)

The first reports of the Cimbri and Teutones' numbers and strength were incredible; later it seemed that they were less than the truth. Three hundred thousand armed men were marching, and much greater numbers of women and children were said to be marching with them. They were seeking land to support their vast hordes and cities in which to settle and live, just as they had heard the Gauls did, when they seized the best lands from the Etruscans*, which they still occupied. Who these people were and where they came from to fall on Gaul and Italy like a thunder cloud was anybody's guess, since they had no contact with southern peoples and had already travelled a long way. They most likely were German tribes, whose territory extends to the northern ocean. This idea is supported by their great size, the light blue color of their eyes, and the fact that the German word for plunderers is 'Cimbri'.

Plutarch, *Life of Marius*, 11.2–6 [ca. 115 CE]

A portion of the army camp was on a gentle slope; part of it was approached from level ground. Augustus had believed that these winter quarters could keep the Germanies in check and indeed in subjection, and never thought of such a disaster as to have the Germans actually attack our legions. Therefore nothing had been done to add to the strength of the position or of the fortifications; the armed forces seemed sufficient.

Tacitus, *Histories*, 4.23 [ca. 110 CE]

Quinctilius Varus and the loss of three legions in Germany (9 CE)

I will set forth the details of this terrible calamity, the most serious the Romans had suffered since Crassus' disaster in Parthia [53 BCE], in my larger work, as others have done. Here I can only grieve for the disaster as a whole. An army unparalleled in bravery, the first of the Roman armies in discipline, energy, and experience in the field of battle, was surrounded through its general's neglect, the enemy's treachery, and fortune's unkindness.... Entrapped by forests, marshes, and ambuscades, the army was annihilated almost to a man by the same enemy whom it had been accustomed to slaughter like cattle, whose life or death had depended entirely on the wrath or pity of the Roman people.

Velleius Paterculus, Roman Histories, 2.119 [ca. 30 CE]

[Augustus] endured two serious and disgraceful defeats, both in Germany: those of Lollius and Varus. The first [17 BCE] was more humiliating than serious, but the second was almost fatal, since three legions were massacred with their general, lieutenants, and all the auxiliaries. When he received this news, Augustus posted night watches throughout the city to prevent further disturbances, and he prolonged the terms of governors of provinces so that the allies might remain loyal because of the presence of experienced men whom they knew. Also, as was the case in the Cimbric and Marsic wars, he vowed games to Jupiter Optimus Maximus if the state's fortunes should improve. In fact, it is said that he was so distraught that for months he refused to cut his beard or hair and would dash his head against the door, crying: "Quinctilius Varus, give me back my legions!" And he observed the day of the disaster each year as one of sorrow and mourning.

Suetonius, Life of Augustus, 22 [early second century CE][3]

Trajan's Dacian campaigns (102/3, 105–6 CE)

The Dacian tribes were situated in the lower Danube region in the Transylvanian plateau. They grew in power and inflicted defeats on Roman armies in the late first century CE. Domitian (81–96 CE) campaigned against Dacia (85–6, 88–9 CE) and recognized Decebalus as a client king of the Romans. The emperor Trajan (98–117 CE) effected the conquest of the realm. The following excerpt from Cassius Dio relays Decebalus' surrender to Trajan.

Decebalus' envoys laid down their arms upon being brought into the Senate. They clasped their hands in the manner of war captives and spoke words as suppliants. In this way they received peace and won back their arms. Trajan celebrated a triumph* and received the title of Dacicus.

Cassius Dio, Roman History, 68.10.1–2 [ca. 205 CE]

The eastern frontier

Pompey's third triumph (September 61 BCE)

His triumph had such a magnitude that, although it was distributed over two days, still the time would not suffice, but much of what had been prepared could not find a place in the spectacle, enough to dignify and adorn another triumphal procession. Inscriptions borne in advance of the procession indicated the nations over which he triumphed. These were: Pontus, Armenia, Cappadocia, Paphlagonia, Media, Colchis,

Iberia, Albania, Syria, Cilicia, Mesopotamia, Phoenicia and Palestine, Judaea, Arabia, and all the power of the pirates by sea and land which had been overthrown. Among these peoples no less than 1,000 strongholds had been captured, according to the inscriptions, and cities not much under 900 in number, besides 800 piratical ships, while 39 cities had been founded. . . . But that which most enhanced his glory and had never been the lot of any Roman before, was that he celebrated his third triumph over the third continent. For others before him had celebrated three triumphs; but he celebrated his first over Libya, his second over Europe, and this his last over Asia, so that he seemed in a way to have included the whole world in his three triumphs.

Plutarch, Life of Pompey the Great, 45.1–5 [ca. 115 CE]

Crassus' disaster at Carrhae (53 BCE)

Crassus was killed by a Parthian named Exathres, although some say that it was a Parthian of another name who killed and decapitated him, cutting off his right hand as he lay on the ground. There is, however, no certain knowledge of this. Some of the Romans present were killed fighting around Crassus; the rest retreated to the hill. The Parthians approached them and told them Crassus had suffered the fate he deserved, but Surena ordered the rest of them to come down from the hill and to have no fear. Some of them then surrendered; others fled in different directions during the night and only a very few of these reached safety. Most were hunted down and killed by Arabs. In the whole campaign it is believed that some 20,000 were killed and 10,000 taken prisoner.

Plutarch, Life of Crassus, 31.6–8 [ca. 115 CE]

Julius Caesar's plans to extend the eastern frontier

Caesar now [44 BCE] . . . planned a lengthy campaign against the Getae and the Parthians. He first planned to attack the Getae, a hardy and warlike people who were neighbors to the Parthians. The Parthians were to be punished for their treachery against Crassus. As an advance force, Caesar sent across the Adriatic 16 infantry legions and 10,000 cavalry.

Appian, Civil Wars, 2.110 [ca. 160 CE]

The Armenian plateau as a 'buffer zone'

From earliest times this country has had an ambiguous national character and geographical situation, since a large extent of its frontier lies adjacent to our own provinces, and it stretches inland to Media. As a result the Armenians are situated between two vast empires, and since they detest Rome and are envious of Parthia, they are too often in turmoil.

Tacitus, Annals, 2.56 [ca. 115 CE]

Parthian subservience and Parthian ambitions

Although the Parthians share a common border with the Romans and are a powerful nation, they have yet so far yielded to the superiority of the Romans and the rulers of our day that they have sent trophies to Rome once set up as memorials of their victory over the Romans. Moreover, Phraates has entrusted his children and grandchildren to Augustus Caesar, and in this slavish manner has secured Caesar's friendship through giving hostages. The Parthians have often turned to Rome in the selection of their king, and even now they are prepared to put their entire authority into Roman hands.

Strabo, *Geography*, 6.4.2 (C 288) [ca. 15 BCE]

In the consulship of Gaius Cestius and Marcus Servilius [35 CE], Parthian noblemen came to Rome without the knowledge of the king Artabanus. Artabanus, loyal to Rome and gentle to his subjects as long as he had Germanicus to fear, soon became arrogant towards us and cruel to his countrymen. He was puffed up by campaigns successfully prosecuted against surrounding nations; he held Tiberius in contempt as a man no longer fit for arms because of his advanced age; and he lusted after Armenia. . . . At the same time he talked in bold and menacing ways about the old boundaries of the Persian and Macedonian empires, and about his intention of taking the territories that Cyrus first held and after him Alexander.

Tacitus, *Annals*, 6.31 [ca. 115 CE]

Trajan's eastern campaign (116–17 CE)

Trajan, who after Augustus set the strength of the Roman state in motion, recovered Armenia from the Persians, took the crown of Armenia Major and appropriated its kingdom. He gave the Albanians a king. He took the Iberians, Bosporans, and Colchians into the trust of Roman control. He occupied the lands of the Osrhoenians and Arabs. He captured the Cardueni and the Marcomedes. He took control of Athemusia, the fairest region of Persis. Seleucia, Ctesiphon, and Babylonia he took and held. He advanced up to the border of India, in Alexander's footsteps. He established a fleet in the Red Sea [Persian Gulf]. He made provinces out of Armenia, Mesopotamia, and Assyria which, situated between the Tigris and Euphrates, are full of well-watered streams like Egypt.

Festus, *Compendium of the Deeds of the Roman People*, 20 [ca. 370 CE]

Trajan planned to divert the Euphrates River through a canal into the Tigris so that he might take his boats along this route and make a bridge of them. But when he learned that this river has a much higher elevation than the Tigris, he refrained from this plan, as he was afraid that the river might rush down in a flood and make the Euphrates unnavigable. So he dragged his boats with hauling-machines across the very narrow space that separates the two rivers. . . . then he crossed the Tigris and entered Ctesiphon. When he had occupied this place he was saluted as imperator* and established his right to the title of Parthicus. The Senate granted him permission to celebrate as many triumphs as he wished, in addition to other honors.

Cassius Dio, *Roman History*, 68.28.1–3 [ca. 205 CE]

The threat of Sassanian Persia (354 CE)

With the situation being thus in Isauria, the Persian king [Sapor] embroiled in local wars, was driving off extremely wild tribes from his frontiers. These tribes are of inconsistent policy: they sometimes make raids upon [Sapor's] territory, and sometimes they aid him in conflicts with us. Nohodares, one of his grandees, received a command to invade Mesopotamia whenever the situation seemed favorable, and he was carefully reconnoitering our territory, planning on a sudden incursion when he found the opportunity. And since all the districts of Mesopotamia, exposed as they are to frontier raids, were protected with frontier-posts and country garrisons, Nohodares turned to the left, attacked the most remote parts of Osrhoëne, and attempted a novel and nearly unprecedented move. If he had succeeded, he would have devastated the whole region like a thunderbolt.

Ammianus Marcellinus, *Histories*, 14.3.1–2 [ca. 390 CE]

There was no marked frontier. The subjects of both peoples did not fear one another and did not suspect an attack, but they intermarried and had joint markets. Whenever the king of either empire commands generals to march against the others they always find the neighboring peoples unguarded. This is because their lands, while being close to each other, are densely populated and yet there was no fort on either side from olden times.

Procopius, *On Buildings*, 3.3.9–14 [ca. 555 CE]

Excerpts from a Byzantine–Persian treaty (562 CE)

The Persians will not allow the Huns, Alani, or other barbarians to pass through the Caspian Gates and invade Roman territory. The Romans will not invade Persian territory. The Saracen allies of both parties are bound by treaty and may not attack the other state. Merchants must import their goods through traditionally appointed toll stations. Ambassadors and envoys of both parties on official journeys are entitled to use public highways in both states and their possessions may not be taxed. Saracen and other barbarian merchants are not allowed to use unknown and little used routes, but must pass through Nisibis and Dara and with formal permission only. If they trespass they will do so under pain of punishment. Wartime refugees and deserters may return to their own state unharmed. Henceforth neither state will accept and admit refugees or emigrants. Neither state will fortify installations near the border. Clients or allies and their territory are not to be attacked.

Menander Protector, *Fragments of the Greek Historians*, ed. Müller [ca. 600 CE][4]

The African frontier[5]

The prefect of Egypt extends Roman frontiers (29 BCE)

Gaius Cornelius Gallus, son of Gnaeus, Roman knight, first prefect of Alexandria and Egypt after the overthrow of the kings by Caesar, son of a god – having been victorious in two battles in the 15 days within which he suppressed the revolt of the Thebaid, capturing five cities – Boresis, Coptus, Ceramice, Diospolis Magna, and Ophiëum – and seizing the leaders of these revolts; having led his army beyond the Nile cataract, a region into which arms had not previously been carried either by the

Roman people or by the kings of Egypt; having subjugated the Thebaid, the common terror of all the kings; and having given audience at Philae to envoys of the king of the Ethiopians, received that king under [Roman] protection, and installed a prince over the Triacontaschoenus, a district of Ethiopia – dedicated this thank offering to his ancestral gods and to the Nile his helpmate.

Corpus Inscriptionum Latinarum, vol. 3, 14.147 (5) [29 BCE][6]

Now Egypt is a Roman province which not only pays a sizable tribute, but also is governed by upright men – the prefects who are sent there from time to time. The man who is sent has the rank of a king, and the administrator of justice is subordinate to him. He has supreme authority over most law suits. Another is the official called the *idiologos*, who looks into all properties without owners which ought to fall to Caesar. Caesar's freedmen attend these, as do stewards, who are entrusted with fairly important affairs. In addition there are three legions, one in the city [Alexandria] and the others in the country. There are also nine Roman cohorts – three in the city, three on the borders of Ethiopia in Syene, as a guard for that region, and three around the remainder of the country. And too there are three cavalry contingents, which are assigned to various critical points.

Strabo, *Geography*, 17.1.12 (C 797) [ca. 15 BCE]

Britain[7]

Claudius' invasion of Britain (43 CE)

To Tiberius Claudius Caesar, son of Drusus, Augustus Germanicus, pontifex maximus[*], holding the tribunician power for the eleventh year, consul[*] five times, acclaimed imperator[*] ..., father of his country, the Roman Senate and people [dedicated this] because he received the surrender of eleven kings of Britain conquered without any defeat and because he was the first to reduce to sovereignty of the Roman people barbarian tribes across the ocean.

Corpus Inscriptionum Latinarum, vol. 6, 920 [51–2 CE]

It is well known that Gaius Caesar [Caligula] was stirred by the idea of invading Britain; but his unhinged mind was swift in retracting; and his grand plans against Germany had failed. The divine Claudius was the author of this great endeavor: legions and auxiliary troops were transported across the Channel, and Vespasian was made a partner in the task – this was his step towards the fame that would soon be his: tribes were subdued, kings captured, and Vespasian was revealed by the fates.

Tacitus, *Agricola*, 13.3 [ca. 98 CE]

[Claudius] in addition enlarged the pomerium[*], in accordance with an ancient custom, by which the expansion of the Empire brings the right to extend the city's boundaries. Yet this right had been exercised by no Roman commander except for L. Sulla and the deified Augustus, even after the subjugation of powerful nations.

Tacitus, *Annals*, 12.23 [ca. 115 CE]

Hadrian's British policy

Son of all the [deified (emperors) Imperator Caesar] Traianus Hadr[ianus Augustus] when the necessity of securing the empire [within its borders] had been forced on him by divine instruction, consul for the second (or third) time . . . having routed [the barbarians and recovered] the province of Britain, he added [a fortified boundary line between] each ocean's shore for 80 miles. The army of the province [built this defensive wall] under the care of [Aulus Platorius Nepos, legate of Augustus with propraetorian power].

Corpus Inscriptionum Latinarum, vol. 7, 498 [117 or 118 CE]

A consolidated empire and stable frontiers

Nor does the younger Africanus [P. Cornelius Scipio Aemilianus Africanus Numantinus, ca. 185–129 BCE] let us keep silent about him. When as censor he was winding up the census and in the sacrifice of suovetaurilia* the scribe was reciting before him from the public tables the formula of prayer in which the immortal gods were asked to make the state of the Roman people better and greater, "It is good and great enough," said Scipio. "So I pray the gods to keep it safe in perpetuity." And on the words he gave order that the formula in the public tables be emended accordingly. From that time on censors have used this modest form of prayer in winding up censuses. For he wisely realized that increase for the Roman Empire was to be asked for in the days when triumphs were sought on the near side of the seventh milestone, but for a people that possessed the greater part of the whole globe it would be greedy to ask for more and abundantly fortunate if they lost nothing of what was already theirs.

Valerius Maximus, *Memorable Deeds and Sayings*, 4.1.10a [ca. 30 CE]

But since Caesar is so distant, and right now is at places which, if we are to look to space, are the world's boundaries, and if we think of what he has achieved, we see that these are the boundaries of the Roman Empire.

Cicero, *In Defense of Balbus*, 64 [56 BCE]

The 'Augustan threshold': Augustus and the stabilized frontier

Augustus governed subjected territories according to Roman custom, but he allowed the allied nations to be governed according to their own traditions. And he did not desire to make any additions to subjected territory or to extend the allied nations by new acquisitions, but rather he thought it best to be content with what was already possessed, and he gave this opinion to the Senate. And so he undertook no war, for the time being at least, but actually gave away certain principalities.

Cassius Dio, *Roman History*, 54.9.1–2 [ca. 205 CE]

The will of Augustus: imperial advice to Tiberius (14 CE)

[Augustus' will] contained a reckoning of the state's resources – the strength of citizens and allies under arms; the number of fleets, client kingdoms under Rome's protection, and provinces; taxes, both direct and indirect; the necessary outlays and customary largesses. Augustus recorded all these in his own hand, with a final clause added (perhaps through fear, perhaps through jealousy) in which he advised that the empire be kept within its present boundaries.

Tacitus, *Annals*, 1.11 [ca. 115 CE]

Yet [Augustus] put the state in order, and not through instituting a monarchy or dictatorship, but by creating the designation of First Citizen. The Empire had been enclosed by the ocean or distant rivers. The legions, provinces, fleets, the entire governmental apparatus, had been centralized. There was law among the citizenry, restraint among the allies; and the capital city itself had been magnificently adorned. There was little that had been accomplished by applied force, and those rare instances were for the sake of the general tranquility.

Tacitus, *Annals*, 1.9 [ca. 115 CE]

Augustus never haphazardly attacked any people, and he did not desire to increase the Empire's boundaries and enhance his military glory. Indeed, he compelled certain barbarian chiefs to swear an oath in the temple of Mars Ultor that they would keep the peace for which they sued in good faith.... The gates of the Temple of Janus Quirinus, which had only been closed twice since the foundation of the Republic, he closed three times during a much shorter time, as a sign that the empire was at peace on land and at sea.[8]

Suetonius, *Augustus*, 21–2 [early second century CE]

I am well aware that many of the events I have recounted and shall go on to describe may seem like trifles unworthy of recording. But I can draw no parallels between my account and the work of those who wrote the ancient history of the Roman people. Immense wars, cities besieged, routed and captured kings, or, when they turned their attention to domestic affairs, wrangles of consul and tribune, disputes concerning agrarian laws, struggles of nobles and commons – these were the themes they treated as they liked. My labor is inglorious and in a narrow field. For this was a time of peace unbroken or weakly challenged, of tragedy in the capital, of a ruler uninterested in extending empire.

Tacitus, *Annals*, 4.32 [ca. 115 CE]

Controlling the fairest parts of land and sea, [the Romans] have on the whole tried to preserve their empire by diplomatic means rather than to extend their power without limit over poor and profitless barbarian tribes, some of whom I have seen negotiating at Rome in order to offer themselves as subjects. But the emperor would not receive them because they are useless to him. They give kings to many other peoples whom they have no need to rule directly. To some of these subject peoples they also make disbursements, thinking it dishonorable to give them up, even though they are expensive. They surround their empire with large armies and they garrison the whole stretch of land and sea like a single fortress.

Appian, *Roman History,* Preface. vii [ca. 160 CE]

For beyond the outermost circle of the world inhabited by men, indeed like a second line of defense in a city's fortifications, you have drawn another circle, one which is more flexible and more easily guarded, and it is here that you have put up your defensive walls and have built border cities; you have populated each of these in different places; and you have given them useful crafts and other amenities. Just like a trench encircles an army camp, all this can be called the circuit and perimeter of the walls.

Aelius Aristides, *Regarding Rome,* 81–2 [ca. 145 CE]

Indeed, at the present your empire's boundaries are of an extent not to be despised, and their interior cannot even be measured. Going to the west from that place where the limit of the Persian empire was then fixed, the rest of your empire is as much greater than the whole of that one. There is nothing that escapes you, not city, not nation, not harbor, not land, unless you have decided that something is of no use. The Red Sea, the cataracts of the Nile, and Lake Maeotis, which men of old used to call the ends of the earth, are for this city [Rome] like "the fence of a courtyard."

Aelius Aristides, *Regarding Rome,* 28 [ca. 145 CE]

Upon assuming imperial power Hadrian [117 CE] immediately returned to the policy of earlier emperors and gave his attention to maintaining peace throughout the world. This was because the nations attacked by Trajan started to revolt; the Moors actually began to attack, and the Sarmatians to wage war, the Britons could not be held in check, Egypt was in the chaos of rioting, and finally Libya and Palestine showed a rebellious spirit. And so [Hadrian] gave up all Roman conquests east of the Euphrates and the Tigris, following, as he used to say, Cato's example, when he used to urge that the Macedonians, since they could not be held down as subjects, should be declared free and independent.

Historia Augusta, Hadrian, 5.1–3 [late fourth century CE]

This, then, is the situation with the different parts of the inhabited world; but since the Romans occupy the best and most renowned portions of it, having surpassed all the earlier rulers on record, it is well worthwhile to add the following account of them, however brief.

Strabo, *Geography,* 17.3.24 (C 839) [ca. 15 BCE]

Client states

Numidia as client state (Adherbal to Roman Senate, 116 BCE)

Conscripted Fathers, my father Micipsa instructed me on his deathbed to consider that I am merely the steward of the kingdom of Numidia, but that the right and legitimate power reside with you. He also commanded me to be as helpful as possible to the Roman people both in times of peace and in war, considering you as kinsmen. He stated that if I were to do this, I would find in your friendship an army and wealth, and protection for my kingdom.

Sallust, Jugurthine War, 14.1 [ca. 40 BCE]

Hegemonial controls: Julius Caesar, Augustus, and the economy of client tribesmen

The deified Caesar crossed over to Britain twice. . . . He won two or three victories over the Britons, although he carried over only two or three legions. He came back with hostages, slaves, and a quantity of booty. Yet at this time some of the chieftains won Augustus Caesar's friendship by sending out embassies and visiting his court. These men have not only made dedications on the Capitoline hill, but they have also succeeded in making virtually the entire island into Roman property. Moreover, since they submit so readily to heavy duties . . . there is no need to garrison the island.

Strabo, Geography, 4.5.3 (C 200) [ca. 15 BCE]

[Augustus] did not take up war, for the present at any rate, but he actually gave away certain dominions – he gave Iamblichus, son of Iamblichus, his ancestral rule over the Arabians, and to Tarcondimotus, son of Tarcondimotus, he gave the kingdom of Cilicia, which his father had held, with the exception of some places on the coast. These places along with Lesser Armenia he gave to Archelaus, since the Mede who had previously held them had died. He entrusted the tetrarchy of a certain Zenodotus to Herod, and to one Mithridates, even though he was a mere boy, he gave Commagene, as its king had executed the boy's father. And because the other Armenians had brought charges against Artaxes and had called his brother Tigranes, who was at Rome, the emperor sent Tiberius to drive Artaxes out and reinstate Tigranes.

Cassius Dio, Roman History, 54.9.2–5 [ca. 205 CE]

A client king (66 CE)[9]

Tiridates spoke: "Master, Arsaces the brother of the kings Vologaesus and Pacorus was my ancestor, and your slave. And now I have come to worship you, my god, as I do Mithras. Whatever destiny you spin out for me will be mine; for you are my fortune and my fate." Nero answered him: "You have done well to come here in person, so that meeting me you might enjoy my grace. For I grant to you what neither your father left you nor your brothers gave to you and preserved for you. I now declare you King of Armenia, so that both you and they will understand that I have the power to take away kingdoms and to grant kingdoms." As he finished speaking, he signalled for Tiridates to ascend by the approach which had been built especially for this occasion, and when Tiridates had been made to sit beneath his feet, he placed the crown on his head.

Cassius Dio, Roman History, 63.5.2–4 [ca. 205 CE]

[Dedicated] to the emperor Caesar Augustus, son of a god, pontifex maximus, holding the tribunician power for the fifteenth year, acclaimed imperator thirteen times, by Marcus Julius Cottius, son of King Donnus, prefect of the following tribes – the Segovii, Segusini, Belacori, Caturiges, Medulii, Tebavii, Adanates, Savincates, Ecdinii, Veaminii, Venisami, Iemerii, Vesubianii, and Quadiates – and by the tribes which are under his command.

Corpus Inscriptionum Latinarum, vol. 3, 14.147 (5) [29 BCE][10]

Disposition of Roman military forces and client states (23 CE)

On either coast Italy was guarded by the fleets at Misenum and Ravenna; a squadron of warships protected the adjacent coast of Gaul. This squadron had been captured by Augustus at the victory at Actium [31 BCE] and sent with strong crews to the town of Forum Iulium. The main strength of our forces, however, were on the Rhine – eight legions poised to deal with the Germans or the Gauls. Three legions watched over the Spains, finally subdued not long before. King Juba received Mauretania as a gift of the Roman people. The rest of Africa was held by two legions; and the same number guarded Egypt. Then, from the Syrian marches right up to the Euphrates, there were four legions for that vast space. On the borders, meanwhile, the Iberian, Albanian, and other monarchs were protected against foreign powers by Rome's might. Rhoemetalces and Cotys' sons held Thrace; the Danube bank was patrolled by two legions in Pannonia and two in Moesia. There were two more in Dalmatia, to the rear of the other four and easy to summon, should Italy need sudden assistance. In any case the capital had a standing army of its own: three urban and nine praetorian cohorts*, mainly recruited from Etruria and Umbria or Old Latium* and the earlier Roman colonies. At selected places in the provinces there were allied warships, cavalry divisions and auxiliary cohorts of almost the same strength; but it was difficult to keep track of them, since they shifted from station to station, and, according to the needs of the moment, they were increased or on occasion reduced.

Tacitus, *Annals*, 4.5 [ca. 115 CE]

A barbarian stipulation

Juthungian envoy to Aurelian (reigned 270–5 CE)

"For you to make peace and obtain its advantages would be best for you, and to settle with us the issues of this war, and in so doing, you would be strengthened by our alliance, to have greater resources against those who attack you. If you should do this, it is just that we get what we used to get from you regularly: gifts of coined and uncoined gold and silver as a guarantee of friendship."

Deuxippus, fragment 6 [after 275 CE]

Soldier and army on the frontier[11]

There is a story that when the armies of Brutus and Cassius were marching together during the civil wars that Brutus' army first arrived at a stream needing to be bridged, but that Cassius' troops were the first in constructing the bridge and effecting a passage. This rigorous discipline made Cassius' men superior to Brutus' men not only in the construction of military works, but also in the general conduct of war.

Frontinus, Stratagems, 4.2.1 [ca. 90 CE]

When they are entrenched, the soldiers go to their tents by companies, in quiet good order. All of their camp duties are carried out with the same discipline, the same concern for security: gathering wood, food supplies, and water, as needed – each party has its assigned task. The time for dinner and breakfast is not left to individual choice: all eat together. A trumpet announces the times for sleep, sentinel duty, and rising. Nothing is done without command. At dawn the rank and file report to their respective centurions, the centurions go to salute the tribunes, the tribunes with all other officers wait upon the commander-in-chief. According to customary practice, he gives them the watchword and other orders to be communicated to the lower ranks. The same precision is maintained on the battlefield. The troops turn about swiftly in the required direction, and, whether advancing to the attack or retreating, all move together at the word of command.

Josephus, Jewish War, 3.85–8 [ca. 75 CE]

There is a small shrine, and in it there is a golden eagle. Every legion in the Roman army has an eagle, and it never leaves winter quarters unless the entire legion sets out. It is affixed to a large pole, which is tapered to a sharp point so that it can be firmly fixed in the ground, and one man carries it.

Cassius Dio, Roman History, 40.18 [ca. 205 CE]

The recruit also should be instructed in constructing a camp. Nothing is so useful and so necessary in time of war. If a camp is built in the right way, the men spend their days and nights in safety inside the rampart, even if the enemy is besieging them. It is as though they are carrying around with them a fortified city wherever they go. But this science has been lost completely, for it has been a long time since anyone built a camp by digging ditches and fixing palisades. The result, as we know, has been that when the barbarians' cavalry attacks, by day or by night, many of our armies have suffered heavy losses.

Vegetius, Epitome of Military Affairs, 1.21 [ca. 400 CE]

Army life

But imperial decisions have relaxed strict legalities in the drawing up of wills for soldiers because of their extreme ignorance. Although they do not employ the established number of witnesses, or transfer their property, or announce their wills in a formal way, nevertheless their testamentary wishes are valid. In addition they are allowed to institute as heirs non-Romans and Latins or to leave them legacies, although as a general rule non-Romans are prohibited from taking an inheritance or legacies by process of civil law, and Latins by the Junian law.[12]

Gaius, *Institutes*, 2.109–10 [second century CE]

Army as emperor-maker

It is necessary before I begin my planned work to consider the condition of the city, the attitude of the armies, the state of the provinces, the strength and weakness throughout the entire world, so that the reader will be able to understand not only the incidents and the outcome of events, which are mostly due to chance, but also their reasons and causes. Even though the news of Nero's death had been greeted with rejoicing, it roused different emotions, not only among the senators and people and city soldiery in Rome, but also among the legions and generals. For the secret of empire had been revealed: that an emperor could be made elsewhere than at Rome.

Tacitus, *Histories*, 1.4 [ca. 110 CE]

A Roman surveyor in the Dacian frontier zone
(101–2 or 105–6 CE)

After we first entered hostile territory, Celsus, our Caesar's earthworks began to demand of me the calculations of measurements. After a prearranged marching length had been determined, two parallel straight lines had to be produced (on the terrain) along which a large defensive structure of palisaded earthworks would arise for the protection of communications. By your invention [Celsus], when part of the earthworks was cut back to the line of sight, the use of the surveying instrument extended these lines. Regarding surveying bridges, we were able to state the width of the rivers from the bank close by, even if the enemy wanted to harrass us.... After our supreme emperor [Trajan] most recently opened up Dacia for us by his victory... I returned to my studies, at leisure as it were.

Die Schriften der römischen Feldmesser, vol. 1, p. 92[13]

A military station on the Damascus–Palmyra road

On a plain completely dry and a source of fear for travelers because of its great expanse and the fate of a neighbor who died from hunger – the worst thing imaginable – you, comrade, have provided a fort, perfectly equipped, you, most valiant guard of the frontier zone, of the cities, and of the emperors honored faithfully all over the earth.... Hence, stranger, continue on your journey with good cheer and, having benefited from a good deed, sing the praise of a magnanimous judge, brilliant in war and peace who, I pray, will, promoted in rank, build more such forts for the emperors, though it is difficult, and will rejoice in children worthy of the deeds of such a father.

Greek and Latin Inscriptions of Syria, vol. 5, 2704 [fourth century CE]

Lands taken from the enemy were given to the commanders and soldiers of the frontier armies, with the proviso that they would continue to have these lands only if their heirs were to enter the military service, and that they should never belong to civilians, for, [Severus Alexander, 222–35 CE] said, men serve with greater zeal when they are defending their own lands. Of course he added to these lands beasts of burden and slaves so that they might be able to work what they had received, and that it might not happen that, because of underpopulation or the old age of the owners, the lands bordering on the barbarians should be left uninhabited, which he thought would be a disgrace.

> *Historia Augusta, Severus Alexander*, 58.4–5 [late fourth century CE]

The discussion of the army raises a further point. Earlier Roman rulers stationed a large number of forces everywhere in frontier districts in order to guard the frontiers, especially in the eastern part, checking the inroads of Persians and Saracens. These troops were called *limitanei*. These the emperor Justinian in the beginning treated so carelessly and miserly that their paymasters were four or five years behind in paying their salaries. When peace was struck between the Romans and Persians these miserable men were compelled to donate the salary owed to them for a certain period to the public treasury, on the pretense that they too would benefit from the blessings of peace. Later he took away from them the very title of an army with no reason. From then on the frontiers of the Roman Empire remained without guards, and the soldiers suddenly had to look to those accustomed to do good deeds.[14]

> Procopius, *Anecdotes*, 24.12–14 [ca. 550 CE]

EDITOR'S NOTES

1   For expansionist ideology in the Augustan poets, see D. Cloud, "Roman Poetry and Anti-Militarism," in *War and Society in the Roman World*, ed. J. Rich and G. Shipley (New York and London, 1993), pp. 113–38, with further sources at 121 n. 2.

2   For aggressive Roman ideological pretensions, see S. P. Mattern, *Rome and the Enemy: Imperial Strategy in the Principate* (Berkeley, Los Angeles, and London, 1999); for the Augustan Principate, see E. S. Gruen, "The Imperial Policy of Augustus," in *Between Republic and Empire: Interpretations of Augustus and his Principate*, ed. K. A. Raaflaub and M. Toher (Berkeley, 1990), pp. 395–416.

3   See C. M. Wells, *The German Policy of Augustus: An Examination of the Archaeological Evidence* (Oxford, 1972).

4   K. Müller, ed., *Fragmenta Historicorum Graecorum* (Paris, 1848–78); translation (with slight modifications) from B. Isaac, *The Limits of Empire: The Roman Army in the East* (Oxford, 1990), p. 261.

5   See B. D. Shaw, *Environment and Society in Roman North Africa: Studies in History and Archaeology* (Aldershot and Brookfield, 1995).

6   Translation from N. Lewis and M. Reinhold, eds, *Roman Civilization: The Republic and the Augustan Age*, vol. 1, 3rd edn. (New York, 1990), p. 600.

7   See H. H. Scullard, *Roman Britain: Outpost of the Empire* (London, 1979).

8   Closing the gates of the temple symbolized universal peace; they had been closed in the time of King Numa and in 235 BCE.

9   See D. C. Braund, *Rome and the Friendly King: The Character of Client Kingship* (London, 1984).

10 Translation from Lewis and Reinhold, eds., *Roman Civilization*, p. 601.

11 See G. R. Watson, *The Roman Soldier* (Ithaca, NY, 1969).

12 By a law (*lex Iunia*), probably of 19 CE, imperfectly manumitted slaves were granted Latin rights of sale and contract, without the right to contract a marriage with a Roman citizen or to make a valid will. See B. Nicholas, *An Introduction to Roman Law* (Oxford, 1962), pp. 74–5.

13 F. Bluhme and K. Lachmann, eds., *Die Schriften der römischen Feldmesser* (repr. Mildesheim, 1967).

14 On Roman frontier societies, see C. R. Whittaker, *Frontiers of the Roman Empire: A Social and Economic Study* (Baltimore and London, 1994).

Glossary

aedile An annually elected magistracy. There were two sets of aediles, one from the plebeians and one from the patrician order (curule aediles). Their main charges were the maintenance of the city of Rome (*cura urbis*), supervision of the grain supply to the city (*cura annonae*), and overseeing the games (*cura ludorum sollemnium*). Holding this office was not essential to the *cursus honorum* (q.v.), but it did confer senatorial dignity.

Aeneas In the Homeric epic saga, Aeneas was a refugee from Troy after the Greeks had sacked the city following a ten-year-long siege (Troy finally succumbed through the Greek ruse of the "Trojan horse"). After many trials and tribulations, Aeneas and his followers ended up in Italy. In Roman legend, Aeneas was the progenitor of the Roman people.

ager publicus "Public land" in Italy which came to the Roman state through conquest or confiscation from rebellious allies. Disputes soon arose as to whether this land should be leased to the wealthy or distributed to the poor. Roman and, after 338 BCE, Latin colonies were established on it. In 367 BCE, the Licinian-Sextian law purportedly restricted the amount of it one citizen could hold to about 350 acres (500 *iugera*). The use of the public land was the focal point of the Gracchan reforms in the late second century BCE.

ass (pl. asses) A large copper coin, which weighed about 12 ounces (one Roman pound). After 211 BCE, the ass weighed about two ounces, and the new silver denarius was worth ten asses.

censor To be elected censor was the crowning achievement of a Roman senatorial career, usually the preserve of ex-consuls. Two men were elected as censors once every five years by the centuriate assembly for an 18-month term. They conducted the census, an official list of all Roman citizens, controlled state contracts, and as the moral arbiters of the state, they reviewed the Senate, expelling those whom they regarded as unfit.

centurion The main professional officer of the Roman army. After Marius, there were six centurions in each of the ten cohorts.

cohort Unit of the Roman legion. There were ten to a legion (600); each divided into six centuries for administrative purposes. By extension, the term was applied to a group of friends and acquaintances which accompanied a provincial governor.

comitium Place of assembly. At Rome comitia (plural) meant an assembly of the Roman people whom a magistrate summoned in groups for legislative or electoral purposes.

consul (pl. consules)   One of the two annually elected chief civil and military magistrates of the Roman Republic. Consuls commanded armies and gave their names to the year. Under the Empire the office continued, with great dignity but a shadow of its former power.

cursus honorum   The hierarchical succession of public offices in a senatorial career. In the second century BCE the progression, after requisite military service, was quaestor-tribune of the plebeians or aedileship, optional-praetor-consul. The crowning achievement of a senatorial career, the censorship, usually went to ex-consuls.

decurion   Local councillor in Latin and Roman colonies and municipalities. They were responsible for the collection of municipal taxes and personally liable in case of default.

denarius (pl. denarii)   A silver Roman coin introduced ca. 211 BCE; equivalent to four sesterces, a small silver coin most commonly used.

dictator   In times of extreme emergency to the state during the history of the Republic, sole power was vested in a dictator, who had 6 months in order to bring the crisis under control. Thereafter the state would revert to the annual magistracies of the consuls. In the late Republic, C. Julius Caesar trampled upon republican institutions, the most dramatic example perhaps being his assumption of a perpetual dictatorship at Rome.

drachma (pl. drachmae)   Greek coin measure; roughly equal to the Roman denarius.

equestrians   The wealthiest non-senatorial class in Roman society. Although a landed interest was essential to it, generally the class may be thought of as consisting in part of the most powerful commercial sector. Some of the equestrians bought up state contracts (see *publicani*), and from the Middle Republican period their interests frequently clashed with those of the senatorial aristocracy.

Etruscans   The most politically and culturally advanced people of pre-Roman Italy, whose greatest period fell in the late seventh and sixth centuries BCE. They were influenced by the Greek culture of southern Italy, and, according to the tradition, an Etruscan dynasty, the Tarquins, ruled Rome at the end of its monarchic period (616–510/509). Etruscan civilization introduced the early Roman community to urbanization, serving as a conduit for Greek cultural influences and contributing some of their own political, cultural, and social institutions to the early Romans.

fasces   A bundle of rods and an axe, a symbol of official authority, carried by the lictors (see **lictor** below) before Roman magistrates.

fetiales   A college of 20 priests, advisers to the Roman Senate on questions of peace and war. Two fetials went out to states with whom Rome agreed to strike treaties, imprecating curses upon the Roman people should they break the covenant. In cases of war, the fetial called Jupiter to witness that the Romans had been wronged; if reparations were not made in 33 days, war was declared, and a fetial traveled to the boundary of the enemy and hurled a symbolic spear into its territory as a declaration of war.

flamines   Roman priests assigned to the worship of individual deities, the three most important of whom were the flamen Dialis (for the worship of Jupiter), the flamen Martialis (for the worship of Mars), and the flamen Quirinalis (for the worship of the ancient god Quirinus). They were always chosen by a pontifical college from the highest Roman nobility, the patriciate.

imperator   The title troops conferred upon their victorious commander, who assumed the title after his name until the close of his magistracy or until after his celebration of a triumph.

imperium   Near-absolute power of Roman commanders in the field and of Roman magistrates in interpreting and executing law; held at first by the monarchs and under the Republic by consuls, military tribunes with consular power (from 445 to 367 BCE), praetors, dictators, and masters of the horse (*magistri equitum*).

interrex In early Rome, an individual appointed by the senators upon the death of a king. In later periods, in the event of the death or resignation of the consuls, one of a group which took the auspices until new consuls were elected.

iugerum (pl. iugera) A Roman land measurement, equal to 0.625 acres.

Latium The region of Latin-speaking peoples which roughly corresponds to modern Lazio, originally bounded by the Tiber and Anio rivers to the northwest and to the east by the Apennine mountains and Monti Lepini.

lictor Attendant of the Roman magistrates with imperium (see **imperium** above) who preceded them, carrying the fasces (see **fasces** above) as a symbol of magisterial authority.

Mamertines ("Sons of Mars") Campanian mercenaries in the service of Rome who seized the Sicilian city of Messene on the straits of Messana ca. 288 BCE. Besieged by the forces of the Syracusan monarch Hiero II, they first made appeal to Carthage, and then to Rome, precipitating events for the First Punic War (264–241 BCE).

manes Roman spirits of the dead; they represented both all the dead souls in the underworld and, in a more specific sense, the family's ancestors.

maniple The name for one of the 30 units, each containing from 120 to 200 men, into which the Roman legion was divided; lost importance after the introduction of the cohort (see **cohort** above).

modius (pl. modii) A dry measure of capacity, equivalent to nearly two English gallons.

ovatio A minor form of the Roman triumph (see **triumph** below); granted to a general whose accomplishment did not merit a triumph.

penates The guardian spirits of the Roman family larder; the chief private cult of the Roman household.

phalanx Greek infantry order of battle; brought to perfection by the reforms of the Macedonian king Philip II ca. 360 BCE.

plebeian The non-elites of the early Roman Republic who struggled to win political rights and concessions from the elites (patricians) in a historical process often called the 'Struggle of the Orders' (traditional dates, 494–287 BCE).[1]

pomerium Consecrated ground running in a strip just outside the city walls of Rome.

pontifex maximus The head of the college of Roman priests who exercised some disciplinary functions over his constituency.

praetor From 197 BCE there were six annually elected praetors. The urban praetor and the peregrine praetor administered justice, but by this time the praetorship had become for the most part a military magistracy, second only to the consuls (see **consul** above).

proconsul The title given to a consul (propraetor stands in the same relationship to praetor) when his command in the field (see **imperium**) was extended beyond the annual magistracy. These promagistracies were exercised within a territorial field of command (*provincia*), as defined by the Senate.

procurator An agent or legal representative; under the emperors they were employees in the civic administration, with diverse duties.

publicani Members of the non-senatorial, equestrian (see **equestrians** above) class who bought public contracts, especially for the collection of public revenue.

Quirites An ancient god whom the Romans claimed to be of Sabine origin; it has plausibly been suggested that the etymology of his name is *co-viri-um*, "assembly of men." When a speaker addressed a Roman assembly as Quirites, he was solemnly invoking hoary antiquity and venerable tradition.

rostra The speaker's platform in the city of Rome, originally on the south side of the meeting place for political assembly (*comitium*).

sesterces Small silver Roman coins which were the most commonly used currency; four to a denarius (often written as HS).

stadia (pl.) A Greek measure of length, equivalent to 125 paces.

suovetaurilia (also solitaurilia) A sacrifice of a pig, a sheep, and a bull at the conclusion of a purification ceremony (*lustratio*).

talent (Attic-Euboean standard) A Greek weight of about 57 lbs (25.86 kg), comprising 60 minae or 6,000 drachmae in monetary terms. If we assume that a day-laborer earned a drachma per day (probably a high estimate; this is the rate attested for skilled laborers on the Athenian Erectheum in the fifth century BCE), then it would have taken that worker some 16 years of uninterrupted labor to earn one talent.

triumph A procession of a victorious Roman general to the temple of Jupiter Optimus Capitolinus, in which the spoils of war were displayed; the crowning military achievement of a Roman aristocratic career.

NOTES

1 For further reading on the 'Struggle,' see the collected essays in K. A. Raaflaub, (ed.), *Social Struggles in Archaic Rome* (Berkeley and Los Angeles, 1986).

Index